Lecture Notes in Computer

Edited by G. Goos, J. Hartmanis, and

Springer
Berlin
Heidelberg
New York
Barcelona
Hong Kong
London
Milan
Paris
Tokyo

Jean-Marc Champarnaud   Denis Maurel (Eds.)

Implementation and Application of Automata

7th International Conference, CIAA 2002
Tours, France, July 3-5, 2002
Revised Papers

 Springer

Series Editors

Gerhard Goos, Karlsruhe University, Germany
Juris Hartmanis, Cornell University, NY, USA
Jan van Leeuwen, Utrecht University, The Netherlands

Volume Editors

Jean-Marc Champarnaud
Université de Rouen, UFR des Sciences et Techniques
LIFAR, 76821 Mont-Saint-Aignan Cedex, France
E-mail: Jean-Marc.Champarnaud@univ-rouen.fr

Denis Maurel
Laboratoire d'Informatique de l'Université de Tours
École Polytechnique de l'Université de Tours, Departement Informatique
64 avenue Jean-Portalis, 37200 Tours, France
E-mail: maurel@univ-tours.fr

Cataloging-in-Publication Data applied for

Bibliographic information published by Die Deutsche Bibliothek
 Die Deutsche Bibliothek lists this publication in the Deutsche Nationalbibliografie;
detailed bibliographic data is available in the Internet at <http://dnb.ddb.de>.

CR Subject Classification (1998): F.1.1, F.4.3, F.3, F.2

ISSN 0302-9743
ISBN 3-540-40391-4 Springer-Verlag Berlin Heidelberg New York

Springer-Verlag Berlin Heidelberg New York
a member of BertelsmannSpringer Science+Business Media GmbH

http://www.springer.de

© Springer-Verlag Berlin Heidelberg 2003
Printed in Germany

Typesetting: Camera-ready by author, data conversion by PTP-Berlin GmbH
Printed on acid-free paper   SPIN: 10872815   06/3142   5 4 3 2 1 0

Preface

The 7th International Conference on Implementation and Application of Automata (CIAA 2002) was held at the Université François Rabelais of Tours, in Tours, France, on July 3–5, 2002.

This volume of Lecture Notes in Computer Science contains all the papers that were presented at CIAA 2002, as well as the abstracts of the poster papers that were displayed during the conference.

The conference addressed issues in automata application and implementation. The topics of the papers presented in this conference ranged from automata applications in software engineering, natural language and speech recognition, and image processing, to new representations and algorithms for efficient implementation of automata and related structures.

Automata theory is one of the oldest areas in computer science. Research in automata theory has always been motivated by its applications since its early stage of development. In the 1960s and 1970s, automata research was motivated heavily by problems arising from compiler construction, circuit design, string matching, etc. In recent years, many new applications of automata have been found in various areas of computer science as well as in other disciplines. Examples of the new applications include statecharts in object-oriented modeling, finite transducers in natural language processing, and nondeterministic finite-state models in communication protocols. Many of the new applications cannot simply utilize the existing models and algorithms in automata theory in the solution to their problems. New models, or modifications of the existing models, are needed to satisfy their requirements. Also, the sizes of the typical problems in many of the new applications are astronomically larger than those used in the traditional applications. New algorithms and new representations of automata are in demand to reduce the time and space requirements of the computation.

The CIAA conference series provided a forum for these new problems and new challenges. In these conferences, both theoretical and practical results related to the application and implementation of automata were presented and discussed, and software packages and toolkits were demonstrated. The participants of the conference series were from both research institutions and industry.

We wish to thank all the program committee members and referees for their efforts in refereeing and selecting papers.

We wish to thank EATCS and ACM SIGACT for their sponsorship, and the following institutions for their donations to the conference:
- CNRS,
- the Scientific Council of the University of Tours,
- the *UFR de Sciences et Techniques* of the University of Rouen,
- the Administrative Council *Région Centre*,
- the Administrative Council *Département d'Indre-et-Loire*,

– the Municipality of Tours,
– the Xerox Research Centre Europe (Grenoble, France).

We also thank the editors of the Lecture Notes in Computer Science series and Springer-Verlag, in particular Ms. Anna Kramer, for their help in publishing this volume.

April 2003   Jean-Marc Champarnaud
                                                              Denis Maurel

Program Committee

Salah Aït-Mokhtar	XRCE Grenoble, France
Marie-Pierre Béal	Université de Marne-la-Vallée, France
Bernard Boigelot	Université de Liège, Belgium
Jean-Marc Champarnaud (Chair)	Université de Rouen, France
Maxime Crochemore	Université de Marne-la-Vallée, France
Gérard Duchamp	Université de Rouen, France
Jacques Farré	Université de Nice, France
José Fortes Gálvez	Universidad de Las Palmas de Gran Canaria, Spain
Oscar Ibarra	University of California at Santa Barbara, USA
Nils Klarlund	AT&T Labs Research, USA
Tomasz Kowaltowski	Universitade Estadual de Campinas, Brazil
Igor Litovsky	Université de Nice, France
Carlos Martín-Vide	Universitad Rovira i Virgili, Spain
Denis Maurel (Chair)	Université de Tours, France
Mehryar Mohri	AT&T Labs Research, USA
Jean-Eric Pin	CNRS, Université Paris 7, France
Kai Salomaa	Queen's University, Canada
Helmut Seidl	Universität Trier, Germany
Sheng Yu	University of Western Ontario, Canada

Organizing Committee

Béatrice Bouchou	Université de Tours, LI
Jean-Marc Champarnaud	Université de Rouen, LIFAR
Michel Crucianu	Université de Tours, LI
Nathalie Friburger	Université de Tours, LI
Denis Maurel	Université de Tours, LI
Mohamed Slimane	Université de Tours, LI

List of Referees

S. Aït-Mokhtar

C. Allauzen

M.-P. Béal

C. Bertelle

B. Boigelot

P. Caron

J.-M. Champarnaud

M. Crochemore

M.J. Daley

Zhe Dang

M. Domaratzki

G. Duchamp

J. Farré

J. Fortes Gálvez

T. Gáal

O. Ibarra

L. Ilie

A. Kempe

N. Klarlund

T. Kowaltowski

I. Litovsky

C. Martín-Vide

D. Maurel

C. Miller

M. Mohri

A. Okhotin

A. Păun

G. Păun

J.-E. Pin

J.-L. Ponty

C. Prieur

B. Ravikumar

J. Sakarovitch

K. Salomaa

H. Seidl

I. Simon

S. Yu

Gaoyan Xie

Sponsoring Institutions

Table of Contents

Abstracts

Edit-Distance of Weighted Automata

Mehryar Mohri

AT&T Labs – Research
180 Park Avenue
Florham Park, NJ 07932, USA
mohri@research.att.com

Abstract. The edit-distance of two strings is the minimal cost of a sequence of symbol insertions, deletions, or substitutions transforming one string into the other. The definition is used in various contexts to give a measure of the difference or similarity between two strings. This definition can be extended to measure the similarity between two sets of strings. In particular, when these sets are represented by automata, their edit-distance can be computed using the general algorithm of composition of weighted transducers combined with a single-source shortest-paths algorithm. More generally, in some applications such as speech recognition and computational biology, the strings may represent a range of alternative hypotheses with associated probabilities. Thus, we introduce the definition of the edit-distance of two distributions of strings given by two weighted automata. We show that general weighted automata algorithms over the appropriate semirings can be used to compute the edit-distance of two weighted automata exactly. The algorithm for computing exactly the edit-distance of weighted automata can be used to improve the word accuracy of automatic speech recognition systems. More generally, the algorithm can be extended to provide an edit-distance automaton useful for rescoring and other post-processing purposes in the context of large-vocabulary speech recognition. In the course of the presentation of our algorithm, we also introduce a new and general *synchronization* algorithm for weighted transducers which, combined with ϵ-removal, can be used to normalize weighted transducers with bounded delays.

1 Introduction

The *edit-distance* of two strings is the minimal cost of a sequence of symbol insertions, deletions, or substitutions transforming one string into the other [18]. It is used in many applications such as computational biology to give a measure of the difference or similarity between two strings.

There exists a classical dynamic-programming algorithm for computing the edit-distance of two strings x_1 and x_2 in time $O(|x_1||x_2|)$, where $|x_i|$, $i = 1, 2$, denotes the length of the string x_i [34]. The algorithm is a special instance of a single-source shortest-paths algorithm applied to a directed graph expanded dynamically. Ukkonen improved that algorithm by reducing the size of the directed graph that needs to be expanded [33]. The complexity of his algorithm is

J.-M. Champarnaud and D. Maurel (Eds.): CIAA 2002, LNCS 2608, pp. 1–23, 2003.

$O(d \max\{|x_1|, |x_2|\})$, where d is the edit-distance of x_1 and x_2. The algorithm is more efficient for strings such that the distance d is small with respect to $|x_1|$ and $|x_2|$. [1]

The definition of edit-distance can be extended to measure the similarity between two sets of strings. It is then the minimum of the edit-distance between any two strings, one in each set. In particular, when these sets are represented by (unweighted) automata, their edit-distance can be computed using the general algorithm of composition of weighted transducers combined with a single-source shortest-paths algorithm [24]. We briefly present that algorithm and point out its generality for dealing with more complex edit-distance models including for example transpositions that can be represented by weighted transducers. The classical dynamic programming algorithm for strings can be viewed in fact as a special instance of that algorithm.

In several applications such as speech recognition, computational biology, handwriting recognition, or topic spotting, the strings may represent a range of alternative hypotheses with associated probabilities given as a weighted automaton. Thus, we introduce the definition of the edit-distance of two distributions of strings given by weighted automata, and give a general algorithm for computing that edit-distance.

Note that the number of hypotheses compactly represented by such weighted automata can be very large in many applications. In speech recognition applications for example, even relatively small automata may contain more than four billion distinct strings. Thus, the use of the classical edit-distance computation for strings seems to be prohibitive here: the number of pairs of strings can be larger than four billion squared. The storage and use of the results would also be an issue. Therefore, it is crucial to keep the compact automata representation of the input strings, and provide an algorithm for computing the edit-distance that takes advantage of that representation.

The edit-distance of weighted automata can be used to improve the word accuracy of automatic speech recognition systems. This was first demonstrated by [32] by reducing automata to their N best strings, later by [19] who gave an algorithm for computing an approximation of the edit-distance and an approximate *edit-distance automaton*. An alternative approach was described by [12] who used an A* heuristic search of deterministic machines and various pruning strategies, some based on the time segmentation of automata, to compute that edit-distance in the context of speech recognition. However, that approach does not produce an edit-distance automaton.

We show that general weighted automata algorithms over the appropriate semirings can be used to compute the edit-distance of two weighted automata *exactly*. More generally, our algorithm can be used to provide an *exact* edit-distance automaton useful for rescoring and other post-processing purposes in the context of large-vocabulary speech recognition. The algorithm is general and can be used in many other contexts such as computational biology.

---

[1] We refer the reader to [7,13] for general surveys of edit-distance and other text processing algorithms.

The paper is organized as follows. We first introduce some preliminary definitions and notation related to semirings and automata that will be used in the rest
of the paper (section 2). In section 3, we introduce various definitions related
to edit-distances, in particular the definition of the edit-distance of weighted
automata. We then give a brief overview of several weighted automata algorithms used to compute the edit-distance of weighted automata (section 4).
They include composition and ϵ-removal of weighted transducers, determinization of weighted automata, and a new and general *synchronization* algorithm for
weighted transducers which, combined with ϵ-removal, can be used to normalize
weighted transducers with bounded delays. Section 5 presents in detail a general
algorithm for computing the edit-distance of two unweighted automata. Finally,
the algorithm for computing the edit-distance of weighted automata, the proof
of its correctness, and the construction of the edit-distance weighted automaton
are given in section 6.

2   Preliminaries

A *weighted automaton* is a finite automaton in which each transition is labeled
with some weight element of a *semiring* in addition to the usual alphabet symbol.

Definition 1 ([16]). *A system* $(\mathbb{K}, \oplus, \otimes, \overline{0}, \overline{1})$ *is a semiring if:*

1. $(\mathbb{K}, \oplus, \overline{0})$ *is a commutative monoid with identity element* $\overline{0}$;
2. $(\mathbb{K}, \otimes, \overline{1})$ *is a monoid with identity element* $\overline{1}$;
3. $\otimes$ *distributes over* $\oplus$;
4. $\overline{0}$ *is an annihilator for* $\otimes$: *for all* $a \in \mathbb{K}, a \otimes \overline{0} = \overline{0} \otimes a = \overline{0}$.

Thus, a semiring is a ring that may lack negation. Some familiar examples are the
Boolean semiring $\mathcal{B} = (\{0, 1\}, \vee, \wedge, 0, 1)$, or the real semiring $\mathcal{R} = (\mathbb{R}_+, +, \times, 0, 1)$
used to combine probabilities. Two semirings particularly used in the following
sections are: the *log semiring* $\mathcal{L} = (\mathbb{R} \cup \{\infty\}, \oplus_{\log}, +, \infty, 0)$ [22] which is isomorphic to $\mathcal{R}$ via a log morphism with:

$$\forall a, b \in \mathbb{R} \cup \{\infty\}, a \oplus_{\log} b = -\log(\exp(-a) + \exp(-b))$$

where by convention: $\exp(-\infty) = 0$ and $-\log(0) = \infty$, and the *tropical semiring*
$\mathcal{T} = (\mathbb{R}_+ \cup \{\infty\}, \min, +, \infty, 0)$ which is derived from the log semiring using the
Viterbi approximation.
   A semiring $(\mathbb{K}, \oplus, \otimes, \overline{0}, \overline{1})$ is said to be *weakly left divisible* if for any x and y
in $\mathbb{K}$ such that $x \oplus y \neq \overline{0}$, there exists at least one z such that $x = (x \oplus y) \otimes z$.
We can then write: $z = (x \oplus y)^{-1} x$. Furthermore, we will assume then that z can
be found in a consistent way, that is: $((u \otimes x) \oplus (u \otimes y))^{-1}(u \otimes x) = (x \oplus y)^{-1} x$
for any $x, y, u \in \mathbb{K}$ such that $u \neq \overline{0}$. A semiring is *zero-sum-free* if for any x and
y in $\mathbb{K}$, $x \oplus y = \overline{0}$ implies $x = y = \overline{0}$. Note that the tropical semiring and the log
semiring are weakly left divisible since the multiplicative operation, $+$, admits
an inverse.

Definition 2. *A* weighted finite-state transducer T *over a semiring* $\mathbb{K}$ *is an 8-tuple* $T = (\Sigma, \Delta, Q, I, F, E, \lambda, \rho)$ *where:*

- Σ *is the finite input alphabet of the transducer;*
- Δ *is the finite output alphabet;*
- Q *is a finite set of states;*
- $I \subseteq Q$ *the set of initial states;*
- $F \subseteq Q$ *the set of final states;*
- $E \subseteq Q \times (\Sigma \cup \{\epsilon\}) \times (\Delta \cup \{\epsilon\}) \times \mathbb{K} \times Q$ *a finite set of transitions;*
- $\lambda : I \to \mathbb{K}$ *the initial weight function; and*
- $\rho : F \to \mathbb{K}$ *the final weight function mapping F to $\mathbb{K}$.*

A *Weighted automaton* $A = (\Sigma, Q, I, F, E, \lambda, \rho)$ is defined in a similar way by simply omitting the output labels.

Given a transition $e \in E$, we denote by $i[e]$ its input label, $p[e]$ its origin or previous state and $n[e]$ its destination state or next state, $w[e]$ its weight, $o[e]$ its output label (transducer case). Given a state $q \in Q$, we denote by $E[q]$ the set of transitions leaving q.

A *path* $\pi = e_1 \cdots e_k$ is an element of E^* with consecutive transitions: $n[e_{i-1}] = p[e_i]$, $i = 2, \ldots, k$. We extend n and p to paths by setting: $n[\pi] = n[e_k]$ and $p[\pi] = p[e_1]$. A cycle π is a path whose origin and destination states coincide: $n[\pi] = p[\pi]$. We denote by $P(q, q')$ the set of paths from q to q' and by $P(q, x, q')$ and $P(q, x, y, q')$ the set of paths from q to q' with input label $x \in \Sigma^*$ and output label y (transducer case). These definitions can be extended to subsets $R, R' \subseteq Q$, by: $P(R, x, R') = \cup_{q \in R, \, q' \in R'} P(q, x, q')$. The labeling functions i (and similarly o) and the weight function w can also be extended to paths by defining the label of a path as the concatenation of the labels of its constituent transitions, and the weight of a path as the $\otimes$-product of the weights of its constituent transitions: $i[\pi] = i[e_1] \cdots i[e_k]$, $w[\pi] = w[e_1] \otimes \cdots \otimes w[e_k]$. We also extend w to any finite set of paths Π by setting: $w[\Pi] = \bigoplus_{\pi \in \Pi} w[\pi]$. An automaton A is *regulated* if the output weight associated by A to each input string $x \in \Sigma^*$:

$$[\![A]\!](x) = \bigoplus_{\pi \in P(I, x, F)} \lambda(p[\pi]) \otimes w[\pi] \otimes \rho(n[\pi])$$

is well-defined and in $\mathbb{K}$. This condition is always satisfied when A contains no ϵ-cycle since the sum then runs over a finite number of paths. It is also always satisfied with k-*closed* semirings such as the tropical semiring [22]. $[\![A]\!](x)$ is defined to be $\overline{0}$ when $P(I, x, F) = \emptyset$.

Similarly, a transducer T is *regulated* if the output weight associated by T to any pair of input-output string (x, y) by:

$$[\![T]\!](x, y) = \bigoplus_{\pi \in P(I, x, y, F)} \lambda(p[\pi]) \otimes w[\pi] \otimes \rho(n[\pi])$$

is well-defined and in $\mathbb{K}$. $[\![T]\!](x, y) = \overline{0}$ when $P(I, x, y, F) = \emptyset$. In the following, we will assume that all the automata and transducers considered are regulated.

A *successful path* in a weighted automaton or transducer M is a path from an initial state to a final state. A state q of M is *accessible* if q can be reached from I. It is *coaccessible* if a final state can be reached from q. A weighted automaton M is *trim* if there is no transition with weight $\bar{0}$ in M and if all states of M are both accessible and coaccessible. M is *unambiguous* if for any string $x \in \Sigma^*$ there is at most one successful path labeled with x. Thus, an unambiguous transducer defines a function.

Note that the second operation of the tropical semiring and the log semiring as well as their identity elements are identical. Thus the weight of a path in an automaton A over the tropical semiring does not change if A is viewed as a weighted automaton over the log semiring or vice-versa.

3 Edit-Distance of Weighted Automata: Definitions

Let Σ be a finite alphabet, and let Ω be defined by $\Omega = \Sigma \cup \{\epsilon\} \times \Sigma \cup \{\epsilon\} - \{(\epsilon, \epsilon)\}$. An element ω of the free monoid Ω^* can be viewed as one of $\Sigma^* \times \Sigma^*$ via the concatenation: $\omega = (a_1, b_1) \cdots (a_n, b_n) \to (a_1 \cdots a_n, b_1 \cdots b_n)$. We will denote by h the corresponding morphism from Ω^* to $\Sigma^* \times \Sigma^*$ and write $h(\omega) = (a_1 \cdots a_n, b_1 \cdots b_n)$.

Definition 3. *An alignment ω of two strings x and y over the alphabet Σ is an element of Ω^* such that $h(\omega) = (x, y)$.*

As an example, $(a, \epsilon)(b, \epsilon)(a, b)(\epsilon, b)$ is an alignment of (aba, bb):

$$x = a\,b\,a\,\epsilon$$
$$y = \epsilon\,\epsilon\,b\,b$$

Let $c : \Omega \to \mathbb{R}_+$ be a function associating some non-negative cost to each element of Ω, that is to each symbol edit operation. For example $c((\epsilon, a))$ can be viewed as the cost of the insertion of the symbol a. Define the cost of $\omega \in \Omega^*$ as the sum of the costs of its constituents: $\omega = \omega_0 \cdots \omega_n \in \Omega^*$: [2]

$$c(\omega) = \sum_{i=0}^{n} c(\omega_i)$$

Definition 4. *The edit-distance $d(x, y)$ of two strings x and y over the alphabet Σ is the minimal cost of a sequence of symbol insertions, deletions, or substitutions transforming one string into the other:*

$$d(x, y) = \min \{c(\omega) : h(\omega) = (x, y)\}$$

---

[2] We are not dealing here with the question of how such weights or costs could be defined. In general, they can be derived from a corpus of alignments using various machine learning techniques such as for example in [28].

In the classical definition of edit-distance, the cost of all edit operations (insertions, deletions, substitutions) is one [18]:

$$\forall a, b \in \Sigma, \; c((a, b)) = 1 \text{ if } (a \neq b) \text{ , 0 otherwise}$$

We will denote by c_1 this specific edit cost function. The definition of edit-distance can be generalized to measure the similarity of two sets of strings X and Y by:

$$d(X, Y) = \inf \{d(x, y) : x \in X, y \in Y\}$$

In some applications such as speech recognition or computational biology, one might wish to measure the similarity of a string x with respect to a distribution Y of strings y with probability $P(y)$. The edit-distance of x to Y can then be defined by the expected edit-distance of x to the strings y:

$$d(x, Y) = E_{P(y)}[d(x, y)]$$

Similarly, the edit-distance of two distributions X and Y is defined by:

$$d(X, Y) = E_{P(x,y)}[d(x, y)]$$

We are particularly interested here in the case where these distributions are given by weighted automata which is typical in the applications already mentioned. More precisely, the corresponding automata are acyclic weighted automata over the log semiring.[3] Let A_1 and A_2 be two acyclic weighted automata over the log semiring $\mathcal{L}$ defined over the same alphabet Σ, their edit-distance is thus given by:

$$d(A_1, A_2) = \sum_{x,y} \exp(-[\![A_1]\!](x) - [\![A_2]\!](y))d(x, y)$$
$$= \sum_{x,y} \exp \{-([\![A_1]\!](x) + [\![A_2]\!](y) - \log d(x, y))\}$$

This equation can be rewritten using the operations of the log semiring.

Definition 5. *The edit-distance of two acyclic weighted automata over the log semiring $\mathcal{L}$, A_1 and A_2, is defined by:*

$$d(A_1, A_2) = \exp(- \bigoplus_{\substack{\log \\ x,y}} ([\![A_1]\!](x) + [\![A_2]\!](y) - \log d(x, y)))$$

We will give an algorithm for computing this edit-distance using general weighted automata algorithms. Note that the computation of $d(A_1, A_2)$ is not trivial a priori since its definition uses operations corresponding to both the tropical semiring (min and + for computing the edit-distance of two strings) and the log semiring ($\oplus_{\log}$ and +).

---

[3] For numerical stability, $- \log$ probabilities are used in practice rather than probabilities.

4 Weighted Automata Algorithms

In this section we give a brief overview of some classical and existing weighted automata algorithms such as composition, determinization, and minimization, and describe a new and general *synchronization* algorithm for weighted transducers.

4.1 Composition of Weighted Transducers

Composition is a fundamental operation on weighted transducers that can be used in many applications to create complex weighted transducers from simpler ones. Let $\mathbb{K}$ be a commutative semiring and let T_1 and T_2 be two weighted transducers defined over $\mathbb{K}$ such that the input alphabet of T_2 coincides with the output alphabet of T_1. Then, the composition of T_1 and T_2 is a weighted transducer $T_1 \circ T_2$ defined for all x, y by [3,10,29,16]:[4]

$$[\![T_1 \circ T_2]\!](x, y) = \bigoplus_z T_1(x, z) \otimes T_2(z, y)$$

There exists a general and efficient composition algorithm for weighted transducers [27,23]. States in the composition $T_1 \circ T_2$ of two weighted transducers T_1 and T_2 are identified with pairs of a state of T_1 and a state of T_2. Leaving aside transitions with ϵ inputs or outputs, the following rule specifies how to compute a transition of $T_1 \circ T_2$ from appropriate transitions of T_1 and T_2:[5]

$$(q_1, a, b, w_1, q_2) \quad \text{and} \quad (q_1', b, c, w_2, q_2') \implies ((q_1, q_2), a, c, w_1 \otimes w_2, (q_1', q_2'))$$

In the worst case, all transitions of T_1 leaving a state q_1 match all those of T_2 leaving state q_1', thus the space and time complexity of composition is quadratic: $O((|Q_1| + |E_1|)(|Q_2| + |E_2|))$. Figures 1 (a)-(c) illustrate the algorithm when applied to the transducers of figures 1 (a)-(b) defined over the tropical semiring $\mathcal{T} = T$.

Intersection of weighted automata and composition of finite-state transducers are both special cases of composition of weighted transducers. Intersection corresponds to the case where input and output labels of transitions are identical and composition of unweighted transducers is obtained simply by omitting the weights. Thus, we can use both the notation $A = A_1 \cap A_2$ or $A_1 \circ A_2$ for the intersection of two weighted automata A_1 and A_2. A string x is recognized by A iff it is recognized by both A_1 and A_2 and $[\![A]\!](x) = [\![A_1]\!](x) \otimes [\![A_2]\!](x)$.

4.2 Determinization of Weighted Automata

A weighted automaton is said to be *deterministic* or *subsequential* [31] if it has a unique initial state and if no two transitions leaving any state share the same input label.

---

[4] Note that we use a *matrix notation* for the definition of composition as opposed to a *functional notation*. This is a deliberate choice motivated in many cases by improved readability.

[5] See [27,23] for a detailed presentation of the algorithm including the use of a transducer filter for dealing with ϵ-multiplicity in the case of non-idempotent semirings.

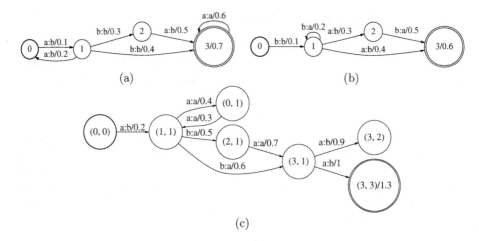

Fig. 1. (a) Weighted transducer T_1 over the tropical semiring. (b) Weighted transducer T_2 over the tropical semiring. (c) Construction of the result of composition $T_1 \circ T_2$. Initial states are represented by bold circles, final states by double circles. Inside each circle, the first number indicates the state number, the second, at final states only, the value of the final weight function ρ at that state. Arrows represent transitions and are labeled with symbols followed by their corresponding weight.

There exists a natural extension of the classical subset construction to the case of weighted automata over a weakly left divisible semiring called *determinization* [20].[6] The algorithm is generic: it works with any weakly left divisible semiring. Figures 2 (a)-(b) illustrate the determinization of a weighted automaton over the tropical semiring. A state r of the output automaton that can be reached from the start state by a path π corresponds to the set of pairs $(q, x) \in Q \times \mathbb{K}$ such that q can be reached from an initial state of the original machine by a path σ with $l[\sigma] = l[\pi]$ and $\lambda(p[\sigma]) \otimes w[\sigma] = \lambda(p[\pi]) \otimes w[\pi] \otimes x$. Thus, x is the *remaining* weight at state q.

Unlike the unweighted case, determinization does not halt for some input weighted automata. In fact, some weighted automata, non *subsequentiable* automata, do not even admit equivalent subsequential machines. We say that a weighted automaton A is *determinizable* if the determinization algorithm halts for the input A. With a determinizable input, the algorithm outputs an equivalent subsequential weighted automaton [20].

There exists a sufficient condition, necessary and sufficient for unambiguous automata, for the determinizability of weighted automata over a tropical semiring based on a *twins property*. There exists an efficient algorithm for testing the twins property for weighted automata [1]. In particular, any acyclic weighted automaton has the twins property and is determinizable.

---

[6] We assume that the weighted automata considered are all such that for any string $x \in \Sigma^*$, $w[P(I, x, Q)] \neq \bar{0}$. This condition is always satisfied with trim machines over the tropical semiring or any zero-sum-free semiring.

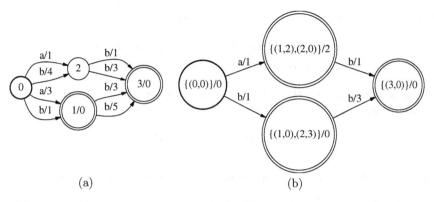

Fig. 2. (a) Weighted automaton A over the tropical semiring. (b) Equivalent subsequential weighted automaton A_2 over the tropical semiring constructed by the determinization algorithm.

4.3 Synchronization

In this section, we present a general algorithm for the *synchronization of weighted transducers*. Roughly speaking, the objective of the algorithm is to synchronize the consumption of non-ϵ symbols by the input and output tapes of a transducer as much as possible.

A synchronization procedure was first presented by [10]. The first explicit synchronization algorithm was given by [11] for transducers with bounded delay, later extended by [2] to transducers with constant emission rate. The algorithm of [11] applies only to transducers with input labels different from the empty string ϵ. We present a simple synchronization algorithm that is not restricted to these transducers, and that applies more generally to *weighted* transducers with bounded delays defined over a semiring $\mathbb{K}$.

Definition 6. *The* delay *of a path π is defined as the difference of length between its output and input labels:*

$$d[\pi] = |o[\pi]| - |i[\pi]|$$

The delay of a path is thus simply the sum of the delays of its constituent transitions. A trim transducer T is said to have *bounded delays* if the delay along all paths of T is bounded. We then denote by $d[T] \geq 0$ the maximum delay in absolute value of a path in T. The following lemma gives a straightforward characterization of transducers with bounded delays.

Lemma 1. *A transducer T has bounded delays iff the delay of any cycle in T is zero.*

Proof. If T admits a cycle π with non-zero delay, then $d[T] \geq |d[\pi^n]| = n|d[\pi]|$ is not bounded. Conversely, if all cycles have zero delay, then the maximum delay in T is that of the simple paths which are of finite number. □

We define the *string delay* of a path π as the string $s[\pi]$ defined by:

$$s[\pi] = \text{suffix of } o[\pi] \text{ of length } |d[\pi]| \quad \text{if } d[\pi] \geq 0$$
$$\text{suffix of } i[\pi] \text{ of length } |d[\pi]| \quad \text{otherwise}$$

and for any state $q \in Q$, the *string delay at q* $S[q]$ by the set of string delays of the paths from an initial state to q:

$$s[q] = \{s[\pi] : \pi \in P(I, q)\}$$

Lemma 2. *If T has bounded delays then the set $s[q]$ is finite for any $q \in Q$.*

Proof. The lemma follows immediately the fact that the elements of $s[q]$ are all of length less than $d[T]$. □

A weighted transducer T is said to be *synchronized* if along any successful path of T the delay is zero or varies strictly monotonically. An algorithm that takes as input a transducer T and computes an equivalent synchronized transducer T' is called a *synchronization* algorithm. We present a synchronization algorithm that applies to all weighted transducers with bounded delays. The following is the pseudocode of the algorithm.

```
Synchronization(T)
 1   F' ← Q' ← E' ← ∅
 2   S ← i' ← {(i, ε, ε) : i ∈ I}
 3   while S ≠ ∅
 4       do  p' = (q, x, y) ← head(S); DEQUEUE(S)
 5           if (q ∈ F and |x| + |y| = 0)
 6               then  F' ← F' ∪ {p'}; ρ'(p') ← ρ(q)
 7               else if (q ∈ F and |x| + |y| > 0)
 8                   then  q' ← (f, cdr(x), cdr(y))
 9                         E' ← E' ∪ (p', car(x), car(y), ρ[q], q')
10                         if (q' ∉ Q')
11                             then  Q' ← Q' ∪ {q'}; ENQUEUE(S, q')
12               for  each e ∈ E[q]
13                   do if (|x i[e]| > 0  and  |y o[e]| > 0)
14                       then  q' ← (n[e], cdr(x i[e]), cdr(y o[e]))
15                             E' ← E' ∪ {(p', car(x i[e]), car(y o[e]), w[e], q')}
16                       else  q' ← (n[e], x i[e], y o[e])
17                             E' ← E' ∪ {(p', ε, ε, w[e], q')}
18                       if (q' ∉ Q')
19                           then  Q' ← Q' ∪ {q'}; ENQUEUE(S, q')
20   return T'
```

To simplify the presentation of the algorithm, we introduce a new state f and add it to Q and F with $\rho[f] = \bar{1}$ and $E[f] = \emptyset$. We denote by $car(x)$ the first symbol of a string x if x is not empty, ϵ otherwise, and denote by $cdr(x)$ the suffix of x such that $x = car(x) \, cdr(x)$.

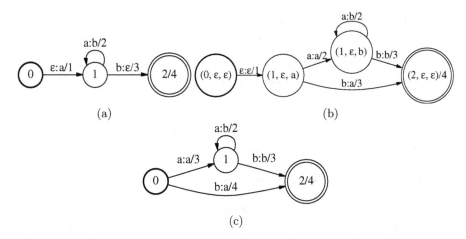

Fig. 3. (a) Weighted automaton A_1 over the tropical semiring. (b) Equivalent synchronized weighted automaton A_2. (c) Synchronized weighted automaton A_3 equivalent to A_1 and A_2 obtained by ϵ-removal from A_2.

Each state of the resulting transducer T' corresponds to a triplet (q, x, y) where $q \in Q$ is a state of the original machine T and where $x \in \Sigma^*$ and $y \in \Delta^*$ are strings over the input and output alphabet of T.

The algorithm maintains a queue S that contains at any time the set of states of T' to examine. Each time through the loop of the lines 3-19, a new state $p' = (q, x, y)$ is extracted from S (line 4) and its outgoing transitions are computed and added to E'. The state p' is final iff q is final and $x = y = \epsilon$ and in that case the final weight at p' is simply the final weight at the original state q (lines 5-6). If q is final but the string x and y are not both empty, then the algorithm constructs a sequence of transitions from p' to (f, ϵ, ϵ) to consume the remaining input and output strings x and y (lines 7-11).

For each transition e of q an outgoing transition e' is created for p' with weight $w[e]$. The input and output labels of e' are either both ϵ if $x\,i[e]$ or $y\,o[e]$ is the empty string, the first symbol of these strings otherwise, and the remaining suffixes of these strings are stored in the destination state q' (lines 12-19). Note that in all cases, the transitions created by the steps of the algorithm described in lines 14-17 have zero delay. The state q' is inserted in S if it has never been found before (line 18-19). Figures 3 (a)-(b) illustrate the synchronization algorithm just presented.

Lemma 3. *Let (q, x, y) correspond to a state of T' created by the algorithm. Then, either $x = \epsilon$ or $y = \epsilon$.*

Proof. Let $p' = (q, x, y)$ be a state extracted from S, it is not hard to verify that if $x = \epsilon$ or $y = \epsilon$, then the destination state of a transition leaving p' created by the algorithm is of the form $q' = (r, \epsilon, y')$ or $q' = (r, x', \epsilon)$. Since the algorithm starts with the states (i, ϵ, ϵ), $i \in I$, by induction, for any state $p' = (q, x, y)$ created either $x = \epsilon$ or $y = \epsilon$. $\qquad\square$

Lemma 4. *Let π' be a path in T' created by the synchronization algorithm such that $n[\pi']$ corresponds to (q', x', y') with $q' \neq f$. Then, the delay of π' is zero.*

Proof. By construction, the delay of each transition created at lines 14-17 is zero. Since the delay of a path is the sum of the delays of its transitions, this proves the lemma.   □

Lemma 5. *Let (q', x', y') correspond to a state of T' created by the algorithm with $q' \neq f$. Then, either $x' \in s[q']$ or $y' \in s[q']$.*

Proof. By induction on the length of π', it is easy to prove that there is a path π' from state (q, x, y) to (q', x', y') iff there is a path from q to q' with input label $x^{-1}i[\pi']x'$, output label $y^{-1}o[\pi']y'$, and weight $w[\pi']$.

Thus, the algorithm constructs a path π' in T' from (i, ϵ, ϵ), $i \in I$, to (q', x', y'), $q' \neq f$ iff there exists a path π in T from i to q' with input label $i[\pi] = i[\pi']x'$, output label $o[\pi] = o[\pi']y'$ and weight $w[\pi] = w[\pi']$. By lemma 4, $|i[\pi']| = |o[\pi']|$. Thus, if $x' = \epsilon$, y' is the string delay of π. Similarly, if $y' = \epsilon$, x' is the string delay of π. By lemma 3, $x' = \epsilon$ or $y' = \epsilon$, thus $y' \in s[q]$ or $x' \in s[q]$.   □

Theorem 1. *The synchronization algorithm presented terminates with any input weighted transducer T with bounded delays and produces an equivalent synchronized transducer T'.*

Proof. By lemmas 4 and 5, if (q', x', y') is a state created by the algorithm with $q' \neq f$, then either $x' = \epsilon$ and $y' \in s[q]$ or $y' = \epsilon$ and $x' \in s[q]$. If T has bounded delays, by lemma 2 $s[q]$ is finite, thus the algorithm produces a finite number of states of the form (q', x', y') with $q' \neq f$.

Let (q, x, ϵ) be a state created by the algorithm with $q \in F$ and $|x| > 0$. $x = x_1 \cdots x_n$ is thus a string delay at q. The algorithm constructs a path from (q, x, ϵ) to (f, ϵ, ϵ) with intermediate states $(f, x_i \cdots x_n, \epsilon)$. Since string delays are bounded, at most a finite number of such states are created by the algorithm. A similar result holds for states (q, ϵ, y) with $q \in F$ and $|y| > 0$. Thus, the algorithm produces a finite number of states and terminates if T has bounded delays.

By lemma 4, paths π' in T' with destination state (q, x, y) with $q \neq f$ have zero delay and the delay of a path from a state (f, x, y) to (f, ϵ, ϵ) is strictly monotonic. Thus, the output of the algorithm is a synchronized transducer. This ends the proof of the theorem.   □

The algorithm creates a distinct state (q, x, ϵ) or (q, ϵ, y) for each string delay $x, y \in s[q]$ at state $q \neq f$. The paths from a state (q, x, ϵ) or (q, ϵ, y), $q \in F$, to (f, ϵ, ϵ) are of length $|x|$ or $|y|$. The length of a string delay is bounded by $d[T]$. Thus, there are at most $|\Sigma|^{\leq d[T]} + |\Delta|^{\leq d[T]} = O(|\Sigma|^{d[T]} + |\Delta|^{d[T]})$ distinct string delays at each state. Thus, in the worst case, the size of the resulting transducer T' is:

$$O((|Q| + |E|)(|\Sigma|^{d[T]} + |\Delta|^{d[T]}))$$

The string delays can be represented in a compact and efficient way using a suffix tree. Indeed, let U be a tree representing all the input and output labels of the paths in T found in a depth-first search of T. The size of U is linear in that of T and a suffix tree V of U can be built in time proportional to the number of nodes of U times the size of the alphabet [15], that is in $O((|\Sigma| + |\Delta|) \cdot (|Q| + |E|))$. Since each string delay x is a suffix of a string represented by U, it can be represented by two nodes n_1 and n_2 of V and a position in the string labeling the edge from n_1 to n_2. The operations performed by the algorithm to construct a new transition require either computing xa or $a^{-1}x$ where a is a symbol of the input or output alphabet. Clearly, these operations can be performed in constant time: xa is obtained by going down one position in the suffix tree, and $a^{-1}x$ by using the suffix link at node n_1. Thus, using this representation, the operations performed for the construction of each new transition can be done in constant time. This includes the cost of comparison of a newly created state (q', x', ϵ) with an existing state (q, x, ϵ), since the comparison of the string delays x and x' can be done in constant time. Thus, the worst case space and time complexity of the algorithm is:

$$O((|Q| + |E|)(|\Sigma|^{d[T]} + |\Delta|^{d[T]}))$$

This is not a tight evaluation of the complexity since it is not clear if the worst case previously described can ever occur, but the algorithm can indeed produce an exponentially larger transducer in some cases.

Note that the algorithm does not depend on the queue discipline used for S and that the construction of the transitions leaving a state $p' = (q, x, y)$ of T' only depends on p' and not on the states and transitions previously constructed. Thus, the transitions of T' can be naturally computed on-demand. We have precisely given an on-the-fly implementation of the algorithm and incorporated it in a general-purpose finite-state machine library (FSM library) [24,26]. Note also that the additive and multiplicative operations of the semiring are not used in the definition of the algorithm. Only $\bar{1}$, the identity element of $\otimes$, was used for the definition of the final weight of f. Thus, to a large extent, the algorithm is independent of the semiring $\mathbb{K}$. In particular, the behavior of the algorithm is identical for two semirings having the same identity elements, such as for example the tropical and log semirings.

4.4 ϵ-Removal

The result of the synchronization algorithm may contain ϵ-transitions (transitions with both input and output empty string) even if the input contains none. An equivalent weighted transducer with no ϵ-transitions can be computed from T' using a general ϵ-removal algorithm [21]. Figure 3 (c) illustrates the result of that algorithm when applied to the synchronized transducer of figure 3 (b).

Since ϵ-removal does not shift input and output labels with respect to each other, the result of its application to T' is also a synchronized transducer.

Note that the synchronization algorithm does not produce any ϵ-cycle if the original machine T does not contain any. Thus, in that case, the computation of the ϵ-closures in T can be done in linear time [21] and the total time complexity of ϵ-removal is $O(|Q'|^2 + (T_\oplus + T_\otimes)|Q'| \cdot |E'|)$, where $T_\oplus$ and $T_\otimes$ denote the cost of the $\oplus$, $\otimes$ operations in the semiring $\mathbb{K}$. Also, on-the-fly synchronization can be combined with on-the-fly ϵ-removal to *directly* create synchronized transducers with no ϵ-transition on-the-fly.

A by-product of the application of synchronization followed by ϵ-removal is that the resulting transducer is *normalized*.

Definition 7. *Let π and π' be two paths of a transducer T with the same input and output labels: $i[\pi] = i[\pi']$ and $o[\pi] = o[\pi']$. We will say that $\pi = e_1 \cdots e_n$ and $\pi' = e'_1 \cdots e'_{n'}$ are identical if they have the same number of transitions ($n = n'$) with the same labels: $i[e_k] = i[e'_k]$ and $o[e_k] = o[e'_k]$ for $k = 1, \ldots, n$. T is said to be normalized if any two paths π and π' with the same input and output labels are identical.*

Note that the definition does not require the weights of two identical paths to be the same.

Lemma 6. *Let T be a synchronized transducer and assume that T has no ϵ-transition. Then, T is normalized.*

Proof. Let π and π' be two paths with the same input and output labels. Since T is synchronized and has no ϵ-transitions, π and π' have the same delay and more precisely the delay varies in the same way along these two paths and are thus identical.   □

5   Computation of the Edit-Distance of Unweighted Automata

The edit-distance $d(X,Y)$ of two sets of strings X and Y each represented by an unweighted automaton can be computed using the general algorithm of composition of transducers and a single-source shortest-paths algorithm [24]. The algorithm applies similarly in the case of an arbitrarily complex edit-distance defined by a weighted transducer over the tropical semiring.

Let A_1 and A_2 be two (unweighted) automata representing the sets X and Y. By definition, the edit-distance of X and Y, or equivalently that of A_1 and A_2, is defined by:

$$d(A_1, A_2) = \inf \{d(x,y) : x \in Dom(A_1), y \in Dom(A_2)\}$$

5.1   Alignment Costs in the Tropical Semiring

Let Ψ be the formal power series defined over the alphabet Ω and the tropical semiring by: $(\Psi, (a,b)) = c((a,b))$ for $(a,b) \in \Omega$.

Lemma 7. *Let $\omega = (a_0, b_0) \cdots (a_n, b_n) \in \Omega^*$ be an alignment, then (Ψ^*, ω) is exactly the cost of the alignment ω.*

Fig. 4. Weighted transducer over the tropical semiring representing Ψ^* with the edit cost function c_1 and $\Sigma = \{a, b\}$.

Proof. By definition of the $+$-multiplication of power series in the tropical semiring:

$$(\Psi^*, \omega) = \min_{u_0 \cdots u_k = \omega} (\Psi, u_0) + \cdots + (\Psi, u_k)$$

$$= (\Psi, (a_0, b_0)) + \cdots + (\Psi, (a_n, b_n))$$

$$= \sum_{i=0}^{n} c((a_i, b_i)) = c(\omega)$$

This proves the lemma.   □

Ψ^* is a rational power series as the closure of the polynomial power series Ψ [29,4]. Thus, by the theorem of Schützenberger [30], there exists a weighted automaton A defined over the alphabet Ω and the semiring $\mathcal{T}$ realizing Ψ^*. A can also be viewed as a weighted transducer T with input and output alphabets Σ. Figure 5 shows the simple finite-state transducer T realizing Ψ^* in the particular case of the edit cost function c_1 and with $\Sigma = \{a, b\}$.

5.2   Algorithm

By definition of composition of transducers and by lemma 7, the weighted transducer $A_1 \circ T \circ A_2$ contains a successful path corresponding to each alignment ω of a string accepted by A_1 and a string accepted by A_2 and the weight of that path is $c(\omega)$.

Theorem 2. *Let U be the weighted transducer over the tropical semiring obtained by: $U = A_1 \circ T \circ A_2$. Let π be a shortest path of U from the initial state to the final states. Then, π is labeled with one of the best alignments of a string accepted by A_1 and a string accepted by A_2 and: $d(A_1, A_2) = w[\pi]$.*

Proof. The result follows directly the previous remark.   □

The theorem provides an algorithm for computing the best alignment between the strings of two unweighted automata A_1 and A_2 and for computing their edit-distance $d(A_1, A_2)$. Any single-source shortest-paths algorithm applied to U can be used to compute the edit-distance and a best alignment. Let $|V|$ denote the sum of the number of states and transitions of an automaton or transducer V. Since the worst case time and space complexity of composition is quadratic, we have: $|U| = O(|A_1||A_2|)$.

When U is acyclic, this is the case in particular when A_1 and A_2 are both acyclic, the total time complexity of the computation of the best alignment and the edit-distance $d(A_1, A_2)$ is $O(|A_1||A_2|)$ since we can then use Lawler's linear-time single-source shortest paths algorithm [17,5]. In the general case, the total complexity of the algorithm is $O(|E| + |Q| \log |Q|)$, where E denotes the set of transitions and Q the set of states of U, using Dijkstra's algorithm implemented with Fibonacci heaps [8,5].

In particular, the time complexity of the computation of the edit-distance for two strings x and y is $O(|x||y|)$. The classical dynamic programming algorithm for computing the edit-distance of two strings can in fact be viewed as a special instance of the more general algorithm just presented.

This algorithm is very general. It extends to the case of automata the classical edit-distance computation and it also generalizes the classical definition of edit-distance. Indeed, any weighted transducer with non-negative weights can be used here without modifying the algorithm. [7] Edit-distance transducers with arbitrary topologies, arbitrary number of states and transitions can be used instead of the specific one-state edit-distance transducer used in most applications. More general transducers assigning non-negative costs to transpositions or to more general weighted context-dependent rules [25] can be used to model complex edit-distances.

6   Computation of the Edit-Distance of Weighted Automata

Our algorithm for computing the edit-distance of two weighted automata is based on weighted composition, determinization, ϵ-removal, and synchronization. More precisely, our algorithm computes -log of that edit-distance:

$$- \log(d(A_1, A_2)) = \bigoplus_{\substack{\log \\ x,y}} [\![A_1]\!](x) + [\![A_2]\!](y) - \log d(x, y)$$

We first show that the cost of the alignment of two strings can be computed using a simple weighted transducer over the log semiring.

---

[7] Transducers with negative weights can be used as well, but the single-source shortest-paths problems of Bellman-Ford would need to be used then in general, which can make the algorithm less efficient in general.

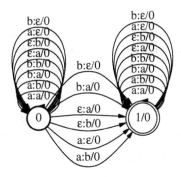

Fig. 5. Weighted transducer over the log semiring representing S with the edit cost function c_1 and $\Sigma = \{a, b\}$. The transition weights and the final weight at state 1 are all equal to 0, since $-\log(c_1(x, y)) = 0$ for $x \neq y$.

6.1 Alignment Costs in the Log Semiring

Let Ψ be the formal power series defined over the alphabet Ω and the log semiring by: $(\Psi, (a, b)) = -\log(c((a, b)))$ for $(a, b) \in \Omega$, and let S be the formal power series S over the log semiring defined by:

$$S = \Omega^* + \Psi + \Omega^*$$

S is a rational power series as a +-product and closure of the polynomial power series Ω and Ψ [29,4]. Thus, by the theorem of Schützenberger [30], there exists a weighted automaton A defined over the alphabet Ω and the semiring $\mathcal{L}$ realizing S. A can also be viewed as a weighted transducer T with input and output alphabets Σ. Figure 5 shows the simple finite-state transducer T realizing S in the particular case of the edit cost function c_1 and with $\Sigma = \{a, b\}$.

Lemma 8. Let $\omega = (a_0, b_0) \cdots (a_n, b_n) \in \Omega^*$ be an alignment, then (S, ω) is equal to -log of the cost of ω.

Proof. By definition of the +-multiplication of power series in the log semiring:

$$(S, \omega) = \bigoplus_{\substack{\log \\ u\,(a_i, b_i)\,v = \omega}} (\Omega^*, u) + (\Psi, (a_i, b_i)) + (\Omega^*, v)$$

$$= \bigoplus_{\substack{\log \\ i=0}}^{n} -\log(c((a_i, b_i))) = -\log(\sum_{i=0}^{n} c((a_i, b_i))) = -\log c(\omega)$$

This proves the lemma. □

The lemma is a special instance of a more general property that can be easily proved in the same way: given an alphabet Σ and a rational set $X \subseteq \Sigma^*$, the power series $\Sigma^* + X + \Sigma^*$ over the log semiring is rational and associates to each string $x \in \Sigma^*$ -log of the number of occurrences of an element of X in x.

6.2   Algorithm

Let A_1 and A_2 be two acyclic weighted automata defined over the alphabet Σ and the log semiring $\mathcal{L}$, and let T be the weighted transducer over the log semiring associated to S.

Let $M = A_1 \circ T \circ A_2$. M can be viewed as a weighted automaton over the alphabet Ω.

Lemma 9. *Let $\omega \in \Omega^*$ be an alignment such that $h(w) = (x, y)$ with $x \in Dom(A_1)$ and $y \in Dom(A_2)$, then:*

$$[\![M]\!](w) = -\log c(\omega) + [\![A_1]\!](x) + [\![A_2]\!](x)$$

Proof. By definition of composition, $[\![M]\!](w)$ represents the value associated by S to the alignment ω with weight $W = [\![A_1]\!](x) + [\![A_2]\!](x)$. By lemma 8 and the definition of power series, S associates to an alignment ω with weight W the following: $-\log c(\omega) + W$. □

The automaton M may contain several paths labeled with the same alignment ω. M is acyclic as the result of the composition of T with acyclic automata, thus it can be determinized. Denote by $\det_{\mathcal{L}}(M)$ the result of that determinization in the log semiring. By definition of determinization, $\det_{\mathcal{L}}(M)$ is equivalent to M but contains exactly one path for each alignment ω between two strings $x \in Dom(A_1)$ and $y \in Dom(A_2)$.

We need to keep for each pair of strings x and y only one path, the one corresponding to the alignment ω of x and y with the minimal cost $c(\omega)$ or equivalently maximal $[\![M]\!](w)$. We will use determinization in the tropical semiring, $\det_{\mathcal{T}}$, to do so. However, to apply this algorithm we first need to ensure that the transducer is normalized so that paths corresponding to different alignments ω but with the same $h(\omega)$ be merged by the automata determinization $\det_{\mathcal{T}}$. By lemma 6, one way to normalize the automaton consists of using the synchronization algorithm, synch, followed by ϵ-removal in the log semiring, $rme_{\mathcal{L}}$.

Theorem 3. *Let N be the deterministic weighted automaton defined by:*

$$N = -\det_{\mathcal{T}}(-rme(\text{synch}(\det_{\mathcal{L}}(A_1 \circ T \circ A_2))))$$

Then for any $x \in Dom(A_1)$ and $y \in Dom(A_2)$:

$$[\![N]\!](x, y) = [\![A_1]\!](x) + [\![A_2]\!](y) - \log d(x, y)$$

Proof. Let $\omega \in \Omega^*$ be an alignment such that $h(w) = (x, y)$ with $x \in Dom(A_1)$ and $y \in Dom(A_2)$, then, by lemma 8:

$$rme_{\mathcal{L}}(\text{synch}(\det_{\mathcal{L}}(A_1 \circ T \circ A_2)))(\omega) = [\![A_1]\!](x) + [\![A_2]\!](y) - \log c(\omega)$$

Since $rme_{\mathcal{L}}(\text{synch}(\det_{\mathcal{L}}(A_1 \circ T \circ A_2)))$ is normalized, by definition of determinization in the tropical semiring, for any $x \in Dom(A_1)$ and $y \in Dom(A_2)$:

$$[\![N]\!](x, y) = \max_{h(\omega)=(x,y)} [\![A_1]\!](x) + [\![A_2]\!](y) - \log c(\omega)$$

$$= [\![A_1]\!](x) + [\![A_2]\!](y) - \log d(x, y) \qquad\qquad\qquad □$$

Since N is deterministic when viewed as a weighted automaton, the shortest distance from the initial state i to the final states F in the log semiring is exactly what we intended to compute:

$$\bigoplus_{\pi \in P(i,F)} w[\pi] = \bigoplus_{\substack{\log \\ x,y}} [\![A_1]\!](x) + [\![A_2]\!](y) - \log d(x,y) = -\log(d(A_1, A_2))$$

This shortest distance can be computed in linear time using a generalization of the classical single-source shortest paths algorithm for acyclic graphs [22]. Thus, the theorem shows that the edit-distance of two automata A_1 and A_2 can be computed exactly using general weighted automata algorithms.

The worst case complexity of the algorithm is exponential but in practice several techniques can be used to improve its efficiency. First, a heuristic pruning can be used to reduce the size of the original automata A_1 and A_2 or that of intermediate automata and transducers in the algorithm described. Additionally, weighted minimization in the tropical and log semirings [20] can be used to optimally reduce the size of the automata after each determinization. Finally, the automaton A is not determinizable in the log semiring but it can be approximated by a deterministic one for example by limiting the number of insertions, deletions or substitutions to some large but fixed number or by using ϵ-determinization [20]. The advantage of a deterministic A is that it is unambiguous and thus it leads to an unambiguous machine M in the sense that no two paths of M correspond to the same alignment. Thus, it is not necessary to apply determinization in the log semiring, $\det_{\mathcal{L}}$, to M.

6.3   Edit-Distance Weighted Automaton

In some applications such as speech recognition, one might wish to compute not just the edit-distance of A_1 and A_2 but an automaton A_3 accepting exactly the same strings as A_1 and such that the weight associated to $x \in Dom(A_3)$ is -log of the expected edit-distance of x to A_2: $[\![A_3]\!](x) = -\log d(x, A_2)$. In such cases, the automaton A_1 is typically assumed to be unweighted: $[\![A_1]\!](x) = 0$ for all $x \in Dom(A_1)$.

More precisely, A_2 is then the weighted automaton, or word lattice, output of the recognizer, and the weight of each sentence is -log of the probability of that sentence given the acoustic information. However, the word-accuracy of a speech recognizer is measured by computing the edit-distance of the sentence output of the recognizer and the reference sentence [32,19]. This motivates the algorithm presented in this section. Assuming that all candidate sentences are represented by some automaton A_1 (A_1 could represent all possible sentences for example or just the sentences accepted by A_2), one wishes to determine for each sentence in A_1 its expected edit-distance to A_2 and thus to compute A_3.

Let $proj_1$ be the operation that creates an acceptor from a weighted transducer by removing its output labels. The following theorem gives the algorithm for computing A_3 based on classical weighted automata algorithms.

Theorem 4. *Let A_1 be an unweighted automaton and A_2 an acyclic weighted automaton over the* log *semiring. Then the edit-distance automaton A_3 can be computed as follows from N:*

$$A_3 = \det_{\mathcal{L}}(\text{proj}_1(N))$$

Proof. Since A_1 is unweighted, by theorem 3, for any $x \in Dom(A_1)$ and $y \in Dom(A_2)$:

$$[\![N]\!](x, y) = [\![A_2]\!](y) - \log d(x, y)$$

To construct A_3 we can omit the output labels of N. $\text{proj}_1(N)$ may have several paths labeled with the same input x. If we apply weighted determinization in the log semiring to it, then by definition the weight of a path labeled with x will be exactly:

$$\bigoplus_{\substack{\log \\ y \in D \text{ om } (A_2)}} [\![A_2]\!](y) - \log d(x, y) = -\log[\sum_{y \in D \text{ om } (A_2)} \exp(-[\![A_2]\!](y) + \log d(x, y))]$$

$$= -\log[\sum_{y \in D \text{ om } (A_2)} \exp(-[\![A_2]\!](y))d(x, y)]$$

$$= -\log d(x, A_2)$$

This proves the theorem. □

The weighted automaton A_3 can be further minimized using weighted minimization to reduce its number of states and transitions [20].

In the log semiring, the weight associated to an alignment with cost zero is $\infty = -\log 0$. Thus, paths corresponding to the best alignments would simply not appear in the result. To avoid this effect, one can assign an arbitrary large cost to perfect alignments.

In speech recognition, using a sentence with the lowest expected word error rate instead of one with the highest probability can lead to a significant improvement of the word accuracy of the system [32,19]. That sentence is simply the label of a shortest path in A_3 and can therefore be obtained from A_3 efficiently using a classical single-source shortest-paths algorithm.

Speech recognition systems often use a rescoring method. This consists of first using a simple acoustic and grammar model to produce a word lattice or n-best list, and then to reevaluate these alternative hypotheses with a more sophisticated model or by using information sources of a different nature. The weighted automaton or word lattice A_3 can be used advantageously for such rescoring purposes.

7   Conclusion

Algorithms for computing the edit-distance of unweighted and weighted automata were given. These algorithms are based on general and efficient weighted automata algorithms over different semirings and classical single-source shortest-paths algorithms. They demonstrate the power of automata theory and semiring theory and provide a complex example of the use of multiple semirings in a single application.

The algorithms presented have applications in many areas ranging from text processing to computational biology. They can lead to significant improvements of the word accuracy in large-vocabulary speech recognition as shown by several experiments [32,19,12]. Recently, several kernels were introduced in computational biology for input vectors representing biological sequences [14,35,9]. These *string kernels* are specific instances of the more general class of *rational kernels* [6] and can all be computed efficiently using the general algorithms presented in sections 5 and 6. They can be generalized to deal properly with probabilistic or weighted sequences. An algorithm for computing such generalized kernels based on general weighted automata algorithms was given in section 6.

Acknowledgments. I thank Cyril Allauzen and Michael Riley for discussions about this work.

References

1. Cyril Allauzen and Mehryar Mohri. Efficient Algorithms for Testing the Twins Property. *Journal of Automata, Languages and Combinatorics*, to appear, 2002.
2. Marie-Pierre Béal and Olivier Carton. Asynchronous sliding block maps. *Informatique Théorique et Applications*, 34(2):139–156, 2000.
3. Jean Berstel. *Transductions and Context-Free Languages*. Teubner Studienbucher: Stuttgart, 1979.
4. Jean Berstel and Christophe Reutenauer. *Rational Series and Their Languages*. Springer-Verlag: Berlin-New York, 1988.
5. T. Cormen, C. Leiserson, and R. Rivest. *Introduction to Algorithms*. The MIT Press: Cambridge, MA, 1992.
6. Corinna Cortes, Patrick Haffner, and Mehryar Mohri. Rational Kernels. In *Advances in Neural Information Processing Systems (NIPS 2002)*, volume to appear, Vancouver, Canada, December 2002.
7. Maxime Crochemore and Wojciech Rytter. *Text Algorithms*. Oxford University Press, 1994.
8. E. W. Dijkstra. A note on two problems in connexion with graphs. *Numerische Mathematik*, 1, 1959.
9. R. Durbin, S.R. Eddy, A. Krogh, and G.J. Mitchison. *Biological Sequence Analysis: Probabilistic Models of Proteins and Nucleic Acids*. Cambridge University Press, Cambridge UK, 1998.
10. Samuel Eilenberg. *Automata, Languages and Machines*, volume A. Academic Press, 1974.
11. Christiane Frougny and Jacques Sakarovitch. Synchronized Rational Relations of Finite and Infinite Words. *Theoretical Computer Science*, 108(1):45–82, 1993.
12. Vaibhava Goel and William Byrne. Task Dependent Loss Functions in Speech Recognition: A* Search over Recognition Lattices. In *Proceedings of Eurospeech'99, Budapest, Hungary*, 1999.

13. Dan Gusfield. *Algorithms on Strings, Trees, and Sequences.* Cambridge University Press, Cambridge, UK., 1997.
14. David Haussler. Convolution kernels on discrete structures. Technical Report UCSC-CRL-99-10, University of California at Santa Cruz, 1999.
15. Shunsuke Inenaga, Hiromasa Hoshino, Ayumi Shinohara, Masayuki Takeda, and Setsuo Arikawa. Construction of the CDAWG for a Trie. In *Proceedings of the Prague Stringology Conference (PSC'01).* Czech Technical University, 2001.
16. Werner Kuich and Arto Salomaa. *Semirings, Automata, Languages.* Number 5 in EATCS Monographs on Theoretical Computer Science. Springer-Verlag, Berlin, Germany, 1986.
17. Eugene L. Lawler. *Combinatorial Optimization: Networks and Matroids.* Holt, Rinehart, and Winston, 1976.
18. Vladimir I. Levenshtein. Binary codes capable of correcting deletions, insertions, and reversals. *Soviet Physics - Doklady*, 10:707–710, 1966.
19. Lidia Mangu, Eric Brill, and Andreas Stolcke. Finding consensus in speech recognition: word error minimization and other applications of confusion networks. *Computer Speech and Language*, 14(4):373–400, 1997.
20. Mehryar Mohri. Finite-State Transducers in Language and Speech Processing. *Computational Linguistics*, 23:2, 1997.
21. Mehryar Mohri. Generic Epsilon-Removal and Input Epsilon-Normalization Algorithms for Weighted Transducers. *International Journal of Foundations of Computer Science*, 13(1):129–143, 2002.
22. Mehryar Mohri. Semiring Frameworks and Algorithms for Shortest-Distance Problems. *Journal of Automata, Languages and Combinatorics*, to appear, 2002.
23. Mehryar Mohri, Fernando C. N. Pereira, and Michael Riley. Weighted Automata in Text and Speech Processing. In *Proceedings of the 12th biennial European Conference on Artificial Intelligence (ECAI-96), Workshop on Extended finite state models of language, Budapest, Hungary.* ECAI, 1996.
24. Mehryar Mohri, Fernando C. N. Pereira, and Michael Riley. The design principles of a weighted finite-state transducer library. *Theoretical Computer Science*, 231:17–32, January 2000.
25. Mehryar Mohri and Richard Sproat. An Efficient Compiler for Weighted Rewrite Rules. In *34th Meeting of the Association for Computational Linguistics (ACL '96), Proceedings of the Conference, Santa Cruz, California.* ACL, 1996.
26. Mohri, Mehryar and Fernando C. N. Pereira and Michael Riley. General-Purpose Finite-State Machine Software Tools. *http://www.research.att.com/sw/tools/fsm*, AT&T Labs – Research, 1997.
27. Fernando C. N. Pereira and Michael D. Riley. Speech recognition by composition of weighted finite automata. In Emmanuel Roche and Yves Schabes, editors, *Finite-State Language Processing*, pages 431–453. MIT Press, Cambridge, Massachusetts, 1997.
28. Eric S. Ristad and Peter N. Yianilos. Learning string edit distance. *IEEE Trans. PAMI*, 20(5):522–532, 1998.
29. Arto Salomaa and Matti Soittola. *Automata-Theoretic Aspects of Formal Power Series.* Springer-Verlag: New York, 1978.
30. Marcel Paul Schützenberger. On the definition of a family of automata. *Information and Control*, 4, 1961.
31. Marcel Paul Schützenberger. Sur une variante des fonctions séquentielles. *Theoretical Computer Science*, 4(1):47–57, 1977.

32. Andreas Stolcke, Yochai Konig, and Mitchel Weintraub. Explicit Word Error Mini-
    mization in N-best List Rescoring. In *Proceedings of Eurospeech'97, Rhodes, Greece*,
    1997.
33. Esko Ukkonen. Algorithms for approximate string matching. *Information and
    Control*, 64:100–118, 1985.
34. Robert A. Wagner and Michael J. Fisher. The string to string correction problem.
    Journal of the Association for Computing Machinery (ACM), 21(1):168–173, 1974.
35. Chris Watkins. Dynamic alignment kernels. Technical Report CSD-TR-98-11,
    Royal Holloway, University of London, 1999.

p-Subsequentiable Transducers

Cyril Allauzen and Mehryar Mohri

AT&T Labs – Research
180 Park Avenue
Florham Park, NJ 07932, USA
{allauzen,mohri}@research.att.com

Abstract. p-subsequential transducers are efficient finite-state transducers with p final outputs used in a variety of applications. Not all transducers admit equivalent p-subsequential transducers however. We briefly describe an existing generalized determinization algorithm for p-subsequential transducers and give the first characterization of *p-subsequentiable transducers*, transducers that admit equivalent p-subsequential transducers. Our characterization shows the existence of an efficient algorithm for testing p-subsequentiability. We have fully implemented the generalized determinization algorithm and the algorithm for testing p-subsequentiability. We report experimental results showing that these algorithms are practical in large-vocabulary speech recognition applications. The theoretical formulation of our results is the equivalence of the following three properties for finite-state transducers: determinizability in the sense of the generalized algorithm, p-subsequentiability, and the twins property.

1 Introduction

Finite-state transducers are automata in which transitions are labeled with both an input and an output symbol. Transducers have been used successfully to create complex systems in many applications such as text and language processing, speech recognition and image processing [9,8,7,12,6].

The time efficiency of such systems is substantially increased when *subsequential transducers* [15], i.e. finite-state transducers with deterministic input, are used. Subsequential machines can be generalized to *p-subsequential transducers* which are transducers with deterministic input with p, $(p \geq 1)$, final output strings [10]. This generalization is necessary in many applications such as language processing to account for finite ambiguities [11].

Not all transducers admit equivalent p-subsequential transducers however. We present the first characterization of *p-subsequentiable transducers*, i.e. transducers that admit equivalent p-subsequential transducers. Our characterization is based on the twins property and leads to an efficient algorithm for testing p-subsequentiability. More generally, our results show the equivalence of the following three fundamental properties for finite-state transducers: determinizability in the sense of a generalized algorithm, p-subsequentiability, and the twins property.

J.-M. Champarnaud and D. Maurel (Eds.): CIAA 2002, LNCS 2608, pp. 24–34, 2003.

This can also be viewed as a generalization of the results known in the case of functional transducers: determinizable functional transducers are exactly those that admit equivalent subsequential transducers [5]. We generalize these results by relaxing the condition on functionality: determinizable transducers are exactly those that admit equivalent p-subsequential transducers and exactly those that admit the twins property.

We have fully implemented the generalized determinization algorithm mentioned above and the algorithm for testing p-subsequentiability. We report experimental results showing that these algorithms are practical in large-vocabulary speech recognition applications.

We first introduce the notation used in the rest of this paper, then briefly describe a generalized determinization algorithm for p-subsequential transducers introduced by [10], present a fundamental characterization theorem, and describe our experimental results.

2 Preliminaries

Definition 1. *A* finite-state transducer $T = (\Sigma, \Delta, Q, I, F, E, \lambda, \rho)$ *is an 8-tuple where* Σ *is a finite input alphabet,* Δ *a finite output alphabet,* Q *a finite set of states,* $I \subseteq Q$ *the set of initial states,* $F \subseteq Q$ *the set of final states,* $E \subseteq Q \times \Sigma \times (\Delta \cup \{\epsilon\}) \times Q$ *a finite set of transitions,* $\lambda : I \to \Delta^*$ *the initial output function mapping* I *to* Δ^*, *and* $\rho : F \to 2^{\Delta^*}$ *the final output function mapping each state* $q \in F$ *to a finite subset of* Δ^*.

Given a transition $e \in E$, we denote by $i[e]$ its input label, $p[e]$ its origin or previous state and $n[e]$ its destination state or next state, $o[e]$ its output label. Given a state $q \in Q$, we denote by $E[q]$ the set of transitions leaving q. We extend the definitions of i, n, p, and E to sets in the following way: $i[\cup_{k \in K} e_k] = \cup_{k \in K} i[e_k]$ and similarly for n, p, and E.

A *path* $\pi = e_1 \cdots e_k$ in T is an element of E^* with consecutive transitions: $n[e_{i-1}] = p[e_i]$, $i = 2, \ldots, k$. We extend n and p to paths by setting: $n[\pi] = n[e_k]$ and $p[\pi] = p[e_1]$. We denote by $P(q, q')$ the set of paths from q to q' and by $P(q, x, q')$ the set of paths from q to q' with input label $x \in \Sigma^*$. These definitions can be extended to subsets $R, R' \subseteq Q$, by: $P(R, x, R') = \cup_{q \in R, \, q' \in R'} P(q, x, q')$. The labeling functions i and o can also be extended to paths by defining the label of a path as the concatenation of the labels of its constituent transitions:

$$i[\pi] = i[e_1] \cdots i[e_k] \qquad o[\pi] = o[e_1] \cdots o[e_k]$$

The set of output strings associated by a transducer T to an input string $x \in \Sigma^*$ is defined by:

$$[\![T]\!](x) = \bigcup_{\pi \in P(I, x, F)} \lambda(p[\pi]) \, o[\pi] \, \rho(n[\pi])$$

$[\![T]\!](x) = \emptyset$ when $P(I, x, F) = \emptyset$. The domain of definition of T is defined as: $Dom(T) = \{x \in \Sigma^* : [\![T]\!](x) \neq \emptyset\}$. A transducer is said to be p-*functional* for some integer p if it associates at most p strings to each input string, that is if

$|[\![T]\!](x)| \leq p$ for any $x \in \Sigma^*$. Two transducers T and T' are *equivalent* when $[\![T]\!] = [\![T']\!]$.

A *successful path* in a transducer T is a path from an initial state to a final state. A state $a \in Q$ is *accessible* if q can be reached from I. It is *coaccessible* if a final state can be reached from q. T is *trim* if all the states of T are both accessible and coaccessible. T is *unambiguous* if for any string $x \in \Sigma^*$ there is at most one successful path labeled with x. An unambiguous transducer is thus *p-functional*, with $p = \max_{q \in F} |\rho(q)|$.

A transducer T is said to be *p-subsequential* [10] for some integer p if it has a unique initial state, if no two transitions leaving the same state share the same input label and if there are at most p final output strings at each final state: $|\rho(f)| \leq p$ for all $f \in F$. T is said to be *p-subsequentiable* if there exists a *p*-subsequential transducer T' equivalent to T.

Given two strings x and y in Σ^*, we say that y is a *suffix* of x if there exists $z \in \Sigma^*$ such that $x = zy$ and similarly that y is a *prefix* of x if there exists z such that $x = yz$. We denote by $x \wedge y$ the longest common prefix of x and y and denote by $|x|$ the length of a string $x \in \Sigma^*$. We extend Σ by associating to each symbol $a \in \Sigma$ a new symbol denoted by a^{-1} and define Σ^{-1} as: $\Sigma^{-1} = \{a^{-1} : a \in \Sigma\}$. $X = (\Sigma \cup \Sigma^{-1})^*$ is then the set of strings written over the alphabet $(\Sigma \cup \Sigma^{-1})$. If we assume that $aa^{-1} = a^{-1}a = \epsilon$, then X forms a group called the *free group generated by* Σ and is denoted by $\Sigma^{(*)}$. Note that the inverse of a string $x = a_1 \cdots a_n$ is then $x^{-1} = a_n^{-1} \cdots a_1^{-1}$. The formula used in our definitions, theorems and proofs should be interpreted as equations in the free group generated by Σ^*.

3   General Determinization Algorithm with *p*-Subsequential Outputs

In this section, we give a brief description of a general determinization algorithm introduced by [10] that takes as input a transducer T and outputs a *p*-subsequential transducer $T' = (\Sigma, \Delta, Q', \{i'\}, F', E', \lambda', \rho')$. A transducer T for which the algorithm terminates and thus generates an equivalent *p*-subsequential transducer is said to be *determinizable*.

The algorithm is a generalization of the subset construction used in the determinization of finite automata. A state in the output transducer T' is a set of pairs (q, z) where q is a state of the input transducer T and $z \in \Sigma^*$ a remainder output string with the following property: if a state q' in T' containing a pair (q, z) can be reached from the initial state by a path with input x and output y, then q can be reached in T from an initial state by a path with input x and output yz.

The pseudocode of the algorithm is given below. Line 1 initializes the set of states, final states, and transitions of T' to the empty set. The algorithm uses a queue S containing the set of states of T' to be considered next. S initially contains the unique initial state of T', i', which is the set of pairs of an initial state i of T and the corresponding initial output string $\lambda(i)$ (line 2).

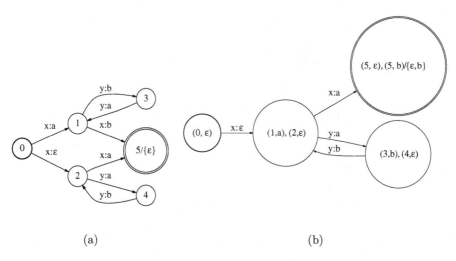

Fig. 1. Generalized determinization of finite-state transducers. (a) Non-deterministic transducer. (b) Construction of equivalent 2-subsequential transducer.

Transducer-Determinization(T)

```
 1  F' ← Q' ← E' ← ∅
 2  S ← i' ← {(i, λ(i)) : i ∈ I}
 3  while  S ≠ ∅
 4        do  p' ← head(S)
 5            DEQUEUE(S)
 6            for  each x ∈ i[E[Q[p']]]
 7                do  y' ← ⋀{zy : (p, z) ∈ p', (p, x, y, q) ∈ E}
 8                    q' ← {(q, y'⁻¹ z y) : (p, z) ∈ p', (p, x, y, q) ∈ E}
 9                    E' ← E' ∪ {(p', x, y', q')}
10                    if  (q' ∉ Q')
11                        then  Q' ← Q' ∪ {q'}
12                              if  Q[q'] ∩ F ≠ ∅
13                                  then  F' ← F' ∪ {q'}
14                                        ρ'(q') ← ⋃{zρ(q) : (q, z) ∈ q', q ∈ F}
15                    ENQUEUE(S, q')
16  return  T'
```

Each time through the loop of lines 3-15, a new subset p' (or equivalently a new state of T') is extracted from S. The algorithm then creates (lines 6-9) a transition with input label $x \in \Sigma$ and output label $y' \in \Sigma^*$ leaving p' if there exists at least one pair $(p, z) \in p'$ such that p admits an outgoing transition with input label x and output label y. y' is then defined as the longest common prefix of all such zy's. The destination state q' of that transition is the subset containing the pairs $(q, y'^{-1}zy)$ such that $(p, z) \in p'$ and (p, x, y, q) is a transition in E. If the destination state q' is new, it is added to Q' (lines 10-11). q' is a final state if it contains at least one pair (q, z), q being a final state. Its final set of output strings is then the union of $z\rho(q)$ over all such pairs (q, z).

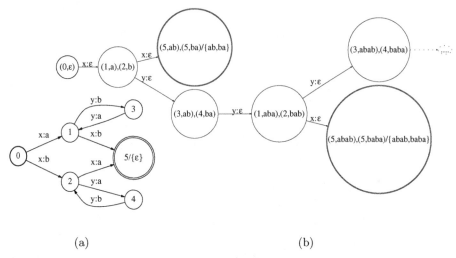

(a)   (b)

Fig. 2. Non-determinizable case. (a) A non-determinizable finite-state transducer; states 1 and 2 are non-twin siblings. (b) Determinization does not halt in this case and creates an infinite number of states.

There are input transducers that are not determinizable, that is for which the algorithm does not terminate. When it terminates, the output transducer T' is equivalent to T. Thus, it does not terminate with any transducer T that is not p-subsequentiable.

Figure 1 (b) illustrates the application of the algorithm to the transducer of figure 1 (a). Figures 2 (a)-(b) show an example of non-determinizable transducer.

The worst case complexity of determinization is exponential. However, in many applications such as large-vocabulary speech recognition such a blow-up does not occur and determinization leads to a significant improvement of speed versus accuracy at a reasonable cost in space [12].

4   Characterization

This section presents a characterization of p-subsequentiable transducers. The characterization is based on the following property.

Definition 2. *Let T be a finite-state transducer. Two states q_1 and q_2 of T are said to be* siblings *if there exist two strings x and y in Σ^* such that both q_1 and q_2 can be reached from I by paths with input label x and there are cycles at q_1 and q_2 both with input label y. Two siblings q_1 and q_2 are said to be* twins *if for any paths $\pi_1 \in P(I, x, q_1)$, $c_1 \in P(q_1, y, q_1)$, $\pi_2 \in P(I, x, q_2)$, $c_2 \in P(q_2, y, q_2)$,*

$$o[\pi_1]^{-1}o[\pi_2] = o[\pi_1 c_1]^{-1}o[\pi_2 c_2] \tag{1}$$

T has the twins property *if any two siblings in T are twins.*

The *twins property* was originally introduced by [4,5] to give a characterization of functional subsequentiable transducers. The decidability of the twins property was also first proved by the same author (see also [3]). The first polynomial-time algorithm for testing the twins property was given by [16], this algorithm was later improved by [2]. More recently, we gave a more efficient algorithm for testing the twins property based on the general algorithm of composition of finite-state transducers and a new characterization of the twins property in terms of combinatorics of words [1].

The following factorization lemma will be useful in several proofs.

Lemma 1. *Let $T = (\Sigma, \Delta, Q, I, F, E, \lambda, \rho)$ be a finite-state transducer, let π be a path from I to state $p \in Q$ and π' a path from I to p' with the same input label $w = i[\pi] = i[\pi']$. Assume that $|w| > |Q|^2 - 1$, then there exist paths $\pi_1, \pi_2, \pi_3,$ $\pi'_1, \pi'_2, \pi'_3,$ such that:*

$$\pi = \pi_1 \pi_2 \pi_3 \quad \pi' = \pi'_1 \pi'_2 \pi'_3 \tag{2}$$

where π_2 and π'_2 are cycles with non-empty input labels and: $i[\pi_k] = i[\pi'_k]$, for $k = 1, 2, 3$.

Proof. Consider the transducer U obtained by composing T and T^{-1}: $U = T \circ T^{-1}$. Since π and π' have the same input label, there exists a path ψ in U with input $o[\pi]$ and output $o[\pi']$. Since $|\psi| = |w| > |Q|^2 - 1$ and U has at most $|Q|^2$ states, ψ goes at least through one non-empty cycle ψ_2: $\psi = \psi_1 \psi_2 \psi_3$. This shows the existence of the common factoring for π and π' since ψ results from matching π and the path obtained from π' by swapping its input and output labels.   □

The following lemma will be used to prove that determinization terminates when the twins property holds.

Lemma 2. *Assume that T has the twins property. Let R be defined by:*

$$R = \{o[\pi']^{-1} o[\pi] : i[\pi] = i[\pi'] = w, |w| \le |Q|^2\}$$

Let q_1 and q_2 be two states of T, π a path from I to q_1, and π' a path from I to q_2 with the same input label: $i[\pi] = i[\pi']$, then $o[\pi']^{-1} o[\pi] \in R$.

Proof. Let w be the common input label of π and π' and assume that $|w| > |Q|^2$. By lemma 1, paths π and π' can be factored in the following way:

$$\pi = \pi_1 \pi_2 \pi_3 \quad \pi' = \pi'_1 \pi'_2 \pi'_3$$

where π_2 and π'_2 are cycles with non-empty input labels and: $i[\pi_k] = i[\pi'_k]$, for $k = 1, 2, 3$. Let $\phi = \pi_1 \pi_3 \in P(I, q_i)$ and $\phi' = \pi'_1 \pi'_3 \in P(I, q_j)$ and $w' = i[\phi] = i[\phi']$. Since T has the twins property, $(o[\pi'_1 \pi'_2])^{-1} o[\pi_1 \pi_2] = o[\pi'_1]^{-1} o[\pi_1]$. Thus: $o[\pi'_1 \pi'_2 \pi'_3]^{-1} o[\pi_1 \pi_2 \pi_3] = o[\pi'_1 \pi'_3]^{-1} o[\pi_1 \pi_3] = o[\phi']^{-1} o[\phi]$. Since $|i[\pi_k]| > 0$, w' is a string strictly shorter than w. By induction, we can find paths $\phi \in P(I, q_1)$ and $\phi' \in P(I, q_2)$, with $i[\phi] = i[\phi'] = w'$, $|w'| \le |Q|^2$ and such that $o[\pi']^{-1} o[\pi] = o[\phi']^{-1} o[\phi]$, thus $o[\pi']^{-1} o[\pi] \in R$. This proves the lemma.   □

The following two lemmas are used in the proof of our main result.

Lemma 3. *Let $x_1, x_2, y_1, y_2 \in \Sigma^*$. Assume that for some integers $r \geq 0$ and $s > 0$, the following holds:*

$$(x_1 y_1^r)^{-1} x_2 y_2^r = (x_1 y_1^{r+s})^{-1} x_2 y_2^{r+s} \tag{3}$$

then:

$$x_1^{-1} x_2 = (x_1 y_1)^{-1} x_2 y_2 \tag{4}$$

Proof. Let $x_1, x_2, y_1, y_2 \in \Sigma^*$ be strings satisfying the hypothesis of the lemma. Without loss of generality, we can assume that $|x_2| \geq |x_1|$. Equality 3 of the lemma can be rewritten as: $y_1^{-r} x_1^{-1} x_2 y_2^r = y_1^{-r-s} x_1^{-1} x_2 y_2^{r+s}$, or: $y_1^s (x_1^{-1} x_2) = (x_1^{-1} x_2) y_2^s$. Repeated applications of this identity lead to:

$$y_1^{sn} (x_1^{-1} x_2) = (x_1^{-1} x_2) y_2^{sn} \tag{5}$$

for any $n \geq 1$. This implies that $x_1^{-1} x_2$ is a string and that it is a prefix of y_1^{sn}. Thus, y_1 is a period of $x_1^{-1} x_2$ [14]. There exist an integer p, and two strings u and v such that $y = vu$ and $x_1^{-1} x_2 = y^p v$. Re-injecting this in equation 5 gives $y_2 = uv$ and completes the proof of the lemma. □

Lemma 4. *Let $T' = (\Sigma, \Delta, Q', \{i'\}, F', E', \lambda', \rho')$ be a p-subsequential transducer equivalent to $T = (\Sigma, \Delta, Q, I, F, E, \lambda, \rho)$. Let $q \in F$ be a final state of T and $q' \in F'$ a final state of F' and assume that there exists $x \in \Sigma^*$ such that $P(I, x, q) \neq \emptyset$ in T and $P(i', x, q') \neq \emptyset$ in T'. Then, there exists a finite set $Z \subset \Delta^{(*)}$ such that for any paths $\pi \in P(I, q)$ and $\pi' \in P(i', q')$, if $i[\pi] = i[\pi']$ then $o[\pi]^{-1} o[\pi'] \in Z$.*

Proof. Let π and π' be two paths satisfying the hypotheses of the lemma. Since T and T' are equivalent, we have $o[\pi]\rho(q) \subseteq [\![T]\!](i[\pi]) = [\![T']\!](i[\pi])$. Since T' is p-subsequential we also have $[\![T']\!](i[\pi]) = o[\pi']\rho'(q')$. Thus:

$$o[\pi]\rho(q) \subseteq o[\pi']\rho'(q') \tag{6}$$

Let $x \in \rho(q)$, there exists y in $\rho'(q')$ such that $o[\pi]x = o[\pi']y$. Define $Z \subset \Delta^{(*)}$ as the finite set $Z = \rho(q)\rho'(q')^{-1}$. Then, $o[\pi]^{-1} o[\pi'] = xy^{-1} \in Z$. This proves the lemma. □

Our main characterization result of this section is given by the following theorem which establishes the equivalence between three properties.

Theorem 1. *Let T be a trim finite-state transducer. Then the following three properties are equivalent:*

1. *T is determinizable;*
2. *T has the twins property;*
3. *T is p-subsequentiable.*

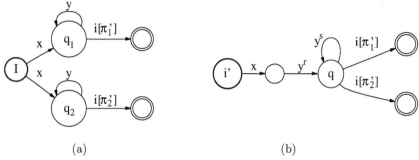

(a)   (b)

Fig. 3. Illustration of the definition of the paths used in the proof of theorem 1. Only the input labels of the paths are indicated. (a) Siblings states q_1 and q_2 in T, paths π_1, c_1, π_2, and c_2 defined as in the definition of the twins property, and paths π_1' and π_2' from q_1 and q_2 to final states. (b) State q in T', path π, and paths μ_1 and μ_2 from q to final states in T'.

Proof. $1 \Rightarrow 3$: By definition of the algorithm, the output of determinization is a p-subsequential transducer.

$3 \Rightarrow 2$: Assume that T is p-subsequentiable and let T' be a p-subsequential transducer equivalent to T. Let q_1 and q_2 be two siblings in T and consider four paths π_1, c_1, π_2, c_2 as in the definition of the twins property. Since T is trim, there exist a path π_1' from q_1 to a final state and a path π_2' from q_2 to a final state. Figure 3 (a) illustrates the definition of these paths. Note that π_1' or π_2' may be an empty if q_1, resp. q_2, is a final state.

Since T' is equivalent to T, there must be a path π in T from the initial state to a state q with input label xy^r with $r \geq 0$, a cycle c at q with input label y^s with $s > 0$, and two paths μ_1 and μ_2, potentially empty, from q to a final state, with input labels respectively $i[\pi_1']$ and $i[\pi_2']$. Figure 3 (b) illustrates the definition of these paths.

By definition of these paths, we have for any $t \geq 0$:

$$i[\pi_1 c_1^{r+st} \pi_1'] = i[\pi c^t \mu_1] \tag{7}$$

The conditions of lemma 4 hold with the final states $n[\pi_1']$ and $n[\mu_1]$ and the paths $\pi_1 c_1^{r+st} \pi_1'$ and $\pi c^t \mu_1$. Thus, there exists a finite set Z such that for any $t \geq 0$:

$$o[\pi_1 c_1^{r+st} \pi_1']^{-1} o[\pi c^t \mu_1] \in Z \tag{8}$$

Since Z is finite, there exist at least two distinct integers t_0 and t_1 such that:

$$o[\pi_1 c_1^{r+st_0} \pi_1']^{-1} o[\pi c^{t_0} \mu_1] = o[\pi_1 c_1^{r+st_1} \pi_1']^{-1} o[\pi c^{t_1} \mu_1] \tag{9}$$

That is:

$$o[\pi_1']zo[\mu_1]^{-1} = o[\pi_1 c_1^{r+st_0}]^{-1} o[\pi c^{t_0}] = o[\pi_1 c_1^{r+st_1}]^{-1} o[\pi c^{t_1}] \tag{10}$$

By lemma 3, this implies:

$$o[\pi_1 c_1^r]^{-1} o[\pi] = o[\pi_1 c_1^{r+s}]^{-1} o[\pi c] \tag{11}$$

We can prove in a similar way that:

$$o[\pi_2 c_2^r]^{-1}o[\pi] = o[\pi_2 c_2^{r+s}]^{-1}o[\pi c]$$ (12)

Thus:

$$o[\pi_1 c_1^{r+s}]^{-1}o[\pi_2 c_2^{r+s}] = o[\pi_1 c_1^r]^{-1}o[\pi_2 c_2^r]$$ (13)

And by lemma 3:

$$o[\pi_1]^{-1}o[\pi_2] = o[\pi_1 c_1]^{-1}o[\pi_2 c_2]$$ (14)

Thus, any two siblings q_1 and q_2 in T are twins, and T has the twins property.

2 $\Rightarrow$ 1: Assume that T has the twins property. Let $\{(q_1, z_1), \ldots, (q_n, z_n)\}$ be a subset created during the execution of the determinization algorithm. By construction, states $q_1, \ldots, q_n$ can all be reached from I by paths labeled with the same input string w.[1] Let z be defined by:

$$z = \bigwedge_{p[\pi]\in I,\, i[\pi]=w} o[\pi]$$ (15)

By definition of the algorithm, for $i = 1, \ldots, n$, there exists a path π_i from I to q_i with input label w such that:

$$z_i = z^{-1}o[\pi_i]$$ (16)

Let $\Pi = \pi_i$ and $\Pi' = \pi_j$ for some $i, j = 1, \ldots, n$. We have:

$$z_j^{-1}z_i = o[\Pi']^{-1}o[\Pi]$$ (17)

Thus, by lemma 2, $z_j^{-1}z_i \in R$ with:

$$R = \{o[\pi']^{-1}o[\pi] : i[\pi] = i[\pi'] = w, |w| \le |Q|^2\}$$ (18)

Define K as the maximum length of the elements of R: $K = \max_{x\in R}|x|$. Since the remainders in the same subset cannot have a common non-empty prefix, for any remainder string z_i, there exists at least on remainder z_j such that $z_i \wedge z_j = \epsilon$, thus $|z_j| + |z_i| = |z_j^{-1}z_i|$. Since $z_j^{-1}z_i \in R$, we have $|z_j^{-1}z_i| \le K$, and thus $|z_i| \le K$. This inequality holds for $i = 1, \ldots, n$, that is any subset remainder belongs to $\Sigma^{\le K}$. Thus, a subset necessarily belongs to $2^{|Q|\times\Sigma^{\le K}}$, which is a finite set. This guarantees the termination of the algorithm and thus the determinizability of T. $\square$

5 Experiments and Results

We have fully implemented the general determinization algorithm presented in section 3. We used a priority queue implemented with a heap to sort the transitions leaving each subset and another priority queue to sort the final output

---

[1] Note that we may have $q_i = q_j$ for some choices of i and j.

strings. Since the computation of the transitions leaving a subset only depends on the states and remainder strings of that subset and on the input transducer, one can limit the computation of the result to just the part that is needed. Thus, we gave an on-the-fly implementation of the algorithm which was incorporated in the FSM library [13].

Our experiments in large-vocabulary speech recognition showed the algorithm to be quite efficient. It took about 5s using a Pentium III 700MHz with 2048 Kb of cache and 4Gb of RAM to construct a *p*-subsequential transducer equivalent to a transducer T with 440,000 transitions representing the mapping from phonemic sequences to word sequences obtained by composition of two transducers.

We also implemented an efficient algorithm for testing the twins property [1]. With our implementation, the *p*-subsequentiality of the transducer T already described could be tested in just 60s using the same machine.

6   Conclusion

A new characterization of *p*-subsequentiable transducers was given. The twins property was shown to be a necessary and sufficient condition for the *p*-subsequentiability of a finite-state transducer without requiring it to be *p*-functional and a necessary and sufficient condition for the general determinizability of transducers. We reported experimental results demonstrating the practicality of our algorithms for testing *p*-subsequentiability and for determinizing transducers in large-vocabulary speech recognition applications.

References

1. Cyril Allauzen and Mehryar Mohri. On the Determinizability of Weighted Automata and Transducers. In *Proceedings of the workshop Weighted Automata: Theory and Applications (WATA)*, Dresden, Germany, March 2002.
2. Marie-Pierre Béal, Olivier Carton, Christophe Prieur, and Jacques Sakarovitch. Squaring transducers: An efficient procedure for deciding functionality and sequentiality. In *Proceedings of LATIN'2000*, volume 1776 of *Lecture Notes in Computer Science*. Springer, 2000.
3. Jean Berstel. *Transductions and Context-Free Languages*. Teubner Studienbucher: Stuttgart, 1979.
4. Christian Choffrut. Une caractérisation des fonctions séquentielles et des fonctions sous-séquentielles en tant que relations rationnelles. *Theoretical Computer Science*, 5:325–338, 1977.
5. Christian Choffrut. *Contributions à l'étude de quelques familles remarquables de fonctions rationnelles*. PhD thesis, (thèse de doctorat d'Etat), Université Paris 7, LITP: Paris, France, 1978.
6. Karel Culik II and Jarkko Kari. Digital Images and Formal Languages. In Grzegorz Rozenberg and Arto Salomaa, editors, *Handbook of Formal Languages*, volume 3, pages 599–616. Springer, 1997.

7. Maurice Gross and Dominique Perrin, editors. *Electronic Dictionnaries and Automata in Computational Linguistics*, volume 377 of *Lecture Notes in Computer Science*. Springer Verlag, 1989.

8. Ronald M. Kaplan and Martin Kay. Regular Models of Phonological Rule Systems. *Computational Linguistics*, 20(3):331–378, 1994.

9. Lauri Karttunen. The Replace Operator. In *33rd Annual Meeting of the Association for Computational Linguistics*, pages 16–23. Association for Computational Linguistics, 1995. Distributed by Morgan Kaufmann Publishers, San Francisco, California.

10. Mehryar Mohri. On some Applications of Finite-State Automata Theory to Natural Language Processing. *Journal of Natural Language Engineering*, 2:1–20, 1996.

11. Mehryar Mohri. Finite-State Transducers in Language and Speech Processing. *Computational Linguistics*, 23(2), 1997.

12. Mehryar Mohri, Fernando C. N. Pereira, and Michael Riley. Weighted Finite-State Transducers in Speech Recognition. *Computer Speech and Language*, 16(1):69–88, 2002.

13. Mohri, Mehryar and Fernando C. N. Pereira and Michael Riley. General-Purpose Finite-State Machine Software Tools. *http://www.research.att.com/sw/tools/fsm*, AT&T Labs – Research, 1997.

14. Dominique Perrin. Words. In M. Lothaire, editor, *Combinatorics on words*, Cambridge Mathematical Library. Cambridge University Press, 1997.

15. Marcel Paul Schützenberger. Sur une variante des fonctions séquentielles. *Theoretical Computer Science*, 4(1):47–57, 1977.

16. Andreas Weber and Reinhard Klemm. Economy of Description for Single-Valued Transducers. *Information and Computation*, 118(2):327–340, 1995.

Bidirectional Push Down Automata

Miguel A. Alonso[1], Víctor J. Díaz[2], and Manuel Vilares[1,3]

[1] Departamento de Computación, Universidade da Coruña
Campus de Elviña s/n, 15071 La Coruña, Spain
{alonso,vilares}@udc.es
http://www.grupocole.org
[2] Departamento de Lenguajes y Sistemas Informáticos, Universidad de Sevilla
Avda. Reina Mercedes s/n, 41012 Sevilla (Spain)
vjdiaz@lsi.us.es
[3] Escuela Superior de Ingeniería Informática, Universidade de Vigo
Campus As Lagoas s/n, 32004 Orense, Spain
vilares@ei.uvigo.es

Abstract. We define a new model of automata for the description of bidirectional parsing strategies for context-free grammars and a tabulation mechanism that allow them to be executed in polynomial time. This new model of automata provides a modular way of defining bidirectional parsers, separating the description of a strategy from its execution.

1 Introduction

The task of designing correct and efficient parsing algorithms can be simplified by separating the definition of the parsing strategy from its tabular execution. This can be accomplished through the use of automata: the actual parsing strategy can be described by means of the construction of a non-deterministic pushdown automaton, and tabulation is introduced by means of some generic mechanism such as memoization. The construction of parsers in this way allows more straightforward proofs of correctness and makes parsing strategies easier to understand and implement.

This approach has been successfully applied to the design of parsing algorithms for context-free grammars that read the input string left-to-right [5,6]. In this article, we define new models of push-down automata which can start reading the input string in any position, spanning to the left and to the right to include substrings which were themselves read in the same bidirectional way. Tabulation techniques are provided in order to execute efficiently these automata.

This article is outlined as follows. Section 2 introduces push-down automata. A bidirectional extension of push-down automata is presented in section 3. Two different tabular frameworks to execute efficiently bidirectional automata are defined in Section 5. These frameworks are applied to predictive and bottom-up head-corner parsing algorithms.

J.-M. Champarnaud and D. Maurel (Eds.): CIAA 2002, LNCS 2608, pp. 35–46, 2003.

2   Push-Down Automata

A Context-Free Grammar (CFG) is a tuple (V_N, V_T, S, P), where V_N is a finite set of non-terminal symbols, V_T a finite set of terminal symbols, $S \in V_N$ is the axiom of the grammar, and P is a finite set of productions (rewriting rules) of the form $A \to \gamma$ with $A \in V_N$ and $\gamma \in (V_T \cup V_N)^*$. Push-Down Automata (PDA) are the operational devices for parsing CFG. Following [3], we define a PDA as a tuple $(V_T, V_S, \Theta, \$_0, \$_f)$ where V_T is a finite set of terminal symbols, V_S is a finite set of stack symbols, $\$_0 \in V_S$ is the initial stack symbol, $\$_f \in V_S$ is the final stack symbol and Θ is a finite set of SWAP, PUSH and POP transitions. A configuration of a PDA is usually defined as a pair $(\xi, a_l \ldots a_n)$, where $\xi \in V_S^*$ is the stack attained and $a_l \ldots a_n$ the part of the input string $a_1 \ldots a_n$ to be read. We consider an alternative and equivalent definition of configuration in which the position l is stored in the top element of ξ. Thus, a configuration is given by the contents of $\hat{\xi}$, a stack of pairs in $V_S \times \mathbb{N}$. The initial configuration is $(\$_0, 0)$. Other configurations are attained by applying transitions as follows:

- The application of a SWAP transition of the form $C \xmapsto{a} F$ to a configuration $\hat{\xi}(C, l)$ yields a configuration $\hat{\xi}(F, l + |a|)$ as a result of replacing C by F and scanning the terminal $a = a_{l+1}$ or the empty string $a = \epsilon$.
- The application of a PUSH transition $C \longmapsto C F$ to a configuration $\hat{\xi}(C, l)$ yields a configuration $\hat{\xi}(C, l)(F, l)$ as a result of pushing F onto C.
- The application of a POP transition of the form $C F \longmapsto G$ to a configuration $\hat{\xi}(C, l)(F, m)$ yields a configuration $\hat{\xi}(G, m)$ as a result of popping C and F, which are replaced by G.

where $C, F, G \in V_S$ and $a \in V_T \cup \{\epsilon\}$. An input string $w = a_1 \ldots a_n$ is succesfully recognized by a PDA if the final configuration $(\$_0, 0)(\$_f, n)$ is attained.

Only SWAP transitions can scan elements from the input string. This is not a limitation, as a scanning push transition $C \xmapsto{a} C F$ could be emulated by the consecutive application of two transitions $C \longmapsto C F'$ and $F' \xmapsto{a} F$, while a scanning pop transition $C F \xmapsto{a} G$ could be emulated by $C F \longmapsto G'$ and $G' \xmapsto{a} G$, where F' and G' are fresh stack symbols.

We call transitions SWAP, PUSH and POP *r-transitions* as they can only read the input string from the left to the right. Thus, push-down automata can only be used to implement unidirectional parsing strategies that read the input string in the same way. As an example of the kind of parsers that can be implemented, a compilation schema[1] of a context-free grammar into a push-down automaton implementing the Earley's parsing strategy [4] is derived. In the resulting automaton, V_T is the set of terminals of the source grammar, V_S is the union of $\{\$_0, \$_f\}$ and a set of dotted productions[2], the initial element $\$_0$ is used to start computations, the final element $\$_f$ is $(S \to \delta\bullet)$ and Θ contains the

---

[1] A compilation schema is a set of rules indicating how to construct an automaton according to a given grammar and parsing strategy.

[2] Dotted productions $A \to \alpha \bullet \beta$ are used to indicate that the part α of the production has been recognized.

[INIT] $\$_0 \overset{\epsilon}{\longmapsto} \$_0\ (S \to \bullet \alpha)$

[PRED] $(A \to \alpha \bullet B\beta) \longmapsto (A \to \alpha \bullet B\beta)\ (B \to \bullet \gamma)$

[SCAN] $(A \to \alpha \bullet a\beta) \overset{a}{\longmapsto} (A \to \alpha a \bullet \beta)$

[COMP] $(A \to \alpha \bullet B\beta)\ (B \to \gamma \bullet) \longmapsto (A \to \alpha B \bullet \beta)$

Fig. 1. Compilation schema for the Earley's strategy

$$\frac{[B,j;C,l]}{[B,j;F,l+|a|]} \quad C \overset{a}{\longmapsto} F \quad a = a_{l+1} \text{ or } a = \epsilon \qquad\qquad \frac{[C,j,l]}{[F,j,l+|a|]} \quad C \overset{a}{\longmapsto} F \quad a = a_{l+1} \text{ or } a = \epsilon$$

$$\frac{[B,j;C,l]}{[C,l;F,l]} \quad C \longmapsto CF \qquad\qquad \frac{[C,j,l]}{[F,l,l]} \quad C \longmapsto CF$$

$$\frac{\begin{array}{c}[C,l;F,m]\\ [B,j;C,l]\end{array}}{[B,j;G,m]} \quad CF \longmapsto G \qquad\qquad \frac{\begin{array}{c}[F,l,m]\\ [C,j,l]\end{array}}{[G,j,m]} \quad CF \longmapsto G$$

Fig. 2. Inference rules for PDA with S^2 items (left-hand) and S^1 items (right-hand)

set of transitions derived by the compilation rules shown in Fig. 1. A **[INIT]** transition is in charge of starting the parsing process. **[LPRED]** transitions predict a non-terminal B placed just after the dot in a given production. Once a production having this non-terminal in its left-hand side has been completely recognized, the dot is advanced by the application of a transition **[COMP]**. Terminals are recognized by **[SCAN]** transitions.

The direct execution of PDA may be exponential with respect to the length of the input string and may even loop. To get polynomial complexity, we must avoid duplicating computations by tabulating traces of configurations called *items*. The amount of information to keep in an item is the crucial point to determine to get efficient executions. Following [3] we know that S^2 items, storing the two elements placed on the top of the configuration stack, can be used to design tabular interpretations which are sound and complete for any parsing strategy.

New items are derived from existing items by means of inference rules of the form $\frac{antecedents}{consequent}$ *conditions* similar to those used in grammatical deduction systems [8], meaning that if all antecedents are present and conditions are satisfied then the consequent item should be generated. Conditions usually refer to transitions of the automaton and to terminals from the input string. The set of inference rules for S^2 items is shown in Fig. 2. Computations start with the item $[\square, 0; \$_0, 0]$ and finish with the item $[\$_0, 0; \$_f, n]$.

$$[\textbf{INIT}]\frac{[\$_0,0,0]}{[S \to \bullet\alpha,0,0]}$$

$$[\textbf{PRED}]\frac{[A \to \alpha \bullet B\beta,j,l]}{[B \to \bullet\gamma,l,l]}$$

$$[\textbf{SCAN}]\frac{\begin{array}{c}[A \to \alpha \bullet a\beta,j,l]\\ [a,l,l+1]\end{array}}{[A \to \alpha a \bullet \beta,j,l+1]}$$

$$[\textbf{COMP}]\frac{\begin{array}{c}[B \to \gamma\bullet,l,m]\\ [A \to \alpha \bullet B\beta,j,l]\end{array}}{[A \to \alpha B \bullet \beta,j,m]}$$

Fig. 3. Deduction steps for the Earley's algorithm

From [3] we also know that if the results of the non-deterministic computations are constrained only by bottom-up propagation of computed facts (e.g. bottom-up and Earley strategies, but not pure top-down strategies) S^1 items storing only the top element of the configuration stack can be used to derive a sound and complete tabular interpretation. The set of inference rules for S^1 items is shown in Fig. 2.[3] Computations start with the item $[\$_0,0,0]$ and finish with $[\$_f,0,n]$. Fig. 3 shows the set of deduction steps corresponding to the parsing schema[4] Earley obtained by applying these inference rules to an automaton resulting from the compilation schema shown in Fig. 1. The worst-case time complexity for the S^2 and S^1 inference rules and for the Earley schema is $\mathcal{O}(n^3)$.

Although PDA can only be used to describe unidirectional strategies, their tabulation technique can be extended to read the input string left-to-right, right-to-left and bidirectionally [7]. This kind of bidirectional tabulation makes possible to implement robust parsers by means of PDA but it does not make possible to specify bidirectional parsing strategies due to PDA transitions does not provide any way of controlling the direction of the parsing process.

---

[3] Although the items involved in these inference rules are usually called S^1 items, actually they are not true S^1 items but $S^{1+\epsilon}$ items due to each item $[C,j,l]$ stores the top element (C,l) of the configuration stack plus the position j of the second element (B,j) [2].

[4] In brief, a parsing schema is a deductive parsing system where inference rules are called *deduction steps* and conditions on the existence of a given terminal a_{l+1} are represented by means of special antecedent items of the form $[a,l,l+1]$ called *hypothesis*.

3   Bidirectional Push-Down Automata

Bidirectional parsing strategies can start computations at any position of the input string and can span to the right and to the left to include substrings which were scanned in a bidirectional way by some subcomputations. As a first step towards the definition of a Bidirectional Push-Down Automata (BPDA), we must adapt configurations in order to be able to represent the discontinuos recognition of the input string. Thus, configurations of a BPDA will be given by the contents of Ξ, a stack of triples in $V_S \times \mathbb{N} \times \mathbb{N}$. The initial configuration is $(\$_0, 0, 0)$. Other configurations are attained by applying transitions as follows:

- The application of a SWAP$_R$ transition of the form $C \overset{a}{\longmapsto}_R F$ to a configuration $\Xi(C, k, l)$ yields a configuration $\Xi(F, k, l + |a|)$ as a result of replacing C by F and scanning the terminal $a = a_{l+1}$ or the empty string $a = \epsilon$ to the right of the substring spanned by C.
- The application of a SWAP$_L$ transition of the form $C \overset{a}{\longmapsto}_L F$ to a configuration $\Xi(C, k, l)$ yields a configuration $\Xi(F, k - |a|, l)$ as a result of replacing C by F and scanning the terminal $a = a_k$ or the empty string $a = \epsilon$ to the left of the substring spanned by C.
- The application of a PUSH$_R$ transition $C \longmapsto_R C F$ to a configuration $\Xi(C, k, l)$ yields a configuration $\Xi(C, k, l)(F, l, l)$. It is expected that F will span a substring inmediatly to the right of the substring spanned by C.
- The application of a PUSH$_L$ transition $C \longmapsto_L C F$ to a configuration $\Xi(C, k, l)$ yields a configuration $\Xi(C, k, l)(F, k, k)$. It is expected that F will span a substring inmediatly to the left of the substring spanned by C.
- The application of a PUSH$_U$ transition of the form $C \overset{a}{\longmapsto}_U C F$ to a configuration $\Xi(C, k, l)$ yields a configuration $\Xi(C, k, l)(F, m, m + |a|)$ as a result of pushing F onto C and scanning the terminal $a = a_{m+1}$ or the empty string $a = \epsilon$. PUSH$_U$ transitions are *undirected* in the sense that a is not necessarily adjacent to the substring spanned by C.
- The application of a POP$_R$ transition of the form $CF \longmapsto_R G$ to a configuration $\Xi(C, k, l)(F, l, m)$ yields a configuration $\Xi(G, k, m)$. The substring spanned by F is adjacent to the right of the substring spanned by C.
- The application of a POP$_L$ transition of the form $CF \longmapsto_L G$ to a configuration $\Xi(C, k, l)(F, m, k)$ yields a configuration $\Xi(G, m, l)$. The substring spanned by F is adjacent to the left of the substring spanned by C.

An input string $a_1 \ldots a_n$ is succesfully recognized by a BPDA if the final configuration $(\$_0, 0, 0)(\$_f, 0, n)$ is attained. SWAP$_R$, PUSH$_R$ and POP$_R$ transitions are the r-transitions corresponding to unidirectional PDA. SWAP$_L$, PUSH$_L$ and POP$_L$ transitions are *l-transitions* that advance "to the left" in the reading of the input string. However, the union of r-transitions and l-transitions is not sufficient to implement bidirectional parsers, we need PUSH$_U$ transitions of the form $C \overset{a}{\longmapsto}_U C F$ to start subcomputations at any position of the input string. We guarantee that, in any computation recognizing the input string, each terminal in the input string is read only once by means of the definition of SWAP$_R$ and SWAP$_L$ transitions (they can not re-read elements which are in the span of the top element of the stack) and the definition of POP_R and POP_L transitions (they can not pop stack elements spanning overlapping substrings). Pop transitions also ensure we read the input string and not a permutation of it.

We define Bidirectional Push-Down Automata (BPDA) as a tuple $(V_T, V_S, \Theta_B, \$_0, \$_f)$ with Θ_B containing $SWAP_R$, $SWAP_L$, $PUSH_R$, $PUSH_L$, POP_R, POP_L and $PUSH_U$ transitions. As an example of the kind of parsers that can be implemented using BPDA, a compilation schema of a context-free grammar into a bidirectional push-down automaton implementing a predictive head-corner parsing strategy is derived. Head-corner parsing strategies can be applied to context-free grammars in which each production has an element of the right-hand side marked as the head of the production. For empty productions $A \to \epsilon$, the empty string ϵ is considered the head of the production. The head-corner relation $>_h$ on $V_N \times (V_N \cup V_T \cup \{\epsilon\})$ is defined by $A >_h X$ if there is a production $A \to \alpha X \beta$ with X the head of the production. If $A \to \epsilon$ then $A >_h \epsilon$. The transitive and reflexive closure of $>_h$ is denoted $>_h^*$. In the resulting automaton, V_T is the set of terminals of the source grammar, V_S is the union of $\{\$_0, \$_f\}$, the set of non-terminals of the source grammar and a set of dotted productions $A \to \alpha \bullet \beta \bullet \gamma$ used to indicate that the part β of the production has been recognized; the initial element $\$_0$ is used to start computations; the final element $\$_f$ is $(S \to \bullet \delta \bullet)$; and Θ_B contains the set of transitions derived by the compilation rules shown in Fig. 4. [**LPRED**] and [**RPRED**] transitions predict a non-terminal to the left and to the right, respectively. Once a production having this non-terminal in its left-hand side has been completely recognized, the dot is advanced by the application of a pair of transitions [**LCOMP1**]-[**LCOMP2**] or [**RCOMP1**]–[**RCOMP2**]. The head-corner of a given non-terminal is found by [**HC$_T$**] and [**HC$_\epsilon$**] transitions. [**HC$_N$**] transitions traverse backwards the chain of head-corners of a given non-terminal. [**LSCAN**] and [**RSCAN**] transitions recognize terminals to the left and to the right, respectively.

4   Context-Free Languages and BPDA

BPDA exactly accepts the class of context-free languages. Given a CFG $\mathcal{G}$, the language accepted by the bidirectional push-down automaton built following the compilation schema shown in Fig. 4 is the language recognized by $\mathcal{G}$. Therefore, the class of context-free languages is included in the class of languages accepted by BPDA. Given a BPDA $\mathcal{A} = (V_T, V_S, \Theta_B, \$_0, \$_f)$ we can construct a CFG $\mathcal{G} = (V_N, V_T, S, P)$ where $V_N \in V_S \times V_S$, $S = \langle \$_0, \$_f \rangle$ and the productions in P are obtained from transitions in Θ_B as follows:

- A production $\langle E, F \rangle \to \langle E, C \rangle a$ for each $C \overset{a}{\longmapsto}_R F \in \Theta_B$ and $E \in V_S$.
- A production $\langle E, F \rangle \to a \langle E, C \rangle$ for each $C \overset{a}{\longmapsto}_L F \in \Theta_B$ and $E \in V_S$.
- A production $\langle C, F \rangle \to \epsilon$ for each $C \longmapsto_R C F \in \Theta_B$ and $E \in V_S$.
- A production $\langle C, F \rangle \to \epsilon$ for each $C \longmapsto_L C F \in \Theta_B$ and $E \in V_S$.
- A production $\langle C, F \rangle \to a$ for each $C \overset{a}{\longmapsto}_U C F \in \Theta_B$ and $E \in V_S$.
- A production $\langle E, G \rangle \to \langle E, C \rangle \langle C, F \rangle$ for each $C F \longmapsto_R G \in \Theta_B$ and $E \in V_S$.

[INIT] $\$_0 \overset{\epsilon}{\longmapsto} \$_0$ (S)

[HC$_T$] $(A) \overset{b}{\longmapsto}_U (A) (B \to \alpha \bullet b \bullet \gamma)$ $A >_h^* B >_h b$

[HC$_N$] $(C \to \bullet\delta\bullet) \overset{\epsilon}{\longmapsto}_R (B \to \alpha \bullet C \bullet \gamma)$ $B >_h C$

[HC$_\epsilon$] $(A) \overset{\epsilon}{\longmapsto}_U (A) (B \to \bullet\bullet)$ $A >_h^* B$

[LPRED] $(B \to \alpha C \bullet \beta \bullet \gamma) \longmapsto_L (B \to \alpha C \bullet \beta \bullet \gamma) (C)$

[RPRED] $(B \to \alpha \bullet \beta \bullet C\gamma) \longmapsto_R (B \to \alpha \bullet \beta \bullet C\gamma) (C)$

[LSCAN] $(B \to \alpha a \bullet \beta \bullet \gamma) \overset{a}{\longmapsto}_L (B \to \alpha \bullet a\beta \bullet \gamma)$

[RSCAN] $(B \to \alpha \bullet \beta \bullet a\gamma) \overset{a}{\longmapsto}_R (B \to \alpha \bullet \beta a \bullet \gamma)$

[LCOMP1] $(C) (C \to \bullet\delta\bullet) \longmapsto_L (C \to \bullet\delta\bullet)$

[LCOMP2] $(B \to \alpha C \bullet \beta \bullet \gamma) (C \to \bullet\delta\bullet) \longmapsto_L (B \to \alpha \bullet C\beta \bullet \gamma)$

[RCOMP1] $(C) (C \to \bullet\delta\bullet) \longmapsto_R (C \to \bullet\delta\bullet)$

[RCOMP2] $(B \to \alpha \bullet \beta \bullet C\gamma) (C \to \bullet\delta\bullet) \longmapsto_R (B \to \alpha \bullet \beta C \bullet \gamma)$

Fig. 4. Compilation schema for a predictive head-corner strategy

– A production $\langle E, G \rangle \to \langle C, F \rangle \langle E, C \rangle$ for each $CF \longmapsto_L G \in \Theta_B$ and $E \in V_S$.

Applying induction in the length of the derivations, we can show that $\langle \$_0, \$_f \rangle \overset{*}{\Rightarrow}$ $a_1 \ldots a_n$ if and only if a computation of $\mathcal{A}$ starting at $(\$_0, 0, 0)$ attains a configuration $(\$_0, 0, 0)(\$_f, 0, n)$ reading $a_1 \ldots a_n$ from the input string, i.e. $\mathcal{G}$ exactly recognizes the language accepted by $\mathcal{A}$. Therefore, the class of languages accepted by BPDA is included in the class of context-free languages.

5   Tabulation of BPDA

As in the case of PDA, the direct execution of BPDA may be exponential with respect to the length of the input string and may even loop. To solve this problem, in this section we extend the S^2 and S^1 tabulation techniques to the case of bidirectional push-down automata.

5.1   The S^2 Framework

From [3] we know that extensions of push-down automata can be tabulated by using S^2 items storing the two elements on the top of the configuration stack. In the case of BPDA, S^2 items are of the form $[B, i, j; C, k, l]$, indicating the part of the input string $a_{k+1} \ldots a_l$ recognized by the top element C and the part $a_{i+1} \ldots a_j$ recognized by the element B placed immediately under C. The set of inference rules for S^2 items is shown in Fig. 5. Computations start with

$$\frac{[B,i,j;C,k,l] \quad C \overset{a}{\longmapsto}_R F}{[B,i,j;F,k,l+|a|] \quad a = a_{l+1} \text{ or } a = \epsilon}$$

$$\frac{[B,i,j;C,k,l] \quad C \overset{a}{\longmapsto}_U C F}{[C,k,l;F,m,m+|a|] \quad a = a_{m+1} \text{ or } a = \epsilon}$$

$$\frac{[B,i,j;C,k,l] \quad C \overset{a}{\longmapsto}_L F}{[B,i,j;F,k-|a|,l] \quad a = a_k \text{ or } a = \epsilon}$$

$$\frac{[B,i,j;C,k,l]}{[C,k,l;F,l,l]} \quad C \longmapsto_R C F$$

$$\frac{[C,k,l;F,l,m]}{[B,i,j;C,k,l]} \quad C F \longmapsto_R G$$
$$\frac{}{[B,i,j;G,k,m]}$$

$$\frac{[B,i,j;C,k,l]}{[C,k,l;F,k,k]} \quad C \longmapsto_L C F$$

$$\frac{[C,k,l;F,m,k]}{[B,i,j;C,k,l]} \quad C F \longmapsto_L G$$
$$\frac{}{[B,i,j;G,m,l]}$$

Fig. 5. Inference rules for S^2 items

the item $[\square,0,0,;\$_0,0,0]$ and finish with $[\$_0,0,0;\$_f,0,n]$. The worst case time complexity with respect to the length n of the input string is $\mathcal{O}(n^5)$.

The application of this set of inference rules to an automaton resulting from the compilation schema shown in Fig. 4 yields the set of deduction steps shown in Fig. 6 (where Φ refers to a dotted production or $\$_0$) which is very close to the set of deduction steps corresponding to the predictive head-corner parsing schema **pHC** defined by Sikkel in [9, chapter 11], also working in $\mathcal{O}(n^5)$ time complexity. The main difference is that predictive steps of the schema **pHC** have stronger constraints with respect to the part of the input string to be considered when seeking for a head-corner. A minor difference is that left-completer and right completer steps have been splited into [**LCOMP1**]–[**LCOMP2**] and [**RCOMP1**]–[**RCOMP2**] pairs.

5.2   The S^1 Framework

The complexity of the tabular framework can be reduced by considering more compact kinds of item. From [3] we also know that a sound and complete tabular interpretation for a given extension of push-down automata can be obtained using S^1 items that store the top element of the configuration stack. In the case of BPDA, S^1 items are of the form $[C,k,l]$, storing the top element C with the corresponding positions k and l of the substring spanned by it. The set of inference rules for S^1 items is derived from the set of inference rules for S^2, as is shown in Fig. 7. Computations start with the item $[\$_0,0,0]$ and finish with $[\$_f,0,n]$. The worst case time complexity with respect to the length n of the input string is $\mathcal{O}(n^3)$.

As an example of the kind of strategies that can be implemented using the S^1 framework, we show in Fig. 8 the compilation schema of a context-free grammar into a bidirectional push-down automaton implementing a bottom-up predictive head-corner parsing strategy. [**HC**$_T$] and [**HC**$_\epsilon$] transitions start the bottom-up recognition of head-corners. [**HC**$_N$] transitions traverse backwards

$$[\text{INIT}] \frac{[\Box, 0, 0; \$_0, 0, 0]}{[\$_0, 0, 0; S, 0, 0]}$$

$$[\text{HC}_T] \frac{\begin{array}{c} [\Phi, s, t; A, l, r] \\ [b, j-1, j] \end{array}}{[A, l, r; B \rightarrow \alpha \bullet b \bullet \gamma, j-1, j]} \quad A >_h^* B >_h b$$

$$[\text{HC}_N] \frac{[A, l, r; C \rightarrow \bullet\delta\bullet, i, j]}{[A, l, r; B \rightarrow \alpha \bullet C \bullet \gamma]} \quad B >_h C$$

$$[\text{HC}_\epsilon] \frac{[\Phi, s, t; A, l, r]}{[A, l, r; B \rightarrow \bullet\bullet, j, j]} \quad A >_h^* B$$

$$[\text{LPRED}] \frac{[A, l, r; B \rightarrow \alpha C \bullet \beta \bullet \gamma, i, j]}{[B \rightarrow \alpha C \bullet \beta \bullet \gamma, i, j; C, i, i]}$$

$$[\text{RPRED}] \frac{[A, l, r; B \rightarrow \alpha \bullet \beta \bullet C\gamma, i, j]}{[B \rightarrow \alpha \bullet \beta \bullet C\gamma, i, j; C, j, j]}$$

$$[\text{LSCAN}] \frac{\begin{array}{c} [A, l, r; B \rightarrow \alpha a \bullet \beta \bullet \gamma, j, k] \\ [a, j-1, j] \end{array}}{[A, l, r; B \rightarrow \alpha \bullet a\beta \bullet \gamma, j-1, k]}$$

$$[\text{RSCAN}] \frac{\begin{array}{c} [A, l, r; B \rightarrow \alpha \bullet \beta \bullet a\gamma, i, j] \\ [a, j, j+1] \end{array}}{[A, l, r; B \rightarrow \alpha \bullet \beta a \bullet \gamma, i, j+1]}$$

$$[\text{LCOMP1}] \frac{\begin{array}{c} [\Phi, j, k; C, j, j] \\ [C, j, j; C \rightarrow \bullet\delta \bullet i, j] \end{array}}{[\Phi, j, k; C \rightarrow \bullet\delta \bullet i, j]}$$

$$[\text{LCOMP2}] \frac{\begin{array}{c} [A, l, r; B \rightarrow \alpha C \bullet \beta \bullet \gamma, j, k] \\ [B \rightarrow \alpha C \bullet \beta \bullet \gamma, j, k; C \rightarrow \bullet\delta \bullet i, j] \end{array}}{[A, l, r; B \rightarrow \alpha \bullet C\beta \bullet \gamma, i, k]}$$

$$[\text{RCOMP1}] \frac{\begin{array}{c} [\Phi, i, j; C, j, j] \\ [C, j, j; C \rightarrow \bullet\delta \bullet j, k] \end{array}}{[\Phi, i, j; C \rightarrow \bullet\delta \bullet j, k]}$$

$$[\text{RCOMP2}] \frac{\begin{array}{c} [A, l, r; B \rightarrow \alpha \bullet \beta \bullet C\gamma, i, j] \\ [B \rightarrow \alpha \bullet \beta \bullet C\gamma, i, j; C \rightarrow \bullet\delta \bullet j, k] \end{array}}{[A, l, r; B \rightarrow \alpha \bullet \beta C \bullet \gamma, i, k]}$$

Fig. 6. Deduction steps for a predictive head-corner parsing schema

$$\frac{[C,k,l]}{[F,k,l+|a|]} \quad \begin{array}{l} C \overset{a}{\longmapsto}_R F \\ a = a_{l+1} \text{ or } a = \epsilon \end{array} \qquad\qquad \frac{[C,k,l]}{[F,m,m+|a|]} \quad \begin{array}{l} C \overset{a}{\longmapsto}_U C\,F \\ a = a_{m+1} \text{ or } a = \epsilon \end{array}$$

$$\frac{[C,k,l]}{[F,k-|a|,l]} \quad \begin{array}{l} C \overset{a}{\longmapsto}_L F \\ a = a_k \text{ or } a = \epsilon \end{array} \qquad\qquad \frac{\begin{array}{c}[F,l,m]\\ [C,k,l]\end{array}}{[G,k,m]} \quad C\,F \longmapsto_R G$$

$$\frac{[C,k,l]}{[F,l,l]} \quad C \longmapsto_R C\,F$$

$$\frac{[C,k,l]}{[F,k,k]} \quad C \longmapsto_L C\,F \qquad\qquad \frac{\begin{array}{c}[F,m,k]\\ [C,k,l]\end{array}}{[G,m,l]} \quad C\,F \longmapsto_L G$$

Fig. 7. Inference rules for S^1 items

[**INIT**] $\$_0 \overset{\epsilon}{\longmapsto} \$_0 \ (S \to \bullet \bullet \alpha)$

[**HC$_T$**] $(A \to \delta_1 \bullet \delta_2 \bullet \delta_3) \overset{a}{\longmapsto}_U \ (A \to \delta_1 \bullet \delta_2 \bullet \delta_3)\,(B \to \alpha \bullet a \bullet \gamma)$

[**HC$_N$**] $(A \to \bullet\beta\bullet) \overset{\epsilon}{\longmapsto}_R \ (B \to \alpha \bullet A \bullet \gamma)$

[**HC$_\epsilon$**] $(A \to \delta_1 \bullet \delta_2 \bullet \delta_3) \overset{b}{\longmapsto}_U \ (A \to \delta_1 \bullet \delta_2 \bullet \delta_3)\,(B \to \bullet\bullet)$

[**LSCAN**] $(B \to \alpha a \bullet \beta \bullet \gamma) \overset{a}{\longmapsto}_L \ (B \to \alpha \bullet a\beta \bullet \gamma)$

[**RSCAN**] $(B \to \alpha \bullet \beta \bullet a\gamma) \overset{a}{\longmapsto}_R \ (B \to \alpha \bullet \beta a \bullet \gamma)$

[**LCOMP**] $(B \to \alpha A \bullet \beta \bullet \gamma)\,(A \to \bullet\delta\bullet) \longmapsto_L \ (B \to \alpha \bullet A\beta \bullet \gamma)$

[**RCOMP**] $(B \to \alpha \bullet \beta \bullet A\gamma)\,(A \to \bullet\delta\bullet) \longmapsto_R \ (B \to \alpha \bullet \beta A \bullet \gamma)$

Fig. 8. Compilation schema for a bottom-up head-corner strategy

the head-corner relation. Terminals are recognized to the left and to the right by [**LSCAN**] and [**RSCAN**] transitions, respectively. Once the right-hand side of a production has been completely recognized, [**LCOMP**] and [**RCOMP**] advance the dot of the production having the left-hand side of that rule to the left or to the right of the dot, respectively.

When the S^1 inference rules are applied to an automaton resulting from the compilation schema shown in Fig. 8, we obtain the set of deduction steps corresponding to the parsing schema **buHC** defined by Sikkel in [9, chapter 11], as shown in Fig. 9, considering that in the parsing schemata framework [9] the antecedent $[A \to \delta_1 \bullet \delta_2 \bullet \delta_3, l, r]$ in steps [**HC$_T$**] and [**HC$_\epsilon$**] can be filtered out as it does not restrict the application of these steps.

$$[\mathbf{INIT}]\frac{[\$_0, 0, 0]}{[S \to \bullet \bullet \alpha, 0, 0]}$$

$$[\mathbf{HC}_T]\frac{\begin{array}{c}[A \to \delta_1 \bullet \delta_2 \bullet \delta_3, l, r] \\ [a, j-1, j]\end{array}}{[B \to \alpha \bullet a \bullet \gamma, j-1, j]}$$

$$[\mathbf{HC}_N]\frac{[A \to \bullet \beta \bullet, i, j]}{[B \to \alpha \bullet A \bullet \gamma, i, j]}$$

$$[\mathbf{HC}_\epsilon]\frac{[A \to \delta_1 \bullet \delta_2 \bullet \delta_3, l, r]}{[B \to \bullet\bullet, j, j]}$$

$$[\mathbf{LSCAN}]\frac{\begin{array}{c}[B \to \alpha a \bullet \beta \bullet \gamma, j, k] \\ [a, j-1, j]\end{array}}{[B \to \alpha \bullet a\beta \bullet \gamma, j-1, k]}$$

$$[\mathbf{RSCAN}]\frac{\begin{array}{c}[B \to \alpha \bullet \beta \bullet a\gamma, i, j] \\ [a, j, j+1]\end{array}}{[B \to \alpha \bullet \beta a \bullet \gamma, i, j+1]}$$

$$[\mathbf{LCOMP}]\frac{\begin{array}{c}[A \to \bullet \delta \bullet, i, j] \\ [B \to \alpha A \bullet \beta \bullet \gamma, j, k]\end{array}}{[B \to \alpha \bullet A\beta \bullet \gamma, i, k]}$$

$$[\mathbf{RCOMP}]\frac{\begin{array}{c}[A \to \bullet \delta \bullet, j, k] \\ [B \to \alpha \bullet \beta \bullet A\gamma, i, j]\end{array}}{[B \to \alpha \bullet \beta A \bullet \gamma, i, k]}$$

Fig. 9. Deduction steps for a bottom-up head-corner parsing schema

6 Conclusions

In order to provide a common framework for the description of bidirectional parsing algorithms for context-free grammars, we have defined a new class of bidirectional push-down automata which works in polynomial time. We have also shown how tabular parsing algorithms can be derived from the automaton describing the parsing strategy, and the tabulation technique associated to the automata model. As illustration, we have considered the case of the predictive head-corner and bottom-up head-corner strategies proposed in [9] but the approach can be applied to the other bidirectional strategies defined in the literature. This approach can also be extended to automata models for extensions of context-free grammars. In this direction, we have investigated a bidirectional version of Linear Indexed Automata for Tree Adjoining Grammars [1].

The use of bidirectional push-down automata to define parsers allowed us to concentrate on the parsing strategy itself, abstracting for details of implementation such as the input positions spanned by a production or the information we must track into items to guarantee the correctness of a parsing strategy.

Acknowledgements. This research has been partially supported by Plan Nacional de Investigación Científica, Desarrollo e Innovación Tecnológica (Grant TIC2000-0370-C02-01), Ministerio de Ciencia y Tecnología (Grant HP2001-0044), Xunta de Galicia (Grants PGIDT01PXI10506PN and PGIDIT02PXIB30501PR) and Universidade da Coruña.

References

1. Miguel A. Alonso, Víctor J. Díaz, and Manuel Vilares. Bidirectional automata for tree adjoining grammars. In *Proc. of the Seventh International Workshop on Parsing Technologies (IWPT-2001)*, pages 42–53, Beijing, China, October 2001. Tsinghua University Press.
2. Eric de la Clergerie. *Automates à Piles et Programmation Dynamique. DyALog : Une Application à la Programmation en Logique.* PhD thesis, Université Paris 7, Paris, France, 1993.
3. Eric de la Clergerie and Bernard Lang. LPDA: Another look at tabulation in logic programming. In Van Hentenryck, editor, *Proc. of the 11th International Conference on Logic Programming (ICLP'94)*, pages 470–486. MIT Press, June 1994.
4. J. Earley. An efficient context-free parsing algorithm. *Communications of the ACM*, 13(2):94–102, 1970.
5. Bernard Lang. Towards a uniform formal framework for parsing. In Masaru Tomita, editor, *Current Issues in Parsing Technology*, pages 153–171. Kluwer Academic Publishers, Norwell, MA, USA, 1991.
6. Mark-Jan Nederhof. An optimal tabular parsing algorithm. In *Proc. of 32nd Annual Meeting of the Association for Computational Linguistics*, pages 117–124, Las Cruces, NM, USA, June 1994. ACL.
7. Mark-Jan Nederhof. Reversible pushdown automata and bidirectional parsing. In J. Dassow, G. Rozenberg, and A. Salomaa, editors, *Developments in Language Theory II*, pages 472–481. World Scientific, Singapore, 1996.
8. Stuart M. Shieber, Yves Schabes, and Fernando C. N. Pereira. Principles and implementation of deductive parsing. *Journal of Logic Programming*, 24(1–2):3–36, July-August 1995.
9. Klaas Sikkel. *Parsing Schemata — A Framework for Specification and Analysis of Parsing Algorithms.* Texts in Theoretical Computer Science — An EATCS Series. Springer-Verlag, Berlin/Heidelberg/New York, 1997.

Finite Automata and Non-self-Embedding Grammars *

Marcella Anselmo[1], Dora Giammarresi[2], and Stefano Varricchio[2]

[1] Dipartimento di Informatica ed Applicazioni,
Università di Salerno I-84081 Baronissi (SA) Italy
anselmo@dia.unisa.it
[2] Dipartimento di Matematica. Università di Roma "Tor Vergata",
via della Ricerca Scientifica, 00133 Roma, Italy.
{giammarr,varricch}@mat.uniroma2.it

Abstract. We consider non-self-embedding (NSE) context-free grammars as a representation of regular sets. We point out its advantages with respect to more classical representations by finite automata, in particular when considering the efficient realization of the rational operations. We give a characterization in terms of composition of regular grammars and state relationships between NSE grammars and push-down automata. Finally we show a polynomial algorithm to decide whether a context-free grammars is self-embedding or not.

1 Introduction

Regular languages play a central role in formal language theory, and indeed in theoretical computer science. Evidence is given by a wide and continued literature, together with a variety of practical problems dealing with regular languages (e.g. compiling, text editing, DNA sequences, and so on). Different properties and questions have been investigated and many points of view have been considered: logical, algebraic, analytical or algorithmic. The fundamental question we deal with in this paper is *representation of a regular language*, indeed defined as an abstract concept.

There are several ways of representing a regular language, each one with its peculiarity, advantages and disadvantages and this results in a richness of the theory. Every time we deal with a regular language, we can choose the most convenient type of representation for it. In this contest, all the procedures to transform a representation into an equivalent one, together with their time and/or space complexity, are of great interest. Regular languages are classically represented by: regular expressions, finite automata (deterministic, non-deterministic, two-way, ...), logical formalisms and regular grammars. We observe that regular grammars are only a different way to represent non-deterministic finite automata. Therefore, if we look for a representation of regular languages which

---

* This work was partially supported by MIUR project **Linguaggi formali e automi:
teoria e applicazioni**.

J.-M. Champarnaud and D. Maurel (Eds.): CIAA 2002, LNCS 2608, pp. 47–56, 2003.

is "better" with respect to finite automata, we have to consider a larger class of grammars. In this paper we focus on a particular family of grammars called *non-self-embedding (NSE) grammars*, strictly including the regular grammars, but still representing regular languages.

A context-free grammar is *self-embedding* (SE) if there is a derivation for a variable A, of type $A \stackrel{*}{\Longrightarrow} \alpha A \beta$ with both α, β non-empty. A context-free grammar is *non-self-embedding* (NSE) if it is not SE. From a result due to Chomsky [2], we know that any NSE grammar generates a regular language. Notice that the vice versa is always true: every regular language admits a NSE grammar representing it (a right-linear grammar is NSE). Despite a poor literature on NSE grammars (we are not aware of any other result), we believe that NSE grammars can be regarded to as an interesting representation for regular languages. Indeed, we exhibit a simple example showing that the representation of a regular language can be much more concise (an exponential gap!) via NSE grammars than via finite automata. This example is, actually, a simple case of a more general situation where the representation by NSE grammars is always more "compact". The idea is to exploit the structure of a grammar that has variables that can be used to generate different instances of the same language.

In this paper we first discuss the consequences of the SE (NSE) property on the grammar structure. We show that a NSE grammar can be expressed in terms of regular grammars. More precisely, we introduce an operation between grammars we call $\oplus$-*composition* that corresponds to the *substitution* operation between languages. Then we characterize the NSE grammars as those grammars that can be obtained by a finite number of $\oplus$-compositions of regular grammars. As immediate consequence, one obtains the Chomsky result, since regular languages are closed under regular substitutions.

We also investigate the realization of rational operations on languages using NSE grammars and we highlight the advantages with respect to finite automata in many situations: for instance in the representation of the square of a language, or, more generally, in the representation of regular expressions containing different instances of the same language. Moreover, we remark that rational operations have a very simple representation in terms of $\oplus$-composition of NSE grammars and that NSE grammars are in general much more concise when we exploit the operation of composition on grammars some of which are identical.

We then study what the SE property yields on push-down automata (PDA). We show that a PDA, obtained by the canonical construction from a NSE grammar, has stack size bounded by some constant. Recall that the vice versa is always true: i.e. PDA with constant stack size recognize regular languages.

In the last part of the paper we give an algorithm that tests whether a context-free grammar is NSE or not. This algorithm has a running time polynomial in the size of the grammar. As consequence, this shows that the SE property has also some relations on decidability results on CFG. Indeed it is well-known that it is undecidable whether a CFG generates a regular language or not.

For lack of space, most of the proofs are omitted from this extended abstract. We refer the interested reader to the full paper [1].

2   Basic Notations and Definitions

We assume the reader familiar with basic formal language theory including finite-state automata, push-down automata, regular expressions and grammars. We will mainly use notations as in [4]. A *context-free grammar* (CFG) will be denoted by $G = (V, T, P, S)$ where V, T, P, S are the sets of *variables, terminals, productions* and the *start* symbol, respectively. We always assume that $V \cap T = \emptyset$. We will use informally the notion of *size* of a grammar as the space needed for its description. By *regular grammar* we indicate a grammar that is either left- or right- linear. We now recall the definition of self-embedding grammar.

Definition 1. *A context-free grammar $G = (V, T, P, S)$ is* self-embedding (SE) *if there exists a variable A such that $A \overset{*}{\Rightarrow} \alpha A \beta$ with $\alpha, \beta \in (V \cup T)^{+}$.*

In this paper we will be interested in *non-self-embedding* (NSE) context-free grammars i.e. satisfying the properties that, for all variables A, any derivation $A \overset{*}{\Rightarrow} \alpha A \beta$ implies that either $\alpha = \epsilon$ or $\beta = \epsilon$. Notice that given a regular language L there exists a NSE grammar for L: in particular a right-linear grammar is NSE. A well-known result states that also the reverse is true. The following theorem is due to Chomsky [2] (see also [3]).

Theorem 1. *The language generated by a NSE grammar is regular.*

3   A Characterization for NSE Grammars

In this section we revisit the Chomsky theorem in a more general framework. In particular we give a Decomposition Theorem stating that the NSE grammars are exactly the context-free grammars obtained as a particular *composition* of regular grammars. We emphasize that such composition operation, corresponds to the operation of substitution on languages. As consequence, NSE grammars are a formalism which is exponentially more compact with respect to non deterministic finite automata.

Definition 2. *Let $G_1 = (V_1, T_1, P_1, S_1)$ and $G_2 = (V_2, T_2, P_2, S_2)$ be two context-free grammars, with $V_1 \cap V_2 = \emptyset$. The $\oplus$-composition of G_1 and G_2 is given by:*

$$G = G_1 \oplus G_2 = (V, T, P, S)$$

where $V = V_1 \cup V_2$, $T = T_1 \backslash V_2 \cup T_2$, $P = P_1 \cup P_2$ and $S = S_1$.

Notice that, if $T_1 \cap V_2 = \emptyset$ then $L(G_1 \oplus G_2) = L(G_1)$. Moreover, by definition, if G is a grammar and $G = G_1 \oplus G_2$, then the corresponding sets of variables, V_1 and V_2, are disjoint. This implies that a derivation of a word w in G can be split in two phases. First, we apply only rules of G_1 (to variables in V_1) starting from its start symbol and get a word w' (on the alphabet T_1). Second, we apply only rules of G_2 (starting from symbols in $T_1 \cap V_2$) and get word w. More formally:

Remark 1. If $G = G_1 \oplus G_2$ then language $L(G)$ can be obtained from $L(G_1)$ by applying a substitution that maps each symbol $A \in T_1 \cap V_2$ to $L_A(G_2)$ where $L_A(G_2)$ is the language generated by the grammar G_2 using A as start symbol.

Similarly, we consider sequences of n applications of $\oplus$-composition, for some n. It is not difficult to verify that the $\oplus$-composition is associative. Let $G_1 \oplus G_2 \oplus \ldots \oplus G_n = G$ with $G_i = (V_i, T_i, P_i, S_i)$, for $i = 1, 2, \ldots, n$ and $G = (V, T, P, S)$. By definition, there should be $V_i \cap V_{i+1} = \emptyset$ for $i = 1, \ldots n - 1$. Moreover, $V = V_1 \cup V_2 \cup \ldots \cup V_n$, $T = T_1 \cup T_2 \cup \ldots \cup T_n \setminus (V_2 \cup \ldots \cup V_n)$, $P = P_1 \cup P_2 \cup \ldots \cup P_n$ and $S = S_1$. The proof of the next lemma can be found in the full paper [1].

Lemma 1. *Let G_1 and G_2 be two NSE grammars, then $G_1 \oplus G_2$ is NSE.*

As consequence of the above lemma, observe that, the $\oplus$-composition of two regular grammars G_1 and G_2 (either left- or right- linear) gives, in general, a non-self-embedding grammar. The main result of this section states that the reverse is also true: every NSE grammar can be obtained as $\oplus$-composition of a finite number of regular grammars. We now give the *Decomposition Theorem*.

Theorem 2. *Let $G = (V, T, P, S)$ be a NSE grammar. Then, there exist n regular grammars $G_1, G_2, \ldots, G_n$, for some n, such that $G = G_1 \oplus G_2 \oplus \ldots \oplus G_n$.*

Proof. (Sketch) The idea of the proof is to "extract" all grammars $G_1, G_2, \ldots, G_n$ from G, one after the other. We start with $G_1 = (V_1, T_1, P_1, S_1)$ that is obtained from G by considering some of G variables as terminals. More precisely, $S_1 = S$ while variables in V_1 are only those ones that are both "reachable" from the start symbol and from which the start symbol can be "reached". All the other G variables will be added to the set of terminals together with G terminals.

Then we proceed by defining in order $G_2, \ldots, G_n$. In general, grammar $G_i = (V_i, T_i, P_i, S_i)$, $i = 2, \ldots, n$, is defined after G_{i-1} as follows. The start symbol S_i is one of the variables of G that is considered terminal in G_{i-1}. Then variables in V_i are G variables that are both "reachable" from S_i and from which S_i can be "reached". The productions in $P_i \subseteq P$ are defined by selecting the rules having V_i variables in the left-hand side. All the symbols on the right-hand side that are not in V_i will constitute the set of terminals T_i.

The key idea behind the proof lies in the order of the G_i's (i.e. the order in which such start vertices S_i are chosen) that is based on a topological ordering of vertices of a particular production graph. This guarantees that, chosen a grammar G_i, the possible G's variables in the right-hand side of rules in P_i do not belong to set V_j for $j < i$. $\qquad\square$

The complete proof can be found in the full paper [1]. We only remark that such proof is constructive, i. e. it gives an effective and efficient (polynomial time) procedure to decompose a NSE grammar in terms of regular grammars.

Observe that Theorem 2 together with Lemma 1 implies that NSE grammars are exactly those grammars obtained as a $\oplus$-composition of regular grammars (either right- or left-linear). Moreover, by Remark 1, one obtains Chomsky result (Theorem 1) as a corollary, since regular languages are closed under substitution.

To conclude, we remark that, despite the decomposition of NSE grammars in left- and right-regular grammars evoke a similarity with two-way finite automata, the two representations are quite different (see Example 1 in the next section).

4   Advantages of NSE Representations

In this section we compare the representation of regular languages by NSE grammars with respect to finite automata (regular grammars). We will see that NSE grammars are much more concise when we exploit the operation of composition on grammars some of which are identical.

We start by defining the rational operations between languages represented via NSE grammars. Rational operations of *union, concatenation* and *star* of languages are basic in the construction of regular languages.

Let $G_1 = (V_1, T_1, P_1, S_1)$ and $G_2 = (V_2, T_2, P_2, S_2)$ be two context-free grammars. Without loss of generality, we assume that the sets of variables V_1 and V_2 are disjoint. We define the following grammars corresponding to the standard constructions for the union, concatenation and star of context-free grammars [4]:

- $G_u = (V_u, T_u, P_u, S_u)$ with $V_u = V_1 \cup V_2 \cup \{S_u\}$, $T_u = T_1 \cup T_2$, $P_u = P_1 \cup P_2 \cup \{S_u \to S_1 | S_2\}$
- $G_c = (V_c, T_c, P_c, S_c)$ with $V_c = V_1 \cup V_2 \cup \{S_c\}$, $T_c = T_1 \cup T_2$, $P_c = P_1 \cup P_2 \cup \{S_c \to S_1 S_2\}$
- $G_s = (V_s, T_s, P_s, S_s)$ with $V_s = V_1 \cup \{S_s\}$, $T_s = T_1$, $P_s = P_1 \cup \{S_s \to S_s S_1 | \epsilon\}$.

Proposition 1. *If the grammars G_1 and G_2 are NSE then the grammars G_u, G_c and G_s are NSE.*

Observe that, when applying rational operations to NSE grammars, the resulting grammar is of the "same" type of the starting ones (while in the automata case we get non-determinism or ϵ-transitions). Moreover the size of the resulting grammar only increases by an additive constant: we add only one production (while in the automata case, we have to add a number of transitions that depends on the number of transitions in the starting automata).

The most interesting case is the concatenation when $L(G_1) = L(G_2)$: when we define the grammar G_c for the square $L' = LL$ of a regular language $L = L(G)$, we do not need to make two disjoint copies of the grammar G. Then, the size of the NSE grammar G_c differs from the size of G only by an additive constant. On the other hand classical constructions give a NFA for $L' = LL$ whose size is at least twice the size of a NFA for L. Observe that this is only one simple case of a typical situation. In fact, by definition, any regular language is obtained as application of rational operations to simpler languages (some of which are often identical!). We observe that the rational operations can be also given in terms of $\oplus$-compositions. More precisely, we define:

$G^+ = (\{S\}, \{S_1, S_2\}, \{S \to S_1 | S_2\}, S)$
$G^\bullet = (\{S\}, \{S_1, S_2\}, \{S \to S_1 S_2\}, S)$
$G^* = (\{S\}, \{S_1\}, \{S \to S S_1 | \epsilon\}, S)$.

Then, it is immediate to verify that $G_u = G^+ \oplus G_1 \oplus G_2$, $G_c = G^\bullet \oplus G_1 \oplus G_2$, $G_s = G^* \oplus G_1$.

We observed that NSE representations are more concise than finite automata ones when the language contains concatenations of copies of same languages. Indeed similar arguments apply to $\oplus$-compositions. We find that NSE grammars are in general much more concise when we exploit the operation of composition on grammars some of which are identical. The next example will show that the difference in size between the two representations can be even exponential.

Example 1. Let $L = \{a^{2^k}\}$. Any NFA for L have at least 2^k states, otherwise it had a loop on its states and would recognize an infinite language.
Let $G = (V, T, P, A_k)$, where $V = \{A_0, A_1, \ldots, A_k\}$, $T = \{a\}$, and

$$P = \{A_k \to A_{k-1}A_{k-1}, \ A_{k-1} \to A_{k-2}A_{k-2}, \ \ldots, \ A_1 \to A_0A_0, \ A_0 \to a\}.$$

It is not difficult to see that G is NSE and that $L(G) = \{a^{2^k}\}$. This shows that the minimal size of a NFA accepting a regular language L can be exponential with respect a NSE grammar generating L.

Notice that G is obtained as composition of very simple grammars exploiting the effect of generating and substituting two copies of the same languages in different occurrences. More precisely, G can be decomposed as $G = G_k \oplus G_{k-1} \oplus \cdots \oplus G_1$, where $G_1 = (\{A_1\}, \{a\}, \{A_1 \to aa\}, \{A_1\})$ and

$$G_i = (\{A_i\}, \{A_{i-1}\}, \{A_i \to A_{i-1}A_{i-1}\}, \{A_i\}), \quad i = 2, \cdots, k.$$

Remark that for every $i = 2, \cdots, k$, $L(G_i \oplus \cdots \oplus G_0)$ can be obtained by applying a substitution that maps A_{i-1} to $L(G_{i-1} \oplus \cdots \oplus G_1)$ (see Remark 1).

5   NSE Grammars and Push-Down Automata

In this section we analyze the relationships between NSE grammars and push-down automata (PDA). The main result states that a context-free grammar is NSE if and only if the corresponding equivalent PDA has a bounded stack.

We recall that a grammar $G = (V, T, P, S)$ is in *canonical form* if its productions are of the kind $A \to a\gamma$ or $A \to \gamma$, with $A \in V$, $a \in T$, and $\gamma \in V^*$. As well known [4], for any context-free grammar G, there exists a context-free grammar G' in canonical form, such that $L(G') = L(G)$. Moreover, $G = (V, T, P, S)$ in canonical form can be easily transformed in an equivalent PDA M_G [4]. More precisely, $M_G = (\{q\}, T, V, \delta, q, S, \emptyset)$, where the transition function δ is defined as: $(q, \gamma) \in \delta(q, a, A)$ if and only if $A \to a\gamma$, with $a \in T \cup \{\epsilon\}$ and $A \in V$. The PDA M_G simulates the leftmost derivations of G:

$$S \overset{*}{\Rightarrow}_\ell w\gamma \iff (q, w, S) \vdash^*_{M_G} (q, \epsilon, \gamma), \quad w \in T^*, \gamma \in V^*. \tag{1}$$

Proposition 2. *Let G be a NSE grammar in canonical form and let M_G the corresponding equivalent PDA defined as above. Then there exists a constant $K > 0$ such that in any computation of M_G the string contained in the stack has length upper-bounded by K.*

Proof. Let $G = (V, T, P, S)$ be a NSE grammar in canonical form and let $k = |V|$ and $h = \max\{|\gamma| \mid A \to \gamma \text{ or } A \to a\gamma, A \in V, a \in T\}$. One can prove by induction on k that for any leftmost derivation $A \overset{*}{\Rightarrow}_\ell w\gamma$, with $A \in V$, $w \in T^*$, and $\gamma \in V^*$, one has $|\gamma| \leq hk$. Let us set $K = hk$. By Eq. (1) if γ appears in the stack in some computation, then $S \overset{*}{\Rightarrow}_\ell w\gamma$ for some $w \in T^*$ and then $|\gamma| \leq K$. □

Since any PDA with bounded stack accepts a regular language, then Proposition 2 gives a new proof of Chomsky Theorem (Theorem 1).

The converse of the previous proposition holds under the hypothesis that all the symbols of the grammar G are *useful*, i.e. they appear inside a derivation of a string of $L(G)$. More precisely let G be a grammar in canonical form, whose symbols are all useful, and let M_G be the corresponding equivalent PDA defined as above. If there exists a constant $K > 0$ such that in any computation of M_G the string contained in the stack has length upper-bounded by K, then G is NSE. The proof goes by contradiction.

Furthermore it is well-known that given a PDA M, one can construct a context-free grammar G_M such that $L(M) = L(G_M)$ [4]. We remark that, in this construction, the first step consists in building a PDA M' having only one state such that $L(M) = L(M')$. In this construction one can easily prove that M' has a *bounded stack* if and only if M has a *bounded stack*. Moreover, from M' one constructs the grammar G_M which is in canonical form and G_M is such that the corresponding equivalent PDA is exactly M'. Therefore, using Proposition 2 and its converse one can state the following proposition.

Proposition 3. *Let M be a PDA and G_M the corresponding equivalent grammar. Then M has bounded stack if and only if G_M is NSE.*

It is interesting to observe that the classical constructions on the equivalence of PDA's and CFG's [3] are polynomial time. Therefore, for a CFG G the equivalent PDA M_G has polynomial size w.r.t. G. Conversely, for a PDA M the equivalent CFG G_M has polynomial size w.r.t. M. Therefore, the representations of regular languages by PDA with bounded stack and by NSE grammars are equivalent in the size up to a polynomial.

6   Test for Self-Embedding Property

We recall that, given a context-free grammar G that generates a language over the alphabet Σ, it is not decidable whether $L(G)$ is regular. (Notice that it is undecidable even whether $L(G) = \Sigma^*$). In this section we describe an algorithm to test whether G is non-self-embedding. If G is non-self-embedding then $L(G)$ is regular. The test is based on the association to G of a labelled directed graph, whose labels are taken in a properly introduced semi-ring. The SE property for G is characterized by the existence of some special paths in the graph. These paths are detected by powering some associated matrix, with entries in the semi-ring.

Let us introduce the semi-ring $C = \{\ell, r, b, 0\}$ equipped with operations sum and product given by the following tables.

+	ℓ	b	r	0
ℓ	ℓ	b	b	ℓ
r	b	b	r	r
b	b	b	b	b
0	ℓ	b	r	0

×	ℓ	b	r	0
ℓ	ℓ	b	b	0
r	b	b	r	0
b	b	b	b	0
0	0	0	0	0

Let G be a unit-free context-free grammar, where the set of variables is $V = \{A_1, A_2, \cdots, A_n\}$. We associate a graph and a matrix with G as follows.

The *Labelled Production Graph* $H(G)$ is a labelled directed graph which vertices are the variables of G, there is an edge $A \to B$ iff there exists a production rule $A \to \alpha B \beta$ in P, and the label of edge $A \to B$ is defined in C by:

$$lab(A \to B) = \begin{cases} \ell & \text{if for every } A \to \alpha B \beta \text{ in } P \text{ it holds } \alpha \neq \epsilon, \beta = \epsilon \\ r & \text{if for every } A \to \alpha B \beta \text{ in } P \text{ it holds } \alpha = \epsilon, \beta \neq \epsilon \\ b & \text{otherwise} \end{cases}$$

The *Transition Matrix* $M(G)$ is a $n \times n$ matrix which entries are defined in C as follows, for any $i, j \in \{1, 2, \cdots, n\}$:

$$M(G)_{i,j} = \begin{cases} 0 & \text{if there is no production rule of type } A_i \to \alpha A_j \beta \text{ in } P \\ lab(A_i \to A_j) & \text{otherwise.} \end{cases}$$

The following algorithm tests whether the grammar G is NSE.

```
SE-TEST(G = (V, E))
 1  for i ← 1 to |V|
 2      do for i ← j to |V|
 3          do M(G)_{i,j} ← 0
 4  for each production A_i→αA_jβ in P
 5      do if α ≠ ε and β = ε
 6          then if M(G)_{i,j} = ℓ or 0
 7              then M(G)_{i,j} ← ℓ
 8              else M(G)_{i,j} ← b
 9          if α = ε and β ≠ ε
10              then if M(G)_{i,j} = r or 0
11                  then M(G)_{i,j} ← r
12                  else M(G)_{i,j} ← b
13              if α ≠ ε and β ≠ ε
14                  then M(G)_{i,j} ← b
15  M^1 ← M(G)
16  M ← M^1
17  for i ← 2 to |V|
18      do M^i ← M^{i-1}M^1
19          M ← M + M^i
20  for i ← 1 to |V|
21      do if M_{i,i} = b
22          then RETURN "G is SE and A_i is SE"
23  RETURN "G is NSE"
```

The algorithm SE-TEST constructs the transition matrix $M(G)$ in lines 4-14. After the execution of the **for** loop in lines 17-19, we find $M = M(G)^{\leq V}$, where for a matrix M and an integer n, we use the notation $M^{\leq n} = M + M^2 + \cdots + M^n$. Finally SE-TEST either returns the message "G is SE and A_i is SE" when it finds that $M(G)_{i,i}^{\leq V} = b$ for some i, or the message "G is NSE" otherwise.

It is easy to see that the running time of the algorithm SE-TEST on $G = (V, T, P, S)$ is polynomial in the size of G (indeed $o(|P| + |V|^4)$).

We want now to prove the correctness of the algorithm SE-TEST. More precisely we claim that the algorithm SE-TEST on a unit-free grammar G returns the message *"G is NSE"* iff G is a non-self-embedding grammar.

A grammar G is self-embedding by definition iff there exists a variable A and a derivation $A \overset{*}{\Rightarrow} \alpha A \beta$ with $\alpha, \beta \neq \epsilon$. Note that no limitations constraint such a derivation, and in particular its length. The following proposition restricts the type and the length of derivations to be tested in order to decide whether a grammar is self-embedding. We say that a derivation $\alpha_0 A_0 \beta_0 \Rightarrow \alpha_1 A_1 \beta_1 \cdots \Rightarrow \alpha_n A_n \beta_n$ is *simple* if $A_h = A_k$, with $1 \leq h < k \leq n$ implies $h = 1$, $k = n$. Therefore the length of a simple derivation in grammar $G = (V, T, P, S)$ is at most $|V|$.

Proposition 4. *Let $G = (V, T, P, S)$ be a unit-free context-free grammar. A variable $A \in V$ is self-embedding iff there exists a derivation $A \overset{*}{\Rightarrow} \alpha A \beta$ such that one of the following two cases holds:*

1. *the derivation is simple and $\alpha, \beta \neq \epsilon$*
2. *the derivation $A \overset{*}{\Rightarrow} \alpha A \beta$ can be split into*

$$A \overset{[i]}{\Rightarrow} \alpha' B \beta' \overset{[j]}{\Rightarrow} \alpha' \alpha'' B \beta'' \beta' \overset{[k]}{\Rightarrow} \alpha' \alpha'' \alpha''' A \beta''' \beta'' \beta'$$

so that the derivations $A \overset{[i]}{\Rightarrow} \alpha' B \beta' \overset{[k]}{\Rightarrow} \alpha' \alpha''' A \beta''' \beta'$ and $B \overset{[j]}{\Rightarrow} \alpha'' B \beta''$ are both simple and either $\begin{cases} \alpha' \alpha''' = \beta'' = \epsilon \\ \alpha'', \beta''' \beta' \neq \epsilon \end{cases}$ or $\begin{cases} \alpha'' = \beta''' \beta' = \epsilon \\ \alpha' \alpha''', \beta'' \neq \epsilon. \end{cases}$

Proof. (Sketch) Let A be a self-embedding variable of G and $A \overset{[n]}{\Rightarrow} \alpha A \beta$ be a derivation with $\alpha, \beta \neq \epsilon$ of minimal length n. If the derivation is not simple then it can be split according to the statement. One can prove that the resulting derivations are both simple by supposing the contrary, removing the derivation from a repeated variable to its next occurrence and showing that we then obtain some new derivation that contradicts the minimality of n. □

Proposition 4 can be translated in terms of the labelled production graph. Let us say that a path in labelled production graph $H(G)$, is of *type ℓ* (r, resp.) if all the edges composing it are labelled ℓ (r, resp.); it is of *type b* otherwise. Proposition 4 implies that G is self-embedding iff there exists a vertex X in $H(G)$ and either X has a loop of type b and length $|V|$ at most or X has two loops of length $|V|$ at most, one of type ℓ and the other one of type r.

Furthermore, this characterization can be easily tested on the transition matrices. Indeed G is SE iff there exists a variable A_i such that $M(G)_{i,i}^{\leq h} = b$.

Example 2. Let $G = (V, T, P, S)$ where $V = \{S, A, B\}$, $T = \{a, b\}$ and P is given by: $S{\to}aSb/AB$, $A{\to}aB/a$ and $B{\to}bA/Bb/b$. Suppose vertices in V are numbered as $A_1 = S$, $A_2 = A$ and $A_3 = B$.

The matrix $M(G)$ is the following one: $M(G) = \begin{vmatrix} b & r & \ell \\ 0 & 0 & \ell \\ 0 & \ell & r \end{vmatrix}$.

The grammar G is SE and all its variables are self-embedding. As an example, A is SE and the derivation $A{\Rightarrow}aB{\Rightarrow}aBb{\Rightarrow}abAb$ satisfies case 2) of Proposition 4. Further this derivation yields in $H(G)$ two loops on B each of length $|V|$ at most: $B \overset{r}{\to} B$ of type r and length $1 < |V|$, and $B \overset{\ell}{\to} A \overset{\ell}{\to} B$ of type ℓ and length $2 < |V|$. Finally these loops on $B = A_3$ imply $M(G)_{3,3}^{\leq h} = b$. Indeed $M(G)_{i,i}^{\leq h} = b$ for $i = 1, 2, 3$. Applying the algorithm SE-TEST on G we have:

$$M^1 = M(G); \quad M^2 = \begin{vmatrix} b & b & b \\ 0 & \ell & b \\ 0 & b & b \end{vmatrix}; \quad M^3 = \begin{vmatrix} b & b & b \\ 0 & b & b \\ 0 & b & b \end{vmatrix}.$$

After the execution of the **for** loop of lines 17-19, $M = M^3 = M(G)^3$. Hence the algorithm finds $M_{1,1} = b$ in line 21 and returns: "G is SE and A_1 is SE".

The previous considerations allow us to claim the correctness of algorithm SE-TEST and state the main result in this section.

Theorem 3. *It is decidable whether a context-free grammar is NSE or not.*

7   Conclusions and Further Directions

Next step of our work will be the comparison of the representation of regular languages by NSE grammars with all the other known formalisms. In particular it would be very interesting to develop efficient algorithms to transform regular expressions to/from NSE grammars as well as finite automata to/from NSE grammars. It could be interesting to study the complexity of an algorithm to transform a finite automaton in a regular expression that has a NSE grammar as intermediate stage of the transformation.

References

1. M. Anselmo, D. Giammarresi, S. Varicchio. Non-Self-Embedding Grammars as representation for Regular Languages. Full paper available at
   www.mat.uniroma2.it/~giammarr/Papers/nse.ps
2. N. Chomsky. A note on phrase-structure grammars, *Information and Control.* Vol 2, pp. 393–395, 1959b.
3. M. A. Harrison. *Introduction to Formal Language Theory.* Addison-Wesley, Reading, MA, 1978.
4. J. E. Hopcroft, R.Motwani and J. D. Ullman. *Introduction to Automata Theory, Languages and Computation - 2nd Edition.* Addison-Wesley, 2001.

Simulation of Gate Circuits in the Algebra of Transients

Janusz Brzozowski and Mihaela Gheorghiu

School of Computer Science,
University of Waterloo,
Waterloo, ON, Canada N2L 3G1
{brzozo,mgheorgh}@uwaterloo.ca

Abstract. We study simulation of gate circuits in algebra C recently introduced by Brzozowski and Ésik. A transient is a word consisting of alternating 0s and 1s; it represents a changing signal. In C, gates process transients instead of 0s and 1s. Simulation in C is capable of counting signal changes, and detecting hazards. We study two simulation algorithms: a general one, A, that works with any state, and $\tilde{A}$, that applies if the initial state is stable. We show that the two algorithms agree in the stable case. We prove the sufficiency of the simulation: all signal changes occurring in binary analysis are also predicted by Algorithm A.

1 Introduction

Asynchronous circuits, in contrast to synchronous ones, operate without a clock. Interest in asynchronous circuits has grown in recent years [4,6,9], because they offer the potential for higher speed and lower energy consumption, avoid clock distribution problems, handle metastability safely, and are amenable to modular design.

Despite its advantages, asynchronous design has some problems, among them, hazards. A hazard is an unwanted signal change, caused by stray delays. A hazard may affect the correctness of a computation. Because hazards are important, much research has been done on their detection. Multiple-valued algebras play an important role here [2]. Recently, Brzozowski and Ésik introduced an infinite-valued algebra C, which subsumes all the previously used algebras [1], and a polynomial-time simulation algorithm based on C. The algorithm is capable not only of detecting hazards, but also of counting the number of signal changes in the worst case; this provides an estimate of the energy consumption.

The purpose of this paper is to compare the Brzozowski-Ésik simulation of a circuit with the binary analysis of the circuit. We prove that all the changes that occur in binary analysis, are also predicted by simulation.

2 The Network Model

The material here is based on [3]. For an integer $n > 0$, $[n]$ denotes $\{1, \ldots, n\}$. Boolean operations AND, OR, and NOT are denoted $\wedge$, $\vee$, and $^-$, respectively. Given a gate circuit with n inputs and m gates, we associate an *input variable* X_i with each input, $i \in [n]$, and a *state variable* s_j with the output of each gate, $j \in [m]$. Input and state

J.-M. Champarnaud and D. Maurel (Eds.): CIAA 2002, LNCS 2608, pp. 57–66, 2003.

Fig. 1. Sample gate circuit

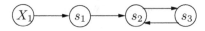

Fig. 2. Network graph for circuit of Fig. 1

variables take values in the binary domain $\mathcal{D} = \{0, 1\}$. Each state variable s_i has an *excitation* S_i, which is the Boolean function of the corresponding gate.

Definition 1. *A network is a tuple* $N = \langle \mathcal{D}, \mathcal{X}, \mathcal{S}, \mathcal{E} \rangle$, *where* $\mathcal{D}$ *is the domain of values,* $\mathcal{X} = \{X_1, \ldots, X_n\}$, *the set of inputs,* $\mathcal{S} = \{s_1, \ldots, s_m\}$, *the set of state variables with associated excitations* $S_1, \ldots, S_m$, *and* $\mathcal{E} \subseteq (\mathcal{X} \times \mathcal{S}) \cup (\mathcal{S} \times \mathcal{S})$, *a set of directed edges. There is an edge between* x *and* y *if and only if the excitation of* y *depends on* x. *The* network graph *is the digraph* $(\mathcal{X} \cup \mathcal{S}, \mathcal{E})$. *Note that* $\mathcal{D}$ *need not be* $\{0, 1\}$.

Example 1. The circuit of Fig. 1 has input X_1, state variables s_1, s_2, s_3, and excitations $S_1 = \overline{X_1}$, $S_2 = s_1 \wedge s_3$, $S_3 = \overline{s_2}$ in domain $\mathcal{D} = \{0, 1\}$. Its network graph is shown in Fig. 2.

A *state* of N is an m-tuple b of values from $\mathcal{D}$ assigned to state variables $s_1, \ldots, s_m$. A *total state* is an $(n+m)$-tuple $c = a \cdot b$ of values from $\mathcal{D}$, the n-tuple a being the values of the inputs, and the m-tuple b, the values of state variables. The dot " $\cdot$ " separates inputs from state variables.

Each excitation S_i is a function of some inputs $X_{j_1}, \ldots, X_{j_l} \in \mathcal{X}$, and some state variables $s_{i_1}, \ldots, s_{i_k} \in \mathcal{S}$, i.e., $S_i = f(X_{j_1}, \ldots, X_{j_l}, s_{i_1}, \ldots, s_{i_k})$, where $f : \mathcal{D}^{l+k} \to \mathcal{D}$. We also treat S_i as a function from $\mathcal{D}^{n+m}$ into $\mathcal{D}$. Thus, let $\tilde{S}_i : \mathcal{D}^{n+m} \to \mathcal{D}$ be $\tilde{S}_i(a \cdot b) = f(a_{j_1}, \ldots, a_{j_l}, b_{i_1}, \ldots, b_{i_k})$, for any $a \cdot b$. From now on we write S_i for $\tilde{S}_i$; the meaning is clear from the context.

For any $i \in [m]$, the value of S_i in total state $a \cdot b$ is denoted $S_i(a \cdot b)$. The tuple $S_1(a \cdot b), \ldots, S_m(a \cdot b)$ is denoted by $S(a \cdot b)$. For any $a \cdot b$, we define the set of unstable state variables as $U(a \cdot b) = \{s_i \mid b_i \neq S_i(a \cdot b)\}$. Thus, $a \cdot b$ is *stable* if and only if $U(a \cdot b) = \emptyset$, i.e., $S(a \cdot b) = b$.

3   Binary Analysis of Networks

In response to changes of its inputs, a circuit passes through a sequence of states as its internal signals change. By analyzing a circuit we mean exploring all possible sequences of states. This section describes a formal analysis model introduced by Muller [10], and later called the *General Multiple Winner* (GMW) model. Our presentation follows that of [3], but here we refer to the GMW model as *binary analysis*.

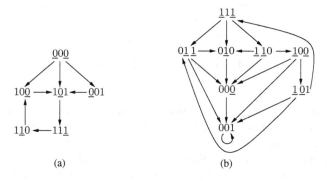

Fig. 3. Sample $G_a(b)$ graphs for circuit of Fig. 1

In this section we use the binary domain, $\mathcal{D} = \{0, 1\}$. We describe the behavior of a network started in a given state with the input kept constant at value $a \in \{0, 1\}^n$, by defining a binary relation R_a on the set $\{0, 1\}^m$ of states of N. For any $b \in \{0, 1\}^m$, $bR_a b$, if $U(a \cdot b) = \emptyset$, i.e., total state $a \cdot b$ is stable, and $bR_a b^K$, if $U(a \cdot b) \neq \emptyset$, and K is any nonempty subset of $U(a \cdot b)$, where by b^K we mean b with all the variables in K complemented. No other pairs of states are related by R_a. As usual, we associate a digraph with the R_a relation, and denote it G_a. In examples, we represent tuples without commas or parentheses, for convenience. Thus $(0, 0, 0)$ is written as 000, *etc.*

For given $a \in \{0, 1\}^n$, and $b \in \{0, 1\}^m$ we define the set of all states reachable from b in relation R_a as $reach(R_a(b)) = \{c \mid bR_a^* c\}$, where R_a^* is the reflexive and transitive closure of R_a. We denote by $G_a(b)$ the subgraph of G_a corresponding to $reach(R_a(b))$.

Example 2. For the circuit in Fig. 1, graph $G_0(000)$ is shown in Fig. 3(a), where unstable variables are underlined. Note that the graph contains no stable states. Graph $G_1(111)$ is shown in Fig. 3(b). Here there is one stable state. To illustrate hazardous behavior, consider path $\pi_1 = 111, 011, 001$. Here s_2 changes once from 1 to 0, and s_3 does not change. However, along path $\pi_2 = 111, 110, 100, 101, 011, 001$, s_2 changes from 1 to 0 to 1 to 0, and s_3 changes from 1 to 0 to 1. If the behavior of π_1 is the intended one, then π_2 violates it. Along π_2 there are unwanted signal pulses: a 1-pulse in s_2, and a 0-pulse in s_3. The first pulse is an example of a *dynamic hazard*, and the second, of a *static hazard*. These pulses can introduce errors in the circuit operation.

4   Transients

While binary analysis is an exhaustive analysis of a circuit, it is inefficient, since the state space is exponential. Simulation using a multi-valued domain is an efficient alternative, if not all the information from binary analysis is needed.

The material here is based on [1]. A *transient* is a nonempty word over $\{0, 1\}$ in which no two consecutive symbols are the same. Thus the set of all transients is

$$\mathbf{T} = 0(10)^* \cup 1(01)^* \cup 0(10)^*1 \cup 1(01)^*0.$$

Transients represent waveforms in a natural way, as shown in Fig. 4.

Fig. 4. Transients as words for waveforms

We use boldface symbols to denote transients, tuples of transients, and functions of transients. For any transient t we denote by $\alpha(\mathbf{t})$ and $\omega(\mathbf{t})$ its first and last characters, respectively. A transient can be obtained from any nonempty binary word by *contraction*, *i.e.*, the elimination of all duplicates immediately following a symbol (*e.g.*, the contraction of 00100011 is 0101). For a binary word s we denote by $\hat{s}$ the result of its contraction. For any $\mathbf{t}, \mathbf{t}' \in \mathbf{T}$, we denote by $\mathbf{tt}'$ the concatenation of t and t'.

The prefix order on $\mathbf{T}$ is denoted $\leq$, and is extended to tuples. For $\mathbf{u} = (\mathbf{u}_1, \ldots, \mathbf{u}_m)$ and $\mathbf{v} = (\mathbf{v}_1, \ldots, \mathbf{v}_m)$ in $\mathbf{T}^m$, we say that u is a prefix of v and write $\mathbf{u} \leq \mathbf{v}$, if $\mathbf{u}_i \leq \mathbf{v}_i$, for all $i \in [m]$.

Extensions of Boolean functions to functions of transients are defined in [1]. Any Boolean function $f : B^n \to B$ is extended to a function $\mathbf{f} : \mathbf{T}^n \to \mathbf{T}$ so that, for any tuple $(\mathbf{t}_1, \ldots, \mathbf{t}_n)$ of transients, f produces the longest transient when $\mathbf{t}_1, \ldots, \mathbf{t}_n$ are applied to the inputs of a gate performing the Boolean function f. We give an example of extended Boolean function next. For more details see [1].

Example 3. Let f to be the two-input OR function and f, its extension. Suppose we want to compute $\mathbf{f}(01, 010)$. We construct a digraph $D(01, 010)$ in which the nodes consist of all the pairs $(\mathbf{t}, \mathbf{t}')$ of transients such that $(\mathbf{t}, \mathbf{t}') \leq (01, 010)$, and there is an edge between any two pairs $\mathbf{p}, \mathbf{p}'$ only if $\mathbf{p} \leq \mathbf{p}'$, and p differs from p' in exactly one coordinate by exactly one letter. The resulting graph is shown in Fig. 5(a). Also, for each node $(\mathbf{t}, \mathbf{t}')$ in the graph we consider as its label the value $f(\omega(\mathbf{t}), \omega(\mathbf{t}'))$. This results in a graph of labels, shown in Fig. 5(b). The value of $\mathbf{f}(01, 010)$ is the contraction of the label sequence of those paths in the graph of labels that have the largest number of alternations between 0 and 1. Therefore, $\mathbf{f}(01, 010) = 0101$.

Let $z(\mathbf{t})$ and $u(\mathbf{t})$ denote the number of 0s and the number of 1s in a transient t, respectively. We denote by $\otimes$ and $\oplus$ the extensions of the Boolean AND and OR operations, respectively. It is shown in [1] that for any $\mathbf{w}, \mathbf{w}' \in \mathbf{T}$ of length > 1, $\mathbf{w} \otimes \mathbf{w}' = \mathbf{t}$, where $\mathbf{t} \in \mathbf{T}$ is such that

$$\alpha(\mathbf{t}) = \alpha(\mathbf{w}) \wedge \alpha(\mathbf{w}'), \quad \omega(\mathbf{t}) = \omega(\mathbf{w}) \wedge \omega(\mathbf{w}'), \quad \text{and} \quad u(\mathbf{t}) = u(\mathbf{w}) + u(\mathbf{w}') - 1.$$

Similarly, $\mathbf{w} \oplus \mathbf{w}' = \mathbf{t}$, where $\mathbf{t} \in \mathbf{T}$ is such that

$$\alpha(\mathbf{t}) = \alpha(\mathbf{w}) \vee \alpha(\mathbf{w}'), \quad \omega(\mathbf{t}) = \omega(\mathbf{w}) \vee \omega(\mathbf{w}'), \quad \text{and} \quad z(\mathbf{t}) = z(\mathbf{w}) + z(\mathbf{w}') - 1.$$

If one of the arguments is 0 or 1 the following rules apply:

$$\mathbf{t} \oplus 0 = 0 \oplus \mathbf{t} = \mathbf{t}, \quad \mathbf{t} \oplus 1 = 1 \oplus \mathbf{t} = 1,$$
$$\mathbf{t} \otimes 1 = 1 \otimes \mathbf{t} = \mathbf{t}, \quad \mathbf{t} \otimes 0 = 0 \otimes \mathbf{t} = 0.$$

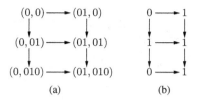

Fig. 5. Graph $D(01, 010)$ with labels

The complement $\bar{\mathbf{t}}$ of $\mathbf{t} \in \mathbf{T}$ is obtained by complementing each character of $\mathbf{t}$. For example, $\overline{1010} = 0101$.

The algebra $C = (\mathbf{T}, \oplus, \otimes, {}^-, 0, 1)$, is called the *change-counting algebra*, and is a commutative de Morgan bisemigroup [1]. We also refer to C as the *algebra of transients*.

We denote by $\mathbf{t} \circ \mathbf{t}'$ concatenation followed by contraction, *i.e.*, $\mathbf{t} \circ \mathbf{t}' = \widehat{\mathbf{t}\mathbf{t}'}$. The $\circ$ operation is associative, and also satisfies for $\mathbf{t}, \mathbf{t}', \mathbf{t}_1, \dots, \mathbf{t}_n \in \mathbf{T}$ and $b \in \{0, 1\}$: 1. if $\mathbf{t} \leq \mathbf{t}'$ then $b \circ \mathbf{t} \leq b \circ \mathbf{t}'$; and 2. $\mathbf{t}_1 \circ \dots \circ \mathbf{t}_n = \widehat{\mathbf{t}_1 \dots \mathbf{t}_n}$.

5   Simulation with Algebra C

A simulation algorithm using algebra C has been proposed in [1]; it generalizes ternary simulation [3,5]. We now give a more general version of the simulation algorithm, and show how it relates to the original version. This parallels the extension of ternary simulation from stable initial state to any initial state [3].

Given any circuit, we use two networks: a binary network $N = \langle \{0, 1\}, \mathcal{X}, \mathcal{S}, \mathcal{E} \rangle$ and the *transient network* $\mathbf{N} = \langle \mathbf{T}, \mathcal{X}, \mathcal{S}, \mathcal{E} \rangle$ having set $\mathbf{T}$ of transients as the domain. The two networks have the same input and state variables, but these variables take values from different domains. A state of network $\mathbf{N}$ is a tuple of transients; the value of the excitation of a variable is also a transient. Excitations in $\mathbf{N}$ are the extensions to C of the Boolean excitations in N. It is shown in [1] that an extended Boolean function depends on one of its arguments if and only if the corresponding Boolean function depends on that argument. Therefore N and $\mathbf{N}$ have the same set of edges.

Binary variables, words, tuples and excitations in N are denoted by italic characters (*e.g.*, s, S). Transients, tuples of transients, and excitations in $\mathbf{N}$ are denoted by boldface characters (*e.g.*, $\mathbf{s}$, $\mathbf{S}$). We refer to components of a tuple by subscripts (*e.g.*, $\mathbf{s}_i$, s_i).

5.1   General Simulation: Algorithm A

We want to record in the value of a variable all the changes in that variable since the start of the simulation, as dictated by its excitation. For variables that are stable initially, since the initial state agrees with the initial excitation, the state transient and the excitation transient will be the same, so at each step we just copy the excitation into the variable. For example, with initial state 0 and excitation 0, if the excitation becomes 01, we set the variable to 01, and so on. For variables that are initially unstable, we first record the initial state, and then the excitation. The operator that gives us the desired result in both cases is $\circ$; thus we have *new_value = initial_value $\circ$ excitation*.

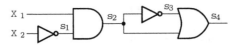

Fig. 6. Circuit with finite simulation

Let $a \cdot b$ be a (binary) total state of $\mathbf{N}$. Algorithm A is defined as follows:

Algorithm A

$s^0 := b$;

$h := 1$;

$s^h := b \circ \mathbf{S}(a \cdot s^0)$;

while $(s^h <> s^{h-1})$ **do**

$\qquad h := h + 1$;

$\qquad s^h := b \circ \mathbf{S}(a \cdot s^{h-1})$;

where $\circ$ is applied to tuples component-wise, i.e., for all m-tuples $\mathbf{u}, \mathbf{v}$ of transients, $\mathbf{u} \circ \mathbf{v} = \mathbf{w}$, where $\mathbf{w}$ is such that $\mathbf{w}_i = \mathbf{u}_i \circ \mathbf{v}_i$, for all $i \in [m]$.

Algorithm A produces a sequence $s^0, s^1, \ldots, s^h, \ldots$, where $s^h = (s_1^h, s_2^h, \ldots, s_m^h) \in \mathbf{T}^m$, for all $h \geq 0$. This sequence can be finite, if we reach $s^{h_0} = s^{h_0-1}$ for some $h_0 > 0$, or infinite otherwise. For convenience, we sometimes consider the finite sequences as being infinite, with $s^h = s^{h_0}$, for all $h > h_0$.

It is shown in [1] that any extended Boolean function $\mathbf{f} : \mathbf{T}^m \to \mathbf{T}$ is *monotonic* with respect to the prefix order, i.e., for any $\mathbf{x}, \mathbf{y} \in \mathbf{T}^m$, if $\mathbf{x} \leq \mathbf{y}$, then $\mathbf{f}(\mathbf{x}) \leq \mathbf{f}(\mathbf{y})$.

Proposition 1. *The sequence resulting from Algorithm A is nondecreasing or monotonic with respect to the prefix order, that is, for all $h \geq 0$, $s^h \leq s^{h+1}$.*

Proof: Since extended Boolean functions are monotonic with respect to the prefix order, so are excitations. We proceed by induction on h.

Basis, $h = 0$: $s^0 = b \leq b \circ \mathbf{S}(a \cdot s^0) = s^1$.

Induction step: $s^h = b \circ \mathbf{S}(a \cdot s^{h-1}) \leq b \circ \mathbf{S}(a \cdot s^h) = s^{h+1}$. ∎

For feedback-free circuits, the sequence resulting from Algorithm A is finite. We can see this if we order the state variables by levels as follows. Level 1 consists of all state variables which depend only on external inputs. Level l consists of all state variables which depend only on variables of level $< l$, and on at least one variable of level $l - 1$. Since the inputs do not change during simulation, level-1 variables change at most once, in the first step of Algorithm A. In general, level-i variables change at most i times. Since the number of levels is finite, our claim follows. Thus the running time of A for feedback-free circuits is polynomial in the number of state variables.

For display reasons, in examples of simulation we write binary states as words, but during computations they are regarded as tuples.

Example 4. Consider the feedback-free circuit in Fig. 6. The excitations are: $\mathbf{S}_1 = \overline{\mathbf{X}_2}$, $\mathbf{S}_2 = \mathbf{X}_1 \otimes s_1$, $\mathbf{S}_3 = \overline{s_2}$, $\mathbf{S}_4 = s_2 \oplus s_3$. For the initial state $a \cdot b = 11 \cdot 1011$, Algorithm A results in Table 1 (left).

Table 1. Results of Algorithms A and Ã

X_1	X_2	s_1	s_2	s_3	s_4	state	X_1	X_2	$\tilde{s}_1$	$\tilde{s}_2$	$\tilde{s}_3$	$\tilde{s}_4$	state
1	1	1	0	1	1	s^0	1	10	0	0	1	1	$\tilde{s}^0$
1	1	10	01	1	1	s^1	1	10	01	0	1	1	$\tilde{s}^1$
1	1	10	010	10	1	s^2	1	10	01	01	1	1	$\tilde{s}^2$
1	1	10	010	101	1010	s^3	1	10	01	01	10	1	$\tilde{s}^3$
1	1	10	010	101	10101	s^4	1	10	01	01	10	101	$\tilde{s}^4$

Table 2. Infinite simulation

X_1	s_1	s_2	s_3	state
0	0	0	0	s^0
0	01	0	01	s^1
0	01	01	01	s^2
0	01	01	010	s^3
...	...	...	...	...

Example 5. For circuits with feedback the simulation sequence may be infinite. Consider the circuit with feedback in Fig. 1. The excitation functions are: $S_1 = \overline{X_1}$, $S_2 = s_1 \otimes s_3$, $S_3 = \overline{s_2}$. We run Algorithm A for this network started in state $a \cdot b = 0 \cdot 000$; the resulting sequence of states, which is infinite, is illustrated in Table 2.

5.2   Simulation with Stable Initial State: Algorithm Ã

Algorithm A above makes no assumptions about the starting state $a \cdot b$. If the network starts in a stable total state and the inputs change, then we have a slightly simpler formulation which we call Algorithm Ã; this is the version used in [1]. Assume **N** is started in stable total state $\tilde{a} \cdot b$ and the input tuple changes to a.

Algorithm Ã

$a = \tilde{a} \circ a;$
$\tilde{s}^0 := b;$
$h := 1;$
$\tilde{s}^h := \mathbf{S}(a \cdot \tilde{s}^0);$
while $(\tilde{s}^h <> \tilde{s}^{h-1})$ **do**
$\qquad h := h + 1;$
$\qquad \tilde{s}^h := \mathbf{S}(a \cdot \tilde{s}^{h-1});$

Example 6. We illustrate Algorithm Ã with the network in Fig. 6, started in stable state $\tilde{a} \cdot b = 11 \cdot 0011$, with the input changing to $a = 10$. The result is shown in Table 1 (right).

It is shown in [1] that the sequence of states resulting from Algorithm Ã is nondecreasing with respect to the prefix order, *i.e.*, Algorithm Ã is monotonic.

For our next result, we modify the circuit model slightly. For each input X_i we add a delay, called *input gate*, with output s_i and excitation $S_i = X_i$. This follows the model of [3]. The following shows that Algorithms A and $\tilde{A}$ are equivalent for any network $\mathbf{N}$ started in a stable state, provided that $\mathbf{N}$ contains input-gate variables.

Theorem 1. *Let* $\mathbf{N}$ *be a network containing input-gate variables. Let* $\tilde{s}^0, \tilde{s}^1, \ldots, \tilde{s}^h, \ldots$ *be the sequence of states produced by Algorithm* $\tilde{A}$ *for* N *started in the stable (binary) total state* $\tilde{a} \cdot b$ *with the input tuple changing to* a. *Then, for all* $h \geq 0$, $\tilde{s}^h = s^h$, *where* $s^0, s^1, \ldots, s^h, \ldots$ *is the sequence of states produced by Algorithm A for* N *started in total state* $a \cdot b$.

Proof: We prove the theorem by induction on h.
Basis, $h = 0$. Since $s^0 = b = \tilde{s}^0$, the basis holds.
First step, $h = 1$. In states $\tilde{s}^0$ and s^0 only input-gate variables can be unstable; therefore only they can change in the first step of $\tilde{A}$, and of A. One easily verifies that $\tilde{s}^1 = s^1$.
Induction step. For any $i \in [m]$, if s_i is an input-gate variable then $s_i^h = s_i^{h-1}$ and $\tilde{s}_i^h = \tilde{s}_i^{h-1}$, because in both algorithms the input-gate variables do not change after the first step. By the induction hypothesis, we have $s_i^h = \tilde{s}_i^h$. If s_i is not an input-gate variable, then it is initially stable in both algorithms, and its excitation does not depend on the input tuple, *i.e.*, $\mathbf{S}_i(a \cdot \mathbf{x}) = \mathbf{S}_i(\mathbf{a} \cdot \mathbf{x})$, for any (internal) state tuple $\mathbf{x}$. Then $s_i^h = \mathbf{S}_i(a \cdot s^{h-1}) = \mathbf{S}_i(\mathbf{a} \cdot \tilde{s}^{h-1}) = \tilde{s}_i^h$. Hence $\tilde{s}_i^h = s_i^h$, for all $i \in [m]$. ∎

6   Covering of Binary Analysis by Simulation

Given the two networks N and $\mathbf{N}$ modeling a gate circuit, we perform the binary analysis for N and Algorithm A for $\mathbf{N}$, both with the same starting total state $a \cdot b$. The binary analysis results in graph $G_a(b)$. Let the state sequence resulting from Algorithm A be $s^0, s^1, \ldots, s^h, \ldots$, where $s^h = (s_1^h, s_2^h, \ldots, s_m^h) \in \mathbf{T}^m$, for all $h \geq 0$.

We now show that binary analysis is covered by Algorithm A. Take any path from the initial state b in graph $G_a(b)$. Suppose the length of the path is h. For each state variable s_i we consider the transient that shows the changes of that variable along the path. We show that this transient is a prefix of the value s_i^h that variable s_i takes in the h-th iteration of Algorithm A.

Example 7. Consider the binary counterpart of the transient network in Fig. 6 with $S_1 = \overline{X_2}$, $S_2 = X_1 \wedge s_1$, $S_3 = \overline{s_2}$, $S_4 = s_2 \vee s_3$. In $G_{11}(1011)$, with the same initial total state as in Example 4, we find a path $\pi = 1011, 1111, 0111, 0001$ of length $h = 3$. If we follow state variable s_3, for example, it changes from 1 to 0 along this path, so the corresponding transient is 10. The value of s_3 in the third step of Algorithm A is $s_3^3 = 101$, which has 10 as a prefix. In fact, this holds for all variables, since $(10, 010, 10, 1) \leq (10, 010, 101, 1010)$.

Definition 2. *Let* $\pi = s^0, \ldots, s^h$ *be a path of length* $h \geq 0$ *in* $G_a(b)$. *Recall that each* s^j *is a tuple* $(s_1^j, \ldots, s_m^j)$. *For any* $i \in [m]$, *we denote by* σ_i^π *the transient* $\widehat{s_i^0 \ldots s_i^h}$, *which shows the changes of the i-th state variable along path* π. *We refer to it as the* history *of variable* s_i *along the path. We define* Σ_i^π *to be* $\widehat{E_i}$, *where* $E_i = S_i(a \cdot s^0) S_i(a \cdot s^1) \ldots S_i(a \cdot s^h)$, *and we call it the* excitation history *of variable* s_i *along path* π. *The histories of all variables along* π *constitute tuple* $\sigma^\pi = (\sigma_1^\pi, \ldots, \sigma_m^\pi)$. *The histories of all excitations along* π *form tuple* $\Sigma^\pi = (\Sigma_1^\pi, \ldots, \Sigma_m^\pi)$.

Note that σ_i^π and Σ_i^π are not always the same. If s_i is unstable initially, they are obviously different, since their first characters are different, that is $s_i^0 \neq S_i(a \cdot s_i^0)$. Even if the variable is stable initially, σ_i^π and Σ_i^π can still be different.

Example 8. An example of a path in graph $G_{11}(1011)$ of the previous example, on which a variable changes fewer times than its excitation is path $\pi = 1011, 0111, 0011$, where $\sigma_3^\pi = 1$, whereas $\Sigma_3^\pi = 101$.

Let s^h be the state produced by Algorithm A after h steps, and let $\pi = s^0, \dots, s^h$ be a path of length $h \geq 0$ in $G_a(b)$, with $s^0 = b$. We prove that $\sigma^\pi \leq s^h$.

Proposition 2. *Let $\pi = s^0, \dots, s^h, s^{h+1}$ be a path in $G_a(b)$, and let $\pi' = s^0, \dots, s^h$. Then, $\sigma^\pi \leq \sigma^{\pi'} \circ S(a \cdot s^h)$.*

Proof: For any variable s_i we have one of the following cases.
Case I, s_i changes during the transition from s^h to s^{h+1}. Then s_i must be unstable in state s^h, i.e., $S_i(a \cdot s^h) \neq s_i^h$, and $s_i^{h+1} = S_i(a \cdot s^h)$, by the definition of binary analysis. Hence $\sigma_i^\pi = \overbrace{s_i^0 \dots s_i^h s_i^{h+1}} = \overbrace{s_i^0 \dots s_i^h} \circ s_i^{h+1} = \sigma_i^{\pi'} \circ S_i(a \cdot s^h)$.
Case II, s_i does not change during the transition from s^h to s^{h+1}. Then $s_i^{h+1} = s_i^h$, by the definition of binary analysis. Then $\sigma_i^\pi = \overbrace{s_i^0 \dots s_i^h s_i^{h+1}} = \overbrace{s_i^0 \dots s_i^h} = \sigma_i^{\pi'} \leq \sigma_i^{\pi'} \circ S_i(a \cdot s^h)$. Thus, our claim holds. ∎

Corollary 1. *For any path $\pi = s^0, \dots, s^h, s^{h+1}$ in $G_a(b)$, with $\pi' = s^0, \dots, s^h$ we have $\sigma^\pi \leq s^0 \circ \Sigma^{\pi'}$.*

Proof: $\sigma^\pi \leq \sigma^{\pi'} \circ S(a \cdot s^h) \leq (\dots((s^0 \circ S(a \cdot s^0)) \circ S(a \cdot s^1)) \circ \dots) \circ S(a \cdot s^h) = s^0 \circ (S(a \cdot s^0) \circ S(a \cdot s^1) \circ \dots \circ S(a \cdot s^h)) = s^0 \circ \Sigma^{\pi'}$. ∎

Proposition 3. *For any path $\pi = s^0, \dots, s^h$ in $G_a(b)$, $\Sigma^\pi \leq \mathbf{S}(a \cdot \sigma^\pi)$.*

Proof: Let $\pi_j = s^0, \dots, s^j$, for all j such that $0 \leq j \leq h$. Then $\sigma^{\pi_0} \leq \sigma^{\pi_1} \leq \dots \leq \sigma^\pi$. Thus $a \cdot \sigma^{\pi_0} \leq a \cdot \sigma^{\pi_1} \leq \dots \leq a \cdot \sigma^\pi$, which means that $a \cdot \sigma^{\pi_0}, a \cdot \sigma^{\pi_1}, \dots, a \cdot \sigma^\pi$ is a subsequence q of nodes on a path p from $a \cdot \alpha(\sigma_1^\pi) \dots \alpha(\sigma_m^\pi) = a \cdot s^0 = a \cdot \sigma^{\pi_0}$ to $a \cdot \sigma^\pi$ in the graph $D(a \cdot \sigma^\pi)$. For any $i \in [m]$, we consider the labeling of graph $D(a \cdot \sigma^\pi)$ with Boolean excitation S_i. Let λ be the sequence of labels of p. The sequence of labels on q is $E_i = S_i(a \cdot s^0), S_i(a \cdot s^1), \dots, S_i(a \cdot s^h)$. Since q is a subsequence of p, $\widehat{E_i} \leq \hat{\lambda}$. By the definition of extended Boolean functions, $\mathbf{S}_i(a \cdot \sigma^\pi)$ is the longest transient obtained by the contraction of the label sequences of paths from $a \cdot \sigma^{\pi_0}$ to $a \cdot \sigma^\pi$ in graph $D(a \cdot \sigma^\pi)$. Hence $\hat{\lambda} \leq \mathbf{S}_i(a \cdot \sigma^\pi)$. By the definition of the excitation history, $\Sigma_i^\pi = \widehat{E_i}$. It follows that $\Sigma_i^\pi \leq \mathbf{S}_i(a \cdot \sigma^\pi)$. ∎

Theorem 2. *For all paths $\pi = s^0, \dots, s^h$ in $G_a(b)$, with $s^0 = b$, $\sigma^\pi \leq s^h$, where s^h is the $(h+1)$st state in the sequence resulting from Algorithm A.*

Proof: We prove the theorem by induction on $h \geq 0$.
Basis, $h = 0$. We have $\pi = s^0 = b = s^0$; hence $\sigma^\pi = s^0 = s^0$, so the claim holds.
Induction hypothesis. The claim holds for some $h \geq 0$, i.e., for all paths π of length h from b in $G_a(b)$, we have $\sigma^\pi \leq s^h$.

Induction step. Let $\gamma = s^0, \ldots, s^h, s^{h+1}$ be a path of length $h + 1$ from b in $G_a(b)$. Then $\pi = s^0, \ldots, s^h$ is a path of length h, and we have

$$
\begin{aligned}
\sigma^\gamma &\leq s^0 \circ \Sigma^\pi && \{ \text{ Cor. 1 } \} \\
&\leq b \circ \mathbf{S}(a \cdot \sigma^\pi) && \{ s^0 = b \text{ and Prop. 3 } \} \\
&\leq b \circ \mathbf{S}(a \cdot s^h) && \{ \text{ induction hypothesis, monotonicity of excitations,} \\
& && \quad \text{and property of } \circ \} \\
&= s^{h+1} && \{ \text{ definition of Algorithm A } \}.
\end{aligned}
$$

∎

Corollary 2. *If Algorithm A terminates with state s^H, then for any path π from b in $G_a(b)$, $\sigma^\pi \leq s^H$.*

Proof: Suppose there exists a path π from b in $G_a(b)$ that satisfies $\sigma_i^\pi > s_i^H$, for some $i \in [m]$. Let h be the length of π. If $h \leq H$, Theorem 2 shows that $\sigma^\pi \leq s^h$. We also have $s^h \leq s^H$, by Prop. 1. So $\sigma^\pi \leq s^H$, and in particular $\sigma_i^\pi \leq s_i^H$, which contradicts our supposition. If $h > H$, then Theorem 2 states that $\sigma^\pi \leq s^h$. By our convention, $s^h = s^H$. So, again we have $\sigma_i^\pi \leq s_i^H$, which is a contradiction. ∎

7   Conclusions

We have proved that all the changes that occur in binary analysis are also detected by simulation. In a companion paper [8] we prove a partial converse of this result.

Acknowledgments. This research was supported by the Natural Sciences and Engineering Research Council of Canada under grant No. OGP0000871.

References

1. Brzozowski, J. A., Ésik, Z.: Hazard algebras. Formal Methods in System Design, to appear.
2. Brzozowski, J. A., Ésik, Z., Iland, Y.: Algebras for hazard detection. Proc. 31st Int. Symp. Multiple-Valued Logic, IEEE Comp. Soc. (2001) 3–12
3. Brzozowski, J. A., Seger, C.-J. H.: Asynchronous circuits. Springer-Verlag (1995)
4. Coates, W. S., Lexau, J. K., Jones, I. W., Fairbanks, S. M., Sutherland, I. E.: A FIFO data switch design experiment. Proc. ASYNC '98, IEEE Comp. Soc. (1998) 4–16
5. Eichelberger, E. B.: Hazard detection in combinational and sequential circuits. IBM J. Res. and Dev. **9** (1965) 90–99
6. Garside, J. D., Furber, S. B., Chang, S.-H.: AMULET3 revealed. Proc. ASYNC '99, IEEE Comp. Soc. (1999) 51–59
7. Gheorghiu, M.: Circuit simulation using a hazard algebra. MMath Thesis, School of Computer Science, University of Waterloo, Waterloo, ON, Canada (2001)
8. Gheorghiu, M., Brzozowski, J. A.: Feedback-free circuits in the algebra of transients. Proc. CIAA 2002, this volume.
9. Kessels, J., Marston, P.: Designing asynchronous standby circuits for a low-power pager. Proc. ASYNC '97, IEEE Comp. Soc. (1997) 268–278
10. Muller, D. E., Bartky, W. C.: A theory of asynchronous circuits. Proc. Int. Symp. on Theory of Switching, Annals of Comp. Lab., Harvard University **29** (1959) 204–243

The Number of Similarity Relations and the Number of Minimal Deterministic Finite Cover Automata

Cezar Câmpeanu[1] and Andrei Păun[2]

[1] Department of Mathematics and Computer Science,
University of Prince Edward Island,
Charlottetown, P.E.I., Canada C1A 4P3
ccampeanu@upei.ca
[2] Department of Computer Science,
University of Western Ontario,
London, Ontario, Canada N6A 5B7
apaun@csd.uwo.ca

Abstract. Finite Deterministic Cover Automata (DFCA) can be obtained from Deterministic Finite Automata (DFA) using the similarity relation. Since the similarity relation is not an equivalence relation, the minimal DFCA for a finite language is usually not unique. We count the number of minimal DFCA that can be obtained from a given minimal DFA with n states by merging the similar states in the given DFA. We compute an upper bound for this number and prove that in the worst case (for a non-unary alphabet) it is $\dfrac{\lceil \frac{4n-9+\sqrt{8n+1}}{8} \rceil !}{(2\lceil \frac{4n-9+\sqrt{8n+1}}{8} \rceil - n + 1)!}$.
We prove that this upper bound is reached, i.e. for any given positive integer n we find a minimal DFA with n states, which has the number of minimal DFCA obtained by merging similar states equal to this maximum.

1 Introduction

Finite languages have many practical applications, for example lexical analysis (e.g. in programming language compilation) and user interface translations [10, 7]. However, the finite languages used in applications are generally very large, which need thousands or even millions of states if represented by deterministic finite automata (DFA) or similar structures. In [1], deterministic finite cover automata (DFCA) are introduced as an alternative representation of finite languages. Experiments have shown that, in many cases, DFCA are much smaller in size than their corresponding minimal DFA [6].

Let L be a finite language and l the length of the longest word(s) in L. Intuitively, a DFCA A for L is a DFA that accepts all words in L and possibly additional words of length greater than l. So, a word w is in L if and only if it is accepted by A (as a DFA), and its length is less than or equal to l, in other

J.-M. Champarnaud and D. Maurel (Eds.): CIAA 2002, LNCS 2608, pp. 67–76, 2003.
© Springer-Verlag Berlin Heidelberg 2003

words, a DFCA will accept a language that "covers" the initial language. Note that checking the length of a word is usually not an extra burden in practice, since the length of an input word is kept anyway in most applications.

The level of a state is the length of the shortest path from the initial state to that state. If two states p and q are similar (as defined in Definition 3), then one "can get rid of" one state of the two using the steps described in Theorem 1, more precisely if two states p and q are similar and the level of state p is less or equal to the level of state q, then we merge state q into p, i.e. we change all incoming transitions to state q, to transitions to state p.

This theorem is actually the basis for the minimization algorithms presented in [1] and [5] (these algorithms construct a minimal DFCA from a given DFA that accepts a finite language). The algorithms are based on computing the similarity relation between states and merging these states.

One can notice that we can have more than one minimal DFCA for a given language L, even if, obviously, the number of states is the same (see Figure 1), so, by relaxing the constraints of such an automaton for a finite language, we pay the price of losing the uniqueness of the minimal element.

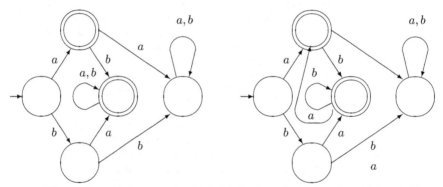

Fig. 1. Two distinct minimal DFCA for $L = \{a, ab, ba, aba, abb, baa, bab\}$

A natural question may now arise: *"How many distinct automata can an algorithm that is merging states yield?"*

We answer to this question by proving that for an alphabet with more than one letter, this maximum is $\frac{k_0!}{(2k_0-n+1)!}$, where n is the number of states in the minimal DFA, $k_0 = \lceil \frac{4n-9+\sqrt{8n+1}}{8} \rceil$, and this upper-bound is reached (Theorem 3).

In the next section, we give the basic definitions and notation, as well as some of the basic results on cover languages and automata.

2   Preliminaries

We assume the reader to be familiar with the basic notations of formal languages and with finite automata, cf. e.g. [3], [8], [9].

In the following we will consider that $L \subset \Sigma^*$ is a finite language over an alphabet Σ and l the length of the longest word(s) in L. The cardinality of a finite set A is $\#A$, the set of words over a finite alphabet Σ is denoted Σ^*, and the empty word is λ. The length of a word $w \in \Sigma^*$ is denoted $|w|$. The set of words over Σ of length at least (respectively, at most, equal) n is denoted $\Sigma^{\geq n}$ (respectively $\Sigma^{\leq n}$, Σ^n); $\Sigma^{>n} = \Sigma^{\geq n} \setminus \Sigma^n$.

For a DFA $A = (\Sigma, Q, q_0, \delta, F)$, we can assume without loosing the generality that $Q = \{0, 1, \ldots, n-1\}$, $n \geq 2$ and $q_0 = 0$.

Please, refer to [1] for the following definitions and results.

Definition 1. *A language L' over Σ is called a cover language of L if $L' \cap \Sigma^{\leq l} = L$.*

Definition 2. *A deterministic finite cover automaton (DFCA) for L is a deterministic finite automaton (DFA) A such that the language accepted by A, i.e., $L(A)$, is a cover language of L.*

Definition 3. *Let $x, y \in \Sigma^*$. We define the similarity relation on words:*

$$x \sim_L y \text{ if for all } z \in \Sigma^* \text{ such that } xz, yz \in \Sigma^{\leq l}, \ xz \in L \text{ iff } yz \in L,$$

and we write $x \not\sim_L y$ if $x \sim_L y$ does not hold.

Definition 4. *Let $A = (Q, \Sigma, \delta, 0, F)$ be a DFA (or DFCA). For each state $q \in Q$, we define $level(q) = \min\{|w| \mid \delta(0, w) = q\}$, and out of the minimal w, we denote with $x_A(q)$ the smallest in the lexicographic order.*
(level(q) is the length of the shortest path, $x_A(q)$, (in the directed graph associated with the automaton) from the initial state to q)

When the automaton A is understood, we write x_q instead of $x_A(q)$. The length of x_q is equal to $level(q)$; $level(q)$ is defined for each $q \in Q$, since we consider only connected/minimal DFA.

Definition 5. *Let $A = (Q, \Sigma, \delta, 0, F)$ be a DFCA for L. Let $p, q \in Q$ and $m = \max\{level(p), level(q)\}$. We say that $p \sim_A q$ (the states p and q are similar) if for every $w \in \Sigma^{\leq l-m}$, $\delta(p, w) \in F$ iff $\delta(q, w) \in F$.*

The relations $\sim_L$, and $\sim_A$ are called similarity relations for words, and respectively for states.

Lemma 1. *Let $A = (Q, \Sigma, \delta, 0, F)$ be a DFCA of L. Let $s, p, q \in Q$ such that $level(s) \leq level(p) \leq level(q)$. The following statements hold:*

1. *If $s \sim_A p$, $s \sim_A q$, then $p \sim_A q$.*
2. *If $s \sim_A p$, $p \sim_A q$, then $s \sim_A q$.*
3. *If $s \sim_A p$, $p \not\sim_A q$, then $s \not\sim_A q$.*
4. *If $s \sim_A p$, $s \not\sim_A q$, then $p \not\sim_A q$.*

Theorem 1. *(Merging theorem) Let $A = (Q, \Sigma, \delta, s, F)$ be a DFCA of L. Suppose that for $p, q \in Q$, $p \sim_L q$, $p \neq q$ and $level(p) \leq level(q)$. Then we can construct a DFCA, $A' = (Q', \Sigma, \delta', s, F')$ for L, such that $Q' = Q - \{q\}$, $F' = F - \{q\}$, and*

$$\delta'(t, a) = \begin{cases} \delta(t, a) & if\ \delta(t, a) \neq q, \\ p & \delta(t, a) = q \end{cases}$$

for each $t \in Q'$ and $a \in \Sigma$.

We say that state q is merged into state p if we can apply the above theorem for p and q.

Corollary 1. *A DFCA A is a minimal DFCA for L if and only if no two distinct states of A are similar.*

We denote by $\equiv_A$ the equivalence relation on states of an DFA A.

Lemma 2. *Let $A = (Q, \Sigma, \delta, 0, F)$ be a DFCA of L. Then $p \equiv_A q$ implies $p \sim_A q$.*

Theorem 2. *Any minimal DFCA of L has the same number of states.*

3   Counting the Number of Minimal DFCA Obtained by Merging States from the Minimal DFA

The following lemma will be useful in the subsequent results:

Lemma 3. *Let $A = (Q, \Sigma, \delta, 0, F)$ be a minimal DFA of a finite language L. If two distinct states have the same level, they are not similar.*

Proof. Assume that $level(p) = level(q)$, and $p \sim q$, therefore $\delta(p, w) \in F$ iff $\delta(q, w) \in F$, for all $w \in \Sigma^{\leq l-level(p)}$.

Since $\delta(p, w) \notin F$ and $\delta(q, w) \notin F$, for all $w \in \Sigma^{>l-level(p)}$, it follows that $p \equiv_A q$, which contradicts the minimally of A. $\square$

For $A = (\Sigma, Q, 0, \delta, F)$ a minimal DFA accepting the finite language L, we denote $Sim_s = \{q \in Q \mid s \sim_A q,\ level(s) \leq level(q)\}$ for all $s \in Q$. We can always obtain a minimal DFCA for L by merging any state s into any state p if $s \in Sim_p$. Denote by $Merged = \{s \in Q \mid s \in Sim_q,\ q \neq s\}$ the merged states, and by $non\text{-}Merged = Q - Merged$, the states that cannot be merged into other states. For any DFCA $C = (\Sigma, non\text{-}Merged, 0, \delta_C, F_C)$ obtained by merging states, the transitions between any two states that cannot be merged are unchanged, so $\delta_C(p, a) = q$ iff $\delta(p, a) = q$ for all $p, q \in non\text{-}Merged$ and $a \in \Sigma$. We use the name of skeleton for these states and transitions. Any minimal DFCA obtained by merging similar states will have the same skeleton.

Lemma 4. *With $A, Sim_s, Merged$ and the skeleton defined in the previous paragraph, we have: for any state $q \in non\text{-}Merged - \{0\}$, there is at least one state $p \in non\text{-}Merged$ such that $\delta_C(p, a) = q$, for some $a \in \Sigma$.*

Proof. Assume that there exists a skeleton state q that is reachable only from merging states. Since x_q is the shortest string with $\delta(0, x_q) = q$, consider the state $s \in Merged$ and a word w, with $\delta(0, w) = s$, $\delta(s, a) = q$, and $wa = x_q$. It is obvious that $level(s) = |w| < level(q)$. Since s can be merged (because of $s \in Merged$) with some state p such that $(level(p) \leq level(s))$ in the DFCA, we have $\delta_C(0, x_q) = \delta_C(p, a)$. So $x_q y \in L$ iff $\delta(p, ay) \in F_C$, for all $y \in \Sigma^{\leq l - level(q)}$, i.e. $q \sim_A \delta(p, a)$. Since $level(\delta(p, a)) \leq level(q)$, and $q \in non\text{-}Merged - \{0\}$, it follows that $\delta_C(p, a) = q$. $\qquad\square$

Corollary 2. *Any two distinct DFCA obtained by merging similar states are not isomorphic.*

Proof. Since all DFCA contain the same skeleton, the only transitions that are changed in the minimal DFA are those from skeleton states to merged states. Therefore, different transitions between the same states of the skeleton will produce different languages, otherwise we would have two distinct minimal DFA for the same language, since any minimal DFCA is also a minimal DFA for the corresponding cover language. $\qquad\square$

Therefore, the maximal number of minimal DFCA that can be obtained by merging states is

$$\prod_{p \in Merged} \#\{s \in non\text{-}Merged \mid p \in Sim_s\}. \tag{1}$$

Lemma 5. *In the worst case, each state that is merged must have at least an incoming transition from a state that is not merged.*

Proof. Assume that there is a state q, such that all incoming transitions to q are from $Merged$. Then this state does not influence the resulting DFCA (it becomes unreachable after merging the other states in $Merged$), and therefore, its similarities $\#\{s \in non\text{-}Merged \mid q \in Sim_s\}$ must not be considered in formula 1 for counting the number of DFCA produced by merging similar states. $\qquad\square$

The merged states have incoming transitions from other skeleton states so that distinct DFCA can be produced.

One has to notice from the merging theorem (Theorem 1) that the transitions are redirected after each merging. This is actually making the difference between the minimal DFCA obtained from the DFA: all the minimal DFCA have the same states, the same transitions that appear in the minimal DFA between these states (i. e. the skeleton) plus some "loop backs" produced by merging states. These loop backs are the only difference between the minimal DFCA obtained in this way. So, if we make sure that each merging state has at least one incoming transition from skeleton states, then we add at least a new transition to the skeleton in the minimal DFCA.

Lemma 6. *In the worst case, the sink state has the level less than $l + 1$, or it will not help in producing any more different minimal DFCA.*

Proof. Assume that sink state, $sink$ has level $l + 1$; then the last final state, $last$, has level l. If there are at least two final states, then $last \in Merged$, $sink \in Merged$, and $\delta(s, a) \neq sink$, for all $s \in Merged$ and $a \in \Sigma$, so we apply Lemma 5.

If $last$ is the only final state, then any two states $p, q \in Q - \{sink, last\}$ are not similar. Indeed, if they have the same level we apply Lemma 3, if $level(p) < level(q)$, then $\delta(q, w) = last$, for some $w \in \Sigma^*$. Of course, we also have $|x_q| + |w| = l$ (cannot be less since the level of $last$ is l and cannot be longer than l, because this is the longest length of the words in L). From $level(p) < level(q)$ we deduce that $|x_p| + |w| < |x_q| + |w| = l$, so $\delta(p, w) \neq last$ and $|w| \leq l - max(level(p, level(q)))$, therefore $p \not\sim q$. The number of minimal DFCA is in this case only $n - 1$, where n is the number of states in the minimal DFA. □

In the following we will find an expression for the maximum of formula 1 and an example of a minimal DFA that reaches the computed bound.

Remark 1. To produce several distinct minimal DFCA we need to have "choices" in merging states. The only possibility when we can have such "choices" (according to Lemma 1) is the following: a high level state is similar with several lower level states and the lower level states are not similar with each other; in this case we have more than one possibility of merging, leading to distinct non-isomorphic DFCA. From the Theorem 1 we know that we always merge higher level states into lower level states.

Theorem 3. *a) The maximal number of distinct, non-isomorphic minimal deterministic finite cover automata obtained from merging states from a minimal DFA with n states is: $\frac{k_0!}{(2k_0 - n + 1)!}$, where $k_0 = \lceil \frac{4n - 9 + \sqrt{8n+1}}{8} \rceil$.*

b) For any $n > 1$ there is a minimal DFA with n states that has the number of minimal DFCA obtained from merging states exactly the number given in part a) (i.e. the upper bound is reached).

Proof. We first prove the following statements that will help us in counting the maximal number of distinct DFCA obtained by merging similar states. All of the following statements are proved in the worst case:

1. The skeleton states are present on all levels up to $k_0 - 1$, where k_0 is the highest level a state can have in the minimal DFA.
2. The states that are merged have the highest levels possible.
3. There is at most one state that will be merged on any level in the DFA.

4. We can have at most one skeleton state for each level.
5. The number of DFCA obtained by merging states from the minimal DFA which satisfies the aforementioned properties and has the highest level for its states k_0 is $\frac{k_0!}{(2k_0-n+1)!}$.

(1) From the Lemma 4 and Lemma 5 we get that for each state (but the start state) there is an incoming transition in our original DFA from a skeleton state, so if the highest level a state can have in the DFA is k_0, then we have at least a skeleton state on each level from 0 to $k_0 - 1$ (otherwise, the maximum level in DFA is less than k_0).

(2) Because in the worst case the number of similarities has to be as large as possible, for each state q we must have as many states as possible such that $q \in Sim_s$. Therefore, the level of merged states have to be higher than as many skeleton states as possible.

(3) Assume that there are at least two states $p, q \in Merged$ on some level r. They cannot be similar, because of Lemma 3, and cannot be both similar with another state of a lower level, because of Lemma 1 (if they are both similar with a lower level state then they will be also similar with each other). So, the set of states of our automaton is partitioned into at least two disjoint parts, all the states that are similar with p are in one of these partitions (and maybe we have also a set of states non similar with any of these states of level r). Because $\{s \mid p \in Sim_s\} \cap \{s \mid q \in Sim_s\} = \emptyset$, the formula for the number of minimal DFCAs has lower factors, since $(2r)! > (r!)^2$. It is clear that the worst case is when we have a single partition (according to the states on level r), meaning that in the worst case we have at most one merged state on each level (one can also prove this by induction on the maximal level of the automaton).

(4) If we have two or more skeleton states on the same level we are not in the worst case, since one can get more (possible) similarities just by taking one of the skeleton states from the same level and making it a new start state (level 0), the old start state being "pushed" at level one. Then the level of every state is increased by one, thus making possible that more merged states are similar with this newly level 0 state (all the merged states that had lower level than this state can now be similar with it), i.e. the sets $(\{s \mid p \in Sim_s\})_{p \in Merged}$, may have one element more.

(5) According to the previous remarks, we have at least one skeleton state on each level up to level $k_0 - 1$, and we have at most one skeleton state on each level, so we must have exactly one skeleton state on each level, from 0 to $k_0 - 1$.

We also know that we cannot have more than one merged state on a level and these states must have their levels as large as possible.

Let us count how many distinct DFCA we produce in this worst case. First, let us see how many states are merged: we have k_0 skeleton states on the levels from 0 to $k_0 - 1$ and possibly the sink state, so the rest of $n - k_0 - 1$ are merged states. These states must have the highest levels, so they are at level $k_0, k_0 - 1, \ldots$ down to some level k_1, one for each level, therefore $k_1 = k_0 - (n - k_0 - 1) + 1 = 2k_0 - n + 2$.

The maximal number of skeleton states that can be similar with a state $p \in Merged$ is the number of states that have their levels less than p, which is exactly $level(p)$ since the skeleton states are one per level.

Then, the maximal number of DFCA obtained in this way is:

$$(2k_0 - n + 2)(2k_0 - n + 3)\ldots(k_0 - 1)k_0 = \frac{k_0!}{(2k_0 - n + 1)!} \text{ for } \frac{n}{2} \le k_0 < n.$$

To finish proving the first statement of the theorem, we have to find for each given n the $k_0 = l$ such that the formula $\frac{k_0!}{(2k_0 - n + 1)!}$ for $\frac{n}{2} \le k_0 < n$ reaches its maximum. After an easy analysis, we obtain that this is equivalent to finding the smallest k_0 for which the inequality $\frac{k_0!}{(2k_0 - n + 1)!} \ge \frac{(k_0 + 1)!}{(2k_0 - n + 3)!}$ holds.

We distinguish two cases: 1) $n = 2m$ (n is even) and 2) $n = 2m + 1$ (n is odd).

Case 1) $n = 2m$:
we rewrite the formula in the form $\frac{(m + k)!}{(2k + 1)!} \ge \frac{(m + k + 1)!}{(2k + 3)!}$, $(k = k_0 - m)$, which implies that $8k^2 + 18k + 10 - n \ge 0$, and the solutions are all integers $k \ge \frac{-9 + \sqrt{8n + 1}}{8}$ (we consider only the positive solutions, of course).

Because we are looking for the smallest k_0 with this property, we get $k_0 = \lceil \frac{4n - 9 + \sqrt{8n + 1}}{8} \rceil$.

Case 2) $n = 2m + 1$:
we rewrite the formula in the form $\frac{(m+k+1)!}{(2k+2)!} \ge \frac{(m+k+2)!}{(2k+4)!}$ $(k = k_0 - m - 1)$, which implies that $8k^2 + 26k + 21 - n \ge 0$, and the solutions are all integers $k \ge \frac{-13 + \sqrt{8n + 1}}{8}$.

So, in this case, k_0 becomes: $k_0 = m + k + 1 = \lceil \frac{4n - 9 + \sqrt{8n + 1}}{8} \rceil$.

Let us prove now the b) part of the theorem by giving a construction for the worst case minimal DFA:

Consider that the DFA has n states and that the maximum is reached in the formula $\frac{k_0!}{(2k_0 - n + 1)!}$, for some k_0 computed using the formula from part a), then we know that all the minimal DFCA have $k_0 + 1$ states.

We construct the minimal DFA $A = (Q, \Sigma, \delta, s, F)$ as follows:
$Q = \{0, 1, \ldots n - 1\}$, $\Sigma = \{a, b\}$ $s = 0$, $F = Q - \{k_0\}$,
$\delta(p, a) = p + 1$, for all $p = 0, \ldots, n - 2$, $p \ne k_0 - 1, n - 1$,
$\delta(p, b) = p + 1$, for all $p = 0, \ldots, 2k_0 - n$, and $p = k_0, \ldots, n - 2$,
$\delta(p, b) = p + n - k_0$, for all $p = 2k_0 - n, \ldots, k_0 - 1$,
$\delta(k_0 - 1, a) = n - 1$, $\delta(n - 1, a) = n - 1$, $\delta(n - 1, b) = n - 1$.

This automaton has the first $k_0 + 1$ states non similar (the skeleton states) and the next states are similar with all the states that have the level lower than them (but the sink state); one can easily see that the given DFA is minimal and satisfies all the properties given before for the worst case, so the actual number

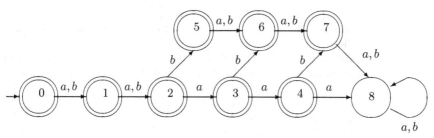

Fig. 2. The minimal DFA with maximum number of DFCA for $n = 9$, $k_0 = \lceil \frac{27+\sqrt{73}}{8} \rceil = 5$, so the number of distinct (non-isomorphic) DFCA is: $\frac{5!}{(2*5-9+1)!} = 60$

of minimal DFCA that are obtained by merging similar states from the given minimal DFA is $\frac{k_0!}{(2k_0-n+1)!}$. □

4   Final Remarks

One may notice that there are minimal cover automata for a finite language L that cannot be obtained by merging all the similar states from the minimal DFA accepting L; such an example is depicted in Figure 1. A subsequent paper will deal with counting all the minimal non-isomorphic DFCA for a given finite language L; we expect that the result from the current paper to be also useful in the general case.

Acknowledgements. We are grateful to the anonymous referees for their comments that proved very useful in improving the presentation of the paper. This research is supported by the Natural Sciences and Engineering Research Council of Canada grant OGP0041630 and a graduate scholarship.

References

1. C. Câmpeanu, N. Sântean and S. Yu, "Minimal Cover-Automata for Finite Languages", *Proceedings of the Third International Workshop on Implementing Automata* WIA'98 (1998), 32–42 and *TCS* vol 267 (2001), 3–16.
2. C. Dwork and L. Stockmeyer, "A Time Complexity Gap for Two-Way Probabilistic Finite-State Automata", *SIAM Journal on Computing*, vol.19 (1990), 1011–1023.
3. J. E. Hopcroft and J.D. Ullman, *Introduction to Automata Theory, Languages and Computation* Addison-Wesley, (1979).
4. J. Kaneps, R. Frievalds, "Running Time to Recognize Non-Regular Languages by 2-Way Probabilistic Automata", in *ICALP'91, LNCS*, Springer-Verlag, New-York/Berlin (1991) vol 510, 174–185.
5. A. Păun, N. Sântean and Sheng Yu, "An $O(n^2)$ algorithm for Minimal Cover-Automata for Finite Languages", *Proceedings of the 5th International Conference on Implementation and Application of Automata* CIAA'00 (2000), 243–251.

6. N. Sântean, *Towards a Minimal Representation for Finite Languages: Theory and Practice*, MSc Thesis, Department of Computer Science, The University of Western Ontario, (2000).

7. J. M. Champarnaud and D. Maurel, *Automata Implementation*, Proceedings of Third International Workshop on Implementing Automata, LNCS 1660, Springer, (1999).

8. A. Salomaa, *Formal Languages* Academic Press, (1973).

9. S. Yu, "Regular languages", in *Handbook of Formal Languages, Vol I*, eds. G. Rozenberg and A. Salomaa, Springer-Verlag, (1997), 41–110.

10. D. Wood and S. Yu, *Automata Implementation*, Proceedings of Second International Workshop on Implementing Automata, LNCS 1436, Springer, (1998).

Regex and Extended Regex

Cezar Câmpeanu[1], Kai Salomaa[2], and Sheng Yu[3]

[1] Department of Mathematics and Computer Science, UPEI
Charlottetown, PE C1A 4P3
ccampeanu@upei.ca
[2] Computing and Information Science Department
Queen' s University
Kingston, Ontario K7L 3N6, Canada
ksalomaa@cs.queensu.ca
[3] Department of Computer Science
University of Western Ontario
London, Ontario N6A 5B7, Canada
syu@csd.uwo.ca

Abstract. Regex are used in many programs such as Perl, Awk, Python, egrep, vi, emacs etc. It is known that regex are different from regular expressions. In this paper, we give regex a formal treatment. We make a distinction between regex and extended regex; while regex present regular languages, extended regex present a family of languages larger than regular languages. We prove a pumping lemma for the languages expressed by extended regex. We show that the languages represented by extended regex are incomparable with context-free languages and a proper subset of context-sensitive languages.

Keywords: Regular expressions, regex, extended regex, formal languages, programming languages

1 Introduction

It is known that the practical "regular expressions" are different from the theoretical ones. The practical "regular expressions" [2] are often called regex. Regex are used in many environments, like Perl, Python, Awk, egrep, lex, vi, emacs, etc. Regex were developed under the influence of theoretical regular expressions. For example, the regex in Lex [4] are similar to theoretical regular expressions. However, regex are quite different in many other environments. Many regex in use now can express a larger family of languages than the regular languages. For example, Perl regex [1] can express $L_1 = \{a^n b a^n \mid n \geq 0\}$ and $L_2 = \{ww \mid w \in \{a, b\}^*\}$. However, Perl regex cannot express the language $L_3 = \{a^n b^n \mid n \geq 0\}$. It is relatively easy to show that a language can be expressed by a regex. For example, L_1 can be expressed by a Perl regex $(a*)b\backslash 1$ and L_2 by $((a|b)*)\backslash 1$. However, it is usually difficult to show that a language

J.-M. Champarnaud and D. Maurel (Eds.): CIAA 2002, LNCS 2608, pp. 77–84, 2003.
© Springer-Verlag Berlin Heidelberg 2003

cannot be expressed by certain devices. For example, how do we prove that L_3 cannot be expressed by a Perl regex? It is clear that there is a need for some formal treatment of regex. This is the main purpose of the paper.

Regex are defined differently in different environments. However, in some sense, there is a common subset of the definitions. In this paper, we first give a formal definition of regex and extended regex according to the common subset of the definitions given in different environments. Then we prove a pumping lemma for extended regex languages. We also show that the family of extended regex languages is a proper subset of the family of context-sensitive languages, and it is incomparable with the family of context-free languages.

2   Basic Definition of Regex and Extended Regex

Let Σ be an ordered set of all printable letters except that each of the following letters is written with an escape character $\backslash$ in front of it: $(,), \{, \}, [,], \$, |, \backslash, ., ?, *,$ and $+$. In addition, Σ also includes $\backslash n$ and $\backslash t$ as the new line and tab character, respectively. In the following, we give the definition of regex as well as the language it defines. For an expression e, we use $L(e)$ to denote the set of all words that match e, i.e., the language e defines.

Basic form of regex:

(1) For each $a \in \Sigma$, a is a regex and $L(a) = \{a\}$. Note that for each $x \in \{(,), \{, \}, [,], \$, |, \backslash, ., ?, *, +\}$, $\backslash x \in \Sigma$ and is a regex and $L(\backslash x) = \{x\}$. In addition, both $\backslash n$ and $\backslash t$ are in Σ and are regex, and $L(\backslash n)$ and $L(\backslash t)$ denote the languages consisting of the new line and the tab, respectively.
(2) For regex e_1 and e_2,
　　　$(e_1)(e_2)$ (concatenation),
　　　$(e_1)|(e_2)$ (alternation), and
　　　$(e_1)*$ (Kleene star)
are all regex, where $L((e_1)(e_2)) = L(e_1)L(e_2)$, $L((e_1)|(e_2)) = L(e_1) \cup L(e_2)$, and $L((e_1)*) = (L(e_1))*$. Parentheses can be omitted. When they are omitted, alternation, concatenation, and Kleene star have the increasing priority.
(3) A regex is formed by using (1) and (2) a finite number of times.

Shorthand form:

(1) For each regex e, $(e)+$ is a regex and $(e)+ \equiv e(e)*$.
(2) The character '.' means any character except '$\backslash n$'.

Character classes:

(1) For $a_{i_1}, a_{i_2}, \ldots, a_{i_t} \in \Sigma$, $t \geq 1$, $[a_{i_1} a_{i_2} \ldots a_{i_t}]$ is a regex and $[a_{i_1} a_{i_2} \ldots a_{i_t}] \equiv a_{i_1} | a_{i_2} | \ldots | a_{i_t}$.
(2) For $a_i, a_j \in \Sigma$ such that $a_i \leq a_j$, $[a_i\text{-}a_j]$ is a regex and $[a_i\text{-}a_j] \equiv a_i | a_{i+1} | \ldots | a_j$.
(3) For $a_{i_1}, a_{i_2}, \ldots, a_{i_t} \in \Sigma$, $t \geq 1$, $[\hat{\ } a_{i_1} a_{i_2} \ldots a_{i_t}]$ is a regex and $[\hat{\ } a_{i_1} a_{i_2} \ldots a_{i_t}] \equiv b_{i_1} | b_{i_2} | \ldots | b_{i_s}$, where $\{b_{i_1}, b_{i_2}, \ldots, b_{i_s}\} = \Sigma - \{a_{i_1}, a_{i_2}, \ldots, a_{i_t}\}$.

(4) For $a_i, a_j \in \Sigma$ such that $a_i \leq a_j$, $[\char`\^ a_i\text{-}a_j]$ is a regex and $[\char`\^ a_i\text{-}a_j] \equiv$
    $b_{i_1}|b_{i_2}|\ldots|b_{i_s}$, where $\{b_{i_1}, b_{i_2}, \ldots, b_{i_s}\} = \Sigma - \{a_i, a_{i+1}, \ldots, a_j\}$.
(5) Mixture of (1) and (2), or (3) and (4), respectively.

Anchoring:

(1) Start-of-line anchor $\char`\^$.
(2) End-of-line anchor $\$$.

We call an expression that satisfies the above definitions a *regex*. Note that
the empty string is not a regex.

Example 1. The expression "$\char`\^ .*\$$" is a regex, which matches any line including
the empty line.

Example 2. The expression "[A-Z][A-Za-z0-9]*" matches any word starting with
a capital letter and followed by any number of letters and digits.

It is clear that regex can express only regular languages. However, the following construct, which appears in Perl, Emacs, etc., is not a regular construct.

Back reference:

'$\backslash m$', where m is a number, matches the content of the mth pair of parentheses before it.

Note that the pairs of parentheses in a regex are ordered according to the
occurrence sequence of their left parentheses. Note also that if the mth pair of
parentheses are in a Kleene star and '$\backslash m$' is not in the same Kleene star, then
'$\backslash m$' matches the content of the mth pair of parentheses in the last iteration of
the Kleene star. A more formal definition is given later. We first look at several
introductory examples.

Example 3. The expression "$(a*)b\backslash 1$" defines the language

$$\{a^n b a^n \mid n \geq 0\}.$$

Example 4. The expression "$(The)(file ([0-9][0-9])).*\backslash 3$" matches any string
that contains "The file " followed by a two-digit number, then any string, and
then the same number again.

Example 5. For the expression $e = (a * b) * \backslash 1$, $aabaaabaaab \in L(e)$ and
$aabaaabaab \notin L(e)$.

There appears to be no convenient way to recursively define the set of extended regex α satisfying the condition that any back reference in α occurs after
the corresponding parenthesis pair. Thus below we first define an auxiliary notion of semi-regex and the extended regex are then defined as a restriction of
semi-regex.

Definition 1. *A* semi-regex *is a regex over the infinite alphabet*

$$\Sigma \cup \{\backslash m \mid m \in N\}$$

where N is the set of natural numbers. Let α be a semi-regex. The matching parenthesis pairs of α are numbered from left to right according to the occurrence of the left parenthesis (the opening parenthesis) of each pair.

A semi-regex α is an extended *regex if the following condition holds. Any occurrence of a back reference symbol $\backslash m$ ($m \in N$) in α is preceded by the closing parenthesis of the mth parenthesis pair of α.*

Below we define the matches of an extended regex and the language defined by an extended regex. Intuitively, a match of an extended regex α is just a word denoted by the regex when each back reference symbol $\backslash m$ is replaced by the contents of the subexpression β_m corresponding to the mth pair of parentheses in α. Due to the star operation, a given subexpression occurrence β_m may naturally "contribute" many subwords to a match. Following the convention used e.g. in Perl, $\backslash m$ will be replaced by the contents of the last (rightmost) occurrence of β_m appearing before this occurrence of $\backslash m$.

The condition that each back reference symbol occurs after the corresponding parenthesis pair guarantees that a match as defined below cannot contain circular dependencies.

We denote the set of occurrences of subexpressions of an extended regex α as $\mathrm{SUB}(\alpha)$. Distinct occurrences of an identical subexpression are considered to be different elements of $\mathrm{SUB}(\alpha)$. A match of an extended regex α is defined as a tree T_α following the structure of α. Naturally, due to the star operation, T_α may make multiple copies of parts of the structure of α.

Definition 2. *A* match *of an extended regex α is a finite (directed, ordered) tree T_α. The nodes of T_α are labeled by elements of $\Sigma^* \times \mathrm{SUB}(\alpha)$ and T_α is constructed according to the following rules.*

(i) *The root of T_α is labeled by an element (w, α), $w \in \Sigma^*$.*

(ii) *Assume that a node u of T_α is labeled by (w, β) where $\beta = (\beta_1)(\beta_2) \in \mathrm{SUB}(\alpha)$. Then u has two successors that are labeled, respectively, by (w_i, β_i), $i = 1, 2$, where $w_1, w_2 \in \Sigma^*$ have to satisfy $w = w_1 w_2$.*

(iii) *Assume that a node u of T_α is labeled by (w, β) where $\beta = (\beta_1) \mid (\beta_2) \in \mathrm{SUB}(\alpha)$. Then u has one successor that is labeled by one of the elements (w, β_i), $i \in \{1, 2\}$.*

(iv) *Assume that a node u of T_α is labeled by (w, β) where $\beta = (\beta_1)* \in \mathrm{SUB}(\alpha)$. Then u has $k \geq 1$ successors labeled by*

$$(w_1, \beta_1), \ldots, (w_k, \beta_1)$$

where $w_1 \cdots w_k = w$, $w_i \neq \lambda$, $i = 1, \ldots, k$. If $w = \lambda$, u has a single successor u_1 labeled by (λ, β) and u_1 is a leaf of T_α.

(v) *If (w, a), $a \in \Sigma$, occurs as a label of a node u then necessarily u is a leaf and $w = a$.*

(vi) *If $(w, \backslash m)$ occurs as a label of a node u then u is a leaf and $w \in \Sigma^*$ is determined as follows. Let β_m be the subexpression of α enclosed by the mth pair of parentheses and let u_{β_m} be the previous node of T_α in the standard left-to-right ordering that is labeled by an element where the second component is β_m that precedes u in the left-to-right ordering of the nodes. (Note that all nodes where the label contains β_m are necessarily independent and hence they are linearly ordered from left to right.) Then we choose w to be the first component of the label of u_{β_m}. Finally, if β_m does not occur in the label of any node of T_α then we set $w = \lambda$.*

The language denoted by an extended regex α *is defined as*

$$L(\alpha) = \{w \in \Sigma^* \mid (w, \alpha) \text{ labels the root of some match } T_\alpha\}.$$

Above the somewhat complicated condition (vi) means just that a back reference symbol $\backslash m$ is substituted by the previous occurrence of the contents of the subexpression β_m corresponding to the mth parenthesis pair. It is possible that β_m does not appear in the label of any node of T_α if β_m occurs inside a Kleene star and in (iv) we choose zero iterations of the star operation. In this case the contents of $\backslash m$ will be λ.

If the nondeterministic top-down construction of T_α produces a leaf symbol violating one of the conditions (v) or (vi), then the resulting tree is not a well-formed match of α. The fact that a back reference symbol $\backslash m$ has to occur after the expression corresponding to the mth parenthesis pair guarantees that in (vi) the label of u_{β_m} can be determined before the label of u is determined.

Example 6. Let $\alpha = (((a|b)*)c\backslash 2)*$. Then $L(\alpha) = L_1^*$ where

$$L_1 = \{wcw \mid w \in \{a, b\}^*\}.$$

In the above examples, and in what follows, for simplicity we often omit several parenthesis pairs and only the remaining parentheses are counted when determining which pair corresponds to a given back reference.

3   A Pumping Lemma for Extended Regex Languages

There are several pumping lemmas for regular languages [3,5], which are useful tools for showing that certain languages are not regular languages. In the following, we prove a pumping lemma for extended regex languages and give several examples to show how to use the lemma to prove that certain languages are not extended regex languages.

For a string (word) $x \in \Sigma^*$, denote by $|x|$ the length of x in the following.

Lemma 1. *Let α be an extended regex. Then there is a constant N such that if $w \in L(\alpha)$ and $|w| > N$, there is a decomposition $w = x_0 y x_1 y x_2 \ldots x_m$, for some $m \geq 1$, such that*

1. $|x_0 y| \leq N$

2. $|y| \geq 1$,

3. $x_0 y^j x_1 y^j \ldots x_m \in L$ for all $j > 0$.

Proof. Let $N = |\alpha| 2^t$ where t is the number of back-references in α. Let $w \in L(\alpha)$ and $|w| > N$. By the definition of N it is clear that some part of w matches a Kleene star or plus in α that has more than one iteration, because each back reference that does not appear inside a Kleene star can at most double the length of the word it matches.

Let $w = x_0 y z$ and y is the first nonempty substring of w that matches a Kleene star or plus. In order to satisfy $|x_0 y| \leq N$, we let y match the first iteration of the star or plus. In other words, we have $e*$ or $e+$ in the extended regex; the y in $x_0 y$ matches e and is the first iteration of the star or plus. Then we have $|x_0 y| \leq N$ and $|y| \geq 1$. There are the following two cases: Case 1, $e*$ (or $e+$) is not back-referenced. Then it is clear that the lemma holds for $m = 1$. Case 2, $e*$ (or $e+$) is back-referenced. Let $z = x_1 y x_2 y x_3 \ldots x_m$ where y's are all the back-references of y. Then we have $w = x_0 y x_1 y x_2 y x_3 \ldots x_m$, and it is clear that $x_0 y^j x_1 y^j x_2 y^j \ldots x_m \in L(\alpha)$ for all $j \geq 1$.

Note that in the case that e in $(e)*$ (or $(e)+$), rather than $e*$ (or $e+$), is back-referenced and y matches e, the lemma clearly holds for $m = 1$.

Example 7. Consider some special cases of regex for the pumping lemma. Let $e_1 = (ab|ba)(\backslash 1)*$. Then the constant N for the pumping lemma is $|e_1| \times 2 = 24$. Since the Kleene star is not referenced, any word w that matches e_1 and $|w| > N$ can be decomposed into xyz such that $|xy| \leq N$, $|y| \geq 1$, and $xy^j z \in L(e_1)$ for all $j > 0$. For example, $w = (ba)^{13}$. Then $x = ba$, $y = ba$, and $z = (ba)^{11}$.

Let $e_2 = bab((a|b)c\backslash 2)*$. Then $N = 28$. Again the Kleene star is not referenced. So, any word $w \in L(e_2)$ and $|w| > N$ can be decomposed into xyz such that $|xy| \leq N$, and $|y| \geq 1$, and $xy^j z \in L(e_2)$ for any $j > 0$. For example, let $w = babacabcbbcbacabcbacaacaacaaca$. Then $x = bab$, $y = aca$, and $z = bcbbcbacabcbacaacaacaaca$.

Let $e_3 = (a*)b\backslash 1bb\backslash 1bbb$. Then $N = 14 \times 2^2 = 56$. Any word $w \in L(e_3)$ and $|w| > N$ can be decomposed into $x_0 y x_1 y x_2 y x_3$ such that $|x_0 y| \leq N$, $|y| \geq 1$, and $x_0 y^j x_1 y^j x_2 y^j x_3 \in L(e_3)$ for all $j > 0$.

Next we show how the pumping lemma is used.

Example 8. The language $L = \{a^n b^n \mid n > 0\}$ cannot be expressed by an extended regex.

Proof. Assume that L is expressed by an extended regex. Let N be the constant of Lemma 1. Consider the word $a^N b^N$. By Lemma 1, $a^N b^N$ has a decomposition $x_0 y x_1 y x_2 \ldots x_m$, $m \geq 1$, such that (1) $|x_0 y| \leq N$, (2) $|y| \geq 1$, and (3) $x_0 y^j x_1 y^j \ldots x_m \in L$ for all $j > 0$. According to (1) and (2), $y = a^i$ for some $i > 0$. But then the word $x_0 y^2 x_1 y^2 \ldots x_m$ is clearly not in L. It is a contradiction. Therefore, L does not satisfy Lemma 1 and, thus, L cannot be expressed by any extended regex.

Similarly, we can prove that the language $\{a^n b^n c^n \mid n \geq 1\}$ is not an extended regex language. As an application of the pumping lemma we get also the following.

Lemma 2. *The family of extended regex languages is not closed under complementation.*

Proof. The language

$$L_1 = \{a^m \mid m > 1 \text{ is not prime }\}$$

is expressed by the extended regex $(aaa*)\backslash 1(\backslash 1)*$. Assume that the complement of L_1, L_1^c, is an extended regex language and apply Lemma 1 to L_1^c. This implies that there exist $n_1 \geq 0$, $n_2 \geq 1$ such that for all $j > 0$,

$$a^{n_1 + j \cdot n_2} \in L_1^c.$$

This is a contradiction since it is not possible that $n_1 + j \cdot n_2$ is prime for all $j > 0$.

We can note also that the language L_1 in the proof of Lemma 2 is an extended regex language over a one-letter alphabet that is not context-free. In particular, this means that there are extended regex languages that do not belong to the Boolean closure of context-free languages.

4 Other Properties of Regex and Extended Regex Languages

Here we prove that every extended regex language is a context-sensitive language. We also show the relationship between extended regex languages and context-free languages.

Theorem 1. *Extended regex languages are context-sensitive languages*

Proof. It suffices to show that each extended regex language is accepted by a linear-bounded automaton (LBA), i.e., a nondeterministic Turing machine in linear space. For a given extended regex, if there is no back reference, we can simply construct a finite automaton that will accept all words that match the regex.

For handling back references, we need store each string that matches a subexpression that is surrounded by a pair of parentheses for later use. If there are m pairs of parentheses in the extended regex, we need m buffers. We store the part of the input strings that match the content of the ith pair of parentheses in the ith buffer.

For a given extended regex, we first label all the parentheses with their appearance number. For example, the extended regex "$(a * (ba*)\backslash 2)b$" would become "$(_1 a * (_2 ba*)_2 \backslash 2)_1 b$". Note that for a fixed extended regex the number of parenthesis pairs is a constant that does not depend on the input word, and hence the numbering can be done easily in linear space. Then we construct a nondeterministic finite automaton (NFA) which treats each labeled parenthesis and each back reference as an input symbol.

Then we build a Turing machine which works according to the NFA as follows. It reads the input symbols and follows the transitions of the NFA. For a $(_i$ transition, it does not read input symbol but starts to store the next matching input symbols into the ith buffer. For a $)_i$ transition, it also does not read any input symbol but stops storing the matching input symbols into the ith buffer. Whenever there is a back reference in the extended regex, say "$\backslash i$", it just compares the string with the content of the ith buffer. It accepts the input string if there is a way to reach a final state when just finishes reading the input. Note that if the ith pair of parentheses are in a Kleene star, it may store input symbols in the ith buffer several times. Then "$\backslash i$" always matches the latest word stored in the ith buffer.

Each buffer needs at most the space of the input word, and there are a constant number of buffers. Thus, an extended regex language is accepted by an LBA and, thus, is a context-sensitive language.

Theorem 2. *The family of extended regex languages is incomparable with the family of context-free languages.*

Proof. The language $L = \{a^n b a^n b a^n \mid n \geq 1\}$ is clearly an extended regex language. It can be expressed as "$(a+)b\backslash 1b\backslash 1$". However, L is not a context-free language. We know that $\{a^n b^n \mid n \geq 0\}$ is a context-free language, but it is not an extended regex language as we have proved in Section 3.

Theorem 3. *The family of extended regex languages is a proper subset of the family of context-sensitive languages.*

References

1. N. Chapman, *Perl — The Programmer's Companion*, Wiley, Chichester, 1997.
2. Jeffrey E.F. Friedl *Mastering Regular Expressions*, O'Reilly & Associates, Inc., Cambridge, 1997.
3. J.E. Hopcroft and J.D. Ullman, *Introduction to Automata Theory, Languages, and Computation*, Addison-Wesley, Reading, 1979.
4. M.E. Lesk, "Lex - a lexical analyzer generator", *Computer Science Technical Report* (1975) 39, AT&T Bell Laboratories, Murray Hill, N.J.
5. S. Yu, "Regular Languages", in *Handbook of Formal Languages*, G. Rozenberg and A. Salomaa eds. pps. 41–110, Springer, 1998.

Prime Decompositions of Regular Prefix Codes

Jurek Czyzowicz[1], Wojciech Fraczak[2], Andrzej Pelc[1], and Wojciech Rytter[3]

[1] Département d'informatique, Université du Québec en Outaouais, Canada
[2] Solidum Systems Corp, Ottawa, Canada and
Département d'informatique, Université du Québec en Outaouais, Canada
[3] Instytut Informatyki, Uniwersytet Warszawski, Poland and
Department of Computer Science, Liverpool University U.K.

Abstract. One of the new approaches to data classification uses finite state automata for representation of prefix codes. An important task driven by the need for the efficient storage of such automata in memory is the decomposition of prefix codes into prime factors. We investigate properties of such prefix code decompositions. A linear time algorithm is designed which finds the prime decomposition $F_1 F_2 \ldots F_k$ of a regular prefix code F given by its minimal deterministic automaton.

1 Introduction

A simple basic operation of formal languages is their concatenation. However, the complexity of the inverse operation of decomposing a language L into a nontrivial concatenation $L_1 L_2$ is not well understood. A concatenation is trivial if one of L_1, L_2 consists exactly of the empty string. A language is *prime* if it cannot be expressed as a non-trivial concatenation of two languages. The prime factorization is the decomposition into prime factors. It has been proved in [1] that the problem of primality is undecidable for context-free languages. Although for regular languages this problem is decidable [1], the decomposition of a regular language into primes may not be unique. Algorithmic issues of this problem are also of interest: it has been left open in [1] whether primality of a language L is an NP-complete problem, even in the case of a finite language L.

In this paper we consider decomposition problems for the class of *regular prefix codes*. Regular prefix codes are languages recognized by finite automata and such that no word is a prefix of another. The representation of the code is a deterministic finite automaton (*dfa*, in short). From a practical point of view precisely this type of languages forms the basis of some classification algorithms in hardware-based technology. Our main results show that decomposition problems for regular prefix codes are much easier than for general regular languages. Our algorithms have linear time complexity. The factorization of a regular prefix code into prime prefix codes is unique, while the factorization of an arbitrary regular language could be not unique. Our results are especially interesting for infinite regular prefix codes.

The practical applications of prefix code decomposition show that the classical theory of finite automata and formal languages can play an important role in

J.-M. Champarnaud and D. Maurel (Eds.): CIAA 2002, LNCS 2608, pp. 85–94, 2003.

modern technology of data classification. Data classification is one of the central problems in network information processing. Packets arriving from a communication channel have to be accepted or rejected, or more generally, divided into several classes, based on their content. There are three fundamental approaches to data classification, used in modern technology: network processor approach, used by such companies as Intel, Motorola, and Vitesse, content addressable memory (CAM) approach [2], used, e.g., by Netlogic, IDT, and Kawasaki, and dedicated chip approach based on finite state automata, used, e.g., by Agere, Raqia, and Solidum Systems Corp. [3]. The first approach is software based, while the last two are implemented in hardware. Among the three, the approach using a dedicated chip is by far the fastest: it enables classifying data packets at wire speed, i.e., it permits to complete the classification as soon as the last bit of the packet is read. In particular, the mechanism of data classification used by Solidum Systems Corp., see http://www.solidum.com, is built around programmable classification processors that can be configured to closely inspect packets for vital information. Based on a programmable state machine technology and on an openly distributed pattern description language PAX PDL [4,5, 6], Solidum's scalable and forward-compatible classification processors simultaneously parse, identify, and tag packets. The information collected can then be used to make intelligent routing and switching decisions. Prefix codes are of particular importance to data classification, due to the fact that in such languages a classification decision concerning an input word can be made on-line without the risk of having to change the decision later, when more bits arrive. Language decomposition and computation of prime components are the most important theoretical tools used in this technology. Each classification task requires a specific finite state automaton to carry it out. However, due to the large size of these automata and to their large number, it is impossible to store all these objects simultaneously. Fortunately, prefix codes corresponding to these automata can be decomposed into *primes*, i.e., undecomposable prefix codes. It turns out that, in practice, those prime factors are often the same for many prefix codes. Consequently, it is enough to store a relatively small number of simple automata which are building blocks for all others. Whence the necessity of efficient computation of prime components of a given prefix code. Another advantage of having a decomposition of prefix codes into primes is that it facilitates updates. Very often a classification task yielded, e.g., by a routing problem, changes over time [7] which requires an update of a part of the corresponding automaton. In such situations we often need to replace only some of the prime factors and are able to reuse the remaining ones.

Prefix codes over a finite alphabet constitute a free monoid, see, e.g., [8]. Thus, every prefix code admits a unique decomposition into primes. In this paper we present an $O(n)$-time algorithm for finding prime components of a regular prefix code F given by the minimal *dfa* (*min-dfa*) A_F of size n. (We assume that the size of the alphabet is bounded, hence the number of transitions is linear in the number of states.) The algorithm finds a decomposition

$$F = F_1 F_2 \ldots F_k$$

into a concatenation of prime prefix codes in linear time (and thus it also decides if the given prefix code is prime). When F is a finite prefix code, this decomposition is relatively easy to find and one can prove that the sum of sizes of the *min-dfas* of all the prime components is $O(n)$. However, in the general case, when A_F contains loops, the sum of sizes of the prime components may sometimes be $\Omega(n^2)$. Despite that, our decomposition algorithm runs in time $O(n)$ and the computed succinct representation of the decomposition is of $O(n)$ size.

2   Definitions and Basic Facts

We consider the alphabet $\Sigma = \{1, 2, \ldots, m\}$. The language containing all words will be denoted by Σ^* and the empty word by ε. We say that v is a prefix (*left factor*) of w if there exists u such that $vu = w$. Let E, F be languages over Σ. We define: $EF^{-1} \overset{\text{def}}{=} \{v \in \Sigma^* \mid \exists w \in F\ vw \in E\}$ and $F^{-1}E \overset{\text{def}}{=} \{v \in \Sigma^* \mid \exists w \in F\ wv \in E\}$. $F^{-1}E$ and EF^{-1} are the left and right quotient of language E by language F, respectively. If $\{w\}$ is a singleton set, then we will write wE, $w^{-1}E$, and Ew^{-1} instead of $\{w\}E$, $\{w\}^{-1}E$, and $E\{w\}^{-1}$, respectively.

Definition 1. *A language $F \subset \Sigma^*$ is called a* prefix code *iff F does not contain two different words such that one is a prefix of the other. Prefix codes $\{\varepsilon\}$ and $\emptyset$ are called* trivial.

In this paper we consider only regular prefix codes, i.e., the ones which are recognized by finite automata.

Definition 2. *A deterministic finite automaton (dfa) $A = (Q, \delta, s, F)$ consists of a finite set Q of states, a partial transition function $\delta : Q \times \Sigma \mapsto Q$, an initial state $s \in Q$, and a set of final states $F \subseteq Q$.*

Lemma 1 ([9]). *For any language E, the following properties are equivalent: (1) E is a prefix code. (2) E is empty or the minimal dfa (min-dfa) accepting E has a single terminal state without outgoing transitions.*

Let $E_1, E_2, \ldots, E_m$ be languages over $\Sigma = \{1, 2 \ldots, m\}$. The *switch composition*, denoted $[E_1 : E_2 : \ldots : E_m]$, is defined by:

$$[E_1 : E_2 : \ldots : E_m] \overset{\text{def}}{=} \bigcup_{i \in \Sigma} i \cdot E_i \tag{1}$$

E.g., if $\Sigma = \{1, 2, 3\}$, we have $[\emptyset : \{\varepsilon\} : \{1\}] = 1\emptyset \cup 2\{\varepsilon\} \cup 3\{1\} = \{2, 31\}$.

Prefix codes are closed with respect to concatenation, switch composition, and left quotient by a word. I.e., if $E_1, E_2, \ldots, E_m$ are prefix codes and w is a word then $E_1 E_2$, $[E_1 : E_2 : \ldots : E_m]$, and $w^{-1}E_1$ are prefix codes.

Definition 3. *A non-empty prefix code which cannot be represented by a concatenation of two non-trivial prefix codes is called a* prime prefix code *(or simply a* prime).

Since non-empty prefix codes form a free monoid, we have the following lemma.

Lemma 2. *Every non-empty prefix code E admits a unique decomposition, $E = P_1 P_2 \ldots P_k$, into non-trivial primes.*

Let E, F be two prefix codes. We say that G is a *common right divisor* of E and F, denoted by $G \in \text{CD}(E, F)$, if and only if there exist two prefix codes E_1, F_1 such that $E_1 G = E$ and $F_1 G = F$. Note, that at least one common right divisor exists, it is $\{\varepsilon\}$. Also, $\emptyset$ is a common right divisor of E and F if and only if $E = F = \emptyset$. We say that $G \in \text{CD}(E, F)$ is *the greatest common right divisor*, $\text{GCD}(E, F)$, if there is no other prefix code $G' \in \text{CD}(E, F)$ such that $G' = G''G$, for a prefix code G''. We have $\text{GCD}(E, \emptyset) = E$ for each prefix code E.

One can prove that the greatest common right divisor always exists and it is unique.

Theorem 1. *Let $F_1, F_2, \ldots, F_m$ be prefix codes. Then $[F_1 : \ldots : F_m]$ is a prime if and only if $\text{GCD}(F_1, \ldots, F_m) = \{\varepsilon\}$.*

Proof. We prove the left-to-right implication by contradiction.
If $\text{GCD}(F_1, \ldots, F_m) \neq \{\varepsilon\}$ then two cases are possible:

1. $\text{GCD}(F_1, \ldots, F_m) = \emptyset$, then $[F_1 : \ldots : F_m] = \emptyset$. This is not a prime.
2. $\text{GCD}(F_1, \ldots, F_m) = F$ is a non-trivial prefix code. Thus, $[F_1 : \ldots : F_m] = [F_1'F : \ldots : F_m'F] = [F_1' : \ldots : F_m'] F$ for some prefix codes $F_1', \ldots, F_m'$. This is not a prime.

The right-to-left implication is also proved by contradiction.
Suppose $[F_1 : \ldots : F_m]$ is not a prime, i.e., $[F_1 : \ldots : F_m] = FP$ for some non-trivial prefix codes F and P. Thus, $P \in \text{CD}(F_1, \ldots, F_m)$ and hence $\{\varepsilon\} \neq \text{GCD}(F_1, \ldots, F_m)$.   □

Since in data classification applications prefix codes are mostly generated using concatenation and switch operations the following observation is useful to store prefix codes as lists of prime factors. Let $E, F, E_1, \ldots, E_m$ be prefix codes over an m-letter alphabet, and let $\mathcal{PF}(F)$ denote the list of prime factors of F. We have

$$\mathcal{PF}(EF) = \mathcal{PF}(E) \cdot \mathcal{PF}(F) \tag{2}$$

$$\mathcal{PF}([E_1 : \ldots : E_m]) = [E_1 G^{-1} : \ldots : E_m G^{-1}] \cdot \mathcal{PF}(G) \tag{3}$$

where $G = \text{GCD}(E_1, E_2, \ldots, E_m)$.

If two prefix codes F_1 and F_2 are given as lists of their prime factors, finding their greatest common right divisor, $\text{GCD}(F_1, F_2)$, is straightforward and consists in identifying the longest common suffix of F_1 and F_2 seen as words over primes. If $\mathcal{PF}(F_1) = E_1 E_2 \ldots E_k$ and $\mathcal{PF}(F_2) = G_1 G_2 \ldots G_r$, then $\text{GCD}(F_1, F_2) = E_i E_{i+1} \ldots E_k$, where i is the smallest integer such that $E_i E_{i+1} \ldots E_k$ is a suffix of $G_1 G_2 \ldots G_r$. If there is no such i then $\text{GCD}(F_1, F_2) = \{\varepsilon\}$.

3 Prime Decomposition of Regular Prefix Codes

From the results of the previous section it is relatively easy to find the prime decomposition of a finite prefix code. In order to find an efficient and general algorithm for decomposition of all regular prefix codes we will introduce below an approach based on so-called *D-articulation states*. In [1] the general problem of decomposition of languages into a *concatenation* of other languages was addressed. It has been proved that every decomposition $A = B \cdot C$ of a regular language A (B and C not necessarily regular) implies a decomposition $A = B' \cdot C'$ such that B' and C' are regular with $B' \subseteq B$ and $C' \subseteq C$.

Theorem 2. *Let E, F, G be non-empty prefix codes such that $E = FG$. E is regular if and only if F and G are.*

Proof. Since regular sets are closed with respect to concatenation, one implication is obvious.

Let $Q(A) \stackrel{\text{def}}{=} \{w^{-1}A \mid w \in \Sigma^*\} \setminus \emptyset$, for any language A. The set $Q(A)$ is exactly the set of states of minimal deterministic (possibly infinite) automata for A, see e.g., [9, Theorem 8.1] or [10].

If $E = FG$ with E, F, G being non-empty prefix codes, then there is an injection $i : Q(F) \hookrightarrow Q(E)$, e.g., $i(w^{-1}F) \stackrel{\text{def}}{=} w^{-1}E = w^{-1}(FG)$. If E is regular, then $Q(E)$ is finite. Because of the existence of i, $Q(F)$ must be finite, i.e., F is regular. On the other hand, G is regular since $G = F^{-1}E$, see [9, Proposition 3.1] or [10]. $\square$

In order to determine the primality of a prefix code F we will need to look for *D-articulation states* of *min-dfa* A_F accepting F.

Definition 4. *Let $A_F = (Q, \delta, i, \{t\})$ be min-dfa recognizing a non-empty prefix code F. A state $s \in Q$ is called a* D-articulation state *if every path from i to t passes through s.*

Lemma 3. *A D-articulation state of a deterministic finite automaton A remains a D-articulation state after minimization of A.*

In the remainder of this section we will show how the prime decomposition problem of a prefix code may be efficiently solved through the determination of D-articulation states of its *min-dfa*.

To determine the prime decomposition of a prefix code F we suppose that it is given as its *min-dfa* A_F. We will suppose that its size (i.e., its number of states) is equal to n. The decomposition algorithm will find a sequence of prefix codes $F_1, F_2, \ldots, F_k$ such that $F = F_1F_2 \ldots F_k$. Each prefix code F_i, for $i \in [1, k]$, will be reported by the algorithm as a *dfa* A_{F_i}. As in some cases the sum of sizes of A_{F_i}, for $i \in [1, k]$, may be as high as $\Omega(n^2)$, cf. Example 1 at the end of Section 4, it would seem to be the lower bound for the time complexity of such an algorithm. However, each A_{F_i} may be obtained as a so-called projection of A_F. A projection of A_F will have the same set of states but the initial and final states may be different. This will allow us to construct an $O(n)$ time algorithm reporting all factors.

Definition 5. *Let* $A = (Q, \delta, i, \{t\})$ *be a dfa accepting a prefix code* F, *and let* s, s' *be two states from* Q. *We denote by* $A(s, s')$ *the finite automaton having the same states as* A, *with* s *designated as initial state and* s' *- the only terminal state, such that all the out-coming transitions of* s' *have been discarded.*

More formally, $A(s, s') \stackrel{\text{def}}{=} (Q, \delta', s, \{s'\})$, *where, for all* $x \in Q$, $\alpha \in \Sigma$:

$$\delta'(x, \alpha) \stackrel{\text{def}}{=} \begin{cases} \text{not defined} & \text{if } x = s' \\ \delta(x, \alpha) & \text{otherwise} \end{cases} \tag{4}$$

Note that after replacing i by s and t by s' we get a *dfa*, but not minimal, in general, since it may contain useless (sink) and unreachable states. In particular, if $s' \neq t$, t becomes a sink state as the new final state s' is unreachable from t. Any such projection produces a prefix code automaton.

To show the correctness of the primality testing algorithm we first prove the following.

Theorem 3. *A prefix code* F *is prime if and only if its min-dfa has no D-articulation state.*

Proof. To prove the right-to-left implication we suppose that $F = F_1 F_2$ and we will conclude that A_F must have a D-articulation state. Let i_i and t_i be initial and terminal states, for prefix code automaton A_{F_i}, $i = 1, 2$, respectively. The construction of A_F is the following.

Let A' be a *dfa* whose set of states is the union of states of A_{F_1} and A_{F_2}, where t_1 and i_2 are identified as the same state. The set of transitions of A' is the union the transition sets of F_1 and F_2. Finally we take as its initial state $i = i_1$ and its terminal state $t = t_2$. It is obvious that A' accepts $F_1 F_2$. Note that the automaton is actually deterministic and $F_A = \min(A')$ is the automaton for F. By construction $t_1 (= s_2)$ is a D-articulation state in A' and thus also in A_F (Lemma 3).

For the left-to-right implication we suppose that a is a D-articulation state of $A_F = (Q, \delta, i, \{t\})$ and we will prove that F is not a prime. Consider $A_{F_1} = A_F(i, a)$ and $A_{F_2} = A_F(a, t)$. Note that A_{F_2} may have a loop on state a but A_{F_1} may not. Take any word $w \in F$ and the process of its acceptance by A_F. Let $w = xy$, where x is such a prefix of w, that reading the last symbol of w we visit state a for the first time. Clearly, x is accepted by A_{F_1} and y is accepted by A_{F_2}. Thus F is a concatenation of two prefix codes defined by the automata $A_F(i, a)$ and $A_F(a, t)$.   □

The following lemma follows directly from the definition of the D-articulation state.

Lemma 4. *Let* $A = (Q, \delta, i, \{t\})$ *be a dfa with at least two different D-articulation states* a_1 *and* a_2. *Then one of the two states, say* a_1, *is such that on every path from* i *to* t *in* A *the first occurrence of* a_1 *always precedes the first occurrence of* a_2. *Moreover, on each of these paths, the last occurrence of* a_1 *precedes the last occurrence of* a_2.

The sequence of D-articulation states of a prefix code automaton A will be called a *spine* of A. Lemma 4 yields an ordering on the states of the spine of A. Thus we will write $a_1 \prec a_2$ if on every complete path in A, the first occurrence of a_1 precedes the first occurrence of a_2 (and, by consequence the same happens to the last occurrences of both states).

Theorem 4. *Let A_F be the min-dfa for a prefix code F, having k D-articulation states. Then F is decomposable into $k + 1$ primes, $F = F_1 F_2 \ldots F_{k+1}$.*

Proof. Let $\{a_1, \ldots, a_k\}$ be the set of D-articulation states of $A_F = (Q, \delta, i, \{t\})$ ordered by $\prec$ relation. The proof goes by induction on k. It is sufficient to prove that $F = F'F''$, such that F' is accepted by $A_{F'}$ with $k-1$ D-articulation states and F'' is a prime prefix code. Let $A_{F'} = A_F(i, a_k)$ and $A_{F''} = A_F(a_k, t)$.

By construction, $F = F'F''$. Observe that, as a_k is the last D-articulation state, by Proposition 4, there is no other state which belongs to every complete path in $A_{F''}$. Thus, by Theorem 3, F'' is prime. We show that $A_{F'}$ has $k-1$ D-articulation states. By construction of $A_{F'}$, all paths in $A_{F'}$ are exactly sub-paths in A_F from i to the first occurrence of a_k.

However, by Lemma 4, on every path in A_F, before the first occurrence of a_k there was the first occurrence of each state a_i for $1 \leq i \leq k - 1$. Thus each state a_i, $1 \leq i \leq k-1$ is a D-articulation state in $A_{F'}$ and no other state in $A_{F'}$ is a D-articulation state. $\qquad\square$

It follows from Theorems 3 and 4 that finding the prime decomposition of a prefix code is equivalent to determining the D-articulation states of its *min-dfa*. Hence we concentrate on the latter task in the next section.

4   Finding D-Articulation States

In this section we present an algorithm which finds all D-articulation states in a *min-dfa* A of a prefix code, in linear time in the size of A. Let G be an n-node directed graph corresponding to a *min-dfa* $(Q, \delta, i, \{t\})$. (Recall that we consider bounded size alphabets, hence the number of edges in G is $O(n)$.) We assume that every node of G is on some directed path from i to t.

Definition 6. *Let v be a node and $\pi = (p_1, \ldots, p_k)$ be a simple directed path in G. Define* FIRST$[v, \pi]$ *to be the smallest index j for which there is a directed path from p_j to v node-disjoint with π. Similarly define* LAST$[v, \pi]$ *to be the largest r for which there is a directed path from v to p_r node-disjoint with π.*

We first give a general overview of the algorithm.

Algorithm Find-D-articulation-states

1. Find any simple directed path $\pi = (p_1, \ldots, p_k)$ from i to t.
   Call this path the *backbone*.
   { Use *Depth-First-Search* [11] on G starting from i. }
2. For each node $v \notin \pi$ compute $\text{FIRST}[v, \pi]$ and $\text{LAST}[v, \pi]$.
3. For each node $v \notin \pi$ add the edge (p_j, p_m) to the graph G,
   where $j = \text{FIRST}[v, \pi]$) and $m = \text{LAST}[v, \pi]$.
4. Output D-articulation states of G as those nodes $p_l \in \pi$ for
   which there is no arc $p_j p_m$ with $j < l < m$.

We now give a more detailed description of the algorithm, show that it runs in linear time, and prove its correctness.

Computation of *left* and *right* labels.

Label all nodes of $\pi = (p_1, \ldots, p_k)$ with 0. Initially, all other nodes are unlabeled. We define the following procedure *Modified-DFS(s)*, for $s \in [1, k]$. It is a version of DFS which starts from p_s using edges outside π. It backtracks whenever a labeled node is encountered. Assign label of value s to all newly visited nodes which were previously not labeled. Call the label assigned in this way to a node v, "the *left* label of v".

The whole algorithm computing *left* labels for all nodes outside the backbone is as follows:

$$\textbf{for } s = 1 \textbf{ to } k \textbf{ do } \textit{Modified-DFS}(s).$$

Similarly we compute *right* labels, processing the reverse graph of G (where all edges are reversed) in the reverse order, i.e., from $s = k$ down to 1.

Lemma 5. *For every node v, its* left *label is equal to* $\text{FIRST}[v, \pi]$ *and its* right *label is equal to* $\text{LAST}[v, \pi]$. *Moreover, by the algorithm above, the values* $\text{FIRST}[v, \pi]$ *and* $\text{LAST}[v, \pi]$ *are computed in linear time.*

Proof. By construction, node v obtains left label l if there exists a path from p_l to v outside of the backbone, and there is no such path starting at p_j, for $j < l$. Hence, $l = \text{FIRST}[v, \pi]$. A similar argument holds for $\text{LAST}[v, \pi]$ and the right label of v. The algorithm takes linear time since each edge is processed at most twice. □

Implementation of Part 4 of the main algorithm.

At the beginning of Part 4 we have the graph augmented by the arcs added in Part 3. Define an integer vector, A, of length k, as follows. $A[j]$ is the highest index of a node of the backbone $\pi = (p_1, \ldots, p_k)$, which is the end of an arc starting in p_j. (We consider edges of the backbone as arcs, so if no arc starting from p_j was added, we have $A[j] = j+1$.) Computing A takes linear time in the number of added arcs, i.e., $O(n)$. Now compute the vector B, where $B[j] = \max(A[1], \ldots, A[j-1])$. This vector can be computed in time

$O(k)$. $B[j] = r$ means that the highest index of a destination node of an arc starting in p_s, for $s < j$, is p_r. Hence $B[j] = j$ iff p_j is a D-articulation state. (Clearly nodes outside of the backbone cannot be D-articulation states.)

It follows that the entire algorithm runs in linear time in n. The correctness of the algorithm follows from the following lemma.

Lemma 6. *A node is a D-articulation state iff it is one of the backbone nodes p_l and there is no edge $p_j p_m$ with $j < l < m$ at the end of the algorithm.*

Proof. Suppose that v is a D-articulation state. Then v must belong to the backbone, for otherwise the backbone would be a path from i to t omitting v. Suppose, for a contradiction, that there is an arc $p_j p_m$ with $j < l < m$. This arc existed in the original graph or has been added in Part 3. In both cases it follows that there is a path from i to t which omits v. This contradicts the definition of a D-articulation state.

Now suppose that v is not a D-articulation state and let R be a path from i to t that does not contain v. Moreover, suppose that v belongs to the backbone, and $v = p_l$. Let j be the largest index smaller than l such that p_j belongs to R, and let m be the smallest index larger than l such that p_m belongs to R. If there is no edge $p_j p_m$ in the original graph then the segment of the path R between p_j and p_m has length at least 2. Let u be any node in this segment. In this case the arc $p_j p_{jm}$ was added in Part 3 when considering node u. Hence the arc $p_j p_m$ is present upon the completion of the algorithm. $\square$

This implies the following result.

Theorem 5. *Let A_F be an n-state min-dfa accepting a prefix code F. The sequence of all D-articulation states of A_F may be found in $O(n)$ time.*

Example 1. Consider the following prefix code F over $\Sigma = \{1, 2\}$,

$$F = \left(12 + 1^2 2 + \ldots + 1^{n-2} 2\right)^* 1^{n-1} = \left(\Sigma_{i=1}^{n-2} 1^i 2\right)^* 1^{n-1}$$

for some $n > 1$. Its *min-dfa* has n states as shown in Fig. 1. Each of its states is a D-articulation state. According to Theorem 4, $F = F_1 F_2 \ldots F_{n-1}$, where $A_{F_i} = A_F(s_i, s_{i+1})$, for $i \in [1, n-1]$. Note that A_{F_i} contains as its set of states $\{s_1, s_2, \ldots, s_{i+1}\}$ and it is minimal. The sum of sizes of A_{F_i}, over $i \in [1, n-1]$, is $2 + 3 + \ldots + n = \Omega(n^2)$. The prefix code F is decomposed into $n - 1$ primes given by the following formula:

$$F_1 = 1 \text{ and } F_i = \left(2 \prod_{j=1}^{i} F_j\right)^* 1, \text{ for } i \in [2, n-1]$$

where $\prod_{j=1}^{i} F_j = F_1 F_2 \ldots F_i$.

For example, for $n = 4$ we have the prime decomposition:

$$\mathcal{PF}\left((12 + 1^2 2)^* 1^3\right) = 1 \cdot (21)^* 1 \cdot (21(21)^* 1)^* 1$$

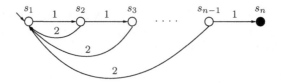

Fig. 1. A prefix code *min-dfa* whose all states are D-articulation states

From the proof of Theorem 4, it follows that the size of the prefix code, expressed as the number of states of its *min-dfa*, is at least as large as the size of each of its prime components. However, the sum of sizes of prime components may be substantially larger than the size of the original prefix code. Example 1 shows that for a prefix code of size n, the sum of sizes of its prime components may be $\Omega(n^2)$. Nevertheless, our algorithm permits to represent all the prime components collectively within an $O(n)$ data structure. Theorems 3, 4, and 5 imply the following result.

Theorem 6. *A prime decomposition of any prefix code accepted by an n-state min-dfa can be found in time $O(n)$ and be represented in $O(n)$ space.*

References

[1] Mateescu, A., Salomaa, A., Yu, S.: On the decomposition of finite languages. Technical Report 222, Turku Centre for Computer Science (1998)
[2] Azgani, S.: Using content-addressable memory for networking applications. Communications Systems Design **5** (1999)
[3] Jenkins, C.: Speed and throughput of programable state machines for classification of OC192 data. In: Network Processors Conference, San Jose, California (2000) 6–24
[4] Bruell, G.: Method and apparatus for defining data packet formats (1997) US Patent 5,680,585.
[5] Nossik, M., Welfeld, F., Richardson, M.: PAX PDL — a non-procedural packet description language. Online publication, Solidum Systems Corp, 1575 Carling Avenue, Ottawa, Ontario, Canada (1998)
    http://www.solidum.com/body/technology/pax-pdl/pax-pdl-00.html.
[6] Czyzowicz, J., Fraczak, W., Iglewski, M., Welfeld, F.: PAX PDL — language for data communication packet description. Technical report, Solidum Systems Corp, 1575 Carling Avenue, Ottawa, Ontario, Canada (2001)
[7] Labovitz, C., Malan, R., Jahanian, F.: Origins of internet routing instability. Technical Report CSE-TR-368-98, University of Michigan (1998)
[8] Pin, J.E.: Variétés de langages formels. Masson, Paris (1984)
[9] Eilenberg, S.: Automata, Languages, and Machines. Volume A. Academic Press (1974)
[10] Hopcroft, J., Ullman, J.: Introduction to Automata Theory, Languages, and Computation. Addison-Wesley (1979)
[11] Cormen, T., Leiserson, C., Rivest, R.: Introduction to Algorithms. The MIT Press (1990)

Implementation of Dictionaries via Automata
and Decision Trees

Abolfazl Fatholahzadeh

Supélec - Campus de Metz
2, rue Édouard Belin, 57078 Metz, France.
Abolfazl.Fatholahzadeh@supelec.fr

Abstract. Finite-state transducers can be used to map a language onto
a set of values. This paper proposes an alternate representation method
for such a mapping, consisting of associating a finite-state automaton
accepting the input language with a decision tree representing the output
values. The advantages of this approach are that it leads to more compact
representations than transducers, and that decision trees can easily be
synthesized by machine learning techniques.

1 Introduction

For the application of large-scale dictionaries two major problems have to be
solved: *fast lookup speed* and *compact representation*. Using *automata* we can
achieve fast lookup by determinization and compact representation by minimization. For providing information for the recognized words one can use the
transducers(i.e., automata with outputs) [13,15,16]. The *goal* of this work is to
propose a competitor to the transducers. Our method combines *automata* and
machine learning theories with following desired properties:

1. The number of the states (and hence the transitions) representing the input
   language of our method is less than compared to the transducers.
2. In constructing transducers, we have to represent every transition by a data
   structure of at least two fields: one for the symbol representing the transition,
   another for the label-value (for short label) associated with the symbol. So
   in order to properly calculate the outputs, the labels set needs to have the
   algebraic structure *e.g.,* semiring in the case of weighted automata [17].
   In our approach the transitions are not labeled with outputs; the cost of
   exploring the automata is low.
3. In most applications (*e.g.,* those of using part of speech tagging) there may
   be (many) identical output values. When you use the transducers there is no
   way to save the amount of space for those identical informations, whereas in
   our approach such economy is allowed.

In order to explain intuitively the benefits of our method, we give a very
simple example in the following. Let $V = \{Asia,Europa\}$ be the output values
of three following countries: $K = \{Iran,Iraq,Ireland\}$. In order to determine the

J.-M. Champarnaud and D. Maurel (Eds.): CIAA 2002, LNCS 2608, pp. 95–105, 2003.
© Springer-Verlag Berlin Heidelberg 2003

output values of any element of K one can *learn* the *decision tree* based on the mutual informations; if the key (of K) ends by *'n/q'* then retrieve *'Asia'* else *'Europa'*.

Our solution is to represent the keys in a finite-state automaton and the output values in a *decision tree*, respectively. Our method has been applied to a number of applications: Who is Who? [11], text classification [7], processing the nationality words and their tagging [9,10] along with the discussions with respect to (w.r.t.) two trie [1], ternary search [2] and perfect hashing [6,4].

In [8] we just briefly sketched our idea without giving the algorithms which will be described in Section 3 of the present paper. In Section 2, we recall some basic notions of both the automata theory and the machine learning used in our algorithms. The experiments and comparisons of our method *w.r.t.* the transducers are outlined in Section 4.

2   Preliminary Considerations

For more informations on automata we refer the reader to [19]. For a general reference on machine learning, the reader is referred to [14].

Recall that an acyclic finite-state automaton is a graph of the form $g = (Q, \Sigma, \delta, q_0, F)$ where Q is a finite set of states, Σ is the alphabet, q_0 is the start state, $F \subseteq Q$ is the accepting states. δ is a partial mapping $\delta : Q \times \Sigma \longrightarrow Q$ denoting *transition*. If $a \in \Sigma$, the notation $\delta(q, a) = \perp$ is used to mean that $\delta(q, a)$ is undefined. Let Σ^* denotes the set containing all strings over Σ including zero-length string, called the empty string ε. The extension of the partial δ mapping with $x \in \Sigma^*$ is a function $\delta^* : Q \times \Sigma^* \longrightarrow Q$ and defined as follows:

$$\delta^*(q, \varepsilon) = q$$
$$\delta^*(q, ax) = \begin{cases} \delta^*(\delta(q, a), x) & \text{if } \delta(q, a) \neq \perp \\ \perp & \text{otherwise.} \end{cases}$$

A finite automaton is said to be (n,m)–automaton if $|Q| = n$ and $|E| = m$ where E denotes the set of the edges (transitions) of g. The property δ^* allows fast retrieval for variable-length strings and quick unsuccessful search determination. The pessimistic time complexity of δ^* is $\mathcal{O}(n)$ *w.r.t.* a string of length n.

A decision tree (dt) is a direct acyclic graph of nodes and arcs. At each *node* a simple test is made; at the *leaves* a decision is made with respect to the class labels (values in our case). The dt is introduced in the machine learning (ML) community [18]. The suitable input for the classification algorithm in ML is the lists of a *fixed* number of *attributes* of the *class* at hand and their values as shown in the left part of Table 1 for 10 restaurants using four attributes. At the top of this tree expressed by way of three rules situated in the right part of Table 1, one can see the attribute age; this indicates that it is most likely that a decision can be made quickly if one first asks for the age of a restaurant. If the answer to this question is 'new' or 'old', then the profit can be predicted by 'down' or 'up', respectively. If the answer is 'midlife', then another question must be posed, about the presence of competition. After this answer is known, the profit trend can be determined.

Table 1. The profit trends of 10 Slow-and-Fast Foods & Its decision tree

Profit	Age	CP[a]	Type	Test	Result
down	old	no	CK	If Age is new	Then Profit is up.
down	midlife	yes	CK	If Age is old	Then Profit is down.
up	midlife	no	HB	If Age is midlife	Then If $\exists$ Competition
down	old	no	HB		Then Profit is down.
up	new	no	HB		Else Profit is up.
up	new	no	CK	Entropy(profit,age)	= 0.4d0
up	midlife	no	CK	Entropy(profit,CP)	= 0.8754887502163469d0
up	new	yes	CK	Entropy(profit,type)	= 1.0d0
down	midlife	yes	HB	Prob(profit,up,age,new)	= 1.0d0
down	old	yes	CK	Prob(profit,up,age,midlife)	= 0.5d0

[a] CP (competition), HB (hamburger) and CK (Chelo–Kabab: Iranian hum).

Table 2. Backward attribute-based Data and Decision Tree.

b_7	b_6	b_5	b_4	b_3	b_2	b_1	KV	Solution-Path	Question	KV
$\star$	$\star$	$\star$	I	r	a	n	Tehran	$(b_1$ n kv Tehran)	$b_1 = $ n?	Tehran
$\star$	$\star$	$\star$	I	r	a	q	Baghdad	$(b_1$ q kv Baghdad)	$b_1 = $ q?	Baghdad
I	r	e	l	a	n	d	Dublin	$(b_1$ d kv Dublin)	$b_1 = $ d?	Dublin

3   Algorithm

We refer to a *key* as a sequence of characters surrounded by empty spaces but containing no internal space. We may use key, word, interchangeably. We write b_i to denote the ith character (from right-to-left) of a key *e.g.*, b_1 and b_5 of *'Iran'* are *'n'* and the null character (shown by $\star$ for convenience), respectively. A *key–value* (or output value noted by kv) is also a sequence of characters surrounded by empty spaces which may have one or more internal spaces. For instance, one may assign to a word a unique ambiguity class, (*e.g.*, *"Adj/Noun"*) although a class represents a set of alternative key–values that a given word can occur with. **Input:** The *user-file* is of the following customary form: $f = \{(k_i, v_i) | i = 1, 2, \ldots, p\}$ where each (k_i, v_i) represents a pair with k_i and v_i standing for a key and key–value, respectively.

Outputs: The (n,m)–automaton and the decision tree. Table 2 shows an example of the learned dt *w.r.t.* $f_1 = \{$(Iran,Tehran),(Iraq,Baghdad), (Ireland,Dublin)$\}$.
Using outputs: Given a string input x, if it can be spelled out using g *i.e.*, $\delta^*(q_0, x) \in F$ then uses *dt* to search *kv*. For instance, *kv* of *'Iran'* *w.r.t.* f_1 is *'Tehran'* because the first solution–path of the learned dt of Table 2 provides us such result. Note that the dt *w.r.t.* $f_2 = \{$(Iran,Asia),(Iraq,Asia)$\}$ has a unique solution-path i.e. (*kvAsia*) - no condition (*i.e.*, question) is required to discriminate the key-value.

3.1   Main Algorithm

Preprocessing: First, by way of the function *FormAutomaton* we form g accepting the input language (K the set of k_i of f). Then, we call the function *FormInputForLearning* along with two input parameters: ℓ (*i.e.*, the length of longest key - calculated by *FormAutomaton*) and f. The output is the suitable data table of $p \times (\ell + 1)$ elements, namely *table* for being used as training examples for learning the key-values. Finally, we learn how the output values can be synthesized by dt. This is done by the function *Classify*, using *table* and *kv*, where *kv* denotes the key–value. So, *kv* is the *target attribute* of the learning process of this phase.

Algorithm 1: Construction from $f = \{(k_i, v_i) | i = 1, 2, \ldots p\}$ and its utilization.

---

func FormDictionnary(f) // **Preprocessing**

$\ell \leftarrow 0$; {ℓ is the global variable standing for the length of the longest key.}
$g \leftarrow$ FormAutomaton(f); {Outputs: ℓ and a (n-m) automaton.}
$table \leftarrow$ FormInputForLearning(f,ℓ); {Output: training samples.}
$dt \leftarrow$ Classify(kv,table); {kv: target attribute. Output: decision tree.}

cnuf

func   UsingDictionary(x)//**Processing,** x is a variable-length string input.

   if $\delta^\star(q_0, x) = q$ such that $q \in F$ **then**
      $kv \leftarrow$ SearchValue(x,dt); {See Table 2.}
   else
      $kv \leftarrow nil$; {x is unknown.}
   end if

cnuf

Processing: It works as follows: if x can be spelled out using g, then the function *SearchValue* uses the learned dt to output the key–value. *SearchValue* examines the current solution–path and stops the search when it succeeds. This function performs no backtracking in its search. Once it selects an attribute to test at a particular level in the tree, it never backtracks to reconsider this choice due to the no existence of 'missing values' (of the attributes) in our method.

3.2   FormAutomaton() - Construction from Keys

J. Daciuk, S. Mihov, B. W.Watson and R.E. Watson [5] in their works describe an elegant algorithms for the incremental construction of minimal acyclic finite state automata and transducers from both sorted and unsorted data. We adapted their former one such that the length of the longest key be calculated for being used later in the construction of suitable input for learning the dt (see 3.3).

Algorithm 2: Construction from sorted keys (K) (Adapted from [5]).

---

func FormAutomaton() // Input: K - the set of sorted keys.

> $Register \leftarrow \emptyset; \ell \leftarrow 0$ {ℓ stands for the length of the longest key.}
> **for** $key \in K$ **do**
>> $lk \leftarrow$ Length(key); $\ell \leftarrow$; Max(lk,ℓ); $cp \leftarrow$ CommonPrefix(key);
>> $ls \leftarrow \delta^*(q_0, cp)$; $cs \leftarrow key[cp + 1 \ldots lk]$;{ls:Last state; cs:Current suffix}
>> **if** HasChildren(ls) **then** ReplaceOrRegister(ls); **fi**
>> AddSuffix(ls,cs); {Creates a branch extending out of the dictionary.}
> **end for**
> ReplaceOrRegister(q_0);

cnuf // Pessimistic time complexity is $\mathcal{O}(p \times \ell \times \log n)$.
func CommonPrefix(key) // The longest prefix of the word to be added.

> **return** $key[1 \ldots \alpha] : \alpha = \max i : \exists q \in Q \ \delta^*(q_0, key[1 \ldots i]) = q$

cnuf// Pessimistic time complexity is $\mathcal{O}(\ell)$
funcReplaceOrRegister(state) //Executes at most $\mathcal{O}(\ell)$ times for each key.

> $child \leftarrow$ LastChild(); {Returns the outgoing transition most recently added.}
> **if not** MarkedAsRegister($child$) **then**
>> **if** HasChildren(ls) **then** ReplaceOrRegister(ls); **fi**
>> **if** $\exists q \in Register(q \equiv_\sim child)$ {$\equiv_\sim$ Same equivalence class - See [5].} **then**
>>> DeleteBranch(child); $LastChild(state) \leftarrow q$;
>> **else**
>>> $Register \leftarrow Register \cup \{child\}$; MarkedAsRegister($child$);
>> **end if**// Memory for the register of states is proportional to **n**.
> **end if**

cnuf // Pessimistic time complexity of adding a state to a register is $\mathcal{O}(\ell)$.

Please refers to [5] for additional descriptions.

3.3   Learning the Output Values

As the left part of Table 2 suggests, we have to construct the suitable input from f wherein the star-symbol in each column corresponding to the null characters of those keys having the length inferior to the longest key, namely 'Ireland'. Note that the meaning of the star-symbol should not be confused with unknown attribute-value which may causes to an impossible classification. The function $FormInputForLearning$ generate the suitable input. Now we are ready to learn the decision tree. This is done by the function $Classify$ using the global input variables: *table* and our target attribute, namely *kv*. If *kv* has only one value, then the decision tree is trivial. Otherwise, construct a tree with the chosen splitting attribute as its root, with its descendants given by a recursive call to $Classify$ on the subtables with the splitting attribute taking each possible value. A subtable is obtained by $GetSubTable$ which returns the subtable of the original table, of entries for which the given attribute takes the given value. That is, in the new table, only the rows for which attribute takes value are included, and the column for attribute is excluded.

Algorithm 3: Learning the output values from $f = \{(k_i, v_i)|i = 1 \ldots p\}$

---

func FormInputForLearning() // Input: $f = \{(k_i, v_i)|i = 1 \ldots, p\}$ and ℓ.

 $table[1][\ell + 1] = $ 'kv'; {kv is our target attribute.}
 for j from ℓ down to 1 {Naming ℓ first attributes.} **do**
  $table[1][j] = concat(\text{'b'}, j)$;
 end for// First row of the data table contain the $\ell + 1$ attributes.
 for i from 2 to p **do**
  $table[i][j] \leftarrow SelectCharacter(key, j, \ell)$ {An asterisk or the j-th character of the key depending on the length of the key and ℓ.}
  $table[i][\ell + 1] \leftarrow v_i$;
 end for
cnuf // Output : $table[p][\ell + 1]$ e.g. Table 2.

func Classify() // Inputs: data table (*i.e.*, $table[p][\ell+1]$) and kv.

 $\Phi \leftarrow$ GetPossibleValues(b); {Returns a list of all the values that appear in the table for a given attribute (b), duplicates deleted.}
 if $|\Phi| = 1${Does kv has only one value? If any, call it v_k.} **then**
  InstallNodeOfTree(kv,v_k); {The leaf of the tree. }
 else
  $b \leftarrow$ BestAttribute(); {Select the best one to test next.}
  for $\phi \in \Phi$ **do**
   $InstallNodeOfTree(b, \phi); table \leftarrow GetSubTable(\phi); Classify()$;
  end for
 end if
cnuf // Output: the decision tree.

function BestAttribute()

 $\Theta \leftarrow$ attributes();{Returns all attributes of the current data table except kv.}
 for $\theta \in \Theta$ **do**
  $e \leftarrow Entropy(\theta)$; Collect (e, θ) into P_θ
 end for
 $b \leftarrow$ Select attribute form P_θ with minimum entropy.
 return(b);
cnuf

func Entropy(θ) // θ stands for an attribute (*e.g.*, b_1)

 $x \leftarrow$ NumberOfRows(); $\Phi \leftarrow$ GetPossibleValues(θ);
 for $\phi \in \Phi$ **do**
  $\psi \leftarrow$ ConditionedEntropy(θ, ϕ); $y \leftarrow$ CountOccurrences(θ, ϕ);
  $z = \psi \times \frac{y}{x}$; Collect z into Z.
 end for
 $e = Sum(Z)$; **return**(e);

cnuf
func ConditionedEntropy(attribute,value)

$S \leftarrow 0$; $V_k \leftarrow$ GetPossibleValues(kv);
for $v_k \in V_k$ **do**
    probability $\leftarrow$ Prob(kv, v_k, attribute,value);
    $S \leftarrow S + $ (probability $\times \log_2$(probability));
end for
return(-S);

cnuf
func Prob(kv, v_k, attribute, value)

$v_1 \leftarrow$ CondCount(kv,v_k attribute value); {How many times does kv take v_k, and attribute takes value?}
$v_2 \leftarrow$ CountOccurrence(attribute,value); {How many times does the specified attribute take the specified value?}
$v_3 \leftarrow$ Coerce(v_2); {Arithmetic precision in double float.}
return($\frac{v_1}{v_3}$);

cnuf

The best attribute to select next is the one with the lowest entropy. The entropy of each attributes in the data table is computed according to the function *Entropy*, and the lowest one selected. The total entropy of an attribute, with respect to a target attribute is a weighted sum of the conditioned entropies given all possible values of the attribute. It represents the expected amount of information left to be determined after the value for attribute has been specified. This value is minimum for the best attribute to be tested next. The conditioned entropy of the target attribute, given that attribute has a particular value is computed from the conditional probabilities (*Prob*). The function *Prob* computes the conditioned probability that the target attribute (*i.e.*, kv) has value v_k (*i.e.*, i'th value of kv), given that a particular attribute has a value. This is computed for a particular set of data by actually computing the frequency with which the target attribute takes the value v_k when the attribute has the specified value, divided by the overall frequency with which the attribute has value, where value is the j'th value of attribute. Note that our classification algorithm is similar to the one used in ID3, with following differences: (1) In ID3 any attribute can be the target attribute whereas the target one is our algorithm is the key-value (kv); (2) In ID3 there should be on place the tests for the appropriateness of the input (*e.g.*, few attributes or data), whereas in our case, thanks to *FormInputForLearning*, this isn't necessary. (3) The memory can be saved by the following data structure of *table*: (a) allocate at most ℓ memory places (string) for each element of the first column (of the table) except the first one (*i.e.*, $table[1][\ell+1]$). (b) represent the other elements - the majority of the cases - just by a short integer. These considerations bring the simplifications and efficiency in our code compared to ID3.

4   Experiments and Comparisons

Based on the main algorithm described in Section 3 we have created implementation of dictionaries. Below, we illustrate the benefits our method by reporting the results using the three following inputs.

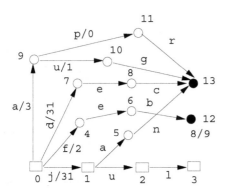

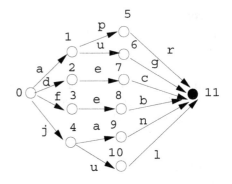

Fig. 1. An acyclic 2-subsequential transducer obtained by the method of Mihov and Maurel [13, Page 150]. A (14,16)–automaton and minimal except for the word *jul*.

Fig. 2. Our solution - a (12,16) unlabeled automaton. The output function (*e.g.*, $kv(feb) = \{28/29\}$) is learned by questions posed about the last character (b1) of the keys of the input language *e.g.*, If b1='c/g/l/n' Then kv=31.

Input 1: Let us consider the following example due to Mihov and Maurel [13, Page 150]: $f = \{(apr, 30), (aug, 31), (dec, 31), (feb, 28/29), (jan, 31), (jul, 31)\}$.

Figure 1 shows the associated transducer - a (14,16)–automaton which can be obtained using their method. Figure 2 reports our solution: a (12,16) unlabeled automaton. The output function is learned via b_1 as the best attribute and the root of the dt of three leaves: (1) If b_1 ='c/g/l/n' Then kv=31; (2) If b_1='r' Then kv=30; (3) If b_1='b' Then kv=28/29.

Input 2: The benefits of our work can be best described in the case of the ambiguous finite–state transducers (AFST). An AFST returns for every accepted input string one or more output strings by following different alternative paths from the initial state to a final state [12]. In addition, there may be a number of other paths that are followed from the initial state up to a certain point where they fail. Following these latter paths is necessary but represents an inefficiency (loss of time). Consider the input alphabet $\{a, b, c\}$ along with the followings input and output languages: $\{cabba, cabca\}$ and $kv(cabca) = \{yzxxy, yzyyy\}$; $kv(cabba) = \{xxxxx, xxyyx, xyzyx\}$ respectively. The output function can easily be characterized using b_2 as shown in Figure 4: a (7,7) automaton along with two decision rules. Figure 3 is due to Kempe [12, Page 158] showing a (13,16) automaton for this input.

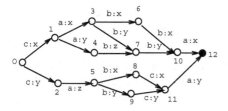

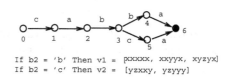

If b2 = 'b' Then v1 = [xxxxx, xxyyx, xyzyx]
If b2 = 'c' Then v2 = [yzxxy, yzyyy]

Fig. 3. Example of ambiguous finite-state transducer shown by a (13,16) automaton [12, Page 158].

Fig. 4. Our alternative - a (7,7) unlabeled automaton along with two decision rules.

Input 3: French linguists divided the French infinitive verbs of the third group (fv3 - irregular ones) into 60 classes ranging from 23 to 82 [3]. Suppose, we are interested in determining the class-number of any verb of fv3. An obvious solution is to use the longest common suffix of each class established by linguists. For instance, one can say that, if a verb (of fv3) ends in '-êtir' then the key-value is 26, and so on. But, our classification *beats* such *'onerous'* classification by providing a cheap one: If the fourth character from right-to-left (b_4) of a recognized verb is 'ê' then the output value is 26. Another path–solution is ($b4$ é b6 q kv 24) meaning that if b4='é' and b6='q' then the output value is 24. Our experiment done on fv3 with 363 (p) verbs outputs a (310,652)–automaton and a decision tree of 109 leaves. Part of the latter is shown below in terms of the path–solutions which is easier to visualize.

(b4 ê kv 26) (b4 é b6 q kv 24) (b4 é b6 * kv 37) (b4 v b6 e b8 p kv 45) (b4 v b6 e b8 * kv 44) (b4 v b6 d kv 42) (b4 v b6 s kv 41) (b4 v b6 u kv 40) (b4 v b6 r kv 39) ... (b4 î b7 c kv 67) (b4 î b7 e b6 n kv 65) (b4 î b7 e b6 p kv 66) (b4 î b7 * b6 n kv 65) (b4 î b7 * b6 p kv 66) (b4 î b7 a kv 64) (b4 î b7 n kv 64) ... (b4 u b6 - kv 82) (b4 u b6 t kv 82) (b4 u b6 a kv 82) (b4 u b6 r kv 82) ... (b4 u b6 * kv 82) (b4 u b6 s kv 72) (b4 u b6 m b3 r kv 34) (b4 u b6 m b3 d kv 74) (b4 u b6 c b3 r kv 33) (b4 u b6 c b3 d kv 73)

Since, we have 60 classes, then the optimization of the dt is desired. This is done by two process. First, by removing the star–tests (*e.g.,* b6='*') in the sub-trees and then by shifting the reduced branches to the rightmost of the current subtree. Shifting is required because careless losses the desired output value. Second, by regrouping the identical output values having the most common branches in the same subtree. We performs this phase when $|V| < p$. Consider the following subtree: {(b4 î b7 * b6 n kv 65) (b4 î b7 * b6 p kv 66), (b4 î b7 a kv 64), (b4 î b7 n kv 64)}, after removing two star–tests (and hence two transfers), the reduced form is: {(b4 î b7 a kv 64),(b4 î b7 n kv 64),(b4 î b6 n kv 65) (b4 î b6 p kv 66)}. By applying the second phase we obtain: {(b4 î b7 a/n kv 64), (b4 î b6 n kv 65),(b4 î b6 p kv 66)}. We omit the optimization algorithm due to the space limitation. The integration of these two phases in our present implementation, as well as, the implementations of *all* alternative techniques mentioned in this paper for the fair comparison (*i.e.*, same data, same machine, same programming language) with our work is desired.

Acknowledgments. I thank Bruce W. Watson for his valuable helps about this work. This work was partially supported by the Conseil Régional de Lorraine.

References

1. Aoe, J–I., Morimoto, K., Shishibori, M., and Park, K. A trie compaction algorithm for a large set of keys. *IEEE Transaction on Knowledge and Data Engineering 8*, 3 (1996), 476–491.
2. Bentley, J., and Sedgewick B. Fast algorithms for sorting and searching strings. In *Annual ACM-SIAM Symposium on Discrete Algorithms* (1996), pp. 1–10.
3. Bescherelle. *L'art de Conjuguer*. Hatier, Paris, 1966.
4. Czech, Z. J., and Majewski, B. S. An optimal algorithm for generating minimal perfect hash function. *Information Processing Letters 43* (1992), 257–264.
5. Daciuk, J., Mihov, S., Watson, B. W., and Watson, R. E. Incremental construction of finite-state automata. *Association for Computational Linguistics 26*, 1 (2000), 3–16.
6. Brain, M. D., and Tharp, A. L. Using trie to eliminate pattern collision in perfect hashing. *IEEE Transaction on Knowledge and Data Engineering 6* (1994), 476–491.
7. Fatholahzadeh, A. DAWG–ID3: Retrieving key-information using graph and classification algorithms. In *International Symposium on Database Technology & Software Engineering, WEB and Cooperative Systems* (2000), Lasker G. E. and Gerhard W. (eds.), 117–124.
8. Fatholahzadeh, A. Experiments with automata and information gain. In *International Conference on Implementation and Application of Automata* (2000), Daley M., Eramian E., and Yu S. (eds.), 252.
9. Fatholahzadeh, A. Nationality word graph for fast information retrieval. In *Collaborative Electronic Commerce Technology and Research* (2000), Williams M. A.and P. Swatman P. (eds.), International Conference on Knowledge Representation, 1–12. Available via www.collecter.org/collUSA.
10. Fatholahzadeh, A. Tagging nationality words using automata. In *ROMMAND: RObust Methods in Analysis of Natural Language Data* (Swiss 2000), Ballim A., Pallotta V., and Ghorbel H. (eds.), 69–76.
11. Fatholahzadeh, A. Online treatment of official names. In *International Conference on Artificial Intelligence* (2001), Arabnia H. R.(ed.), 203–209.
12. Kempe, A. Factorizations of ambiguous finite-state transducers. In *International Conference on Implementation and Application of Automata* (2000), Daley M., Eramian M., and Yu S. (eds.), 157–164.
13. Mihov, S., and Murel, D. Direct construction of minimal acyclic sub-sequential transducers. In *International Conference on Implementation and Application of Automata* (2000), Daley M., Eramian E., and S.Yu (eds.), 150–156.
14. Mitchell, T. M. *Machine Learning*. Mc Graw-Hill, 1997.
15. Mohri, M. On some application of finite-state automata theory to natural language. *Natural Language Engineering 2*, 1 (1996), 1–20.
16. Mohri, M. Finite-state transducers in language and speech processing. *Computational Linguistics 23*, 2 (1997), 269–311.

17. Mohri, M. Generic ϵ−removal algorithm for weighted automata. In *International Conference on Implementation and Application of Automata* (2000), Daley M., Eramian E., and Yu S. (eds.) 26–35.

18. Quinlan, R. *C4.5: Programs for Machine Learning.* Morgan Kaufmann, 1993.

19. Rozenberg G. and Salomaa A. (eds.) *Handbook of Formal Language.* Springer–Verlag, Berlin Heidelberg, 1997.

Feedback-Free Circuits in the Algebra of Transients

Mihaela Gheorghiu and Janusz Brzozowski

School of Computer Science,
University of Waterloo,
Waterloo, ON, Canada N2L 3G1
{mgheorgh,brzozo}@uwaterloo.ca

Abstract. An efficient simulation algorithm using an algebra of transients for gate circuits was proposed by Brzozowski and Ésik. This algorithm seems capable of predicting all the signal changes that can occur in a circuit under worst-case delay conditions. We verify this claim by comparing simulation with binary analysis. For any feedback-free circuit consisting of 1- and 2-input gates and started in a stable state, we prove that all signal changes predicted by simulation occur in binary analysis, provided that wire delays are taken into account. Two types of finite automata play an important role in our proof.

1 Introduction

Detecting signal changes in digital circuits is important, because unwanted (hazardous) signal changes may affect the correctness of computations, and increase the computation time and energy consumption. To address this problem, Brzozowski and Ésik [1] proposed an infinite-valued algebra C of transients, and an efficient simulation algorithm for gate circuits based on this algebra. In a companion paper [2] we compare the simulation of a circuit in C to the traditional binary analysis. We show that simulation of an arbitrary circuit is sufficient: all the changes that occur in binary analysis are also predicted by the simulation. In general, however, simulation is more pessimistic than binary analysis. It is the purpose of this paper to determine how pessimistic the simulation can be.

Here we consider the class of feedback-free gate circuits with stable initial states. Although this is a special case, it is important in practice. For this case, we show that all the changes predicted by simulation also occur in binary analysis, provided that wire delays are taken into account. Our result is limited to gate circuits constructed with 1- or 2-input gates; the general case remains open.

This paper is as self-contained as possible. The reader should see [2] for more details, and [5] for complete background information and proofs.

2 Circuits, Networks, and Binary Analysis

For an integer $n > 0$, $[n]$ denotes $\{1, \ldots, n\}$. Boolean operations OR, NOT, and XOR are denoted $\vee$, $^-$, and $\underline{\vee}$, respectively.

Figure 1(a) shows a gate circuit consisting of an inverter and an OR gate. It has input variable X_1 and state variables s_a and s_b. Each state variable s_i has an *excitation*

J.-M. Champarnaud and D. Maurel (Eds.): CIAA 2002, LNCS 2608, pp. 106–116, 2003.
© Springer-Verlag Berlin Heidelberg 2003

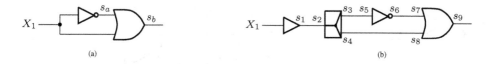

Fig. 1. Circuit C_1 and its complete version

S_i, which is the Boolean function of the corresponding gate. Here, $S_a = \overline{X_1}$, and $S_b = X_1 \lor s_a$. The value of a variable may be different from that of its excitation. This allows us to represent the delay of a gate. A variable normally follows its excitation. However, if the excitation changes quickly, the variable may fail to follow the excitation, because of the inertial nature of the delay.

To account for other delays, we construct the *complete* counterpart of a circuit by adding the following variables. For each input X_i, we add an *input-gate* variable s_i; we represent the input gate by a triangle. We also consider each fork as a *fork gate*,[1] and add a variable for each fork output; we represent a fork gate by a rectangle. Finally, we add a variable for each wire. The excitations of the added variables are identity functions. For our example, see Fig. 1. We add input-gate variable s_1, fork-gate variables s_3 and s_4, wire variables s_2, s_5, s_7, and s_8, and we relabel s_a as s_6 and s_b as s_9. The new excitations are: $S_1 = X_1$, $S_2 = s_1$, $S_3 = S_4 = s_2$, $S_5 = s_3$, $S_6 = \overline{s_5}$, $S_7 = s_6$, $S_8 = s_4$, $S_9 = s_7 \lor s_8$.

Any circuit, complete or not complete, is modeled by a network.

Definition 1. *A network [3] is a tuple $N = \langle \mathcal{D}, \mathcal{X}, \mathcal{S}, \mathcal{E} \rangle$, where $\mathcal{D}$ is the domain of values, $\mathcal{X} = \{X_1, \dots, X_n\}$, the set of inputs, $\mathcal{S} = \{s_1, \dots, s_m\}$, the set of state variables with associated excitations $S_1, \dots, S_m$, and $\mathcal{E} \subseteq (\mathcal{X} \times \mathcal{S}) \cup (\mathcal{S} \times \mathcal{S})$, a set of directed edges. There is an edge between x and y iff the excitation of y depends on x. The* network graph *is the digraph $(\mathcal{X} \cup \mathcal{S}, \mathcal{E})$.*

A *state* of N is an m-tuple b of values from $\mathcal{D}$ assigned to state variables $s_1, \dots, s_m$. A *total state* is an $(n + m)$-tuple $c = a \cdot b$ of values from $\mathcal{D}$, the n-tuple a being the inputs, and the m-tuple b, the state. The value of S_i in $a \cdot b$ is denoted $S_i(a \cdot b)$. The tuple of all $S_i(a \cdot b)$, for $i \in [m]$, is denoted $S(a \cdot b)$. For any $a \cdot b$, the set of unstable state variables is $U(a \cdot b) = \{s_i \mid b_i \neq S_i(a \cdot b)\}$. Thus, $a \cdot b$ is *stable* iff $U(a \cdot b) = \emptyset$. For any state variable $s_i \in \mathcal{S}$, we define its *fan-in set* $\phi(s_i) = \{x \mid x \in \mathcal{X} \cup \mathcal{S}, (x, s_i) \in \mathcal{E}\}$. We call state variables s_i and s_j *related* if $s_i \mathcal{E}^+ s_j$ or $s_j \mathcal{E}^+ s_i$, where $\mathcal{E}^+$ is the transitive closure of $\mathcal{E}$; otherwise, we call them *unrelated*.

For binary analysis we use the binary domain, $\mathcal{D} = \{0, 1\}$. We describe the behavior of a network started in a given state with the input kept constant at value $a \in \{0, 1\}^n$ by defining a binary relation R_a on the set $\{0, 1\}^m$ of states of N. For any $b \in \{0, 1\}^m$, bR_ab, if $U(a \cdot b) = \emptyset$, and bR_ab^K, if $U(a \cdot b) \neq \emptyset$, and K is any nonempty subset of $U(a \cdot b)$, where by b^K we mean b with the variables in K complemented. No other pairs are related by R_a. As usual, we associate a digraph with the R_a relation, and denote it G_a.

---

[1] Our reason for calling input delays and forks *gates* will become clear later.

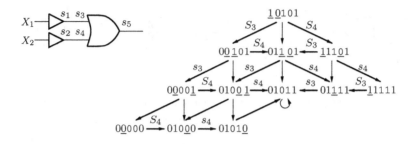

Fig. 2. Circuit C_2 and its binary analysis

For given $a \in \{0,1\}^n$, and $b \in \{0,1\}^m$ we define the set of all states reachable from b in relation R_a as $reach(R_a(b)) = \{c \mid b R_a^* c\}$, where R_a^* is the reflexive and transitive closure of R_a. We denote by $G_a(b)$ the subgraph of G_a corresponding to $reach(R_a(b))$.

Example 1. For the complete circuit in Figure 2, with excitations $S_1 = X_1$, $S_2 = X_2$, $S_3 = s_1$, $S_4 = s_2$, $S_5 = s_3 \vee s_4$, we show $G_{01}(10101)$, where tuples are shown as words, unstable variables are underlined, and boldface features and edge labels are for later use.

3   Transients, Gate Automata, and Extended Functions

A *transient* [1] is a nonempty word over $\{0,1\}$ in which no two consecutive symbols are the same. Thus the set of all transients is

$$\mathbf{T} = 0(10)^* \cup 1(01)^* \cup 0(10)^*1 \cup 1(01)^*0.$$

Transients represent changing signals in a natural way; for instance, transient 010 represents a signal changing from 0 to 1 to 0. For any $\mathbf{t} \in \mathbf{T}$ we denote by $\alpha(\mathbf{t})$ and $\omega(\mathbf{t})$ its first and last characters, respectively, and by $|\mathbf{t}|$, its length. A transient can be obtained from any nonempty binary word by *contraction*, *i.e.*, the elimination of duplicates immediately following a symbol (*e.g.*, the contraction of 00100011 is 0101). For a binary word s we denote its contraction by $\hat{s}$. For any $\mathbf{t}, \mathbf{t}' \in \mathbf{T}$, we denote by $\mathbf{t} \circ \mathbf{t}'$ concatenation followed by contraction, *i.e.*, $\mathbf{t} \circ \mathbf{t}' = \widehat{\mathbf{tt}'}$.

Extensions of Boolean functions to the domain $\mathbf{T}$ of transients were defined in [1]. Here we give an equivalent definition using finite automata, needed for later proofs. For common Boolean functions, [1] gives simpler formulas for computing extensions. For example, let $\oplus$ be the extension of the OR function. Then, for transients $\mathbf{w}, \mathbf{w}'$ of length > 1, $\mathbf{w} \oplus \mathbf{w}' = \mathbf{t}$, where $\mathbf{t}$ is such that

$$\alpha(\mathbf{t}) = \alpha(\mathbf{w}) \vee \alpha(\mathbf{w}'), \quad \omega(\mathbf{t}) = \omega(\mathbf{w}) \vee \omega(\mathbf{w}'), \quad \text{and} \quad z(\mathbf{t}) = z(\mathbf{w}) + z(\mathbf{w}') - 1,$$

where $z(\mathbf{t})$ is the number of 0s in $\mathbf{t}$. Also,

$$\mathbf{t} \oplus 0 = 0 \oplus \mathbf{t} = \mathbf{t}, \quad \text{and} \quad \mathbf{t} \oplus 1 = 1 \oplus \mathbf{t} = 1.$$

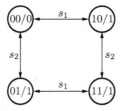

Fig. 3. OR gate automaton

Let s_i be the state variable of a gate, let $\phi(s_i) = \{s_1, \dots, s_k\}$, and let the excitation S_i be Boolean function $f : \{0,1\}^k \to \{0,1\}$. We extend f to $\mathbf{f} : \mathbf{T}^k \to \mathbf{T}$. For any tuple $(\mathbf{t}_1, \dots, \mathbf{t}_k)$ of transients, $\mathbf{f}(\mathbf{t}_1, \dots, \mathbf{t}_k)$ is the longest transient the gate could produce at its output, if its inputs changed as shown by the k transients. Formally, the definition uses a finite automaton to model the gate behavior. For any $j \in [k]$, we denote by e_j the j-th unit tuple in $\{0,1\}^k$ that has a 1 in position j and 0s elsewhere. By taking the component-wise exclusive OR of a tuple $t \in \{0,1\}^k$ with e_j, we obtain the tuple $t' \in \{0,1\}^k$ that differs from t only in the jth component.

Definition 2. *The gate automaton of a gate s_i with Boolean function $f : \{0,1\}^k \to \{0,1\}$ is an (uninitialized) Moore machine $\mathcal{G}_i = (I_i, O, \mathcal{P}_i, \tau_i, o_i)$, where $I_i = \phi(s_i)$ is the input alphabet, $O = \{0,1\}$, the output alphabet, $\mathcal{P}_i = \{0,1\}^k$, the set of states, $\tau_i : \mathcal{P}_i \times I_i \to \mathcal{P}_i$, the transition function defined for $p \in \mathcal{P}_i$, $s_j \in I_i$ as $\tau_i(p, s_j) = p \veebar e_j$, and $o_i : \mathcal{P}_i \to O$, the output function defined for $p \in \mathcal{P}_i$ as $o_i(p) = f(p)$. If $\mathcal{G}_i$ has an initial state p_i^0, then it is denoted by $(\mathcal{G}_i, p_i^0)$.*

Example 2. The automaton of an OR gate with inputs s_1 and s_2 is shown in Fig. 3.

We extend τ_i to words as follows: for the empty word ϵ, $\tau_i(p, \epsilon) = p$, and for any $p \in \mathcal{P}_i$ and $w \in I_i^*$, $\tau_i(p, ws_j) = \tau_i(p, w) \veebar e_j$. Any state of $\mathcal{G}_i$ can be the initial state, depending on the tuple of transients for which we compute the extension. Suppose the initial state is p_i^0. In $(\mathcal{G}_i, p_i^0)$, any input word $u \in I_i^*$ produces an output word v as follows. If u is the empty word, then $v = f(p_i^0)$. Otherwise, $u = u's_j$ produces $v = wf(\tau_i(p_i^0, u))$, where w is the output word of u'. The contraction $\hat{v}$ of v is the *output profile* of u. For any tuple $(\mathbf{t}_1, \dots, \mathbf{t}_k)$ of transients, describing the changes of variables $s_1, \dots, s_k$, we choose $p_i^0 = (\alpha(\mathbf{t}_1), \dots, \alpha(\mathbf{t}_k))$. Thus p_i^0 shows the initial values of $s_1, \dots, s_k$. An input word $u \in I_i^*$ *determines* the unique tuple $(\mathbf{t}_1, \dots, \mathbf{t}_k)$ of transients if $|u|_{s_j} = |\mathbf{t}_j| - 1$, for all $j \in [k]$, where $|u|_{s_j}$ is the number of times s_j occurs in u. There may be several input words determining a given tuple of transients; let $\mathcal{U}(\mathbf{t}_1, \dots, \mathbf{t}_k)$ be the set of all words determining $(\mathbf{t}_1, \dots, \mathbf{t}_k)$. Let $\mathcal{V}(\mathbf{t}_1, \dots, \mathbf{t}_k)$ be the set of output profiles of the words in $\mathcal{U}(\mathbf{t}_1, \dots, \mathbf{t}_k)$, and let $v_{max}(\mathbf{t}_1, \dots, \mathbf{t}_k)$ be the longest profile in $\mathcal{V}(\mathbf{t}_1, \dots, \mathbf{t}_k)$.

Definition 3. *For any Boolean function $f : \{0,1\}^k \to \{0,1\}$, we define its extension $\mathbf{f} : \mathbf{T}^k \to \mathbf{T}$ by $\mathbf{f}(\mathbf{t}_1, \dots, \mathbf{t}_k) = v_{max}(\mathbf{t}_1, \dots, \mathbf{t}_k)$, for all $(\mathbf{t}_1, \dots, \mathbf{t}_k) \in \mathbf{T}^k$.*

Definition 4. *For gate automaton $(\mathcal{G}_i, p_i^0)$, an input word $u \in I_i^*$ is called* worst-case *if u determines $(\mathbf{t}_1, \ldots, \mathbf{t}_k)$, and has the longest output profile among the words in $\mathcal{U}(\mathbf{t}_1, \ldots, \mathbf{t}_k)$, i.e., if $\hat{v} = v_{max}(\mathbf{t}_1, \ldots, \mathbf{t}_k)$, where v is the output word of u.*

Example 3. We illustrate the new concepts of this section. Consider the automaton of Fig. 3, with $p_i^0 = 00$. The output produced by $u = s_1 s_2 s_1$ is $v = 0111$, and its output profile is $\hat{v} = 01$. If $u = s_1 s_1 s_2 s_2$, then $v = 01010$, and $\hat{v} = 01010$. Also

$$\mathcal{U}(010, 010) = \{s_1 s_2 s_1 s_2, \; s_1 s_2 s_2 s_1, s_1 s_1 s_2 s_2, \; s_2 s_1 s_1 s_2, \; s_2 s_1 s_2 s_1, \; s_2 s_2 s_1 s_1\}.$$

We compute $01 \oplus 010$. We find $\mathcal{U}(01, 010) = \{s_1 s_2 s_2, \; s_2 s_1 s_2, \; s_2 s_2 s_1\}$ and $\mathcal{V} = \{01, 0101\}$. Hence $01 \oplus 010 = 0101$. Word $s_2 s_2 s_1$ is worst-case, in contrast to $s_1 s_2 s_2$ or $s_2 s_1 s_2$.

4   Simulation

To simulate a circuit having binary network $N = \langle \{0, 1\}, \mathcal{X}, \mathcal{S}, \mathcal{E} \rangle$, we use the *transient network* $\mathbf{N} = \langle \mathbf{T}, \mathcal{X}, \mathcal{S}, \mathcal{E} \rangle$. The inputs and state variables of N and $\mathbf{N}$ are the same, but in $\mathbf{N}$ they take values in the domain $\mathbf{T}$, and excitations in $\mathbf{N}$ are the extensions to $\mathbf{T}$ of the Boolean excitations in N. Binary variables, words, tuples and excitations in N are denoted by italic characters (*e.g.*, s, S). Transients, tuples of transients, and excitations in $\mathbf{N}$ are denoted by boldface characters (*e.g.*, $\mathbf{s}$, $\mathbf{S}$).

The simulation consists of Algorithm $\tilde{A}$ [1] given below. We want to know what happens when the network starts in a stable binary initial state $\tilde{a} \cdot b$, and the input is changed to a. We set the input of network $\mathbf{N}$ to $\tilde{a} \circ a$, where $\circ$ is applied componentwise. We then change all variable values to the values of their excitations. For feedback-free circuits $\tilde{A}$ always terminates. Let the sequence of states produced by $\tilde{A}$ be $\mathbf{s}^0, \ldots, \mathbf{s}^H$. This sequence is nondecreasing in the prefix order on $\mathbf{T}$; we say that $\tilde{A}$ is *monotonic*.

Algorithm $\tilde{A}$

$\mathbf{a} = \tilde{a} \circ a;$

$\mathbf{s}^0 := b;$

$h := 1;$

$\mathbf{s}^h := \mathbf{S}(\mathbf{a} \cdot \mathbf{s}^0);$

while $(\mathbf{s}^h <> \mathbf{s}^{h-1})$ **do**

  $h := h + 1;$

  $\mathbf{s}^h := \mathbf{S}(\mathbf{a} \cdot \mathbf{s}^{h-1});$

$\mathbf{X}_1$	s_1	s_2	s_3	s_4	s_5	s_6	s_7	s_8	s_9	state
01	0	0	0	0	0	1	1	0	1	$\mathbf{s}^0$
01	01	0	0	0	0	1	1	0	1	$\mathbf{s}^1$
01	01	01	0	0	0	1	1	0	1	$\mathbf{s}^2$
01	01	01	01	01	0	1	1	0	1	$\mathbf{s}^3$
01	01	01	01	01	01	1	1	01	1	$\mathbf{s}^4$
01	01	01	01	01	01	10	1	01	1	$\mathbf{s}^5$
01	01	01	01	01	01	10	10	01	1	$\mathbf{s}^6$
01	01	01	01	01	01	10	10	01	101	$\mathbf{s}^7$

Example 4. For the circuit of Fig. 1(b), the extended excitations are: $\mathbf{S}_1 = \mathbf{X}_1$, $\mathbf{S}_2 = \mathbf{s}_1$, $\mathbf{S}_3 = \mathbf{S}_4 = \mathbf{s}_2$, $\mathbf{S}_5 = \mathbf{s}_3, \mathbf{S}_6 = \overline{\mathbf{s}_5}$, $\mathbf{S}_7 = \mathbf{s}_6$, $\mathbf{S}_8 = \mathbf{s}_4$, $\mathbf{S}_9 = \mathbf{s}_7 \oplus \mathbf{s}_8$. Input $\mathbf{X}_1$ changes from $\tilde{a} = 0$ to $a = 1$, and $b = 000001101$. The result is in the table above.

Theorem 1. *Let $\tilde{\mathbf{N}} = \langle \mathbf{T}, \mathcal{X}, \tilde{\mathcal{S}}, \tilde{\mathcal{E}} \rangle$ be the complete version of a feedback-free network $\mathbf{N} = \langle \mathbf{T}, \mathcal{X}, \mathcal{S}, \mathcal{E} \rangle$. Let $\mathbf{s}^H$ be the result of Algorithm $\tilde{A}$ for $\tilde{\mathbf{N}}$ started in stable binary total state $\tilde{a} \cdot \tilde{b}$, with input $\tilde{a} \circ a$. Let $\mathbf{s}^G$ be the result of Algorithm $\tilde{A}$ for $\mathbf{N}$, started in stable binary total state $\tilde{a} \cdot b$, where $b_i = \tilde{b}_i$, for all $s_i \in \mathcal{S}$, with the same input. Then $\mathbf{s}^H$ and $\mathbf{s}^G$ agree on the variables in $\mathcal{S}$.*

The proof is given in [5]. The theorem shows that adding wire delays to **N** does not affect the number of signal changes in **N**. In other words, simulation takes wire delays into account automatically.

5   Covering of Simulation by Binary Analysis

Let N be the binary network of a complete feedback-free circuit. We start N in stable total state $\tilde{a} \cdot b$, and change the input tuple $\tilde{a}$ to a. In the resulting state $a \cdot b$ only the input gates corresponding to the inputs that change are unstable, all other state variables being stable. Let $G_a(b)$ be the result of the binary analysis of N with initial state $a \cdot b$. Here, by a *path in* $G_a(b)$ we always mean a path starting in state b.

Definition 5. *Let* $\pi = s^0, \dots, s^h$ *be any path in* $G_a(b)$. *Recall that each* s^j *is a tuple* $(s_1^j, \dots, s_m^j)$. *For any* $i \in [m]$, *we denote by* σ_i^π *the transient* $s_i^0 \dots s_i^h$ *showing the changes of* s_i *along* π. *We call* σ_i^π *the* history *of* s_i. *We also define* Σ_i^π *to be* $\widehat{E_i}$, *where* $E_i = S_i(a \cdot s^0) \dots S_i(a \cdot s^h)$ *is the transient showing the changes of* S_i *along* π. *We call* Σ_i^π *the* excitation history *of* s_i. *We denote by* σ^π *the tuple* $(\sigma_1^\pi, \dots, \sigma_m^\pi)$.

Let **N** be the transient counterpart of N, and let the result of Algorithm $\tilde{\text{A}}$ for **N**, with initial state $\tilde{a} \cdot b$, and input $\tilde{a} \circ a$ be $\mathbf{s}^0, \dots, \mathbf{s}^H$. If we find a path π in $G_a(b)$ whose history matches the last state $\mathbf{s}^H$ of the simulation, then π covers all simulation states, due to the monotonicity of Algorithm $\tilde{\text{A}}$. Thus, we are looking for a *matching* path, defined next.

Definition 6. *Let* π *be a path in* $G_a(b)$. *Let* $V \subseteq S$ *be a set of state variables in* N. *Path* π *is* matching on V *if* $\sigma_i^\pi = \mathbf{s}_i^H$, *for all* $s_i \in V$.

Our main result is stated next. The rest of the paper is devoted to its proof.

Theorem 2. *Binary analysis covers simulation in the following sense. There exists a path* π *in* $G_a(b)$ *that is matching on* S, *i.e., that satisfies* $\sigma^\pi = \mathbf{s}^H$.

Let $G'_a(b)$ be the subgraph of $G_a(b)$ in which exactly one unstable variable changes at each step. For example, $G'_a(b)$ is shown in boldface in Fig. 2. The next proposition [5], stated without proof, allows us to restrict ourselves to $G'_a(b)$. Paths π and π' are *equivalent* if they have the same history, *i.e.*, if $\sigma^\pi = \sigma^{\pi'}$.

Proposition 1. *For any path* π *in* $G_a(b)$ *there exists an equivalent path* π' *in* $G'_a(b)$.

Since the circuit is feedback-free, we can arrange the state variables of N in levels as follows: level 0 consists of the input gates; level 1 is comprised of all variables whose fan-in set belongs to level 0, and in general level l consists of all variables whose fan-in variables belong to levels $< l$, and which have at least one fan-in variable in level $l-1$. This level assignment results in even levels containing gate variables and odd levels containing wire variables.[2] We use $level(s_i)$ to denote the level of s_i. The last level of any network is always a gate level, so N has an even number $2L$ of levels. Let $2l$,

---

[2] For this reason we consider input delays and forks as gates.

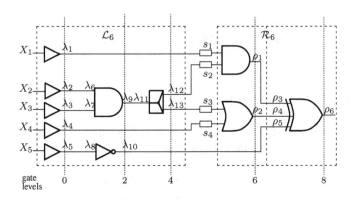

Fig. 4. Sample circuit with partition.

where $0 < l \leq L$, be a gate level of the circuit. Let $V_{2l} = \{s_i \in \mathcal{S} \mid level(s_i) = 2l\}$. Let $V = \bigcup_{s_i \in V_{2l}} \phi(s_i)$. Suppose $V = \{s_1, \ldots, s_K\}$. Note that $s_1, \ldots, s_K$ are all wire variables and are initially stable; they are not necessarily all of level $2l-1$, but they belong to levels $< 2l$. The circuit is partitioned by these variables into two areas, denoted $\mathcal{L}_{2l}$ and $\mathcal{R}_{2l}$. Area $\mathcal{L}_{2l}$ contains the gates of level 0 and those of levels $< 2l$ together with their fan-in variables. Area $\mathcal{R}_{2l}$ contains the gates of level $2l$ and those of levels $> 2l$ together with their fan-in variables. Since the circuit is feedback-free, there are no signals flowing from $\mathcal{R}_{2l}$ to $\mathcal{L}_{2l}$, but there may be wires that connect outputs of gates in $\mathcal{L}_{2l}$ to inputs of gates of levels $> 2l$ in $\mathcal{R}_{2l}$. Formally, $\mathcal{L}_{2l} = \bigcup_{level(s_i)=0} \{s_i\} \cup \bigcup_{0<level(s_i)<2l,}{}_{level(s_i)\ even} (\{s_i\} \cup \phi(s_i))$, and $\mathcal{R}_{2l} = \bigcup_{level(s_i)=2l} \{s_i\} \cup \bigcup_{level(s_i)>2l,}{}_{level(s_i)\ even} (\{s_i\} \cup \phi(s_i))$. Note that $\mathcal{L}_{2l}, V, \mathcal{R}_{2l}$ form a partition of the set $\mathcal{S}$ of state variables in N, $\mathcal{L}_2 = \bigcup_{level(s_i)=0} \{s_i\}$, $\mathcal{R}_{2L+2} = \emptyset$ and $\mathcal{L}_{2L+2} = \mathcal{S}$, if we assume a fictitious gate level $2L + 2$.

Example 5. We illustrate the partition in Fig. 4. Here $l = 3$. We relabel the state variables in $\mathcal{L}_{2l}$ with subscripted λs, and those in $\mathcal{R}_{2l}$, with subscripted ρs.

5.1   Proof of Theorem 2

The proof of Theorem 2 is by induction on l, where $1 \leq l \leq L$. We give only a sketch of the proof here (see [5] for details). We show there exists a path in $G'_a(b)$ that is matching on $\mathcal{L}_{2L+2} = \mathcal{S}$. The basis consists of showing there exists a path that is matching on $\mathcal{L}_2$, i.e., on the input-gate variables. In the induction step we assume we have a path τ that is matching on $\mathcal{L}_{2l}$, and construct a path π that is matching on $\mathcal{L}_{2l+2}$. A preliminary result characterizes π in terms of the *hazard-preserving* and *worst-case* properties defined next.

Definition 7. *Let π be a path in $G_a(b)$, and s_i a state variable that is initially stable. We call π hazard-preserving on s_i if $\sigma_i^\pi = \Sigma_i^\pi$. For $V \subseteq \mathcal{S}$, path π is hazard-preserving on V if it is hazard-preserving on all $s_i \in V$.*

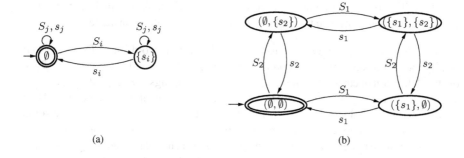

Fig. 5. Delay automata: (a) for variable s_i, and (b) for set $\{s_1, s_2\}$

Definition 8. *Let π be a path in $G_a(b)$, and s_i a gate variable implementing Boolean function $f : \{0,1\}^k \longrightarrow \{0,1\}$ that depends only on state variables. Let $\phi(s_i) = \{s_1, \ldots, s_k\}$. We call π worst-case on s_i if $\Sigma_i^\pi = \mathbf{f}(\sigma_1^\pi, \ldots, \sigma_k^\pi)$. For a set of gate variables $V \subseteq S$, path π is worst-case on V if it is worst-case on each $s_i \in V$.*

Example 6. Consider the graph in Fig. 2. Path $\pi = 10101, 00101, 00001, 01001, 01011$ is hazard-preserving on s_3 and s_4, but not on s_5, since $\sigma_5^\pi = 1$ and $\Sigma_5^\pi = 101$. Path π is worst-case on s_5, but $\pi' = 10101, 11101, 11111, 01111, 01011$ is not, since $\Sigma_5^{\pi'} = 1$ and $10 \oplus 01 = 101$.

Lemma 1. *Path π in $G'_a(b)$ is matching on $\mathcal{L}_{2l+2}$ iff it is matching on $\mathcal{L}_{2l}$, hazard-preserving on V and V_{2l}, and worst-case on V_{2l}.*

5.2 Hazard-Preserving Paths

We now characterize hazard-preserving paths by automata. For $V = \{s_1, \ldots, s_k\} \subseteq S$, let $\Xi(V) = \{S_i \mid s_i \in V\}$, and $\Delta(V) = V \cup \Xi(V)$. Suppose the variables in V are initially stable in $G'_a(b)$, unrelated to each other, and have pairwise distinct excitations. Recall that every state variable represents a delay. We want to describe the hazard-preserving behavior of these delays in $G'_a(b)$, *i.e.*, we are interested in paths on which the k delays do not 'lose' any changes. We describe the hazard-preserving behavior of $s_i \in V$ by the automaton shown in Fig. 5(a); this is $\mathcal{D}_V^i$, the *delay automaton for variable s_i*. The label on a transition of the automaton shows the excitation or variable that changes in that transition. Subscript j ranges over $[k] \setminus i$. The label of each state shows whether s_i is stable (label is $\emptyset$) or unstable (label is $\{s_i\}$) in that state. Changes of excitations or variables other than S_i and s_i do not alter the state, since variables in V are unrelated and have distinct excitations. Variable s_i changes each time it is unstable, so as not to lose any changes.

To describe the hazard-preserving behavior of all $s_i \in V$ at the same time we take the *direct product* [4] $\mathcal{D}_V$ of $\mathcal{D}_V^1, \ldots \mathcal{D}_V^k$.

Example 7. The delay automaton of set $V = \{s_1, s_2\}$ is shown in Fig. 5(b). The nonempty components of a state label show the variables that are unstable.

Let $\mathcal{L}(\mathcal{D}_V)$ be the language accepted by $\mathcal{D}_V$. We call the words in $\mathcal{L}(\mathcal{D}_V)$ *balanced on* V. By the definition of the direct product, we have $\mathcal{L}(\mathcal{D}_V) = \mathcal{L}(\mathcal{D}_V^1) \cap \ldots \cap \mathcal{L}(\mathcal{D}_V^k)$. From the definition of each $\mathcal{D}_V^i$, it follows that $w \in \Delta_V^*$ belongs to $\mathcal{L}(\mathcal{D}_V^i)$ iff $w \downarrow_{\{S_i, s_i\}} = (S_i s_i)^{c_i}$, for some integer $c_i \geq 0$, where $w \downarrow_{\mathcal{A}}$ is the projection of w to alphabet $\mathcal{A}$. Then a word $w \in \Delta_V^*$ is balanced on V iff, for all $s_i \in V$, $w \downarrow_{\{S_i, s_i\}} = (S_i s_i)^{c_i}$, for some integer $c_i \geq 0$. Language $\mathcal{L}(\mathcal{D}_V)$ is a regular subset of the *Dyck language* D_k [6].

We now establish the relation between hazard-preserving paths and delay automata. Let V be defined as before. We limit our interest to paths that are hazard-preserving on V.

To any path π in $G_a'(b)$ we associate $w^\pi \in \Delta_V^*$ called the *path-word on* V as follows: we label each step of the path with S_i if S_i changes, and with s_i if s_i changes in that step, for $S_i \in \Xi(V), s_i \in V$. Other steps are labelled by ϵ. Since the variables of V are unrelated and have distinct excitations, each step has a single label. Path-word w^π is the concatenation of the labels along path π.

Example 8. Consider $G_a(b)$ of Example 1. The subgraph $G_a'(b)$ is shown in Fig. 2 by boldface edges. We choose $V = \{s_3, s_4\}$ and show the labels on edges. The values of s_3, s_4 are also in boldface in each state. For $\pi = 10101, 00101, 01101, 01111, 01011$, $w^\pi = S_3 S_4 s_4 s_3$.

We denote by $\mathcal{H}_V$ the set of all paths in $G_a'(b)$ that are hazard-preserving on V. Let $\mathcal{W}_V = \{w^\pi \mid \pi \in \mathcal{H}_V\}$. The delay automaton is quite general, and applies to any network N and any $G_a'(b)$, as long as we find a set V that satisfies the necessary requirements. For a particular network N and $G_a'(b)$, not all words accepted by the automaton correspond to paths in $G_a'(b)$. We find a necessary and sufficient condition for a balanced word to be a path-word.

Definition 9. *A word* $w \in \mathcal{L}(\mathcal{D}_V)$ *is relevant to* $G_a'(b)$ *iff there exists a path* π *in* $G_a'(b)$ *such that* $w \downarrow_{\Xi(V)} = w^\pi \downarrow_{\Xi(V)}$. *We denote by* $\mathcal{L}(\mathcal{D}_V) \downarrow_{G_a'(b)}$ *the set of all words in* $\mathcal{L}(\mathcal{D}_V)$ *that are relevant to* $G_a'(b)$.

Example 9. For the circuit and $G_a'(b)$ of Example 8, with $V = \{s_3, s_4\}$, the delay automaton $\mathcal{D}_V$ is in Fig. 5 (right), with S_3, s_3, S_4, s_4 taking the roles of S_1, s_1, S_2, s_2, respectively. For example, $S_4 S_3 s_4 s_3$ and $S_3 s_3 S_4 s_4$ are relevant, $S_3 s_3 S_3 S_4 s_3 s_4$ and $S_3 S_4 s_4 S_4 s_3 s_4$ are irrelevant.

We state without proof (see [5] for details) the following proposition that reduces finding a hazard-preserving path to finding a relevant balanced word.

Proposition 2. $\mathcal{W}_V = \mathcal{L}(\mathcal{D}_V) \downarrow_{G_a'(b)}$.

5.3   Worst-Case Paths

We now characterize worst-case paths using gate automata. Let s_i be any gate variable in $\mathcal{S}$, with $\phi(s_i) = \{s_1, \ldots, s_k\}$, and let $(\mathcal{G}_i, p_i^0)$ be its gate automaton, with $p_i^0 =$

$(b_1, \ldots, b_k)$ (the values of $s_1, \ldots, s_k$ in b). For any path π in $G'_a(b)$ we label with s_j each step in which s_j changes, for all $j \in [k]$. The word obtained by concatenating the labels along π is an input word $u^\pi \in I_i^*$ that shows how the fan-in variables of s_i change along π. The output word v^π produced by u^π shows how the excitation S_i changes on π. Let $\mathbf{t}_1, \ldots, \mathbf{t}_k$ be the transients determined by u^π. Then the following hold: 1) $\sigma_j^\pi = \mathbf{t}_j$, for all $j \in [k]$, and 2) $\Sigma_i^\pi = \widehat{v^\pi}$. Let π be a path in $G'_a(b)$ labelled with u^π as above.

Proposition 3. *Path π is worst-case on s_i iff u^π is a worst-case word for $(\mathcal{G}_i, p_i^0)$.*

5.4   Delay Automata and Gate Automata

Having reduced finding a hazard-preserving path to finding a relevant balanced word, and finding a worst-case path to finding a worst-case word, we now state an important lemma that relates these two kinds of words, and guarantees the existence of a path that is both hazard-preserving and worst-case. For any gate variable s_i of a feedback-free circuit, we have a delay automaton $\mathcal{D}_{\phi(s_i)}$ for its fan-in set, and a gate automaton $(\mathcal{G}_i, p_i^0)$.

For any alphabet $\mathcal{A}$, a word $r \in \mathcal{A}^*$ is called *prefix-restricted* if r has a prefix r' having exactly one occurrence of each letter of r. We call r' the *key prefix* of r. For example, word $abaabb$ is prefix-restricted, with key prefix ab, but $aabab$ is not prefix-restricted.

Recall that $I_i = \phi(s_i)$, $\Xi(I_i)$ is the set of the excitations of the variables in I_i, and $\Delta_{I_i} = I_i \cup \Xi(I_i)$ is the alphabet of $\mathcal{D}_{I_i}$. The lemma below relates words over $\Xi(I_i)$ to words over I_i in the following sense. Given any prefix-restricted word over $\Xi(I_i)$, we can always find a worst-case word over I_i, such that an interleaving of the two words is a balanced word. The result is limited to 1- and 2-input gates; we conjecture the result to be true in the general case.

Lemma 2. *Let $(\mathcal{G}_i, p_i^0)$ be the gate automaton of variable s_i, for a 1- or 2-input gate. For any prefix-restricted word $r \in \Xi(I_i)^*$ having key prefix r', there exists a balanced word $w \in \mathcal{L}(\mathcal{D}_{I_i})$ such that $w{\downarrow}_{\Xi(I_i)} = r$, and $w{\downarrow}_{I_i}$ is a worst-case word for $(\mathcal{G}_i, p_i^0)$. Also, w has a prefix w' such that $w'{\downarrow}_{\Xi(I_i)} = r'$, and the output profile of $w'{\downarrow}_{I_i}$ has length 2 if the output profile of $w{\downarrow}_{I_i}$ has length > 1.*

Proposition 2 and Lemma 2 help us construct a path π satisfying the conditions of Lemma 1, and hence conclude the proof of Theorem 2. For details see [5].

6   Conclusions

Our results can be summarized as follows. Assume that we have a feedback-free gate network N, in which state variables are associated with gates only. We perform the binary analysis of N started in a stable state. We extend the Boolean functions in N to functions on transients. This gives us the transient version $\mathbf{N}$ of N. We now simulate $\mathbf{N}$ using algorithm $\tilde{\mathbf{A}}$; for feedback-free circuits this algorithm always terminates. Next, we add wire delays to N, obtaining the complete binary network $\tilde{N}$ and its transient counterpart $\tilde{\mathbf{N}}$. By Theorem 1, the simulation of $\tilde{\mathbf{N}}$ agrees with the simulation of $\mathbf{N}$ on the variables of $\mathbf{N}$. Finally, by Theorem 2, we know that binary analysis of $\tilde{N}$ covers the simulation of $\tilde{\mathbf{N}}$, and hence that of $\mathbf{N}$. In conclusion, we have shown that simulation of feedback-free circuits is not pessimistic, if wire delays are taken into account.

Acknowledgments. This research was supported by the Natural Sciences and Engineering Research Council of Canada under grant No. OGP0000871.

References

1. Brzozowski, J. A., Ésik, Z.: Hazard algebras. Formal Methods in System Design, to appear.
2. Gheorghiu, M., Brzozowski, J. A.: Simulation of gate circuits in the algebra of transients. Proc. CIAA 2002, this volume.
3. Brzozowski, J. A., Seger, C.-J. H.: Asynchronous circuits. Springer-Verlag (1995)
4. Eilenberg, S.: Automata, languages and machines, Academic Press, **A** (1974)
5. Gheorghiu, M.: Circuit simulation using a hazard algebra. MMath Thesis, School of Computer Science, University of Waterloo, Waterloo, ON, Canada (2001)
6. Salomaa, A.: Formal languages, Academic Press (1973)

On Minimizing Cover Automata for Finite Languages in $O(n \log n)$ Time

Heiko Körner

Wallgasse 14,
D–67433 Neustadt/Weinstraße,
Germany

Abstract. A deterministic finite automaton (DFA) $\mathcal{A}$ is called a cover automaton (DFCA) for a finite language L over some alphabet Σ if $L = L(\mathcal{A}) \cap \Sigma^{\leq l}$, with l being the length of some longest word in L. Thus a word $w \in \Sigma^*$ is in L if and only if $|w| \leq l$ and $w \in L(\mathcal{A})$. The DFCA $\mathcal{A}$ is *minimal* if no DFCA for L has fewer states.

In this paper, we present an algorithm which converts an n–state DFA for some finite language L into a corresponding minimal DFCA, using only $O(n \log n)$ time and $O(n)$ space. The best previously known algorithm [2] requires $O(n^2)$ time and space. Furthermore, the new algorithm can also be used to minimize any DFCA, where the best previous method [1] takes $O(n^4)$ time and space.

1 Introduction

Regular languages and finite automata (DFA) are widely used in theoretical computer science and have been studied extensively. However, many applications only deal with finite languages. In this paper we analyze *cover automata* (DFCA) which are capable of parsing these languages as follows. Let L be some finite language and l the length of its longest word(s). A DFCA for L accepts a word w with $|w| \leq l$ if and only if $w \in L$, but it may also accept additional words being longer than l. Thus deciding the membership problem with a DFCA only requires an additional comparison of two integers.

Recently, DFCA have been further elaborated [1,2,3]. Compared with ordinary DFA, corresponding DFCA are much smaller in many cases. As an example, let $L = \{a, aba, ababa\}$. Figure 1 (a) shows a minimal finite automaton accepting L with seven states. The cover automaton in Fig. 1 (b) also accepts some longer words, but only has three states. Hence DFCA are more space efficient.

Păun et.al. [3] have suggested an algorithm for converting an n–state DFA into a corresponding DFCA with the fewest possible number of states. It requires $O(n^2)$ time and space. Another algorithm [1] consuming $O(n^4)$ time and space has been proposed for directly minimizing a DFCA. However, in this paper we shall show that both problems can be solved in $O(n \log n)$ time and $O(n)$ space by decomposing the set of states of the original DFA resp. DFCA accordingly.

The paper is organized as follows. The next section reviews some notation and basic results on DFCA. Section 3 introduces *similarity state decompositions*

J.-M. Champarnaud and D. Maurel (Eds.): CIAA 2002, LNCS 2608, pp. 117–127, 2003.
© Springer-Verlag Berlin Heidelberg 2003

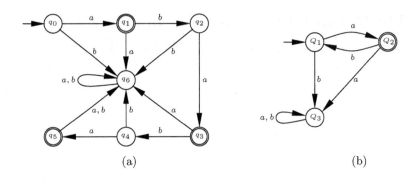

Fig. 1. A minimal DFA (a) and a minimal DFCA (b) for $L = \{a, aba, ababa\}$

(SSD). Given such a decomposition, a minimal DFCA can be easily established. An SSD can be computed with the algorithm presented in Sect. 4. Finally, Sect. 5 contains the complexity analysis and some concluding remarks.

2 Preliminaries

We assume the reader to be familiar with the theory of finite automata as presented in standard books, e.g. [6]. A DFA is a quintuple $\mathcal{A} = (Q, \Sigma, \delta, q_0, F)$, where $Q = \{q_0, \ldots, q_{n-1}\}$ is a finite set of states, Σ is a finite nonempty set of input symbols, $\delta : Q \times \Sigma \to Q$ is a (total) transition function, $q_0 \in Q$ is the initial state, and $F \subseteq Q$ is the set of final states. We extend δ to $Q \times \Sigma^*$ by setting $\delta(q, \varepsilon) = q$ and $\delta(q, aw) = \delta(\delta(q, a), w)$, where $a \in \Sigma$ and $w \in \Sigma^*$. Let $|w|$ be the length of a word $w \in \Sigma^*$. For $k \geq 0$ let $\Sigma^{\leq k} = \{w \in \Sigma^* \mid |w| \leq k\}$. The language recognised by $\mathcal{A}$ is $L(\mathcal{A}) = \{w \in \Sigma^* \mid \delta(q_0, w) \in F\}$.

For the rest of the paper, we assume L to be some fixed finite language. By l we denote the maximal length of a word in L.

Definition 1. *A DFA $\mathcal{A}$ is a deterministic finite cover automaton (DFCA) for L iff $L(\mathcal{A}) \cap \Sigma^{\leq l} = L$. (We then also say that $\mathcal{A}$ covers L.) $\mathcal{A}$ is called minimal if no DFCA for L has fewer states than $\mathcal{A}$.*

All states of a DFCA $\mathcal{A} = (Q, \Sigma, \delta, q_0, F)$ for L are assumed to be useful, i.e., for $q \in Q$ there exists some word $w \in \Sigma^*$ such that $\delta(q_0, w) = q$ (useless states can be easily removed in time linear in the number of states n). This allows us to define $\mathrm{level}_{\mathcal{A}}(q) := \min\{|w| \mid \delta(q_0, w) = q\}$ for all $q \in Q$. We simply write $\mathrm{level}(q)$ when the corresponding DFA is clear from the context. To give an example, in Fig. 1 (a) we have $\mathrm{level}(q_0) = 0$, $\mathrm{level}(q_1) = 1$, $\mathrm{level}(q_2) = 2$, $\mathrm{level}(q_3) = 3$, $\mathrm{level}(q_4) = 4$, $\mathrm{level}(q_5) = 5$, and $\mathrm{level}(q_6) = 1$. By applying a breadth–first–search algorithm [4] to the state transition diagram associated with $\mathcal{A}$, the levels of all states can also be computed in linear time. Clearly, a state $q \in Q$ with $\mathrm{level}_{\mathcal{A}}(q) > l$ can be removed from $\mathcal{A}$ without changing $L(\mathcal{A}) \cap \Sigma^{\leq l}$. Thus for the rest of this paper we assume $\mathrm{level}(q) \leq l$ for all states q of any automata.

Definition 2. *Let $\mathcal{A} = (Q, \Sigma, \delta, q_0, F)$ be a DFA and $p, q \in Q$. We say p and q are similar (denoted $p \sim q$) iff $\delta(p, w) \in F \Leftrightarrow \delta(q, w) \in F$ for all $w \in \Sigma^{\leq l-k}$, where $k = \max\{level(p), level(q)\}$. Otherwise, p and q are dissimilar ($p \not\sim q$).*

For example, concerning the DFA in Fig. 1 (a), it is rather easy to see that q_2 and q_4 are similar. Firstly note that $l = 5$ and $\max\{level(q_2), level(q_4)\} = 4$. Now clearly $\delta(q_2, w) \in F \Leftrightarrow \delta(q_4, w) \in F$ for all $w \in \Sigma^{\leq 5-4} = \{\varepsilon, a, b\}$. However, q_4 and q_5 are dissimilar because $\delta(q_4, \varepsilon) = q_4 \notin F$ and $\delta(q_5, \varepsilon) \in F$.

Note that $\sim$ is reflexive and symmetric, but *not* transitive (see [1] for further properties). A DFCA $\mathcal{A}$ for L is known to be minimal if and only if all states of $\mathcal{A}$ are pairwise dissimilar [2]. However, checking similarity for all pairs of states in a straightforward way consumes at least $\Omega(n^2)$ time. We therefore use a different method to obtain a minimal DFCA, which is presented in the next section.

3 Similarity Decompositions

This section gives an introduction to similarity state decompositions. We shall prove that once such a decomposition is given, it is easy to construct a minimal DFCA for L. We start with the basic definition.

Definition 3. *Let $\mathcal{A} = (Q, \Sigma, \delta, q_0, F)$ be a DFA. We say that $(Q_1, \ldots, Q_r)$ is a similarity state decomposition (SSD) of Q if*

a) $Q_1 \cup \ldots \cup Q_r = Q$
b) $Q_i \cap Q_j = \emptyset$ for all $1 \leq i < j \leq r$
c) $\forall 1 \leq i \leq r \, \forall p, q \in Q_i : p \sim q$
d) $\forall 1 \leq i < j \leq r \, \exists p \in Q_i \, \exists q \in Q_j : p \not\sim q$

For all $q \in Q$ we denote by $[q]$ the set Q_i of the decomposition such that $q \in Q_i$.

Concerning our example in Fig. 1 (a), the reader can easily verify the following properties: $q_0 \sim q_2$, $q_0 \sim q_4$, $q_2 \sim q_4$, $q_1 \sim q_3$, $q_1 \sim q_5$, $q_3 \sim q_5$, $q_0 \not\sim q_1$, $q_0 \not\sim q_6$, and $q_1 \not\sim q_6$. Hence $Q_1 := \{q_0, q_2, q_4\}$, $Q_2 := \{q_1, q_3, q_5\}$, and $Q_3 := \{q_6\}$ form an SSD.

The goal for this section is to show the following theorem.

Theorem 1. *Let $(Q_1, \ldots, Q_r)$ be an SSD for some DFCA $\mathcal{A} = (Q, \Sigma, \delta, q_0, F)$ covering L. Choose $p_i \in Q_i$ such that $level(p_i) = \min\{level(q) \mid q \in Q_i\}$, for all $1 \leq i \leq r$. Define a DFA $\mathcal{B} = (Q', \Sigma, \delta', q_0', F')$ by setting $Q' := \{Q_1, \ldots, Q_r\}$, $q_0' := [q_0]$, $F' := \{[q] \mid q \in F\}$, and*

$$\delta'(Q_i, a) := [\delta(p_i, a)] \, , \quad \text{for all } 1 \leq i \leq r \text{ and } a \in \Sigma \, .$$

Then $\mathcal{B}$ is a minimal DFCA for L.

In Fig. 1 (a), we have $p_1 := q_0$, $p_2 := q_1$, and $p_3 := q_6$. Now, for example, since $\delta(p_2, b) = \delta(q_1, b) = q_2 \in Q_1$, we obtain $\delta'(Q_2, b) = Q_1$. By checking the other transitions we finally end up with the DFCA shown in Fig. 1 (b).

We require three auxiliary results to prove Thm. 1.

Lemma 1. *Let $\mathcal{A}$ and $\mathcal{B}$ be as in Thm. 1. Then $q \in F \Leftrightarrow [q] \in F'$ for all $q \in Q$.*

Proof. By definition, $[q] \in F'$ for all $q \in F$. Now let $[q] \in F'$, i.e., $q \in [p]$ for some $p \in F$. Since we have $p \sim q$, $\text{level}_\mathcal{A}(p) \leq l$ and $\text{level}_\mathcal{A}(q) \leq l$, we conclude that $p \in F \Leftrightarrow \delta(p, \varepsilon) \in F \Leftrightarrow \delta(q, \varepsilon) \in F \Leftrightarrow q \in F$. □

Lemma 2. *Let $\mathcal{A}$ and $\mathcal{B}$ be as given in Thm. 1. Let $w = a_1 \ldots a_k \in \Sigma^{\leq l}$. Then for $0 \leq j \leq k$ there exists some $p \in \delta'(q_0', a_1 \ldots a_j)$ such that $\text{level}_\mathcal{A}(p) \leq j$ and $\delta(p, a_{j+1} \ldots a_k) \in F \Leftrightarrow w \in L(\mathcal{A})$.*

Proof. If $j = 0$, then we can choose $p := q_0$. To prove the claim for $j + 1$, let i such that $Q_i = \delta'(q_0', a_1 \ldots a_j)$. By induction there exists some $p' \in Q_i$ with $\text{level}_\mathcal{A}(p') \leq j$ and $\delta(p', a_{j+1} \ldots a_k) \in F \Leftrightarrow w \in L(\mathcal{A})$. The properties of p_i imply $\text{level}_\mathcal{A}(p_i) \leq \text{level}_\mathcal{A}(p') \leq j$. Since $p_i \sim p'$ and $|a_{j+1} \ldots a_k| = k - j \leq l - j$, we have $\delta(p_i, a_{j+1} \ldots a_k) \in F \Leftrightarrow \delta(p', a_{j+1} \ldots a_k) \in F \Leftrightarrow w \in L(\mathcal{A})$. Now choose $p := \delta(p_i, a_{j+1})$. Then $\text{level}_\mathcal{A}(p) \leq \text{level}_\mathcal{A}(p_i) + 1 \leq \text{level}_\mathcal{A}(p') + 1 \leq j + 1$ and $p \in [\delta(p_i, a_{j+1})] = \delta'(Q_i, a_{j+1}) = \delta'(q_0', a_1 \ldots a_{j+1})$. Also, since $\delta(p, a_{j+2} \ldots a_k)$ equals $\delta(p_i, a_{j+1} \ldots a_k)$, it follows that $\delta(p, a_{j+2} \ldots a_k) \in F \Leftrightarrow w \in L(\mathcal{A})$. □

Lemma 3. *Let $\mathcal{A}$ and $\mathcal{B}$ be as given in Thm. 1. Then $\text{level}_\mathcal{B}([q]) \leq \text{level}_\mathcal{A}(q)$ for all $q \in Q$.*

Proof. Assuming the contrary, let $k := \text{level}_\mathcal{A}(q)$ be the smallest number such that $\text{level}_\mathcal{B}([q]) \geq k + 1$ for some $q \in Q$. Clearly $q \neq q_0$ and $k \geq 1$ because $\text{level}_\mathcal{B}([q_0]) = \text{level}_\mathcal{A}(q_0) = 0$. Let $p \in Q$ and $a \in \Sigma$ such that $\text{level}_\mathcal{A}(p) = k - 1$ and $\delta(p, a) = q$. By our choice of k, $\text{level}_\mathcal{B}([p]) \leq k - 1$. Let $[p] = Q_i$ and $\delta'([p], a) = Q_j$ for suitable i and j. Then $\delta(p_i, a) \in Q_j$. Moreover, $\text{level}_\mathcal{B}([q]) > k$ and $\text{level}_\mathcal{B}(Q_j) \leq \text{level}_\mathcal{B}([p]) + 1 \leq k$ imply that $Q_j \neq [q]$. So there exist $p' \in Q_j$ and $q' \in [q]$ such that $p' \not\sim q'$. Since $[q'] = [q]$, $\text{level}_\mathcal{A}(q') < k$ would contradict our choice of k and q. Hence $\text{level}_\mathcal{A}(q') \geq k$. Thus there exists some $w \in \Sigma^{\leq l-k}$ such that $\delta(p', w) \in F \Leftrightarrow \delta(q', w) \notin F$ and $|w| \leq l - \max\{\text{level}_\mathcal{A}(p'), \text{level}_\mathcal{A}(q')\}$. Since $\text{level}_\mathcal{A}(\delta(p_i, a)) \leq \text{level}_\mathcal{A}(p_i) + 1 \leq \text{level}_\mathcal{A}(p) + 1 = k$ and $\delta(p_i, a) \sim p'$ (both states are in Q_j), we conclude that $\delta(\delta(p_i, a), w) \in F \Leftrightarrow \delta(p', w) \in F$. Similarly, $\text{level}_\mathcal{A}(q) = k$ and $q \sim q'$ imply that $\delta(\delta(p, a), w) = \delta(q, w) \in F \Leftrightarrow \delta(q', w) \in F$. So altogether it follows that $\delta(p_i, aw) \in F \Leftrightarrow \delta(p, aw) \notin F$. However, since $|aw| \leq l - k + 1$ and $\text{level}_\mathcal{A}(p_i) \leq \text{level}_\mathcal{A}(p) = k - 1$, this contradicts $p_i \sim p$. □

We are now prepared for proving the previously stated theorem.

Proof (of Thm. 1). Let $w = a_1 \ldots a_k \in \Sigma^{\leq l}$. By using Lemma 2 with $j = k$, there exists some $p \in \delta'(q_0', w)$ such that $w \in L(\mathcal{A}) \Leftrightarrow \delta(p, \varepsilon) \in F \Leftrightarrow p \in F$ and $\text{level}_\mathcal{A}(p) \leq l$. Also, by Lemma 1, $p \in F \Leftrightarrow [p] = \delta'(q_0', w) \in F' \Leftrightarrow w \in L(\mathcal{B})$. So for all $w \in \Sigma^{\leq l}$ we have $w \in L \Leftrightarrow w \in L(\mathcal{A}) \Leftrightarrow w \in L(\mathcal{B})$. Hence $\mathcal{B}$ covers L.

To show that $\mathcal{B}$ is minimal, assume a DFCA $\mathcal{C} = (\tilde{Q}, \Sigma, \tilde{\delta}, \tilde{q}_0, \tilde{F})$ covering L with $|\tilde{Q}| < |Q'| = r$. For all $1 \leq i \leq r$ let $v_i \in \Sigma^*$ such that $|v_i| = \text{level}_\mathcal{B}(Q_i)$ and $\delta'(q_0', v_i) = Q_i$. Since $|\tilde{Q}| < r$, there exist $1 \leq i < j \leq r$ with $\tilde{\delta}(\tilde{q}_0, v_i) = \tilde{\delta}(\tilde{q}_0, v_j)$. By the properties of an SSD, we can choose $p \in Q_i$ and $q \in Q_j$ with $p \not\sim q$, so it follows there exists some word z with $|z| \leq l - \text{level}_{\mathcal{A}}(p)$, $|z| \leq l - \text{level}_{\mathcal{A}}(q)$, and $\delta(p, z) \in F \Leftrightarrow \delta(q, z) \notin F$. By Lemma 3 we have $|v_i z| \leq l$ and $|v_j z| \leq l$. Now put $j = |v_i|$ and apply Lemma 2 to $w = v_i z$. This leads to some $p' \in Q_i$ with $\delta(p', z) \in F \Leftrightarrow w \in L(\mathcal{A})$ and $\text{level}_{\mathcal{A}}(p') \leq |v_i| \leq l - |z|$, i.e., $|z| \leq l - \text{level}_{\mathcal{A}}(p')$. Since $p \sim p'$, we conclude $\delta(p, z) \in F \Leftrightarrow \delta(p', z) \in F \Leftrightarrow v_i z \in L(\mathcal{A})$. Similarly, $\delta(q, z) \in F \Leftrightarrow v_j z \in L(\mathcal{A})$, so $v_i z \in L \Leftrightarrow v_i z \in L(\mathcal{A}) \Leftrightarrow v_j z \notin L(\mathcal{A}) \Leftrightarrow v_j z \notin L$. But $v_i z \in L(\mathcal{C}) \Leftrightarrow \tilde{\delta}(\tilde{\delta}(\tilde{q}_0, v_i), z) \in \tilde{F} \Leftrightarrow \tilde{\delta}(\tilde{\delta}(\tilde{q}_0, v_j), z) \in \tilde{F} \Leftrightarrow v_j z \in L(\mathcal{C})$, so $\mathcal{C}$ cannot cover L.   □

The crucial question now is how to compute an SSD for a given DFCA. An efficient method for this task is presented next.

4   The Decomposition Algorithm

The algorithm for decomposing the state set of some DFCA $(Q, \Sigma, \delta, q_0, F)$ into an SSD is an (however nontrivial) adaptation of Hopcroft's well known method for minimizing ordinary DFAs [5]. We first sketch the idea, and then prove its correctness. The complexity analysis is given in Sect. 5.

The algorithm manages a decomposition $(Q_1, \ldots, Q_r)$ of Q such that the properties a), b) and d) of an SSD are always satisfied. The initial decomposition is $Q_1 := Q \setminus F$ and $Q_2 := F$. As long as there is some state set Q_i which violates condition c) of an SSD, (i.e. Q_i contains two dissimilar states p and q), Q_i is split into two nonempty parts, where one part (containing p) replaces the current set Q_i, and the other part (containing q) becomes the new state set Q_{r+1}. We then also say that all states in the first part are *separated* from the states in the second part. Now r is increased by one, and the described procedure is repeated until an SSD is found. Clearly, the corresponding main loop executes for at most n times, where $n = |Q|$. Furthermore, once two states p and q have been separated, they remain in different state sets until the algorithm terminates.

Some of the state sets determined during the execution of the algorithm are additionally stored in a first–in–first–out (FIFO) queue T. With each execution of the main loop, the first element of T is extracted from the queue, and possibly causes other state sets of the current decomposition to be split. The smaller part of each such separated state set is then appended to T. At the beginning, T contains only one set, namely F. The main loop eventually terminates as soon as T becomes empty. Hence, if the resulting SSD contains r state sets, then exactly $r - 1$ elements have been appended to (and removed from) T.

From the algorithm shown in Fig. 2 it can be seen that T in fact stores pairs of the form (S, k), where S is some state set as described above, and k is some integer which corresponds to the levels of the states in S. The exact meaning of k will become clear during the correctness proof presented below. Later, we shall also analyze the state sets X and Y which are computed in lines 8–9 (roughly speaking, X and Y contain the dissimilar p's and q's mentioned above).

Before proving the correctness of the algorithm, let us apply it to the example in Fig. 1 (a). Recall that the length l of the longest word in L is five. Starting with $Q_1 := \{q_0, q_2, q_4, q_6\}$ and $Q_2 := \{q_1, q_3, q_5\}$ (line 3), the algorithm reaches

```
1    If F = ∅ Or F = Q Then { Output SSD=(Q); Exit; }
     Compute level(q) for all q ∈ Q;
     Q₁ := Q \ F; Q₂ := F; r := 2;
     Initialize FIFO queue T with the only element (F, 0);
5    While T ≠ ∅ Do { (* main loop *)
        Extract first element (S, k) from T;
        For c ∈ Σ Do {
           X := {p | δ(p, c) ∈ S ∧ level(p) + k < l};
           Y := {q | δ(q, c) ∉ S ∧ level(q) + k < l};
10         For i := r Downto 1 Do {
              If Qᵢ ∩ X ≠ ∅ And Qᵢ ∩ Y ≠ ∅ Then {
                 Choose Z ⊆ Qᵢ such that Qᵢ ∩ X ⊆ Z and Qᵢ ∩ Y ⊆ Qᵢ \ Z;
                 If |Z| ≤ |Qᵢ \ Z| Then {
                    Q_{r+1} := Z;
15                  Qᵢ := Qᵢ \ Z;
                 } Else {
                    Q_{r+1} := Qᵢ \ Z;
                    Qᵢ := Z;
                 }
20               Append (Q_{r+1}, k + 1) to FIFO queue T;
                 r := r + 1;
              }
           }
        }
25   }
     Output SSD=(Q₁, . . . , Q_r);
```

Fig. 2. The algorithm which determines an SSD for some DFCA $(Q, \Sigma, \delta, q_0, F)$

the **For**–loop in line 7 with $S = \{q_1, q_3, q_5\}$, $k = 0$ and $r = 2$ (lines 3, 4, and 6). Now for $c = a$ we get $X = \{p \mid \delta(p, a) \in S \wedge \text{level}(p) + 0 < 5\} = \{q_0, q_2, q_4\}$ and analogously $Y = \{q_1, q_3, q_6\}$ (lines 8 and 9). The inner **For**–loop (line 10) verifies whether Q_i has to be split ($i = 2, 1$). The test in line 11 fails for Q_2 because $Q_2 \cap X = \emptyset$, but for Q_1 we have $Q_1 \cap X = \{q_0, q_2, q_4\}$ and $Q_1 \cap Y = \{q_6\}$. Thus in line 12 the algorithm chooses the only possibility $Z = \{q_0, q_2, q_4\}$, and in lines 17–18 it sets Q_3 to $\{q_6\}$, whereas Q_1 is overwritten with $\{q_0, q_2, q_4\}$. Finally $(\{q_6\}, 1)$ is appended to the currently empty queue T (line 20), and r is increased to three to reflect the new number of sets in the actual decomposition (line 21). Observe that the other instance of the inner **For**–loop with $c = b$ yields $X = \{p \mid \delta(p, b) \in S \wedge \text{level}(p) + 0 < 5\} = \emptyset$ in line 8, so the test in line 11 always fails. Furthermore, during the next iteration of the main loop, T becomes empty again after extracting $(\{q_6\}, 1)$ in line 6, and this time it is easy to see that no more state sets are split. Hence T remains empty, and the algorithm terminates with the desired SSD $(\{q_0, q_2, q_4\}, \{q_1, q_3, q_5\}, \{q_6\})$.

To show the correctness of the algorithm, we first prove some helpful properties.

Lemma 4. *Let* $(S_2, k_2), (S_3, k_3), \ldots, (S_r, k_r)$ *be the complete sequence of elements appended to* T *during the execution of the algorithm. Then* $k_2 \leq \ldots \leq k_r$.

Proof. Let i be the smallest index satisfying $k_i > k_{i+1} \geq 0$. Then (S_i, k_i) has been appended to T due to some pair (S_u, k_u) with $u < i$ and $k_u + 1 = k_i$. Later, (S_{i+1}, k_{i+1}) has been appended to T due to some pair (S_v, k_v) with $u \leq v \leq i$ and $k_v + 1 = k_{i+1}$. But then $k_u + 1 = k_i > k_{i+1} = k_v + 1$ implies $k_u \neq k_v$, i.e., $u \neq v$. Hence $u < v \leq i$, i.e., $u \leq v - 1 < i$, and by our choice of i we have $k_{v-1} \geq k_u = k_i - 1 > k_{i+1} - 1 = k_v$ which in turn contradicts the choice of i. $\square$

Lemma 5. *For two dissimilar states* $p, q \in Q$ *let* $0 \leq m \leq l$ *and* $w \in \Sigma^{\leq m}$ *such that* $level(p) \leq l - m$, $level(q) \leq l - m$, *and* $\delta(p, w) \in F \Leftrightarrow \delta(q, w) \notin F$. *Then* p *and* q *are separated and a pair* (S, k) *with* $p \in S \Leftrightarrow q \notin S$ *and* $k \leq m$ *is appended to* T.

Proof. If $m = 0$, then $w = \varepsilon$ and therefore $p \in F \Leftrightarrow q \notin F$. Moreover, all states have a level of at most l. Thus, from the program lines 1–4, it is easy to see that the claim holds. Now assume $level(p) \leq l - (m + 1)$, $level(q) \leq l - (m + 1)$, and $w = bw'$ for some $b \in \Sigma$ and $w' \in \Sigma^{\leq m}$. Let $p' = \delta(p, b)$ and $q' = \delta(q, b)$. Then $level(p') \leq level(p) + 1 \leq l - m$ and $level(q') \leq l - m$. Additionally, we have $\delta(p', w') = \delta(p, bw') \in F \Leftrightarrow \delta(q, bw') = \delta(q', w') \notin F$. By the induction hypothesis, a pair (S, k') with $p' \in S \Leftrightarrow q' \notin S$ and $k' \leq m$ is appended to T. Now assume $p, q \in Q_j$ for some j when (S, k') is extracted from T in line 6. Consider the instance of the **For**–loop in line 7 when c equals b. Since $level(p) \leq l - (m + 1) < l - m \leq l - k'$ and similarly $level(q) < l - k'$, it is easy to see from lines 8–9 that either $p \in X \wedge q \in Y$ or $q \in X \wedge p \in Y$. Consider the instance of the **For**–loop in line 10 when $i = j$. The condition in line 11 is satisfied, and when line 20 is reached, p and q have been separated. Also, since $k' + 1 \leq m + 1$, line 20 appends a pair to T as claimed.

If p and q were separated before (S, k') is extracted from T, then the corresponding state set either has been split while executing lines 1–4 (in this case the claim follows immediately), or due to some pair (S', k'') with $k'' \leq k'$ by Lemma 4. Then $k'' \leq k' \leq m$, i.e., $k'' + 1 \leq m + 1$, and the claim follows in the same way as presented above. $\square$

Lemma 6. *When creating a new state set* $Q_{r'+1}$ $(r' \geq 2)$ *by splitting some previous state set* Q_i $(i \leq r')$ *into two parts, each part contains a state* p *with* $level(p) \leq l - k_{r'+1}$.

Proof. Before appending the pair $(Q_{r'+1}, k + 1)$ with $k + 1 = k_{r'+1}$ to T in line 20, the program code in lines 8–19 ensures that each part contains a state p with $level(p) + k < l$, i.e. $level(p) \leq l - k_{r'+1}$. $\square$

Lemma 7. *Let* $1 \leq i \leq r$. *Then the state set* Q_i *of the finally computed SSD contains a state* p *with* $level(p) \leq l - k_i$, *where* $k_1 = 0$.

Proof. The claim is trivial if the algorithm terminates in line 1. Otherwise, by line 3, both Q_1 and Q_2 are nonempty. Hence, both sets contain at least one state p with level$(p) \le l = l - k_1 = l - k_2$. Now each time a state set Q_i is split into two parts, both the new state set $Q_{r'+1}$ and the remaining part of Q_i contain a state p with level$(p) \le l - k_{r'+1} \le l - k_i$ by Lemma 6 and 4.   □

Lemma 8. *When creating a new state set $Q_{r'}$ ($r' \ge 2$) it holds that*

$$\forall 1 \le j < r' \, \forall p \in Q_j \, \forall q \in Q_{r'} : \max\{level(p), level(q)\} \le l - k_{r'} \implies p \nsim q \ .$$

Proof. The claim can be easily verified if $r' = 2$. For $r' \ge 2$ let Q_i be the state set from which $Q_{r'+1}$ has been separated. If $j < i$, let $\tilde{Q}_1, \ldots, \tilde{Q}_i$ denote the status of the decomposition after creating $\tilde{Q}_i$. Then $Q_{r'+1} \subseteq \tilde{Q}_i$ and $Q_j \subseteq \tilde{Q}_j$. By Lemma 4, $l - k_{r'+1} \le l - k_i$, thus the claim follows from the induction hypothesis for $r' = i$. Similarly, if $j > i$, let $\tilde{Q}_1, \ldots, \tilde{Q}_j$ be the status of the decomposition after creating $\tilde{Q}_j$. Then again $Q_{r'+1} \subseteq \tilde{Q}_i$ and $Q_j \subseteq \tilde{Q}_j$, and the claim follows analogously.

It remains to prove the claim for $j = i$. Consider the pair (S, k) (line 6) and the symbol $c \in \Sigma$ (line 7) of the algorithm which caused $Q_{r'+1}$ to be created. Then (S, k) equals $(\tilde{Q}_t, k_t)$ for some $t \le r'$, where $\tilde{Q}_1, \ldots, \tilde{Q}_t$ was the actual decomposition after generating $\tilde{Q}_t$. Now we reconstruct what happened just before creating $Q_{r'+1}$. Firstly, line 20 implies $k_{r'+1} = k + 1 = k_t + 1$. Secondly, from lines 8–9 we see that $X = \{p \mid \delta(p, c) \in \tilde{Q}_t \wedge \text{level}(p) \le l - (k_t + 1)\}$ and $Y = \{q \mid \delta(q, c) \notin \tilde{Q}_t \wedge \text{level}(q) \le l - (k_t + 1)\}$. Furthermore, analyzing line 12 (with Q_i representing the still unsplit state set) yields

$$\forall p \in Z : (\text{level}(p) > l - (k_t + 1)) \vee p \in X$$

and

$$\forall q \in Q_i \setminus Z : (\text{level}(q) > l - (k_t + 1)) \vee q \in Y \ .$$

Now assume $p \in Z$ and level$(p) \le l - k_{r'+1} = l - (k_t + 1)$. Then $p \in X$ and $p' \in \tilde{Q}_t$ for $p' := \delta(p, a)$. Since level$(p) \le l - (k_t + 1)$, we have level$(p') \le l - k_t$. Similarly, $q \in Q_i \setminus Z$ and level$(q) \le l - k_{r'+1}$ implies $q' := \delta(q, a) \notin \tilde{Q}_t$ (which means $q' \in \tilde{Q}_1 \cup \ldots \cup \tilde{Q}_{t-1}$) and level$(q') \le l - k_t$. Therefore the induction hypothesis for $r' = t$ yields $p' \nsim q'$. So there is some $w \in \Sigma^{\le k_t}$ such that $\delta(p', w) \in F \Leftrightarrow \delta(q', w) \notin F$, and the word $cw \in \Sigma^{\le k_t + 1}$ can be used to show that p and q are dissimilar.   □

The correctness of the algorithm follows now.

Theorem 2. *Given a DFCA $\mathcal{A} = (Q, \Sigma, \delta, q_0, F)$ covering L, the algorithm in Fig. 2 correctly determines a corresponding SSD.*

Proof. Clearly the properties a) and b) of an SSD are satisfied. To prove d), assume $1 \le u < v \le r$ and let $\tilde{Q}_1, \ldots, \tilde{Q}_{r'}$ be the first decomposition status which satisfies $Q_u \subseteq \tilde{Q}_{u'}$ and $Q_v \subseteq \tilde{Q}_{v'}$ for some $1 \le u', v' \le r'$ with $u' \ne v'$. Clearly $2 \le r' \le v$. Now either $u' = r'$ or $v' = r'$, and Lemma 8 implies

$\forall p \in \tilde{Q}_{u'} \ \forall q \in \tilde{Q}_{v'} : \ \max\{\text{level}(p), \text{level}(q)\} \leq l - k_{r'} \implies p \not\sim q$. Moreover, $\tilde{Q}_{u'}$ contains a state p with $\text{level}(p) \leq l - k_{r'}$ by Lemma 6 (or, for $r' = 2$, by Lemma 7). Now if $u = u'$, then Lemma 6 and 4 ensure this property also holds for Q_u. Similarly, if $u \neq u'$, then Q_u must have been created after $\tilde{Q}_{r'}$, i.e. $u > r'$, and Lemma 7 and 4 again imply a state $p \in Q_u$ with $\text{level}(p) \leq l - k_u \leq l - k_{r'}$. Applying the same arguments to $\tilde{Q}_{v'}$ and Q_v, we see that property d) of an SSD holds. Finally, by Lemma 5, dissimilar states are always separated. From this property c) follows. □

5 Complexity

We now sketch an implementation for the algorithm which consists of two parts. The first one deals with the preprocessing work which corresponds to the first four program lines. It also verifies whether the algorithm terminates in line 1 (however this case is trivial and skipped in the following discussion). The second part contains the body of the **While**–loop.

We start with studying the data structure used for managing the current decomposition $\{Q_1, \ldots, Q_r\}$. Each state set Q_i is represented by a double–linked list of length $|Q_i|$. A simple implementation for this is to manage an array *link* of size n, where $link[j]$ contains *prev* and *next* indices indicating the states before and after q_j in its corresponding list. In order to know where each list begins, we manage an additional array *head* with again n elements, where $head[i]$ stores the index of the first element of Q_i (for $i > r$ the index is undefined). Furthermore, the function *getindex* maps Q to $\{1, \ldots, r\}$, where $getindex(q) = j$ iff $[q] = Q_j$. Another array contains the levels for all states in Q and can be computed with the breadth–first–search method [4] in $O(n)$ time. This bound also applies to the other preprocessing work done before reaching the **While**–loop in line 5.

An efficient implementation for the FIFO queue T is required. Whenever a pair (S, k_i) is appended to T, we have $S = Q_i$ at that point of time. Thus S does not need to be saved if we keep track of all parts which are later separated from Q_i. Thus when Q_i is created, we start to manage a single–linked (and initially empty) list $children_i$ of indices. Each time a state Q_j with $j > i$ is separated from Q_i, j is added to $children_i$. Now T can be implemented by a linear size array T' storing k_i for $2 \leq i \leq r$, and an index h for T' representing the head of the queue. Then line 6 becomes $T'[2] := 0$ and $h := 2$, and line 20 becomes $T'[r+1] := k + 1$. To extract (S, k) from T, we collect the set C of all indices associated with the tree at root h, using the *children* pointers. Also, we put $k := T'[h]$ and $h := h + 1$. Then $S = \{q \in Q_j \mid j \in C\}$, and thus extracting (S, k) takes $\Theta(|S|)$ time. Note that testing the condition in line 5 is equivalent to verifying $h \leq r$.

Additional data structures are necessary for implementing the **While**–loop. For each $q \in Q$ and $a \in \Sigma$ we require the set $\delta^{-1}(q, a) := \{p \in Q \mid \delta(p, a) = q\}$ to be stored in a single–linked list. There are two additional linear size arrays *count* and *newindex* with $count[i]$ and $newindex[i]$ initialized with zero, for all $1 \leq i \leq n$. Finally, we define two more functions b and c with domain $\{1, \ldots, n\}$

by setting $b(i) = |\{q \in Q_i \,|\, \text{level}(q) < l\}|$ and $c(i) = |Q_i|$ for $i = 1, 2$, and $b(i) = c(i) = 0$ for $i > 2$. All initial settings can be easily calculated in $O(n)$ time and space (regarding $|\Sigma|$ as a constant).

The meaning of b and c is as follows. While executing the **While**–loop, it always holds that $b(i) = |\{q \in Q_i \,|\, \text{level}(q) < l - k\}|$ and $c(i) = |Q_i|$, for all $1 \leq i \leq r$, where k has been determined in line 6. It is easy to update c whenever state sets are split, but managing b requires for all $1 \leq i \leq l$ a single–linked list R_i containing the set $\{q \,|\, \text{level}(q) = l - i\}$. Again, these lists can be determined in linear time. Now each time k increases by one due to line 6 (see the proof of Lemma 4), we in turn decrease $b(\text{getindex}(q))$ by one for all $q \in R_k$. Then clearly b is correctly managed. Since each list R_i is only required once, the overall additional time complexity added to the loop is linear.

Lines 8–23 are processed in three steps. Using $count$ for temporary data, the first step computes $|Q_i \cap X|$ and $|Q_i \cap Y|$ for all $1 \leq i \leq r$, where X and Y are as specified in line 8 resp. 9. The states are split during the second step, using $newindex$ to hold the indices of the new states. The last step exchanges the positions of some state sets and cleans up the auxiliary data structures.

The first step is as follows. For each $q \in S$ and $p \in \delta^{-1}(q, a)$, provided that $\text{level}(p) < l - k$, we increase $count[\text{getindex}(p)]$ by one. Since the automaton is deterministic, each state p occurs at most once. Afterwards we clearly have $|Q_i \cap X| = count[i]$ and $|Q_i \cap Y| = b_i - count[i]$ for all $1 \leq i \leq r$.

To seperate the states, we always choose $Z := Q_i \cap X$, $Q_{r+1} := Z$, and $Q_i := Q_i \setminus Z$ as in lines 12, 14, and 15. (Later, Q_i and Q_{r+1} are exchanged if the condition in line 13 is not satisfied.) For each $q \in S$ and $p \in \delta^{-1}(q, a)$ with $\text{level}(p) < l - k$, we put $i := \text{getindex}(p)$ and test the two conditions $count[i] > 0$ and $b_i - count[i] > 0$. If both hold then p must be moved from Q_i to Q_s, where $s = newindex[i]$. If $s = 0$ then the new state set has not yet been created. We then assign $r := r+1$, $newindex[i] := r$, and setup Q_r to only contain p. If $s > 0$, we directly insert p into Q_s. Note that each case can be processed in constant time.

During the third step, for all $q \in S$ and $p \in \delta^{-1}(q, a)$, we assign $count[i] := 0$ and $newindex[i] := 0$, where $i = \text{getindex}(p)$. But before doing so, if $s > 0$ (with $s = newindex[i]$), we verify whether $c(i) < c(s)$ holds, indicating that Q_i and Q_s must be exchanged. Since $count[i] = c(s)$, exchanging Q_i and Q_s can be accomplished in $O(|Q_i| + |Q_s|) = O(c(i) + c(s)) = O(2 \cdot c(s)) = O(count[i])$ time, mainly for updating the corresponding $getindex$ entries.

Note that resetting $newindex[i]$ to zero prevents Q_i and Q_s from being exchanged twice. So the consumed time for exchanging all state sets cannot exceed $O(\sum_{1 \leq i \leq n} count[i]) = O(\sum_{q \in S} |\delta^{-1}(q, a)|)$. This bound also applies to the other work done during all three steps, and thus to the complete body of the loop (lines 6–24), regarding $|\Sigma|$ as a constant. Moreover, the automaton is deterministic, thus for all $c \in \Sigma$ we have $\delta^{-1}(p, c) \cap \delta^{-1}(q, c) = \emptyset$ if $p \neq q$, and hence $\sum_{q \in Q} |\delta^{-1}(q, c)| \leq n$. Finally, when splitting a state set, only the smaller part is appended to T. Thus for all $q \in Q$ a state set S containing q can be extracted from T for at most $O(\log n)$ times. Altogether this yields the following result.

Theorem 3. *An SSD can be determined in $O(n \log n)$ time and $O(n)$ space.*

Corollary 1. *An n-state DFCA can be minimized within the same bounds.*

Proof. We can easily accomplish the construction in Thm. 1 in linear time. □

Corollary 2. *An n-state DFA accepting a finite language can be converted into a minimal DFCA using $O(n \log n)$ time and linear space.*

Proof. The DFA is also a DFCA. □

Thus the new algorithm significantly improves the previously known methods for converting and minimizing cover automata. Also, we assume that the $O(n \log n)$ time bound is tight, and state this conjecture as an open problem.

Acknowledgement. I would like to thank Michael Clausen, Natalie Packham, Sheng Yu, and the anonymous referees for helpful comments.

References

1. Câmpeanu, C., Sântean, N., Yu, S.: Minimal Cover–Automata for Finite Languages. In: Champarnaud, J.-M., Maurel, D., Ziadi, D. (eds.): Third International Workshop on Implementing Automata (WIA'98). Lecture Notes in Computer Science, Vol. 1660. Springer-Verlag, Berlin Heidelberg New York (1998) 32–42
2. Câmpeanu, C., Păun, A., Yu, S.: An Efficient Algorithm for Constructing Minimal Cover Automata for Finite Languages. International Journal of Foundations of Computer Science (2000), to appear
3. Păun, A., Sântean, N., Yu, S.: An $O(n^2)$ Algorithm for Constructing Minimal Cover Automata for Finite Languages. In: Yu, S., Păun, A. (eds.): Implementation and Application of Automata (CIAA 2000). Lecture Notes in Computer Science, Vol. 2088. Springer-Verlag, Berlin Heidelberg New York (2000) 243–251
4. Corman, T.H., Leiserson, C.E., Rivest, R.L.: Introduction to Algorithms. MIT Press, Cambridge (1990)
5. Hopcroft, J.E.: An $n \log n$ algorithm for minimizing the states in a finite automaton. In: Kohavi, Z., Paz. A. (eds.): The Theory of Machines and Computations. Academic Press, New York (1971) 189–196
6. Hopcroft, J.E., Ullman, J.D.: Introduction to Automata Theory, Languages and Computation. Addison–Wesley, Reading, MA (1979)

Compilation of Constraint-Based Contextual Rules for Part-of-Speech Tagging into Finite State Transducers*

Jorge Graña[1], Gloria Andrade[1], and Jesús Vilares[2]

[1] Departamento de Computación, Universidad de La Coruña
Campus de Elviña s/n, 15071 - La Coruña, Spain
{grana,andrade}@dc.fi.udc.es
[2] Departamento de Informática, Universidad de Vigo
Campus de As Lagoas, 32004 - Orense, Spain
jvilares@uvigo.es

Abstract. With the aim of removing the residuary errors made by pure stochastic disambiguation models, we put forward a hybrid system in which linguist users introduce high level contextual rules to be applied in combination with a tagger based on a Hidden Markov Model. The design of these rules is inspired in the Constraint Grammars formalism. In the present work, we review this formalism in order to propose a more intuitive syntax and semantics for rules, and we develop a strategy to compile the rules under the form of Finite State Transducers, thus guaranteeing an efficient execution framework.

1 Introduction

In the context of the use of the tools for *part-of-speech tagging* (POST) developed in the GALENA and CORGA projects[1], our projects for the automatic processing of the Spanish and Galician languages, a repeated request from the linguist partners has been the design of a formalism to introduce high level contextual rules. The purpose of these rules is to remove the residuary errors that pure stochastic taggers systematically make, allowing them to improve the usual performances of 95-97% of success.

The *constraint grammars* formalism (CGs) [3] was a good candidate on the basis of its good results: on concrete languages, such as English [7], performances can reach 99% of precision with a set of about 1 000 contextual rules; and, in general, performances are better than those of the pure stochastic taggers particularly when training and application texts are not from the same style and

* This work has been partially supported by the Spanish Government (under projects TIC2000-0370-C02-01 and HP2001-0044), and by the Galician Government (under project PGIDT01PXI10506PN).

[1] GALENA means *Generation of Natural Language Analyzers* and CORGA means *Reference Corpus of Current Galician*. See http://coleweb.dc.fi.udc.es for more information on both projects.

J.-M. Champarnaud and D. Maurel (Eds.): CIAA 2002, LNCS 2608, pp. 128–137, 2003.

source. However, comparison is difficult since some ambiguities are not resolved by CGs. That is, CGs return a set of more than one tag in some cases, which makes it necessary to combine this technique with another one.

Furthermore, the syntax and semantics of the rules involved in CGs are not very intuitive, since they try to solve problems other than tagging. In fact, they join tagging and certain steps of parsing, even though both analyses are traditionally treated in separate modules. These aspects definitely lead us to design a new formalism for contextual rules. Furthermore, these rules will be oriented to operate together with our tagger, a second order *hidden Markov model* (HMM) with linear interpolation of uni-, bi-, and trigrams as smoothing technique [2].

The aim of the present work is to describe the new formalism of contextual rules. This formalism is mainly inspired in CGs, but some aspects from other rule-based environments, such as *transformation-based error-driven learning* [1] or *relaxation labelling* [5], have been also considered. After this, we focus the discussion on the efficient execution of the rules, for which we design a strategy that compiles them into *finite state transducers* (FSTs). Finally, we make some reflections about time and space complexity of the FSTs obtained.

2   Contextual Rules Based on Constraints

The heterogeneous nature of languages for building contextual rules is a current problem: there is no standard, and there are many differences between languages. Basically, all systems use rules of this kind: if a certain *constraint* or condition is satisfied (for instance, the word following the current word is a verb), then a concrete *action* is executed (for instance, to select the tag substantive). Actions are usually limited to selection or deletion of one of the possible tags. However, constraints involved in the rules can vary greatly in the type of the condition and in the syntax used.

Our formalism omits syntactic components from the rules, represents the same range of conditions as that covered by the rule-based environments cited above, but with a more intuitive and legible syntax, and allows us to express preceding and following contexts on the basis of both tags and words, whether those words are ambiguous or not. The rules can be classified in three different groups: local rules, barrier rules and special rules.

2.1   Local Rules

The rules that conform this group present the following syntax:

```
<action> (<tag>) ([not] <position> <condition> {<values>}, ...);
```

In `<action>`, we specify the mission of the rule. The possible actions to execute are:

- `select`, to select one of the possible tags of the current word,

- **delete**, to remove one of those tags,
- and **force**, to fix the tag for the current word, even though this tag is not present in the set of possible tags for that word.

The field `<position>` must be replaced by an integer indicating which is the word affected by the condition of the rule: 0 for the current word, -1 for the previous one, 1 for the next one, and so on. The possible values for `<condition>` and their corresponding semantics are:

- **is**, which is true when the set of possible tags of the word affected by the condition and the set of tags `<values>` specified in the rule are equal,
- **contains**, which is true when the set of possible tags of the word affected by the condition contains the set of tags `<values>` specified in the rule,
- and **belongs**, which is true when the word affected by the condition is present in the set of words `<values>` specified in the rule.

Conditions can be combined with the usual logic connectives:

- for negation, we can use the keyword **not** in front of the condition,
- for logic-and, we can write several conditions delimited by commas in the same rule,
- and for logic-or, we can write the conditions in separate rules, all these rules involving the same `<action>` and `<tag>` fields.

The following example illustrates the aspect presented by the rules included in this group[2]:

```
force (Det) (1 belongs {sobre}, not 1 is {P});
```

This rule fixes determiner as the tag of the current word, when the next one is the word **sobre** and is not a preposition.

2.2   Barrier Rules

These rules do not refer a concrete position, but navigate leftwards or rightwards from the current word, by replacing the field `<direction>` by `-*` or `+*`, respectively, in the following syntax:

```
<action> (<tag>) (<direction> <condition-1> {<values-1>}
                  barrier <condition-2> {<values-2>}, ...);
```

The general constraint of the rule is established by the condition `<condition-1>` expressed before the keyword **barrier**, and the boundary for navigation is established by `<condition-2>`. This allows us to express situations like the following:

```
select (Adj) (-* contains {S} barrier is {V});
```

where if before the current word there is another word that can be a substantive, and between those two words there is no verb, the current word will be an adjective.

---

[2] To simplify, in this work, we use **Adj** for adjective, **Det** for determiner, **P** for preposition, **Pron** for pronoun, **S** for substantive, and **V** for verb.

2.3 Special Rules

Finally, we have a group for special rules, that always execute an action. Their syntax is:

```
<action> always (<tag>);
```

In this case, the possible actions are only `select` and `delete`, because the action `force` would produce an output text with all the words tagged with the same tag `<tag>`. An example could be the following:

```
delete always (ForeignWord);
```

When it is sure that the input text to be processed is written only in the local language, we can use this rule to remove the tag `ForeignWord` from all ambiguous words that can be a foreign word and something else. These rules could be called also *rare rules*, since they are not commonly used.

2.4 A Practical Example

In Table 1, we show how an initial trellis with ambiguous words evolves step by step when a certain set of contextual rules is applied on it. We have marked with boxes the points where individual rules match. The last row contains the final trellis obtained after the application of the whole set of rules.

Table 1. Evolution of a trellis when a set of contextual rules is applied on it

Rule	Trellis
select (S) (1 is {V});	El sobre está sobre la mesa Pron P V P Det S [S] S Pron V V V
delete (V) (-2 contains {P,V});	El sobre está sobre la mesa Pron S V P Det S S Pron [V] V
select (P) (-2 belongs {bajo,sobre}, -1 is {V});	El sobre está sobre la mesa Pron S V [P] Det S S Pron V
force (Det) (1 belongs {sobre}, not 1 is {P});	El sobre está sobre la mesa [Pron] S V P Det S Pron
	El sobre está sobre la mesa Det S V P Det S Pron

The correct sense of this sentence is the following: *The envelope is on the table.* Therefore, we can observe in the final trellis that some tagging conflicts have been solved. However, the trellis still contains ambiguities. This behaviour is normal, since the application of contextual rules does not guarantee the removal of all ambiguities; but now we could apply the Viterbi algorithm [6] with a greater possibility of success. It is necessary to remember that we are in the context of a hybrid system for POST, and rules operate together with a HMM-based tagger.

3   Compilation of Contextual Rules into FSTs

Instead of processing the input stream forward and backward repeatedly, looking for the matching of the conditions involved in the rules, it is advisable to perform a previous compilation step that translates the rules into finite state transducers. These structures always treat the input stream linearly forward and allow us to apply contextual rules more efficiently.

3.1   Definition of the Input Alphabet

In order to work with FSTs, we need an alphabet, i.e. the set of symbols that conform the input streams. Since rules will be applied on trellises, in which ambiguous words can appear, a first alternative was to use pairs as elements of the alphabet. In these pairs, the first component would be a word, and the second one would be the set of tags associated to that word in the trellis. However, it would need to perform operations on sets in order to transit adequately between the states of the FSTs, and those operations could involve too high a computational effort for every single transition. Therefore, this approach was rejected.

A better mechanism for the symbolic compilations of the rules is the assignment of integers to words and tags. Furthermore, in order to obtain FSTs which are as compact as possible, we do not consider the whole tagset and the whole dictionary of our system, but only the set of tags and the set of words that appear in the rules (we will call these sets TR and WR, respectively). In this way, the exact correspondence is the one shown in Table 2: 0 is reserved for the empty string ε; -1 and 1 will be the beginning and the end of sentence, respectively; the tags that appear in the rules will be numbered forward from 3 to n, and stored in a structure that we will call *mini-tagset*; the words that appear in the rules will be numbered backward from -3 to $-m$, and stored in a structure that we will call *mini-dictionary*; and finally, -2 and 2 will be reserved as wildcards to represent any other words or tags, respectively, that do not appear in the rules, but can appear in a new sentence to be tagged and in its corresponding trellis.

Table 2. Mapping for words and tags that can appear in trellises

$w \in WR$	$w \notin WR$	Start	ε	End	$t \notin TR$	$t \in TR$
$-m, \ldots, -4, -3$	-2	-1	0	1	2	$3, 4, \ldots, n$

Table 3. A mini-tagset and a mini-dictionary

Mini-tagset	Mini-dictionary
Det → 3	bajo → -3
P → 4	sobre → -4
S → 5	
V → 6	

Table 4. A trellis and its corresponding mapping

El	sobre	está	sobre	la	mesa	-2	-4	-2	-4	-2	-2
Pron	P	V	P	Det	S	2	4	6	4	2	5
	S		S	Pron	V		5		5	3	6
	V		V				6		6		

The set of rules used in the example of Table 1 involves four tags and two words, so we can build the mini-tagset and mini-dictionary shown in Table 3. By using these structures and the mapping explained above, we can transform the initial trellis of that example into the one shown in Table 4.

Now, we collect all the integers of this new trellis by columns and add the marks of beginning and end of sentence in order to obtain the corresponding input stream for a cascade of FSTs implementing the contextual rules:

```
-1 -2  2 -4  4  5  6 -2  6 -4  4  5  6 -2  2  3 -2  5  6  1
```

The FSTs will translate this input stream into an output stream with the same aspect. After this, we apply the inverse procedure to retrieve the final trellis obtained from the application of the contextual rules.

3.2   Building an FST for Every Contextual Rule

The next step consists in the construction of an individual FST for every contextual rule to be applied. Firstly, we describe this process intuitively by using the following rule:

```
select (S) (1 is {V});
```

A possible version of the corresponding FST is shown in Fig. 1. In this case, the action must be represented first (from state 0 to state 2), since the condition (from state 2 to 5) affects a word that appears afterwards. In both cases, action and condition, the word must be represented before its possible tags. We will draw arcs with thick lines for words and arcs with normal lines for tags.

- **Action.** In this rule, the current word can be any word, hence we use the wildcard -2 and all the words present in the mini-dictionary (bajo and sobre) in the label of the arc from state 0 to 1. In a trellis, only tags can be modified, not words. This is the reason why these three possible cases for words are translated into themselves. The action of the rule, i.e. to select the tag

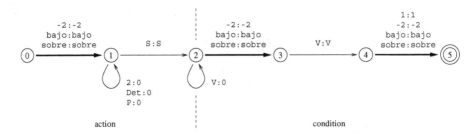

Fig. 1. Fictitious FST for the rule select (S) (1 is {V});

substantive, is represented by the arc $1 \xrightarrow{\text{S:S}} 2$, which does not modify the tag, and by the loops in states 1 and 2, which remove the rest of possible tags by translating them into the empty string 0. We use two loops instead of only one because we assume that the tags will always appear in a predefined order (usually, the lexicographic order, which should coincide with the order defined in the mapping), and that this order will not be broken by any sequence of iterations with different tags in the same loop. These hypotheses are not critical in practice, and allow us to build more compact FSTs. Be that as it may, the most important aspect is that an arc keeping the tag substantive is mandatory and cannot be included in any optional loop.

— **Condition.** The same reasoning made above is applicable to the word involved in the condition (the arc from state 2 to 3). The rule requires this word to be precisely a verb, hence the presence of only one arc for its tags ($3 \xrightarrow{\text{V:V}} 4$, which does not modify the tag since we are implementing a condition, not an action). This is enough for the example under consideration, since verb is the last tag in the mini-tagset. However, it is a better alternative not to allow state 4 to be the final state of this FST, because in general it cannot be guaranteed that verb is the unique tag. Therefore, another word or the end of sentence must appear after the tag (hence the final arc from state 4 to 5).

The FST presented above is fictitious and has been shown only to facilitate understanding. In practice, words and tags must be replaced by their integers associated in the mapping, producing the corresponding real implementation of the FST shown in Fig. 2.

The designing and building of FSTs becomes more difficult when the condition is complex. For instance, the construction of transducers for barrier rules or for local rules with inclusions or negations is much more complicated than for the simple equality shown above. Nevertheless, this process of symbolic compilation has been implemented for all the rule schemes covered by our formalism. Since it is not possible to describe the whole compilation process here, we include only one more example in order to illustrate how FSTs always prove to be a robust frame to perform any operation involved in this kind of contextual rules. In this case, we consider the generic barrier rule

$$\texttt{select } (t_s) \ (+ * \texttt{ is } \{t_j, t_k, \ldots, t_l\} \texttt{ barrier is } \{t_x, t_y, \ldots, t_z\})$$

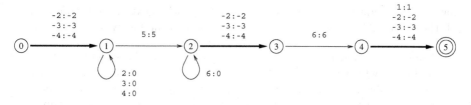

Fig. 2. Real FST for the rule `select (S) (1 is {V})`;

The aspect of the abstract version of the corresponding FST is shown in Fig. 3.

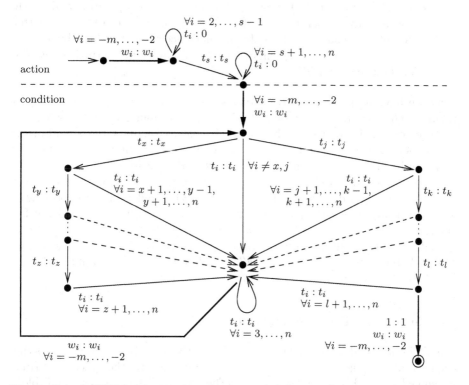

Fig. 3. Generic FST for the barrier rule `select` (t_s) $(+ *$ is $\{t_j, t_k, \ldots, t_l\}$ **barrier is** $\{t_x, t_y, \ldots, t_z\})$

3.3 Making the FSTs Operative

Let us consider, for instance, a simple transducer which transforms 3 into 4 when 1 appears before the 3. This FST will produce the output stream 1 4 only if the input stream is exactly 1 3. However, we want this FST to produce the same effect for any other sequences of symbols containing 1 3 as substring. In order to do this, we need to apply a normalization process on the FST. That is, once we have built a transducer for every contextual rule, the next phase is to normalize all these FSTs. The normalization process requires the following steps:

- Compilation and closure of the alphabet. Once we have defined the input alphabet, which we will call Σ, it is necessary to create a FST to transform every symbol into itself. Then, we obtain Σ^*, where $*$ is the closure operation, in order to be able to process input strings with more than one symbol.
- For every transducer T, we perform the following operations:
  - $a = p_1(T)$, where p_1 is the first project operation, i.e. every arc $q \xrightarrow{x:y} r$ is replaced by $q \xrightarrow{x} r$ or by $q \xrightarrow{x:x} r$. Therefore, a can be seen as an automaton or as a transducer that does not change its input.
  - $\Gamma = \Sigma^* - (\Sigma^* \cdot a \cdot \Sigma^*)$, where $-$ is the subtraction operation and $\cdot$ is the concatenation operation. In this way, we obtain in Γ a transducer that accepts the complement of the language accepted by a (and by T).
  - Finally, $N = \Gamma \cdot (T \cdot \Gamma)^*$, in order to obtain in N the normalized version of the transducer T.

Once we have normalized all transducers, we can form a cascade by applying them in sequence, taking the output of an FST as input for the following one. Another option is to build only one FST able to simulate the simultaneous application of all contextual rules by only one pass over the input stream. This FST can be obtained by composing all individual transducers.

The operations of closure, project, subtraction, concatenation, composition, etc., are well-defined in the theory of FSTs, and there are tools available which implement all these procedures. In our case, we have used the free version of *FSM Library: General-purpose finite-state machine software tools*, available in `http://www.research.att.com/sw/tools/fsm/`, implemented by Mohri, Pereira and Riley from the *AT&T* laboratories [4]. This library has allowed us to build the final operative version of our FSTs.

3.4   Space and Time Complexities

The FSTs obtained have always operated correctly and rapidly, which shows that the general compilation procedure is robust. For instance, the spaces and times consumed by the FSTs corresponding to the rules of Table 1 appear in Table 5, where T_i is the FST of each individual rule, and T_{1234} is the composition of the four preceding FSTs. It is important to note that, in theory, the time complexity of the FST obtained by composition is linear respect to the length of the input, and does not depend on the number of rules. But in practice, even though in a hybrid system for POST a small set of contextual rules (between 50 and 100) is expected to be sufficient, the computational cost of the composition operation is very high, and it is more advisable to perform a sequential application of the rules by executing the cascade of the corresponding individual FSTs: for time, 0.247 vs. 1.717 seconds, in a Pentium III 450 MHz. under Linux operating system; and for space, 20 160 vs. 2 931 156 bytes, in all cases with only 4 contextual rules.

Table 5. Spaces and times for a set of FSTs and for their corresponding composition

FSTs	Initial FST			Normalized FST				
	number of states	number of arcs	size in bytes	number of states	number of arcs	size in bytes	compilation in seconds	execution in seconds
T_1	6	16	348	19	142	2 520	0.245	0.051
T_2	11	32	664	58	520	9 036	0.878	0.072
T_3	8	26	532	39	346	6 024	0.586	0.070
T_4	7	23	472	20	145	2 580	0.251	0.054
Total	32	97	2 016	136	1 153	20 160	1.960	0.247
T_{1234}	-	-	-	30 244	160 513	2 931 156	11.773	1.717

4 Conclusion and Future Work

We have presented a strategy to compile constraint-based contextual rules for part-of-speech tagging under the form of finite state transducers. The purpose of these contextual rules is to remove the residuary errors that pure stochastic taggers make. These contextual rules must be introduced by linguists, and therefore we also provide a new formalism with intuitive syntax and semantics. Transducers have proved to be a very formal and robust execution framework for contextual rules, but there are still some aspects that should be investigated further. In the context of our hybrid system for POST, where contextual rules operate in combination with a HMM-based tagger, it is necessary to perform experiments with the purpose of selecting the best order in which to apply these two disambiguation techniques. Another aspect of future work, in this case for situations where it is possible to detect that residuary errors are systematic, is the automatic generation of specific contextual rules for these errors.

References

1. Brill, E. (1994). Some advances in rule-based part of speech tagging. In *Proceedings of the Twelfth National Conference on Artificial Intelligence (AAAI-94)*.
2. Graña, J.; Chappelier, J.-C.; Vilares, M. (2001). Integrating external dictionaries into part-of-speech taggers. In *Proc. of the Euroconference on Recent Advances in Natural Language Processing (RANLP-2001)*, pp. 122–128.
3. Karlsson, F.; Voutilainen, A.; Heikkilä, J.; Anttila, A. (1995). Constraint grammar: a language-independent system for parsing unrestricted text. *Mouton de Gruyer*, Berlin.
4. Mohri, M. (1997). Finite-state transducers in language and speech processing. *Computational Linguistics*, vol. 23(2), pp. 269–311.
5. Padró, L. (1996). POS tagging using relaxation labelling. In *Proceedings of the 16th International Conference on Computational Linguistics (COLING-96)*.
6. Viterbi, A.J. (1967). Error bounds for convolutional codes and an asymptotically optimal decoding algorithm. *IEEE Trans. Information Theory*, vol. IT-13 (April).
7. Voutilainen, A.; Heikkilä, J. (1994). An English constraint grammar (ENGCG): a surface-syntactic parser of English. In Fries, Tottie and Schneider (eds.), *Creating and using English language corpora*, Rodopi.

Finite State Lazy Operations in NLP

Franck Guingne[1,2] and Florent Nicart[1,2]

[1] L.I.F.A.R. Université de Rouen,
Faculté des Sciences et des Techniques,
76821 Mont Saint Aignan Cedex, France
{guingne,nicart}@dir.univ-rouen.fr
[2] X.R.C.E., Xerox Research Center Europe
38240 Meylan
{Franck.Guingne,Florent.Nicart}@xrce.xerox.com

Abstract. Finite state networks can represent dictionaries and lexical relations. Traditional finite-state operations like composition can produce huge networks with prohibitive computation space and time. For a subset of finite state operations, these drawbacks can be avoided by using virtual networks, which rely on structures that are partially built on demand. This paper addresses the implementation of virtual network operations in xfst (XEROX Finite State Technology software). The example of "priority union" which is particularly useful in NLP, is developed.

1 Introduction

Finite-state techniques are widely used in various areas of Natural Language Processing (NLP) [5,6,9] such as morphological analysis, tokenization [12] and part-of-speech disambiguation. Finite-state transducers, which are a generalization of finite-state automata, can be used to efficiently represent lexical relations. Such "lexical transducers" have many advantages: they take up little memory, are robust, and are available as complete products for commercial applications.

In addition to memory considerations, existing finite-state automata can be powerfully and flexibly combined together into new automata using finite-state operations such as, for example, union, priority union, intersection and composition.

Because of memory and time considerations, the full computation of such new automata may be intractable. Lazy finite-state algorithms make it possible to perform these operations partially, building them on demand at runtime as required to handle specific inputs. Lazy algorithms have already been designed with success to handle operations on automata such as determinization (see [1] for an application to pattern matching). Our aim here is to implement the so-called "virtual networks" and their algorithms based on lazy evaluation.

In the next section, we will introduce finite state transducers (FST) by giving some definitions and computational considerations. In the third section, we will explain the advantages of xfst "virtual networks" [7] and how they work. The priority union will be taken as example.

J.-M. Champarnaud and D. Maurel (Eds.): CIAA 2002, LNCS 2608, pp. 138–147, 2003.
© Springer-Verlag Berlin Heidelberg 2003

2   Transducers

A Finite-State Transducer (FST) [13] is a machine that encodes a relation between two regular languages. It behaves like a FSA (Finite State Automaton), also called an acceptor. For each accepted word from the input language, a FST returns one or more related words of the output language.

2.1   Definitions and Operations

Definitions. A FST is a 6-tuple $(\Sigma, \Omega, Q, I, F, E)$ where: Σ is the *input* alphabet, Ω is the *output* alphabet, Q is the (finite) *set of states*, $I \subset Q$ is the set of *initial* states, $F \subset Q$ is the set of *final* states, $E \subseteq Q \times (\Sigma \cup \{\epsilon\}) \times \Omega^* \times Q$ a finite set of *transitions*.

As the input side of a FST can be seen as a FSA, we similarly define a *transition function* δ mapping $Q \times (\Sigma \cup \{\epsilon\})$ to 2^Q by $\delta(q, a) = \{q' \mid \exists(q, a, b, q') \in E\}$. It can be extended to input words in a mapping δ^* from $Q \times \Sigma^*$ to 2^Q.

Given a FST $T = (\Sigma, \Omega, Q, I, F, E)$, a *path* from p_1 to q_n in T is a sequence $(p_i, a_i, b_i, q_i)_{i=1,n}$ of edges of E such that $q_i = p_{i+1}, i = 1 \ldots n - 1$. A *successful path* is a path from an initial state to a final state. A *word* w is *recognized* by a transducer if and only if $\exists i \in I \mid \delta^*(i, w) \cap F \neq \emptyset$.

Transducers arc only able to express a class of relations: *the regular ones* (the link between finite state transducers and regular relations can be shown in analogy to Kleene's theorem [8]). The construction of transducers from regular relations can be performed in the same way as for automata from regular expressions [3]. Empty transitions (ϵ-transitions) are simply replaced by (ϵ, ϵ). In this way, we can define union, concatenation and closure of transducers.

We will use the term finite-state network to cover both simple automata and transducers. By convention, our networks have one initial state, shown as the leftmost state in our diagrams, and we can apply them in both directions: from the upper side to lower side and *vice versa*. The final state is represented as a double circle. We use *upper side* for the input side and *lower side* for output side. Notice that the following definitions on regular operations could be writ-

Lexical side :

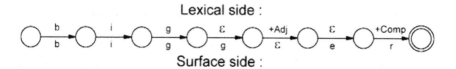

Surface side :

Fig. 1. A path in a *lexicon transducer* for English with "Lexical side" as upper side and "Surface side" as lower side. "+Adj", "+Comp" are atomic symbols.

ten without using ϵ-transitions [2], but we use them here to produce simpler constructions.

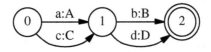

Network A

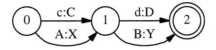

Network B

Fig. 2. The two networks used in our examples.

Union. Given two FSTs $T_1 = (\Sigma_1, \Omega_1, Q_1, i_1, F_1, E_1)$ and $T_2 = (\Sigma_2, \Omega_2, Q_2, i_2, F_2, E_2)$, encoding the relations R_1 and R_2, respectively, the relation $R_3 = R_1 \cup R_2$ is encoded by the FST

$$T_3 = T_1 \cup T_2. \qquad (1)$$

such that: $T_3 = (\Sigma_1 \cup \Sigma_2, \Omega_1 \cup \Omega_2, Q_1 \cup Q_2 \cup \{i_3\}, \{i_3\}, F_1 \cup F_2, E_3)$, with $E_3 = E_1 \cup E_2 \cup \{(i_3, \epsilon, \epsilon, i_1), (i_3, \epsilon, \epsilon, i_2)\}$.

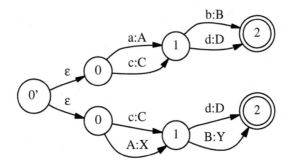

Fig. 3. Union of networks A and B, ϵ is the identity relation $\epsilon : \epsilon$.

Concatenation. Given two FSTs $T_1 = (\Sigma_1, \Omega_1, Q_1, i_1, F_1, E_1)$ and $T_2 = (\Sigma_2, \Omega_2, Q_2, i_2, F_2, E_2)$, encoding the relations R_1 and R_2, respectively, the relation $R_3 = R_1 \cdot R_2$ is encoded by the FST

$$T_3 = T_1 \cdot T_2. \qquad (2)$$

such that: $T_3 = (\Sigma_1 \cup \Sigma_2, \Omega_1 \cup \Omega_2, Q_1 \cup Q_2, \{[i_1]\}, F_2, E_3)$, with $E_3 = E_1 \cup E_2 \cup \{(f_1, \epsilon, \epsilon, i_2) \mid f_1 \in F_1\}$.

Kleene Star. Given a FST $T = (\Sigma, \Omega, Q, \{i\}, F, E)$, encoding the relation R, the relation $R^* = \bigcup_{k \in \mathbb{N}} R^k$ is recognized by the FST

$$T^* = \bigcup_{k \in \mathbb{N}} T^k. \tag{3}$$

such that $T^* = (\Omega, \Sigma, Q \cup \{i_1\}, \{i_1\}, \{i\}, E_1)$ and $E_1 = E \cup \{(i_1, \epsilon, \epsilon, i)\} \cup \{(f, \epsilon, \epsilon, i) \mid f \in F\}$.

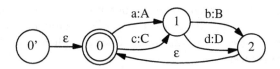

Fig. 4. The Kleene star of the network A.

Composition. Given two FSTs $T_1 = (\Sigma, \Omega, Q_1, \{i_1\}, F_1, E_1)$ and $T_2 = (\Omega, \Gamma, Q_2, \{i_2\}, F_2, E_2)$, encoding the relations R_1 and R_2, respectively, the relation $R_3 = R_1 \circ R_2$ is encoded by the FST

$$T_3 = T_1 \circ T_2. \tag{4}$$

such that: $T_3 = (\Sigma, \Gamma, Q_1 \times Q_2, \{i_1\}, \{i_2\}, F_1 \times F_2, E_3)$, with $E_3 = \{((q_1, q_2), a, b, (q_1', q_2')) \mid \exists c \in \Omega \cup \{\epsilon\} \mid (q_1, a, c, q_1') \in E_1 \text{ and } (q_2, c, b, q_2') \in E_2\}$

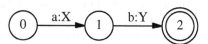

Fig. 5. Result of "network A composed with network B".

2.2   Computational Considerations

A very common operation on FSTs in NLP is the composition of several transducers. Let us consider it to examine some computational problems.

The simplest way to perform the operation is to simulate the composition by applying a string or a set of strings on the input of the first transducer, retrieving on its output the related string set and applying that string set to the input of the second network, and so on for each stage of the composition. But at each level of the composition, the strings of the output string set that are accepted as input by the next transducer belong to the intersection of the output language of the transducer with the input language of the subsequent transducer. That is, in the general case, multiple strings may be generated at each level of the composition, but some or all of them may be rejected or filtered out by the next transducer. A more efficient way to perform composition of several transducers is to pre-compile a single FST corresponding to the relation between the very first input language and the very last output language. In this way, the single pre-composed transducer directly maps an applied string to the final result without producing any intermediate results.

In some cases, however, compiling a single transducer will require a huge amount of memory. In the case of composition, in the worst case, the number of states in the composed network is the product of the number of states in the original networks.

Another reason for why compiling is not possible can be that the desired behavior cannot be predicted in advance. As an example of unpredictability, consider the following case. A transducer T for morphological analysis is composed of four transducers:

$$T \equiv T_1 \circ T_1 \circ T_3 \circ T_4 \tag{5}$$

Morphological analysis means mapping a surface string to a string that can be read as a morphological analysis of the input string, e.g., the French word "pensons" to "penser+Verb+PInd+1P+Pl", indicating the first-person plural present indicative form of the verb "penser". Let T_1 be a filter that blocks certain words, and T_4 be a transducer that provides a mapping between Unicode strings and another character encoding or transliteration for the language. And let us assume that there is a set of alternative filters, say T_{11}, T_{12}, T_{13}, and T_{14}, and a set of alternative encoding transducers, say T_{41}, T_{42}, T_{43}, and T_{44}, that are appropriate in various contexts and which are selected by the user at runtime. The precompilation of T to serve all possible combinations of filters and encodings would require constructing 16 different variants in this simple example. In interactive systems, users could conceivably control dozens of options affecting the final behavior of a transducer, which could raise the number of variants to several thousands.

3   Virtuality

To avoid precompilation in such cases, the final transducer can be built virtually.

3.1   Principles

The aim is to work with an object that represents the result of the combinations of the original networks (virtual operation can also be a unary operation like virtual determinization), and to build the true result network incrementally, in a "lazy" fashion, as required in real use. Typically, when we apply a virtual operation on a real network or networks, we obtain a virtual network that has the same properties as a real one and can participate in further virtual operations. Although it is not directly exploitable, the virtuality mechanism makes the lazy evaluation transparent for the end user.

Thus, a "virtual transducer" can be represented by a tree whose leaves are "physical transducers" and whose non-terminal nodes are operators such as union, intersection, concatenation, composition, or negation. Each time we need to use parts of the virtual transducer, this tree is partially evaluated as required to build the physical states and arcs to handle the actual input.

In this way, the resulting transducer is available immediately, instead of waiting for a long computational time, and memory is used only for the parts of the final transducer that are actually used. The price to pay is somewhat slower operations since they need to construct physical states and arcs at runtime to work.

Different Types of Virtuality. Basically, the principle of lazy operations [11] is evaluating variables or functions only when they are needed and not necessarily keeping the result. In the present case, it is advantageous to retain in memory the compiled physical parts of the network since they can be re-used often, networks act as if cached, so, for example, an operation will take more time to execute the first time, and will execute more quickly when repeated.

We can now distinguish two types of virtual networks: virtual networks on states, and virtual networks on arcs.

In virtual networks on states, the states are virtual. To follow a path in a virtual transducer, we need to realize all the states on this path (make them physical). This requires the arc set of each state to be physically constructed.

In the second type of virtual network, the arcs are virtual. That is, we just need to realize arcs that are on the requested path, not the whole arc set of all the states that are on the path. What we are working on is an implementation of the first type of virtual network, based on the original implementation designed by Ronald M. Kaplan, John Maxwell and Lauri Karttunen. In this version, we need two special functions in order to realize states: an "arc set function" that builds the outgoing arcs of the state being realized, and a "finality function" that decides whether a state being realized must be final or not.

Concretely, when virtual operations are applied, a new network is built that contains just a virtual initial state and is associated with a data structure de-

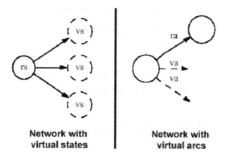

Network with   Network with
virtual states   virtual arcs

Fig. 6. Two types of virtuality.

scribing the type of virtual operation and giving the two appropriate "arc set" and "finality" functions. This virtual initial state is associated with each initial state of the original physical or virtual networks.

Arc Set Functions. For a state to be realized, we need to build its whole set of outgoing arcs according to rules, depending on the virtual operation being performed from the set of outgoing arcs of each associated original state. Physical arcs are created that point to new virtual states. These virtual states are associated with physical (resp. virtual) state(s) in the original physical (resp. virtual) network(s). The rules for creating the new arc set must be locally decidable since the function can only access information about the current virtual state and its associated states.

For example, in a virtual network given by the virtual union of two networks, the arc set function will create an arc for all the arcs in the arc set of the two associated states with the same labels. This arc will point to a virtual state that will be associated with all the destination states of the matching arcs. This is fully decidable because all of the words in both of the two networks will be present in the resulting network.

However, in the case of the virtual intersection, we will need to do the same work and build arcs that will later be revealed to be useless. This is due to words in each network that can be prefixes of words in the other network. In such a case, the decidability of the virtual operation will rely on the finality function.

Finality Functions. When a virtual state is realized, the finality function will decide if the physical version of this state has to be final according to rules depending on the virtual operation performed. In the general case, it corresponds to the logical definition of the operation. To continue with the examples previously taken, the finality function for a "virtual union" will perform a logical OR between the finality value of all the associated states, whereas it will perform a logical AND for a "virtual intersection".

3.2   The Priority Union

Let us see in more detail the behavior of our virtual networks by taking the virtual priority union[4] as an example. We can give two similar definitions of the priority union depending on the sides of the transducers we apply it on. On the upper side, the priority union will give the whole set of string pairs of the first transducer, and the strings pairs from the second transducer whose upper string is not recognized by the first transducer. Mathematically:

$$T_1 \overset{p}{\bigcup} T_2 \equiv T_1 \cup (\neg upper(T_1) \circ T_2), \tag{6}$$

with $upper(T_1)$ means the upper side of T_1.

The other definition is:

$$T_1 \bigcup_p T_2 \equiv T_1 \cup (T_2 \circ \neg lower(T_1)), \tag{7}$$

with $lower(T_1)$ means the lower side of T_1.

The type of priority union to be used depends on the side of the resulting transducer we plan to apply strings on. The priority union is very useful in NLP because it permits lookup on transducers or dictionaries in a sequential way. More precisely, it can replace batch programs that try lookup on a sequence of dictionaries and stop at the first lookup that returns a non-empty point.

Our current implementation works in a binary way, that is each virtual state is associated with a pair of states from the original networks. If these states are non-deterministic, which means states have multiple arcs with the same symbol on the input side, several virtual states and state pairs are created. As each virtual state corresponds to a pair of states in the original networks, both of the "finality" and "arc set" functions deal with the following cases:

- A : (state from Net1, state from Net2);
- B : (state from Net1, No state);
- C : (No state, state from Net2).

Moreover, the initial state is the object of a particular treatment for two reasons: since the priority union of two transducers contains the whole relation described by the first one, all arcs from its initial state are copied without any selection and point to new virtual state with state pairs of type A. Two networks could occur whose initial states both own loop arcs with same label. These loop arcs must not be reproduced on the initial state of the resulting network in order not to be concatenated with the network they do not belong to. To avoid this, we ensure that the initial state of the resulting network is not associated with the pair made of the initial states of the original networks.

Following these considerations let us explain the work of the two "virtual" functions. The treatment made by the arc set function is quite simple. In cases B and C, it just has to copy the arc set of the associated state and make it point to virtual states of the same type (respectively B or C). In case A, two arc sets have to be processed: arcs that match on the upper (lower) side between the two arc sets produce arcs labeled with the labels of the matched arcs from the second network, and point to a new virtual state corresponding to the target of the matching arcs in the two networks (type A). Other arcs (that do not match with other arcs in the other network) are replicated and point to a virtual state of type B or C, depending on whether they belong to the first or to the second network. As for the virtual intersection, the arc set function cannot locally determine whether a pair of matching arcs is useful or not, and let the finality function decide. The finality function has to determine the finality of a given virtual state according to the type of this state. Type B and C are easy to process. They correspond respectively to paths that are only in the first network, or only in the second one. In these cases the function has just to return the finality of the

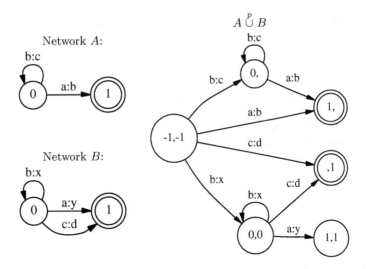

Fig. 7. The priority union (on the upper side) of network A and network B.

single associated state. The case A, however, corresponds to paths that have been followed in both networks. Then the function needs to apply the logical formula on the finality of the associated states:

$$\neg Finality(StateA) \wedge Finality(StateB) \tag{8}$$

This allows adding successful paths in the resulting network that come from the second network and cannot be found in the first.

4   Conclusion and Future Work

Virtual operations are useful because some operations on transducers can't be realized without them. This is the case when we manipulate large transducers. Sometimes, we don't need the whole result of an operation. For example, to perform some lookups on a normalized German lexicon, we need to compose the lexicon network with a normalization filter network. In our test (on a Sparc Ultra 10 with 150 MHZ CPU, 128 Mo memory), this composition took 27 seconds, and lookups were immediate. With the virtual composition, the result is immediate and lookups remain instantaneous.

Some modifications must be done in the virtual priority union implementation to treat one-sided epsilons. Some optimizations can be added in order to manage more efficiently the memory used by virtual transducers. We also plan to consider the weighted case [10] and to extend virtuality to weighted networks.

Acknowledgments. Many thanks to Kenneth R. Beesley, Jean-Marc Champarnaud, Tamas Gaal, Lauri Karttunen and Andre Kempe for their comments.

References

1. A. V. Aho. 1990. Algorithms for Finding Patterns in Strings, in Handbook of Theoretical Computer Science. Volume A: Algorithms and Complexity, (J. van Leeuwen, ed.), Elsevier, 255–300.
2. J.-M. Champarnaud, J.-L. Ponty and D. Ziadi. 1997. From a regular expression to an automaton, Intern. J. of Computer Math., Vol. 72, 415–431, 1999.
3. L. Karttunen. 1994. Constructing Lexical Transducers. In The Proceedings of the Fifteenth International Conference on Computational Linguistics. Coling 94, I, pages 406–411, Kyoto, Japan.
4. L. Karttunen. 1998. The Proper Treatment of Optimality in Computational Phonology. FSMNLP'98. International Workshop on Finite-State Methods in Natural Language Processing, June 29-July 1, 1998, pages 1–12, Bilkent University, Ankara, Turkey.
5. L. Karttunen. 2000. Applications of Finite-State Transducers in Natural Language Processing, Lecture Notes in Computer Science,in CIAA'2000, S. Yu and A. Paun eds., Springer Verlag, 2088(2001), 34–46.
6. L. Karttunen (J-P. Chanod, G.Grefenstette, A.Schiller). 1996. Regular Expressions for Language Engineering. Natural Language Engineering 2(4) 305–328.
7. L. Karttunen, T. Gaal, and A. Kempe 1997. Xerox Finite-State Tool. Technical Report. Xerox Research Centre Europe, Grenoble. June 1997. Meylan, France.
8. S. Kleene, Representation of events in nerve nets and finite automata, automata studies, Ann. Math. Stud., Princeton University Press 34 (1956), 3
9. M. Mohri. 1996. On Some Applications of Finite-State Automata Theory to Natural Language Processing, journal of natural language engineering, 2: 61–80.
10. M. Mohri, F. C. N. Pereira, and M. Riley. A Rational Design for a Weighted Finite-State Transducer Library. In Derick Wood and Sheng Yu, editors, Proceedings of the Second International Workshop on Implementing Automata (WIA '97). volume 1436 of Lecture Notes in Computer Science, pages 144–158. Springer-Verlag, Berlin-NY, September.
11. M. Riley, F. Pereira, and E. Chun. 1995., Lazy transducer composition: a flexible method for on-the-fly expansion of context dependent grammar networks, in IEEE Automatic Speech Recognition Workshop, pages 139–140, Snowbird, UT.
12. R. M, Kaplan. and P. Newman. 1997. Lexical resource reconciliation in the Xerox Linguistic Environment. In D. Estival, A. Lavelli, K. Netter, and F. Pianesi (editors), Computational environments for grammar development and linguistic engineering, pp. 54–61. Proceedings of a workshop sponsored by the Association for Computational Linguistics, Madrid, Spain, July 1997
13. S. Eilenberg. 1974. Automata, Languages and Machines, Volume A.

State Complexity of Basic Operations on Nondeterministic Finite Automata

Markus Holzer[1] and Martin Kutrib[2]

[1] Institut für Informatik, Technische Universität München
Arcisstraße 21, D-80290 München, Germany
holzer@informatik.tu-muenchen.de
[2] Institut für Informatik, Universität Giessen
Arndtstraße 2, D-35392 Giessen, Germany
kutrib@informatik.uni-giessen.de

Abstract. The state complexities of basic operations on nondeterministic finite automata (NFA) are investigated. In particular, we consider Boolean operations, catenation operations – concatenation, iteration, λ-free iteration – and the reversal on NFAs that accept finite and infinite languages over arbitrary alphabets. Most of the shown bounds are tight in the exact number of states, i.e. the number is sufficient and necessary in the worst case. For the complementation tight bounds in the order of magnitude are proved. It turns out that the state complexities of operations on NFAs and deterministic finite automata (DFA) are quite different. For example, the reversal and concatenation have exponential state complexity on DFAs but linear complexity on NFAs. Conversely, the complementation can be done with linear complexity on DFAs but needs exponentially many states on NFAs.

1 Introduction

Motivated by several applications and implementations of finite automata in software engineering, programming languages and other practical areas in computer science, the state complexity of deterministic finite automata has been studied in recent years. For example, the state complexity of the intersection of DFAs has been studied in [14]. A tight bound of 2^n states for the reversal has been shown in [7], whereas catenations and other operations are the main topic of [15]. For the important case of finite languages results have been obtained in [1]. A state-of-the-art survey can be found in [13]. Related to the problem of finding upper bounds for the state complexity is the problem of efficiently simulating nondeterministic automata by deterministic ones. For example, transforming a certain type of NFA to a DFA gives an upper bound for the corresponding NFA state complexity of complementation. Results concerning the simulation problems have been shown in [8,9,11].

As pointed out in [13] there are several good reasons why the size of DFAs is a natural and objective measure for regular languages. E.g. the size of a DFA is linear to the number of states of a DFA, but this is not necessarily true for

J.-M. Champarnaud and D. Maurel (Eds.): CIAA 2002, LNCS 2608, pp. 148–157, 2003.
© Springer-Verlag Berlin Heidelberg 2003

NFAs. On the other hand, the influence of the degree of nondeterminism on the power and limitations of certain devices is an important question in descriptional complexity theory. Finite automata with limited nondeterminism have been considered in [6] where an infinite nondeterministic hierarchy of regular languages has been proved. The issue of quantifying inherent nondeterminism in regular languages is dealt with in [3]. The relation between ambiguity and the amount of nondeterminism is considered in [4].

We expect that examining the state complexity of basic operations on NFAs will enhance the understanding of the relations between nondeterminism, ambiguity and the power of finite automata.

2   Preliminaries

We denote the powerset of a set S by 2^S. The empty word is denoted by λ, the reversal of a word w by w^R, and for the length of w we write $|w|$. For the number of occurrences of a symbol a in w we use the notation $\#_a(w)$.

A *nondeterministic finite automaton* (NFA) is a system $\langle S, A, \delta, s_0, F \rangle$, where (1) S is the finite set of *internal states*, (2) A is the finite set of *input symbols*, (3) $s_0 \in S$ is the *initial state*, (4) $F \subseteq S$ is the set of *accepting (or final) states*, and (5) $\delta : S \times A \to 2^S$ is the *transition function*.

The set of rejecting states is implicitly given by the partitioning, i.e. $S \setminus F$.

If not otherwise stated throughout the paper we assume that the NFAs are always *reduced*. This means that there are no unreachable states and that from any state a final state can be reached. An NFA is said to be *minimal* if its number of states is minimal with respect to the accepted language. Since every n-state NFA with λ-transitions can be transformed to an equivalent n-state NFA without λ-transitions [5] for state complexity issues there is no difference between the absence and presence of λ-transitions. For convenience, we consider NFAs without λ-transitions only.

As usual the transition function δ is extended to a function $\Delta : S \times A^* \to 2^S$ reflecting sequences of inputs as follows: $\Delta(s, wa) = \bigcup_{s' \in \Delta(s,w)} \delta(s', a)$, where $\Delta(s, \lambda) = \{s\}$ for $s \in S$, $a \in A$, and $w \in A^*$. In the sequel we always denote the extension of a given δ by Δ.

Let $\mathcal{A} = \langle S, A, \delta, s_0, F \rangle$ be an NFA, then a word $w \in A^*$ is *accepted* by $\mathcal{A}$ if $\Delta(s_0, w) \cap F \neq \emptyset$. The *language accepted* by $\mathcal{A}$ is $L(\mathcal{A}) = \{w \in A^* \mid w \text{ is accepted by } \mathcal{A}\}$.

The next two preliminary results involve NFAs directly. They are key tools in the following sections, and can be proved by a simple pumping argument.

Lemma 1. *Let $p \geq 1$ be an arbitrary integer. Any NFA that accepts the language $\{a^p\}^+$ resp. $\{a^p\}^*$ needs at least $p+1$ resp. p states.*

The $(p+1)$th state is necessary since the initial state has to be a non-accepting one. If we modify the language to $\{a^p\}^*$ then the initial state could be equal to the accepting state.

3   Boolean Operations

We start our investigations with Boolean operations on NFAs that accept languages over arbitrary alphabets. In the case when the finite automaton is deterministic it is well-known that in the worst case the Boolean operations union, intersection and complementation have a state complexity of $m \cdot n$, $m \cdot n$ and m, respectively. However, the state complexity of NFA operations is essentially different. At first we consider the union.

Theorem 2. *For any integers $m, n \geq 1$ let $\mathcal{A}$ be an m-state and $\mathcal{B}$ be an n-state NFA. Then $m + n + 1$ states are sufficient and necessary in the worst case for an NFA $\mathcal{C}$ to accept the language $L(\mathcal{A}) \cup L(\mathcal{B})$.*

Proof. In order to construct an $(m + n + 1)$-state NFA for the language $L(\mathcal{A}) \cup L(\mathcal{B})$ we simply use a new initial state and connect it to the states of $\mathcal{A}$ and $\mathcal{B}$ that are reached after the first state transition.

Now we are going to show that $m + n + 1$ states are necessary in the worst case. Let $\mathcal{A}$ be an m-state NFA that accepts the language $\{a^m\}^*$ and $\mathcal{B}$ an n-state NFA that accepts $\{b^n\}^*$.

Let $\mathcal{C}$ be an NFA for the language $L(\mathcal{A}) \cup L(\mathcal{B})$. In order to reject the inputs a^i, $1 \leq i \leq m - 1$, but to accept the input a^m the NFA $\mathcal{C}$ needs at least $m - 1$ non-accepting states $s_1, \ldots, s_{m-1}$ from each of which a final state is reachable. Similarly, $\mathcal{C}$ needs at least $n - 1$ states $s'_1, \ldots, s'_{n-1}$ for processing the inputs b^i, $1 \leq i \leq n - 1$.

Denote by P_a resp. P_b the set of states that are reachable by inputs of the form a^i resp. b^i for $i \geq 1$. None of the final states may be reachable from the states in $P_a \cap P_b$. Otherwise words of the form $a^i b^j$ or $b^i a^j$ would be accepted.

It follows that neither the s_i nor the s'_i may belong to the intersection $P_a \cap P_b$. But, trivially, they do belong to P_a resp. to P_b. Now consider all words $\{a^m\}^+$. There must exist a final state s_m that accepts infinitely many of them. Thus, s_m is reachable from s_m itself. The same holds for a state s'_n for the words in $\{b^n\}^+$. It follows $s_m \in P_a$ and $s'_n \in P_b$ but $s_m \notin P_a \cap P_b$ and $s'_n \notin P_a \cap P_b$. Finally, the initial state s_0 must be a final state since $\lambda \in L(\mathcal{A}) \cup L(\mathcal{B})$, but $s_0 \neq s_m$ and $s_0 \neq s'_n$ since otherwise $\{a^m\}^i b^n$ or $\{b^n\}^i a^m$ would be accepted for some $i \in \mathbb{N}$. Altogether, $P_a \cup P_b$ must contain at least $m + n$ different states that are not equal to the initial state. $\qquad \square$

When we are concerned with finite languages the state complexity of the union can be reduced by three states. For these upper bounds in the deterministic case see [2]. We may assume w.l.o.g. that minimal NFAs for finite languages not containing the empty word have only one final state. Since such NFAs do not contain any cycles they do contain at least one final (sink) state for which the transition function is not defined. Now a given minimal NFA with more than one final state is modified such that a sink state becomes the only final state. Therefore simply the transition function has to be extended. If the finite language contains the empty word, then in addition the initial state is a second final one.

Corollary 3. *For any integers $m, n \geq 2$ let $\mathcal{A}$ be an m-state NFA and $\mathcal{B}$ be an n-state NFA. If $L(\mathcal{A})$ and $L(\mathcal{B})$ are finite, then $m+n-2$ states are sufficient and necessary in the worst case for an NFA $\mathcal{C}$ to accept the language $L(\mathcal{A}) \cup L(\mathcal{B})$.*

Proof. We can adapt the proof of the previous theorem as follows. Since NFAs for finite languages do not contain any cycles, for the construction of the NFA $\mathcal{C}$ we do not need a new initial state (this saves one state). Moreover, we can merge both initial states (this saves the second one) and both final sink states (this saves the third one). Now the construction of $\mathcal{C}$ is straightforward.

The finite languages $\{a^m\}$ and $\{b^n\}$ are witnesses for the necessity of the number of states for the union in the worst case. An NFA that accepts the language $\{a^m\}$ needs at least $m + 1$ states. Otherwise it would run through cycles. By the same argumentation as in the proof of Theorem 2 and merged initial and sink states we obtain at least $(m + 1) + (n + 1) - 2$ states for an NFA that accepts $\{a^m\} \cup \{b^n\}$. □

The complementation of NFA languages is an expensive task at any rate. It is well known [10] that 2^n is the tight upper bound on the number of states necessary for a deterministic finite automaton to accept an (infinite) n-state NFA language. Since the complementation operation on deterministic finite automata neither increases nor decreases the number of states (simply exchange final and non-final states) we obtain an upper bound for the state complexity of the complementation on NFAs.

Corollary 4. *For any integer $n \geq 1$ the complement of an n-state NFA language is accepted by a 2^n-state NFA.*

Unfortunately, this expensive upper bound is tight in the order of magnitude. Currently it is open whether the exact upper bound is necessary in the worst case. Basically, the idea is to construct an efficiently acceptable language such that nondeterminism cannot do anything for an efficient acceptance of its complement.

Theorem 5. *For any integer $n > 2$ there exists an n-state NFA $\mathcal{A}$ such that any NFA that accepts the complement of $L(\mathcal{A})$ needs at least 2^{n-2} states.*

Proof. For $k \geq 0$ let $L_k = \{a, b\}^* a\{a, b\}^k b\{a, b\}^*$. It is clear that L_k is accepted by the $(k + 3)$-state NFA depicted in Figure 1.

Intuitively, $\mathcal{A}$ has to guess the position of an input symbol a which is followed by k arbitrary input symbols and a symbol b. In order to accept the complement of L_k a corresponding NFA $\mathcal{B} = \langle S', \{a, b\}, \delta', s'_0, F' \rangle$ has to verify that the input

Fig. 1. A $(k + 3)$-state NFA accepting $\{a, b\}^* a\{a, b\}^k b\{a, b\}^*$.

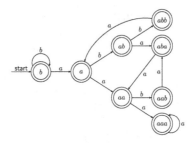

Fig. 2. A minimal NFA accepting L_2 of Theorem 5.

has no substring $a\{a,b\}^k b$. Therefore, after reading a symbol a $\mathcal{B}$ must be able to remember the next k input symbols. Altogether this needs 2^{k+1} states.

More formally, we consider the input words of length $k+1$. Observe that for each of these words w the concatenation ww belongs to the complement of L_k. Let $S(w)$ be $\{s \in S' \mid s \in \Delta'(s_0', w) \wedge \Delta'(s, w) \cap F' \neq \emptyset\}$, and v, v' be two arbitrary different words from $\{a,b\}^{k+1}$. Assume $S(v) \cap S(v') \neq \emptyset$. It follows $\Delta'(s_0', vv') \cap F' \neq \emptyset$ and $\Delta'(s_0', v'v) \cap F' \neq \emptyset$ and, therefore, vv' and $v'v$ are accepted by $\mathcal{B}$.

But this is a contradiction since there exists a position $1 \leq p \leq k+1$ at which v has a symbol a and v' a symbol b or vice versa. Thus either vv' or $v'v$ is of the form $x_1 \cdots x_{p-1} a x_{p+1} \cdots x_{k+1} y_1 \cdots y_{p-1} b y_{p+1} \cdots y_{k+1}$ and, therefore, belongs to L_k. From the contradiction follows $S(v) \cap S(v') = \emptyset$. Since there exist 2^{k+1} words in $\{a,b\}^{k+1}$ the state set S' has to contain at least 2^{k+1} states. □

The situation for finite languages over an ℓ-letter alphabet, $\ell \geq 2$, is quite different, since the upper bound of the transformation to a deterministic finite automaton is different. In [11] it has been shown that $O(\ell^{\frac{n}{\log_2 \ell + 1}})$ states are an upper bound for deterministic finite automata accepting a finite n-state NFA language.

Corollary 6. *For any integers $\ell, n > 1$ the complement of a finite n-state NFA language over an ℓ-letter alphabet is accepted by an $O(\ell^{\frac{n}{\log_2 \ell + 1}})$-state NFA.*

Note, that for $\ell = 2$ the upper bound is $O(2^{\frac{n}{2}})$. A slight modification of the proof of the previous theorem yields:

Theorem 7. *For any integers $\ell > 1$ and $n > 2$ there exists a finite n-state NFA language L over an ℓ-letter alphabet such that any NFA that accepts the complement of L needs at least $\Omega(\ell^{\frac{n}{2 \cdot \log_2 \ell}})$ states.*

Proof. For $\ell > 1$ let $A = \{a_1, \ldots, a_\ell\}$ be an alphabet. Let $k \geq 0$ be an integer. A finite language L_k is defined by $A^j a_1 A^k y$, where $0 \leq j \leq k$ and $y \in A \setminus \{a_1\}$. The NFA depicted in Figure 3 accepts L_k with $2k + 3$ states. Trivially L_k is also accepted by an NFA with $2k + 4$ states.

An NFA $\mathcal{B}$ for the complement works similar to the corresponding NFA in the previous proof. It need not remember $k + 1$ input symbols exactly, but whether

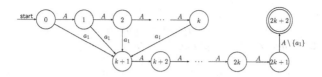

Fig. 3. A $(2k + 3)$-state NFA accepting L_k of Theorem 7.

a symbol has been a_1 or not. Since previously we argued with words of finite lengths it follows immediately that $\mathcal{B}$ needs at least 2^{k+1} states. Additionally the length of the prefix A^j has to be tracked. For this purpose the state set has to be doubled such that we have a lower bound of 2^{k+2} states. Transforming $2 = \ell^{\log_\ell 2} = \ell^{\frac{1}{\log_2 \ell}}$ we obtain the lower bound $\ell^{\frac{k+2}{\log_2 \ell}} \in \Omega(\ell^{\frac{n}{2 \cdot \log_2 \ell}})$. $\qquad\square$

Next we are going to prove a tight bound for the remaining Boolean operation, the intersection.

Theorem 8. *For any integers $n, m \geq 1$ let $\mathcal{A}$ be an m-state and $\mathcal{B}$ be an n-state NFA. Then $m \cdot n$ states are sufficient and necessary in the worst case for an NFA to accept the language $L(\mathcal{A}) \cap L(\mathcal{B})$.*

Proof. Clearly, the NFA defined by the cross-product of $\mathcal{A}$ and $\mathcal{B}$ accepts the language $L(\mathcal{A}) \cap L(\mathcal{B})$ with $m \cdot n$ states.

As witness languages for the fact that the bound is reached in the worst case define $L_k = \{w \in \{a, b\}^* \mid \#_a(w) \equiv 0 \pmod{k}\}$ for all $k \in \mathbb{N}$. An NFA that accepts L_k with k states is easily constructed.

Identically, L'_k is defined to be $\{w \in \{a, b\}^* \mid \#_b(w) \equiv 0 \pmod{k}\}$. It remains to show that an NFA $\mathcal{C}$ that accepts $L_m \cap L'_n$ for $m, n \geq 1$, needs at least $m \cdot n$ states.

Consider the input words $a^i b^j$ and $a^{i'} b^{j'}$ with $0 \leq i, i' \leq m - 1$ and $0 \leq j, j' \leq n - 1$, and assume $\mathcal{C} = \langle S, A, \delta, s_0, F \rangle$ has less than $m \cdot n$ states. Since there are $m \cdot n$ such words, for at least two of them the intersection

$$\{s \in S \mid s \in \Delta(s_0, a^i b^j) \wedge \Delta(s, a^{m-i} b^{n-j}) \cap F \neq \emptyset\} \cap \Delta(s_0, a^{i'} b^{j'})$$

is not empty. This implies $a^{i'} b^{j'} a^{m-i} b^{n-j} \in L_m \cap L'_n$. Since either $i \neq i'$ or $j \neq j'$ it follows $i' + m - i \not\equiv 0 \pmod{m}$ or $j' + n - j \not\equiv 0 \pmod{n}$, a contradiction. $\qquad\square$

4   Catenation Operations

Now we turn to the catenation operations. In particular, tight bounds for concatenation, iteration and λ-free iteration will be shown. Roughly speaking, in terms of state complexity these are efficient operations for NFAs. Again, this is essentially different when deterministic finite automata come to play. For example, in [15] a bound of $(2m - 1) \cdot 2^{n-1}$ states has been shown for the DFA-concatenation, and in [12] a bound of $2^{n-1} + 2^{n-2}$ states for the iteration.

Theorem 9. *For any integers $m, n \geq 1$ let $\mathcal{A}$ be an m-state NFA and $\mathcal{B}$ be an n-state NFA. Then $m + n$ states are sufficient and necessary in the worst case for an NFA $\mathcal{C}$ to accept the language $L(\mathcal{A})L(\mathcal{B})$.*

Proof. The upper bound is due to the observation that in $\mathcal{C}$ one has simply to connect the final states in $\mathcal{A}$ with the states in $\mathcal{B}$ that follow the initial state.

The upper bound is reached for the concatenation of the languages $L(\mathcal{A}) = \{a^m\}^*$ and $L(\mathcal{B}) = \{b^n\}^*$. The remaining proof follows the idea of the proof of Theorem 2. □

In case of finite languages one state can be saved.

Lemma 10. *For any integers $m, n \geq 1$ let $\mathcal{A}$ be an m-state NFA and $\mathcal{B}$ be an n-state NFA. If $L(\mathcal{A})$ and $L(\mathcal{B})$ are finite, then $m + n - 1$ states are sufficient and necessary in the worst case for an NFA $\mathcal{C}$ to accept the language $L(\mathcal{A})L(\mathcal{B})$.*

Proof. Since for finite languages $\mathcal{A}$ and $\mathcal{B}$ must not contain any cycles the initial state of $\mathcal{B}$ is not reachable after the construction of the previous theorem. Thus, it can be deleted what yields an upper bound of $m + n - 1$ states.

As witnesses for the tightness consider the languages $\{a^{m-1}\}$ and $\{b^{n-1}\}$. They are accepted by m-state resp. n-state NFAs. Clearly, any NFA for the concatenation needs at least $m + n - 1$ states. □

The constructions yielding the upper bounds for the iteration and λ-free iteration are similar. The trivial difference between both operations concerns the empty word only.

Theorem 11. *For any integer $n > 2$ let $\mathcal{A}$ be an n-state NFA. Then $n + 1$ resp. n states are sufficient and necessary in the worst case for an NFA to accept the language $L(\mathcal{A})^*$ resp. $L(\mathcal{A})^+$.*

Proof. Let $\mathcal{A} = \langle S_A, A_A, \delta_A, s_{0,A}, F_A \rangle$ be an n-state NFA. Then the transition function of an n-state NFA $\mathcal{C} = \langle S, A, \delta, s_0, F \rangle$ that accepts the language $L(\mathcal{A})^+$ is for $s \in S$ and $a \in A$ defined as follows: $\delta(s, a) = \delta_A(s, a)$ if $s \notin F_A$, and $\delta(s, a) = \delta_A(s, a) \cup \delta_A(s_{0,A}, a)$ if $s \in F_A$.

The other components remain unchanged, i.e., $S = S_A$, $s_0 = s_{0,A}$, and $F = F_A$.

If the empty word belongs to $L(\mathcal{A})$ then the construction works fine for $L(\mathcal{A})^*$ also. Otherwise an additional state has to be added: Let $s_0' \notin S_A$ and define $S = S_A \cup \{s_0'\}$, $s_0 = s_0'$, $F = F_A \cup \{s_0'\}$, and for $s \in S$ and $a \in A$: $\delta(s, a) = \delta_A(s, a)$ if $s \notin F_A \cup \{s_0'\}$, $\delta(s, a) = \delta_A(s, a) \cup \delta_A(s_{0,A}, a)$ if $s \in F_A$, and $\delta(s, a) = \delta_A(s_{0,A}, a)$ if $s = s_0'$.

In order to prove the tightness of the bounds for any $n > 2$ let

$$L_n = \{w \in \{a, b\}^* \mid \#_a(w) \equiv n - 1 \pmod{n}\}$$

The language L_n is accepted by an n-state NFA. At first we show that $n + 1$ states are necessary for $\mathcal{C} = \langle S, \{a, b\}, \delta, s_0, F \rangle$ to accept $L(\mathcal{A})^*$.

Contrarily, assume $\mathcal{C}$ has at most n states. We consider words of the form a^i with $0 \leq i$. The shortest four words belonging to $L(\mathcal{A})^*$ are λ, a^{n-1}, a^{2n-2}, and a^{2n-1}. It follows $s_0 \in F$. Moreover, for a^{n-1} there must exist a path $s_0 \vdash s_1 \vdash \cdots \vdash s_{n-2} \vdash s_n$ where $s_n \in F$ and $s_1, \ldots, s_{n-2}$ are different non-accepting states. Thus, $\mathcal{C}$ has at least $n-2$ non-accepting states.

Assume for a moment F to be a singleton. Then $s_0 = s_n$ and for $1 \leq i \leq n-3$ the state s_0 must not belong to $\delta(s_i, a)$. Processing the input a^{2n-1} the NFA cannot enter s_0 after $2n-2$ time steps. Since $a \notin L(\mathcal{A})^*$ the state s_0 must not belong to $\delta(s_0, a)$.

On the other hand, $\mathcal{C}$ cannot enter one of the states $s_1, \ldots, s_{n-3}$ since there is no transition to s_0. We conclude that $\mathcal{C}$ is either in state s_{n-2} or in an additional non-accepting state s_{n-1}. Since there is no transition such that $s_{n-2} \in \delta(s_{n-2}, a)$ in both cases there exists a path of length n from s_0 to s_0. But a^n does not belong to $L(\mathcal{A})^*$ and we have a contradiction to the assumption $|F| = 1$.

Due to our assumption $|S| \leq n$ we now have $|F| = 2$ and $|S| - |F| = n - 2$. Let us recall the accepting sequence of states for the input a^{n-1}: $s_0 \vdash s_1 \vdash \cdots \vdash s_{n-2} \vdash s_n$. Both s_0 and s_n must be accepting states. Assume $s_n \neq s_0$. Since a^{2n-2} belongs to $L(\mathcal{A})^*$ there must be a possible transition $s_0 \vdash s_1$ or $s_n \vdash s_1$. Thus, a^{2n-2} is accepted by s_n. In order to accept a^{2n-1} there must be a corresponding transition from s_n to s_n or from s_n to s_0. In both cases the input a^n would be accepted. Therefore $s_n = s_0$.

By the same argumentation the necessity of a transition for the input symbol a from s_0 to s_0 or from s_0 to s_n follows. This implies that a is accepted. From the contradiction follows $|S| > n$.

As an immediate consequence we obtain the tightness of the bound for $L(\mathcal{A})^+$. In this case $s_0 \in F$ is not required. Thus, just one final state is necessary.   □

The state complexity for the iterations in the finite language case is n resp. $n - 1$. Without proof we state:

Lemma 12. *For any integer $n > 1$ let $\mathcal{A}$ be an n-state NFA. If $L(\mathcal{A})$ is finite, then $n - 1$ resp. n states are sufficient and necessary in the worst case for an NFA to accept the language $L(\mathcal{A})^*$ resp. $L(\mathcal{A})^+$.*

5 Reversal

The last operation under consideration is the reversal. For deterministic automata one may expect that the state complexity is linear. But it is not. In [15] for infinite languages a tight bound of 2^n has been shown. A proof of a tight bound for finite languages can be found in [1]. It is of order $O(2^{\frac{n}{2}})$ for a two-letter alphabet. From the following efficient bounds for NFAs it follows once more that nondeterminism is a powerful concept.

Theorem 13. *For any integer $n > 3$ let $\mathcal{A}$ be an n-state NFA. Then $n + 1$ states are sufficient and necessary in the worst case for an NFA $\mathcal{C}$ to accept the language $L(\mathcal{A})^R$.*

Fig. 4. A $(k+3)$-state and a $(k+4)$-state NFA accepting L_k and L_k^R of Theorem 13.

Proof. Basically, the idea is to reverse the directions of the transitions. This works fine for NFAs whose set of final states is a singleton or whose initial state is not within a loop. In general we are concerned with more than one accepting state and have to add a new initial state. If, in addition, the old initial state is part of a loop, then its role cannot be played by the new one and we obtain an $(n+1)$-state NFA.

The language $L_k = a^k\{a^{k+1}\}^*(\{b\}^* \cup \{c\}^*)$ for $k \geq 1$, may serve as an example for the fact that the bound is reached. The $(k+3)$-state NFA $\mathcal{A}$ that accepts L_k and the $(k+4)$-state NFA $\mathcal{C}$ that accepts L_k^R are depicted in Figure 4.

The necessity of $k+4$ states can be seen as follows. Since accepted inputs may begin with an arbitrary number of b's or c's we need two states s_b and s_c to process them. This cannot be done by the initial state because the loops would lead to acceptance of words with prefixes of the form b^*c^* or c^*b^*.

Obviously, a loop of $k+1$ states is needed in order to verify the suffix $\{a^{k+1}\}^*a^k$. If one in this sequence would be equal to s_b (s_c), then it would have a loop for b's (c's) and, hence, inputs of the form $c^*a^*b^*a^k$ ($b^*a^*c^*a^k$) would be accepted. For similar reasons the new initial state cannot be within a loop. Altogether it follows that $\mathcal{C}$ needs at least $k+4$ states what proves the tightness of the bound.   □

The fact that NFAs for finite languages do not have any cycle leads once more to the possibility of saving one state compared with the infinite case.

Lemma 14. *For any integer $n \geq 1$ let $\mathcal{A}$ be an n-state NFA. If $L(\mathcal{A})$ is finite, then n states are sufficient and necessary in the worst case for an NFA to accept the language $L(\mathcal{A})^R$.*

Proof. Recall from the proof of Corollary 3 that for every minimal n-state NFA that accepts a non-empty finite language there exists an equivalent n-state NFA that has only one final state. By the construction of the previous proof we obtain an $(n+1)$-state NFA that has an unreachable state. It is the unique former final state. The bound follows if the state is deleted.

Let for $n \geq 1$ the language L_n defined to be $\{a, b\}^{n-1}$. Trivially, L_n is accepted by an n-state NFA. Since $L_n = L_n^R$ the assertion follows.   □

The bound for the reversal of finite NFA languages is in some sense strong. It is sufficient and reached for all finite languages. Finally, Table 1 summarizes the shown state complexity bounds for NFAs.

Table 1. Comparison of the NFA and DFA state complexities (ℓ is the number of states, t is the number of final states of the 'left' automaton).

	NFA		DFA	
	finite	infinite	finite	infinite
$\cup$	$m+n-2$	$m+n+1$	$O(mn)$	mn
$\sim$	$O(\ell^{\log_2 \ell+1})$	$O(2^{n-2})$	n	n
$\cap$	(mn)	mn	$O(mn)$	mn
R	n	$n+1$	$O(2^{\frac{n}{2}})$	2^n
$\cdot$	$m+n-1$	$m+n$	$O(mn^{t-1}+n^t)$	$(2m-1)2^{n-1}$
$*$	$n-1$	$n+1$	$2^{n-3}+2^{n-4}$	$2^{n-1}+2^{n-2}$
$+$	n	n		

References

1. Câmpeanu, C., Čulik, K., Salomaa, K., and Yu, S. *State complexity of basic operations on finite languages.* Fourth International Workshop on Implementing Automata, LNCS 2214, pp. 60–70.
2. Câmpeanu, C., Sântean, N., and Yu, S. *Minimal cover-automata for finite languages.* Theoret. Comput. Sci. 267 (2001), 3–16.
3. Goldstine, J., Kintala, C., and Wotschke, D. *On measuring nondeterminism in regular languages.* Inform. Comput. 86 (1990), 179–194.
4. Goldstine, J., Leung, H., and Wotschke, D. *On the relation between ambiguity and nondeterminism in finite automata.* Inform. Comput. 100 (1992), 261–270.
5. Hopcroft, J. E. and Ullman, J. D. *Introduction to Automata Theory, Language, and Computation.* Addison-Wesley, Reading, Massachusetts, 1979.
6. Kintala, C. M. and Wotschke, D. *Amounts of nondeterminism in finite automata.* Acta Inf. 13 (1980), 199–204.
7. Leiss, E. *Succinct representation of regular languages by Boolean automata.* Theoret. Comput. Sci. 13 (1981), 323–330.
8. Mereghetti, C. and Pighizzini, G. *Optimal simulations between unary automata.* STACS 1998, LNCS 1373, 1998, pp. 139–149.
9. Mereghetti, C. and Pighizzini, G. *Unary automata simulations and cyclic languages.* International Workshop on Descriptional Complexity of Automata, Grammars and Related Structures, 1999, pp. 145–153.
10. Meyer, A. R. and Fischer, M. J. *Economy of description by automata, grammars, and formal systems.* IEEE Symposium SWAT 1971, pp. 188–191.
11. Salomaa, K. and Yu, S. *NFA to DFA transformation for finite languages over arbitrary alphabets.* J. Aut., Lang. and Comb. 2 (1997), 177–186.
12. Yu, S. *Regular languages.* In Rozenberg, G. and Salomaa, A. (eds.), *Handbook of Formal Languages I.* Springer, 1997, chapter 2, pp. 41–110.
13. Yu, S. *State complexity of regular languages.* J. Aut., Lang. and Comb. 6 (2001), 221–234.
14. Yu, S. and Zhuang, Q. *On the state complexity of intersection of regular languages.* SIGACT News 22.3 (1991), 52–54.
15. Yu, S., Zhuang, Q., and Salomaa, K. *The state complexities of some basic operations on regular languages.* Theoret. Comput. Sci. 125 (1994), 315–328.

Adaptive Automata – A Revisited Proposal

João José Neto and César Bravo

Escola Politécnica da Universidade de São Paulo
Av. Prof. Luciano Gualberto sn Travessa 3 n° 158
CEP 05508-900 São Paulo SP BRASIL
joao.jose@poli.usp.br
lupus@usp.br

Abstract. This paper impose further discipline to the use of adaptive automata [Jos94], [Iwa00] by restricting some of their features, in order to obtain devices that are easier to create and more readable, without loosing computational power. An improved notation is proposed as a first try towards a language for adaptive paradigm programming.

Keywords: adaptive devices, rule-driven formalisms, self-modifying machines, adaptive automata, adaptive paradigm.

1 Introduction

In [Jos01], the structure and the operation of adaptive rule-based devices have been formally stated. Structured pushdown automata [Jos93] are a variant of classical pushdown automata, in which states are clustered into mutually recursive finite-state sub-machines, which restrict the usage of the control pushdown store to the handling of return states only. Adaptive automata are self-modifying rule-driven formalisms whose underlying non-adaptive devices are the structured pushdown automata. Structured pushdown automata are fully equivalent to classical pushdown automata.

However, despite these features, adaptive automata sometimes lack simplicity, turning them difficult to understand and maintain.

The proposal described in this paper imposes some restrictions to the use of the features of the model in order to obtain devices that are easier to create and understand, without loosing any of the their original computational power.

2 Adaptive Automata

In order to Adaptive automata perform self-modification, adaptive actions attached to their state-transition rules are activated whenever the transition is applied.

The Underlying Structured Pushdown Automata. A finite-state automaton is composed of a set of states, a finite non-empty alphabet, a transition function, an initial state and a set of final states. Transitions map ordered pairs specifying the current state and the current input symbol into a new state.

J.-M. Champarnaud and D. Maurel (Eds.): CIAA 2002, LNCS 2608, pp. 158–168, 2003.

There are two types of transitions from state A to state B:

(a) Transitions $(A, \alpha) \rightarrow B$, which consume an input symbol α; and

(b) Empty transitions $(A, \epsilon) \rightarrow B$, which do not modify the input.

A structured pushdown automaton also exhibits a set of states, a finite non-empty alphabet, an initial state, a set of final states, a pushdown alphabet and a transition function, including internal transitions, like those shown for finite-state automata, and external transitions, responsible for the calling and returning scheme. Beside the two types of internal transitions, sub-machines allow special call and return transitions:

(a) Transitions $(A, \epsilon) \rightarrow (\downarrow B, X)$ from state A, calling a sub-machine whose initial state is X. B is the return state, to which the control will be passed upon a return transition is performed by the called sub-machine. B is pushed onto the pushdown store when these transitions are executed.

(b) Transitions $(C, \epsilon) \rightarrow (\uparrow B, B)$ from some state C in the current sub-machine's set of final states. State B, which represents any state tha has been previously pushed onto the pushdown store by the sub-machine that called the current one, is popped out of the pushdown store and the caller sub-machine is then resumed at the popped state.

The Adaptive Mechanism. Adaptive actions change the behavior of an adaptive automaton by modifying the set of rules defining it. In adaptive automata, the adaptive mechanism consists of executing one adaptive action attached to the state transition rule chosen for application before the rule is performed, and a second one after applying the subjacent state transition rule.

The adaptive mechanism of adaptive automata is described in [Jos01]: it is defined by attaching a pair of (optional) adaptive actions to the subjacent non-adaptive rules defining their transitions, one for execution before the transition takes place and another for being performed after executing the transition.

At each execution step of an adaptive automaton, the device's current state, the contents of the top position in the pushdown storage and the current input symbol determine a set of feasible transitions to be applied. In deterministic cases, the set is either empty (no transition is allowed) or it contains a single transition (in this case, that transition is immediately applied). In non-deterministic cases, more than one transition are allowed to be executed in parallel. In sequential implementations, a backtracking scheme chooses to apply one among the set of allowed transitions.

Adaptive actions are formulated as calls to adaptive parametric functions. These ones describe the modifications to apply to the adaptive automaton whenever they are called. These changes are described and executed in three sequential steps: (a) An optional adaptive action may be specified for execution prior to applying the specific changes to the automaton. (b) A set of elementary adaptive actions specifies the modifications performed by the adaptive action being described. (c) Another optional adaptive action may performed after the specific modifications are applied to the automaton.

Elementary adaptive actions specify the actual modifications to be imposed to the automaton. Changes are performed through three classes of adaptive actions, which specify a transition pattern against which the transitions in use are to be tested: (a) Inspection-type actions (introduced by a question mark in usual notation), which search the current set of transitions in the automaton for transitions whose shape match the given pattern (b) Elimination-type adaptive actions (introduced by a minus sign in usual notation), which eliminate from the current set of transitions in the automaton all transitions matching the given shape. (c) Insertion-type adaptive actions (introduced by a plus sign in usual notation), which add to the set of current transitions a new one, according to the specified shape.

The adaptive mechanism turn a usual automaton into an adaptive one by allowing its set of rules to change dynamically.

3   Improving the Formulation of Adaptive Automata

In this section we discuss some of the main drawbacks of the traditional version of the formalisms used for representing adaptive automata in previous publications.

The Notation. The notation used to represent adaptive automata is the first source of drawbacks to be considered in our study, for the simplicity of the model relies on the use of notations with the adequate features: a good notation is expected to be at least compact, simple, expressive, unambiguous, readable, and easy to learn, understand and maintain.

The notations for adaptive automata and structured pushdown automata generally differ in details, but there are two main classes of notations: graphical ones, are better for human visualization, and symbolic ones, which are more compact and machine-readable.

We compared notations still in use, and chose an algebraic and a graphical one, according to their characteristics and functionality:

Transition type	Symbolic notation	Graphical notation
Transition consuming α	$(A, \alpha) \rightarrow B$	$\bigcirc^A \xrightarrow{\alpha} \bigcirc^B$
Empty transition	$(A, \epsilon) \rightarrow B$	$\bigcirc^A \xrightarrow{\epsilon} \bigcirc^B$
Initial state	Explicitly indicated	$\rightarrow \bigcirc$
Final state	Explicitly indicated	$\odot$

For structured pushdown automaton, the final choice preserves the notation established for finite-state automata to denote internal transitions in submachines. The symbol ϵ (the empty string) has been preserved in both finite-state and structured pushdown notations in order to maintain compatibility with traditional well-established notations. The following table adds notation for expressing (empty-transition) sub-machines calls and returns:

Transition type	Symbolic notation	Graphical notation
Call sub-machine X from state A, returning to state B	$(A, \epsilon) \rightarrow (\downarrow B, X)$	$\bigcirc^A \xRightarrow{X} \bigcirc^B$
Return to state R after executing the called sub-machine X in its final state C	$(C, \epsilon) \rightarrow (\uparrow R, R)$ for all possible R	

For adaptive automata, all transitions not calling adaptive actions are denoted as stated above. Adaptive transitions make reference up to a pair of adaptive actions, $\mathcal{B}$ (before-action) and $\mathcal{A}$ (after-action). Their notation is summarized in the table below.

A restriction on the transitions to which adaptive actions may be attached, restricts them to be attached to internal transitions only avoiding superposition of the effects of two different sources of complexity in the same transition rule.

Transition type	Symbolic notation	Graphical notation
Adaptive transition with "before" adaptive action attached	$(A, \alpha) \rightarrow B[\mathcal{B}\bullet]$	$\bigcirc^A \xrightarrow[\mathcal{B}\bullet]{\alpha} \bigcirc^B$
Adaptive transition "after" adaptive action attached	$(A, \alpha) \rightarrow B[\bullet\mathcal{A}]$	$\bigcirc^A \xrightarrow[\bullet\mathcal{A}]{\alpha} \bigcirc^B$
Adaptive transition with both adaptive action attached	$(A, \alpha) \rightarrow B[\mathcal{B} \bullet \mathcal{A}]$	$\bigcirc^A \xrightarrow[\mathcal{B}\bullet\mathcal{A}]{\alpha} \bigcirc^B$

In the general case, adaptive actions $\mathcal{B}$ and $\mathcal{A}$ are representations of parametric calls to adaptive functions, which have the general form M $(p_1, p_2, \ldots, p_n)$ where $p_1, p_2, \ldots, p_n$ are n arguments passed to an adaptive function named M.

Adaptive actions are symbolically declared apart from the adaptive automaton, and they comprehend a header and a body. In the header, the name and the formal parameters of the adaptive function arc defined, followed by a section in which the names of all variables and generators are declared.

The body part is formed by an optional adaptive function call to be executed on entry, followed by a set of elementary adaptive actions, responsible by the modifications to be performed. A furhter optional call specifies another adaptive function to be executed on exit. Both calls are denoted in the usual way, as mentioned above.

There are three types of elementary adaptive actions: insertion, elimination and inspection actions. The notation chosen for the elements of the declaration of an adaptive function is shown in the table below. No graphic notation is yet suggested for adaptive functions.

Element of the declaration	Symbolic notation
Adaptive function name	M
Parameters	$(p_1, p_2, \ldots, p_n)$
Variables	$v_1, v_2, \ldots, v_n$
Generators	$g_1^*, g_2^*, \ldots, g_n^*$
Inspection actions	$?\,[\,\text{pattern}\,]$
Elimination actions	$-\,[\,\text{pattern}\,]$
Insertion actions	$+\,[\,\text{pattern}\,]$
Pattern	Any transition

Graphical notations have been tried [Alm95] that showed to be effective in some particular cases, where the self-modifications to be performed are small and easily visible. It is difficult to represent graphically the operation of adaptive functions in their full generality. We chose to adopt symbolic descriptions for adaptive functions, even when graphical notation is used to describe the adaptive automata they refer to. In order to provide an acceptable notation for dealing with sets and predicates, we chose to adopt the usual notation of predicate calculus, including quantifiers, for expressing adaptive functions.

The Underlying Model. The underlying model for adaptive automata is the structured pushdown automaton. Sub-machines may be considered as improved finite-state automata that are allowed to recursively call each other. The best feature of this arrangement is that structured pushdown automata turn out to be easier to design and understand than pushdown automata.

Pushdown machines may be considered excessively complex for some applications, for which finite-state automata have being used successfully. In these cases, some means should be provided to avoid the presence of unnecessary features in the underlying non-adaptive automaton.

In the special cases for which a simple finite state mechanism is enough, we may suppress the pushdown storage from the notationm reducing the remaining sub-machine into a simple finite-state machine.

The device resulting from the suggested simplification becomes an adaptive finite-state automaton, and may be formally stated just as published before in section 4 of [Jos01].

The Adaptive Mechanism. The principle of this mechanism consists in modifying the set of rules of the adaptive automaton by performing two adaptive actions, one before and another one after executing the underlying state-transition rule. However, one may ask whether a pair of adaptive actions is really a need. A element that substantially contributes to harden understanding adaptive devices is the structure of the adaptive functions themselves.

Adaptive functions are allowed to perform a pair of adaptive actions, one before and another after the modifications the adaptive function is expected to perform.

The set of parameters allowed in adaptive functions is another feature that is questionable when we search for simplicity: is it really needed to allow an arbitrary number of parameters? Should it be better to limit the number of parameters to a minimum? What should this minimum be? Should adaptive functions have no parameters at all? In the case of allowing parametric adaptive functions, should parameter types be controlled instead of arbitrarily chosen? Should adaptive functions be allowed as parameters?

Elementary adaptive actions are another source of complexity, since no restrictions are imposed to their use. Some questions may be posed concerning these elements of the formulation of adaptive automata: Should multiple variables be allowed in inspecting and eliminating elementary adaptive actions? Should looping be allowed within elementary adaptive actions?

In the following text we propose answers to several questions posed here, with the intent of achieving for adaptive automata a formulation according to our simplicity goals.

Adaptive Actions. In adaptive automata, this adaptive mechanism consists of executing the pair of adaptive actions attached to a rule at the time it is chosen for application. The first adaptive action in the pair is executed before the rule is performed, while the second one is executed after applying the subjacent state-transition rule. We limit to one the number of adaptive actions attached to the corresponding subjacent rule. Indeed, [Iwa00] shows a proof for the following theorem, stating that there is no need of attaching a pair of adaptive actions per rule, but the use of a single one is enough.

Theorem 1. *The result of the execution of any adaptive action is equivalent to a non-empty sequence of elementary adaptive actions.*

Proof. This theorem is fully demonstrated in [Iwa00] by simulating the device with the specified restrictions. □

Further simplifications may be achieved by using the following theorem:

Theorem 2. *For each rule defining an adaptive automaton, there is an equivalent set of rules, all of which have at most one attached (after-) adaptive action.*

Proof. This theorem may be proved by using the previous one and by showing that each adaptive transition having an attached before-adaptive action may be decomposed into a sequence of two simpler ones: the first one is an empty transition having as its attached after-adaptive action the before-adaptive action in the original transition; the second one is a copy of the original transition, from which the before-adaptive action has been removed. □

Theorem 3. *For each adaptive function that calls a pair of attached adaptive actions there is an equivalent set of simpler adaptive functions, all of which have at most one attached (after-) adaptive action.*

Proof. The proof of this theorem follows from the result of the previous one, and is based on showing that each adaptive function F that calls a before-adaptive action B may be decomposed into a sequence of two simpler ones in the following way: F becomes a copy of B's body, followed by a call to an auxiliary function F_1, where F_1 is a copy of F from which the call to B has been removed. □

4   Improving the Formulation of the Underlying Model

Structured pushdown automata use their pushdown store in two extremely limited situations, in which no symbol is consumed from the input string: (a) when a sub-machine is called, the return state is pushed onto the pushdown store before control is passed to the starting state of the sub-machine being called, and (b) when a sub-machine finishes its activity, a return state is popped from the pushdown store, and a return is made to that state in the calling sub-machine.

In this section we propose some changes to the underlying structured pushdown automata. These suggestions rely on the following theorem.

Theorem 4. *Adaptive (structured pushdown) automata are equivalent to adaptive finite-state automata.*

Proof. Proving that an adaptive structured pushdown automaton may simulate an adaptive finite-state automaton is straightforward. The opposite clause of the theorem is proved by simulating the pushdown store with states and transitions of adaptive finite-state automata. The resulting model allows performing the same work without using explicit memory. Such simulation may be sketched in three steps:

- We can suppose, without lost of generality, that all sub-machines in the adaptive automaton have single initial and final states.
- For sub-machines that are not self-embedded, substituting all sub-machine calls by an equivalent empty adaptive transition is enough. Indeed, if a calling sub-machine N invokes submachine M, we replace the following adaptive transition in N:

$$\bigcirc^q \xrightarrow[\bullet\mathcal{A}(q)]{\alpha} \bigcirc^p$$

for the original sub-machine call:

$$\bigcirc^q \xRightarrow{M} \bigcirc^p$$

where ϵ is the empty word and $\bullet\mathcal{A}(q)$ is an adaptive function which performs a macro expansion of the call to sub-machine M by replicating its topology in the exact place where the former call was, in such a way that the initial state of submachine M is reached, by a unique empty transtition from state q and the state p is reached by a unique empty transition from the unique final state of M. Note that the adaptive function $\bullet\mathcal{A}$ is executed only once. Such replacements finishes in a finite number of steps since, by hyphotesis, there are no self-embedding in M.

- If any sub-machine in the adaptive automaton is self-embedded, then it suffices to substitute every self-sub-machine call (top of the following table) by the adaptive transition (bottom of the table). Rhombuses represent the body of sub-machine M:

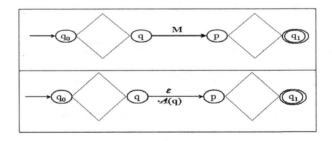

Where, again, the ϵ is the empty word but now $\bullet\mathcal{A}$ is an adaptive function with the following effect shown in the last box.

Note that this adaptive function duplicates the sub-machine topological structure and the states q_0, q_1, q and p. It must be clear, also, that this process can be a non-stopping one, but anyway it is a safe way to simulate the adaptive (structured pushdown) automata with an adaptive finite-state automata.   □

Improving the Formulation of the Adaptive Mechanism. The adaptive mechanism is indeed an important source of complexity in the formulation of adaptive automata which may be simplified in several aspects, some of which are the following: (a) by limiting to one the number of adaptive actions attached to each rule and/or called inside adaptive functions (b) by restricting the nature and number of parameters allowed for adaptive functions (c) by avoiding multiple variables to be inspected at the same time in a single inspection (d) by avoiding loops within elementary adaptive actions (e) by avoiding adaptive functions passed as parameters. Unfortunately, if we impose too much simplifications to the formulation, it becomes less expressive, requiring more clauses to perform the desired effect. However, by restricting the formulation, simpler facts are expressed by each adaptive action, rendering the formulation easier to understand. The hints above surely help searching for a cleaner and more effective formulation. This is a challenge yet to be overcome.

5   Illustrating Example

In this section, we chose a Non-deterministic Adaptive Finite Automaton, and used it to solve the well-known string-matching problem of determining whether a given string is a sub-string of some text. One classical solution for this problem is as follows: (a) Create a non-deterministic finite-state automaton that solves the problem. Constructing such automaton is straightforward: at its initial state, a loop consumes any symbol in its alphabet; next, a simple path consuming the sequence of symbols in the string we are looking for, and, at the end of this path, a unique final state consumes any further alphabet symbols. The explicit non-determinism in this automaton is located at the beginning of the path that accepts the required pattern. (b) Use a standard method to eliminate the non-deterministic transitions in the automaton. (c) Use a standard algorithm to minimize the resulting deterministic automaton.

In [Hol00] an algorithm is presented that constructs directly the desired deterministic finite-state automaton; it has the advantage of eliminating the need to eliminate non-deterministic transitions, since the complexity of this process is exponential. Additionally, in this method the full automaton must be constructed and minimized a priori.

Our approach avoids the exponential transformation, and does not require any unnecessary *a priori* work: we start from an initial adaptive non-deterministic finite-state automaton and let it process a text sample; whenever a text being analyzed activates a non-deterministic transition, the execution of the corresponding adaptive function performs the required topological transformations in order to render it deterministic. By doing so, our approach uses an incremental strategy to force them to perform in a deterministic way all transitions they execute, without changing the remaining non-deterministic transitions present in their formulation.

5.1   An Exact String Matching Non-deterministic FSA

Here we follow [Hol00]; the straightforward non-deterministic finite-state automaton is constructed for accepting the pattern **aba**, over the alphabet $\Sigma = \{a, b\}$:

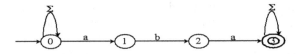

Fig. 1. A non-deterministic finite-state automaton

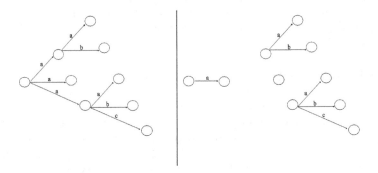

Fig. 2. Eliminating non-deterministic transitions.

5.2   An Equivalent Adaptive FSA for Exact String Matching

Now, let us turn the attention to our adaptive approach. In figure 2 (left) a non-determinism is present. In order to remove such non-determinism, we introduce a new state (fig. 2, right).

Now, in order to make it reachable, from the newly created state, all states that were reachable through all transitions departing from the conflicting states, we add further transitions leaving the new state and arriving to the target states, consuming the appropriate symbols, as shown in fig. 3. These operations may be sketched as an adaptive function B, in fig. 4.

This adaptive function receives a state and a token as parameters. In this formulation, it declares three variables and one generator; in line 3 quantifiers are used to allow testing whether there is more than one transition departing from

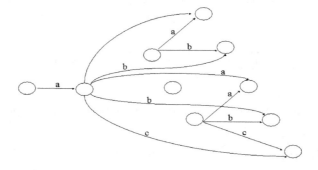

Fig. 3. Inserting transitions connecting the new state to the automaton

1	$B(q, \sigma) = \{$	declaring name and parameters of B
2	$p, n*, r, a;$	declaring variables (n is a generator)
3	$(!p)(?[(q, \sigma) \to p]) \{$	only if there are more than one rule with this shape,
4	$+[(q, \sigma) \to n]$	add a new transition with his shape with destination n
5	$(\forall p)(?[(q, \sigma) \to p]) \{$	for all transitions emerging from state q
6	$(\forall a)(\forall r)(?[(p, \alpha) \to r]) \{+[(n, \alpha) \to r] \}$	insert corresponding transitions departing from n
7	$-[(q, s) \to p] \} \} \}$	after all insertions, remove the original transition

Fig. 4. Adaptive function B that dynamically eliminates non-deterministic transitions from our non-deterministic adaptive finite-state automaton

the state received as the first parameter, and consuming the symbol received as the second parameter; if the answer is negative, then the query (the clause introduced by a question mark in this notation) will produce an empty result, and in this case the clause in braces (comprehending lines 4, 5, 6, 7) will not be executed. Otherwise, in line 4 a new transition is created from the current state to a new one, by means of generator n. Line 5 states that for each output transition, a proper output transition is generated and the original transition is deleted. The resulting adaptive non-deterministic finite-state automaton is shown in figure 5.

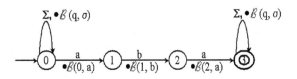

Fig. 5. Adaptive non-deterministic finite-state automaton

6   Conclusions

The proposed simplification to the formulation of adaptive automata seems to be reasonably expressive, compact and readable, allowing them to be stated in a rather intuitive form. Most features and development practices already established are preserved and respected to a large extent.

The proposed formulation caused almost no impacts to the power of adaptive automata, so the net result of its use will be a significant increase in the readability and soundness of the formulation without loss of the devices computational power.

From the programming point of view, our proposal has also advantages over the earlier notations, allowing programmers to build and debug adaptive automata in a more expedite way, resulting better products and a far better documentation.

References

[Alm95] Almeida Junior, J.R. STAD - Uma ferramenta para representação e simulação de sistemas através de statecharts adaptativos. São Paulo 1995, 202p. Doctoral Thesis. Escola Politécnica, Universidade de São Paulo.[In Portuguese]

[Hol00] Holub, Jan. Simulation of Non-deterministic Finite Automata in Pattern Matching. PhD Dissertation Thesis, Faculty of Electrical Engineering, Czech Technical University, February 2000, Prague.

[Iwa00] Iwai, M. K. Um formalismo gramatical adaptativo para linguagens dependentes de contexto. São Paulo 2000, 191p. Doctoral Thesis. Escola Politécnica, Universidade de São Paulo.

[Jos93] José Neto, J. Contribuição à metodologia de construção de compiladores. São Paulo, 1993, 272p. Thesis (Livre-Docência) Escola Politécnica, Universidade de São Paulo.[In Portuguese]

[Jos94] José Neto, J. Adaptive automata for context-dependent languages. ACM SIGPLAN Notices, v.29, n.9, p.115–24, 1994.

[Jos01] José Neto, J. Adaptive automata for syntax learning. XXIV Conferencia Latinoamericana de Informática CLEI'98, Quito - Ecuador, Centro Latinoamericano de Estudios em Informatica, Pontificia Universidad Católica Del Ecuador, tomo 1, pp.135–146. 19 a 23 de Outubro de 1998.

Efficient Automaton-Based Recognition for Linear Conjunctive Languages

Alexander Okhotin

Department of Computing and Information Science,
Queen's University, Kingston, Ontario, Canada K7L 3N6.
okhotin@cs.queensu.ca

Abstract. This paper studies practical algorithms for dealing with a particular family of cellular automata, which has recently been proved computationally equivalent to linear conjunctive grammars. The relation between these grammars and these automata resembles that between regular expressions and finite automata: while the former are better suited for human use, the latter are considerably easier to implement. In this paper, an algorithm for converting an arbitrary linear conjunctive grammar to an equivalent automaton is proposed, and different techniques of reducing the size of existing automata are studied.

1 Introduction

Linear conjunctive grammars [2] are linear context-free grammars augmented with an explicit intersection operation. The language family they generate is closed under all set-theoretic operations [3] and is known to contain many classical non-context-free languages, such as $\{a^n b^n c^n \mid n \geqslant 0\}$, $\{wcw \mid w \in \{a, b\}^*\}$ and the language of all derivations in a given finite string rewriting system [3], as well as other interesting languages, such as $\{ba^2 ba^4 b \ldots ba^{2n-2} ba^{2n} b \mid n \geqslant 0\}$.

In spite of their increased generative capacity, linear conjunctive grammars can be parsed with virtually the same quadratic-time methods as linear context-free grammars [2]. In an attempt to generalize these recognition methods, the paper [4] investigated a certain simple family of automata and established their computational equivalence to linear conjunctive grammars. These automata are basically one-dimensional cellular automata with the tape gradually shrinking in course of the computation; they can be simulated in $(n^2 + n)/2 + C$ elementary table lookup operations, which makes them very suitable for practical use. However, the grammar to automaton construction methods of [4] were mainly aimed at establishing the computational equivalence of the two formalisms and are very inefficient in the sense of the number of states generated; additionally, they require the grammar to be in a certain normal form, which is also inconvenient.

In this paper we develop a new practical algorithm to construct an automaton out of an arbitrary grammar and study various techniques of reducing the number of states in these automata. The language $\{wcw \mid w \in \{a, b\}^*\}$ is used to illustrate the methods of this paper, which allow to convert the original grammar for this language [2] to an automaton of 158 states and then reduce this automaton to 35 states, while the methods of [4] yield 222 states.

J.-M. Champarnaud and D. Maurel (Eds.): CIAA 2002, LNCS 2608, pp. 169–181, 2003.
© Springer-Verlag Berlin Heidelberg 2003

The algorithms developed in this paper have been implemented in the parser generator for conjunctive grammars [5].

2   Preliminaries

2.1   Linear Conjunctive Grammars

Conjunctive grammars were introduced in [2] as an extension of context-free grammars with an explicit intersection operation.

Definition 1. *A conjunctive grammar is a quadruple $G = (\Sigma, N, P, S)$, where Σ and N are disjoint finite nonempty sets of terminal and nonterminal symbols; P is a finite set of grammar rules of the form*

$$A \to \alpha_1 \& \ldots \& \alpha_n \quad (A \in N;\ n \geqslant 1;\ \text{for all } i,\ \alpha_i \in (\Sigma \cup N)^*), \qquad (1)$$

where the strings α_i are distinct and their order is considered insignificant; $S \in N$ is a nonterminal designated as the start symbol.

   For each rule of the form (1) and for each i $(1 \leqslant i \leqslant n)$, $A \to \alpha_i$ is called a conjunct. Let $conjuncts(P)$ denote the sets of all conjuncts.

A conjunctive grammar generates strings by deriving them from the start symbol, generally in the same way as the context-free grammars do. Intermediate strings used in course of a derivation are defined as follows:

Definition 2. *Let $G = (\Sigma, N, P, S)$ be a conjunctive grammar. The set of conjunctive formulae $\mathcal{F} \subset (\Sigma \cup N \cup \{\text{`(`}, \text{`\&`}, \text{`)`}\})^*$ is defined inductively: (i) The empty string ϵ is a formula; (ii) Any symbol from $\Sigma \cup N$ is a formula; (iii) If $\mathcal{A}$ and $\mathcal{B}$ are nonempty formulae, then $\mathcal{AB}$ is a formula. (iv) If $\mathcal{A}_1, \ldots, \mathcal{A}_n$ $(n \geqslant 1)$ are formulae, then $(\mathcal{A}_1 \& \ldots \& \mathcal{A}_n)$ is a formula.*

There are two types of derivation steps:

1. A nonterminal can be rewritten with a body of a rule enclosed in parentheses
   - $s'As'' \overset{G}{\Longrightarrow} s'(\alpha_1 \& \ldots \& \alpha_n)s''$, if $A \to \alpha_1 \& \ldots \& \alpha_n \in P$ and $s'As'' \in \mathcal{F}$,
   where $s', s'' \in (\Sigma \cup N \cup \{\text{`(`}, \text{`\&`}, \text{`)`}\})^*$.
2. A conjunction of one or more identical terminal strings enclosed in parentheses can be replaced with one such string without the parentheses –
   $s'(w \& \ldots \& w)s'' \overset{G}{\Longrightarrow} s'ws''$, if $s'As'' \in \mathcal{F}$.

Definition 3. *Let $G = (\Sigma, N, P, S)$ be a conjunctive grammar. The language of a formula is the set of all terminal strings derivable from the formula: $L_G(\mathcal{A}) = \{w \in \Sigma^* \mid \mathcal{A} \overset{G}{\Longrightarrow}^* w\}$. Define $L(G) = L_G(S)$.*

Let us now restrict general conjunctive grammars to obtain the subclass of linear conjunctive grammars:

Definition 4. *A conjunctive grammar $G = (\Sigma, N, P, S)$ is said to be linear, if each rule in P is of the form*

$$A \to u_1 B_1 v_1 \& \ldots \& u_m B_m v_m \quad (m \geqslant 1, \; u_i, v_i \in \Sigma^*, \; B_i \in N) \qquad (2a)$$

$$A \to w \quad (w \in \Sigma^*) \qquad (2b)$$

It has been proved in [2] that every linear conjunctive grammar can be effectively transformed to an equivalent grammar of the following form:

Definition 5. *A linear conjunctive grammar $G = (\Sigma, N, P, S)$ is said to be in the linear normal form, if each rule in P is of the form*

$$A \to bB_1 \& \ldots \& bB_m \& C_1 c \& \ldots \& C_n c \quad (m, n \geqslant 0;$$
$$m + n \geqslant 1; \; B_i, C_j \in N; \; b, c \in \Sigma), \qquad (3a)$$

$$A \to a \quad (A \in N, a \in \Sigma), \qquad (3b)$$

$$S \to \epsilon, \quad \text{only if } S \text{ does not appear in right parts of rules} \qquad (3c)$$

Example 1. The following linear conjunctive grammar for the well-known non-context-free language $\{wcw \mid w \in \{a, b\}^*\}$, quoted from [2], will be used as an example throughout this paper:

$$S \to C\&D$$
$$C \to aCa \mid aCb \mid bCa \mid bCb \mid c$$
$$D \to aA\&aD \mid bB\&bD \mid cE$$
$$A \to aAa \mid aAb \mid bAa \mid bAb \mid cEa$$
$$B \to aBa \mid aBb \mid bBa \mid bBb \mid cEb$$
$$E \to aE \mid bE \mid \epsilon$$

2.2 The Corresponding Automata

Let us give a definition of a particular family of one-dimensional cellular automata, which is known to be equivalent to linear conjunctive grammars [4].

Definition 6. *An automaton is a quintuple $M = (\Sigma, Q, I, \delta, F)$, where Σ is the input alphabet, Q is a finite nonempty set of states, $I : \Sigma \to Q$ is a function that sets the initial states, $\delta : Q \times Q \to Q$ (a binary operator on Q) is the transition function, and $F \subseteq Q$ is the set of final states.*

An automaton $M = (\Sigma, Q, I, \delta, F)$ takes a nonempty string $w = a_1 \ldots a_n$ ($a_i \in \Sigma$, $n \geqslant 1$) as an input, converts it to the string of states $I(a_1) \ldots I(a_n)$ (see Figure 1(a)) and then proceeds to constructing new strings of states out of existing strings of states by replacing a string of the form $q_1 \ldots q_m$ with the string $\delta(q_1, q_2), \delta(q_2, q_3), \ldots, \delta(q_{m-1}, q_m)$, as shown in Figure 1(b). This is being done until the string of states shrinks to a single state; then the string is accepted if and only if this single state belongs to the set F.

Now let us formally define the computation of an automaton.

Fig. 1. One step of computation.

Definition 7. *An instantaneous description (ID) of an automaton* $(\Sigma, Q, I, \delta, F)$ *is an arbitrary nonempty string over* Q. *The successor of an ID* $q_1 q_2 \ldots q_n$ *(where* $n \geqslant 2$*), denoted as* $\bar{\delta}(q_1 q_2 \ldots q_n)$, *is the ID* $q'_1 q'_2 \ldots q'_{n-1}$, *such that* $q'_i = \delta(q_i, q_{i+1})$ *for all* i. *A sequence of IDs* $\alpha_1, \ldots, \alpha_n$ *(*$n \geqslant 1$*) is called a computation of the automaton if* $\alpha_{i+1} = \bar{\delta}(\alpha_i)$ *for all* i *(*$1 \leqslant i < n$*) and* $|\alpha_n| = 1$.

Note that the successor of an ID is uniquely determined, and therefore the automaton is deterministic and the computation starting from a definite string of states has a definite outcome:

Definition 8. *For each ID* $q_1 \ldots q_n$ *(*$n \geqslant 1$*), denote the outcome of the computation starting from* $q_1 \ldots q_n$ *as* $\Delta(q_1 \ldots q_n) = \bar{\delta}^{n-1}(q_1 \ldots q_n) \in Q$.

It is left to define the initial ID of the automaton on the given input:

Definition 9. *Let* $M = (\Sigma, Q, I, \delta, F)$ *be an automaton. For each string* $w = a_1 \ldots a_n \in \Sigma^+$, *define* $I(w) = I(a_1) \ldots I(a_n)$. *The computation of the automaton* M *on the string* w *is the computation starting from the ID* $I(w)$. *The string* w *is accepted iff* $\Delta(I(w)) \in F$; *the language accepted by the automaton is defined as* $L(M) = \{w \mid w \in \Sigma^+, \Delta(I(w)) \in F\}$.

One evident limitation of these automata is their inability to accept or reject the empty string; however, this is only a technical limitation which does not affect their generative power on longer strings.

Let us quote two theoretical results obtained in [4], which show computational equivalence of linear conjunctive grammars and these automata.

Theorem 1. *For every linear conjunctive grammar* $G = (\Sigma, N, P, S)$ *there exists and can be effectively constructed an automaton* $M = (\Sigma, Q, I, \delta, F)$, *such that* $L(M) = L(G) \pmod{\Sigma^+}$.

Theorem 2. *For every automaton* M *there exists and can be effectively constructed a linear conjunctive grammar* G, *such that* $L(G) = L(M)$.

3   Construction of Automata

In this section we review the construction that was used in [4] in the proof of the computational equivalence of automata and grammars, and then generalize this construction to obtain a practical method of converting an arbitrary linear conjunctive grammar to an equivalent automaton.

3.1   A Method for Grammars in the Linear Normal Form

The idea of construction [4] is to simulate the recognition algorithm for linear conjunctive grammars in the linear normal form developed in [2]. In order to simulate the computation of this algorithm, each state of the automaton "remembers" the set of nonterminals that derive the corresponding substring, as well as the first and the last symbols of this substring.

Let $G = (\Sigma, N, P, S)$ be a linear conjunctive grammar in the linear normal form. We construct the automaton $M = M(G) = (\Sigma, Q, I, \delta, F)$, where $Q = \Sigma \times 2^N \times \Sigma$, $I(a) = (a, \{A \mid A \to a \in P\}, a)$, $\delta((b, R_1, b'), (c', R_2, c)) = (b, \{A \mid \exists A \to bB_1\& \ldots bB_m\&C_1c\& \ldots \&C_nc : \forall i, j\ B_i \in R_2, C_j \in R_1\}, c)$ and $F = \{(a, R, b) \mid a, b \in \Sigma,\ R \subseteq N,\ S \in R\}$.

The correctness of this construction is stated in the following lemma [4]:

Lemma 1. Let $w \in \Sigma^+$ be an arbitrary nonempty string and let $\Delta(I(w)) = (b, R, c)$. Then, for each nonterminal $A \in N$, $A \stackrel{G}{\Longrightarrow}{}^* w$ if and only if $A \in R$.

A practical implementation of this construction can define Q to be the minimal subset of $\Sigma \times 2^N \times \Sigma$ that contains $I(a)$ for all $a \in \Sigma$ and $\delta(q', q'')$ for every two states q', q'' in this set. This can be computed as follows:

```
let Q = {I(a) | a ∈ Σ}                      /* use I as defined above */
    while new states can be added to Q
        for all q', q'' ∈ Q
            add δ(q', q'') to Q              /* use δ as defined above */
```

As we shall show later in Section 4, this construction still can create many superfluous states, but in the practical cases it yields much less states than $|\Sigma|^2 \cdot 2^{|N|}$ given by the straightforward construction.

For instance, the grammar from Example 1, after being transformed to the linear normal form, has 13 nonterminals, which gives an upper bound of $3 \cdot 2^{13} \cdot 3 = 73728$ states, meaning the table δ of more than five billion entries. On the other hand, the given construction method yields only 222 states, and, consequently, δ table of around fifty thousand entries.

3.2   A Method for Arbitrary Grammars

The goal of the construction is again an automaton that is able to compute the sets of nonterminals deriving each substring. However, the conjuncts can now be of the form $A \to uBv$ or $A \to w$ for strings u and v of unbounded length, while the automata still operate only with pairs of states that are apart only by one input symbol, and we still have to compute $\Delta(I(a_1 \ldots q_n))$ out of $\Delta(I(a_1 \ldots q_{n-1}))$ and $\Delta(I(a_2 \ldots q_n))$ only.

The proposed solution is to fix some base set of strings over $\Sigma \cup N$ that we are interested in, such that the subset of those of them that derive some terminal string bwc could be determined solely by the symbols b, c and by the knowledge of which strings from this base set derive the terminal strings bw and wc. Once this collection is constructed, this functional dependency could be encoded in the definition of the transition function δ.

The simplest base set satisfying this condition is the set of all nonempty substrings of $\{\alpha \mid A \to \alpha \in conjuncts(P)\}$, but it in fact contains numerous superfluous strings. For instance, if we want to recognize the string bac, then keeping track of both ba and ac is not needed. We shall now propose one possible more efficient method of constructing the base set of strings. Given an arbitrary linear conjunctive grammar $G = (\Sigma, N, P, S)$, let us define the set of incomplete strings $Items \subseteq \Sigma^+ \cup \Sigma^* N \Sigma^*$ as $Items = \{S\} \cup Items_{uB} \cup Items_{uBv} \cup Items_w$, where

$$Items_{uB} = \bigcup_{A \to uBv \in conjuncts(P)} \{yB \mid \exists x \in \Sigma^* : xy = u, |yB| < |uBv|\}, \quad (4a)$$

$$Items_{uBv} = \bigcup_{A \to uBv \in conjuncts(P)} \{uBx \mid \exists y \in \Sigma^* : xy = v, |uBx| < |uBv|\}, \quad (4b)$$

$$Items_w = \bigcup_{A \to w \in conjuncts(P)} \{x \mid \exists y \in \Sigma^* : xy = w, |x| < |w|\} \quad (4c)$$

Let us also define the following augmented version of this set: $\overline{Items} = Items \cup \{\alpha \mid \alpha \neq \epsilon, A \to \alpha \in conjuncts(P)$ for some $A \in N\}$.

Lemma 2. Let $a \in \Sigma$. Denote NULLABLE $= \{A \mid A \in N, A \Longrightarrow^* \epsilon\}$. Then,

$$(\{a\} \cup \{a\} \cdot \text{NULLABLE} \cup \text{NULLABLE} \cdot \{a\}) \cap \overline{Items} = \{\alpha \mid \alpha \in \overline{Items}, \alpha \Longrightarrow^* a, \alpha \notin N\} \quad (5)$$

Lemma 3. Let bwc $(b, c \in \Sigma, w \in \Sigma^*)$ be an arbitrary string of length 2 or more. Let $X_1 = \{\alpha \mid \alpha \in Items, \alpha \Longrightarrow^* bw\}$, $X_2 = \{\alpha \mid \alpha \in Items, \alpha \Longrightarrow^* wc\}$. Then,

$$(\{b\} \cdot X_2 \cup X_1 \cdot \{c\}) \cap \overline{Items} = \{\alpha \mid \alpha \in \overline{Items}, \alpha \Longrightarrow^* bwc, \alpha \notin N\} \quad (6)$$

Once the set (6) is computed, the set of *nonterminals* that derive the string bwc can be determined by the following closure operation:

Definition 10. Let $G = (\Sigma, N, P, S)$ be a linear conjunctive grammar, let $R \subseteq (\Sigma \cup N)^+$. Define the set closure$(R)$ as the least subset of $R \cup N$ that includes R and contains every $A \in N$, such that there is a rule $A \to \alpha_1 \& \ldots \& \alpha_m \in P$, for which $\alpha_i \in closure(R)$ for all i.

Lemma 4. If $X \cap \overline{Items} = \{\alpha \mid \alpha \in \overline{Items}, \alpha \Longrightarrow^* w, \alpha \notin N\}$ for some $w \in \Sigma^+$ and $X \subseteq (\Sigma \cup N)^+$, then

$$closure(X) \cap Items = \{\alpha \mid \alpha \in Items, \alpha \Longrightarrow^* w\} \quad (7)$$

Now it suffices to write down the mentioned results in the form of a construction. Define the new automaton as $(\Sigma, Q, I, \delta, F)$, where $Q = \Sigma \times 2^{Items} \times \Sigma$, the initial states are defined as

$$I(a) = (a, \, closure(\{a\} \cup \{a\} \cdot \text{NULLABLE} \cup \text{NULLABLE} \cdot \{a\}) \cap Items, \, a) \quad (8)$$

for all $a \in \Sigma$, the transition function δ is defined as

$$\delta((b, X_1, c'), (b', X_2, c)) = (b, \, closure(b \cdot X_2 \cup X_1 \cdot c) \cap Items, \, c) \quad (9)$$

for every $(b, X_1, c'), (b', X_2, c) \in Q$, and the set of final states is

$$F = \{(b, X, c) \mid (b, X, c) \in Q, \, S \in X\} \quad (10)$$

Lemma 5. *For each string $w \in \Sigma^+$, let $\Delta(I(w)) = (b, R, c)$. Then, for every incomplete string $\alpha \in Items$, $\alpha \overset{G}{\Longrightarrow}{}^* w$ if and only if $\alpha \in R$.*

Consider the grammar for $\{wcw \mid w \in \{a, b\}^*\}$ from Example 1. The set $Items$ equals $\{S, C, D, A, B, E, aC, aA, aB, bC, bA, bB, cE\}$. The cardinality of $\Sigma \times 2^{Items} \times \Sigma$ is again $3 \cdot 2^{13} \cdot 3 = 73728$. However, if we rule out obviously unreachable states in the same way as suggested in Section 3.1, the algorithm will construct the following 158 states:

$(a, \emptyset, a)$	$(a, \{C, E, aA\}, a)$	$(b, \{D, A, bB\}, a)$	$(a, \{A, E, aC\}, b)$
$(a, \emptyset, b)$	$(a, \{C, E, aA\}, b)$	$(b, \{D, A, bB\}, b)$	$(a, \{A, E, aA\}, a)$
$(a, \emptyset, c)$	$(a, \{C, E, aB\}, a)$	$(c, \{D, A, cE\}, a)$	$(a, \{A, E, aA\}, b)$
$(b, \emptyset, a)$	$(a, \{C, E, aB\}, b)$	$(a, \{D, B, aA\}, a)$	$(a, \{A, E, aB\}, a)$
$(b, \emptyset, b)$	$(b, \{C, E, bC\}, a)$	$(a, \{D, B, aA\}, b)$	$(a, \{A, E, aB\}, b)$
$(b, \emptyset, c)$	$(b, \{C, E, bC\}, b)$	$(b, \{D, B, bB\}, a)$	$(b, \{A, E, bC\}, a)$
$(c, \emptyset, a)$	$(b, \{C, E, bA\}, a)$	$(b, \{D, B, bB\}, b)$	$(b, \{A, E, bC\}, b)$
$(c, \emptyset, b)$	$(b, \{C, E, bA\}, b)$	$(c, \{D, B, cE\}, b)$	$(b, \{A, E, bA\}, a)$
$(c, \emptyset, c)$	$(b, \{C, E, bB\}, a)$	$(a, \{D, aA\}, a)$	$(b, \{A, E, bA\}, b)$
$(a, \{S, C, D, aA\}, a)$	$(b, \{C, E, bB\}, b)$	$(a, \{D, aA\}, b)$	$(b, \{A, E, bB\}, a)$
$(a, \{S, C, D, aA\}, b)$	$(a, \{C, aC\}, a)$	$(b, \{D, bB\}, a)$	$(b, \{A, E, bB\}, b)$
$(b, \{S, C, D, bB\}, a)$	$(a, \{C, aC\}, b)$	$(b, \{D, bB\}, b)$	$(a, \{A, aC\}, a)$
$(b, \{S, C, D, bB\}, b)$	$(a, \{C, aA\}, a)$	$(c, \{D, cE\}, a)$	$(a, \{A, aC\}, b)$
$(c, \{S, C, D, cE\}, c)$	$(a, \{C, aA\}, b)$	$(c, \{D, cE\}, b)$	$(a, \{A, aA\}, a)$
$(a, \{C\}, a)$	$(a, \{C, aB\}, a)$	$(a, \{A\}, a)$	$(a, \{A, aA\}, b)$
$(a, \{C\}, b)$	$(a, \{C, aB\}, b)$	$(a, \{A\}, b)$	$(a, \{A, aB\}, a)$
$(b, \{C\}, a)$	$(b, \{C, bC\}, a)$	$(b, \{A\}, a)$	$(a, \{A, aB\}, b)$
$(b, \{C\}, b)$	$(b, \{C, bC\}, b)$	$(b, \{A\}, b)$	$(b, \{A, bC\}, a)$
$(a, \{C, E\}, a)$	$(b, \{C, bA\}, a)$	$(c, \{A\}, a)$	$(b, \{A, bC\}, b)$
$(a, \{C, E\}, b)$	$(b, \{C, bA\}, b)$	$(a, \{A, E\}, a)$	$(b, \{A, bA\}, a)$
$(b, \{C, E\}, a)$	$(b, \{C, bB\}, a)$	$(a, \{A, E\}, b)$	$(b, \{A, bA\}, b)$
$(b, \{C, E\}, b)$	$(b, \{C, bB\}, b)$	$(b, \{A, E\}, a)$	$(b, \{A, bB\}, a)$
$(a, \{C, E, aC\}, a)$	$(a, \{D, A, aA\}, a)$	$(b, \{A, E\}, b)$	$(b, \{A, bB\}, b)$
$(a, \{C, E, aC\}, b)$	$(a, \{D, A, aA\}, b)$	$(a, \{A, E, aC\}, a)$	$(a, \{B\}, a)$

$(a, \{B\}, b)$	$(b, \{B,E,bA\}, a)$	$(a, \{E\}, a)$	$(a, \{aC\}, a)$
$(b, \{B\}, a)$	$(b, \{B,E,bA\}, b)$	$(a, \{E\}, b)$	$(a, \{aC\}, b)$
$(b, \{B\}, b)$	$(b, \{B,E,bB\}, a)$	$(b, \{E\}, a)$	$(a, \{aC\}, c)$
$(c, \{B\}, b)$	$(b, \{B,E,bB\}, b)$	$(b, \{E\}, b)$	$(a, \{aA\}, a)$
$(a, \{B,E\}, a)$	$(a, \{B,aC\}, a)$	$(a, \{E,aC\}, a)$	$(a, \{aA\}, b)$
$(a, \{B,E\}, b)$	$(a, \{B,aC\}, b)$	$(a, \{E,aC\}, b)$	$(a, \{aB\}, a)$
$(b, \{B,E\}, a)$	$(a, \{B,aA\}, a)$	$(a, \{E,aA\}, a)$	$(a, \{aB\}, b)$
$(b, \{B,E\}, b)$	$(a, \{B,aA\}, b)$	$(a, \{E,aA\}, b)$	$(b, \{bC\}, a)$
$(a, \{B,E,aC\}, a)$	$(a, \{B,aB\}, a)$	$(a, \{E,aB\}, a)$	$(b, \{bC\}, b)$
$(a, \{B,E,aC\}, b)$	$(a, \{B,aB\}, b)$	$(a, \{E,aB\}, b)$	$(b, \{bC\}, c)$
$(a, \{B,E,aA\}, a)$	$(b, \{B,bC\}, a)$	$(b, \{E,bC\}, a)$	$(b, \{bA\}, a)$
$(a, \{B,E,aA\}, b)$	$(b, \{B,bC\}, b)$	$(b, \{E,bC\}, b)$	$(b, \{bA\}, b)$
$(a, \{B,E,aB\}, a)$	$(b, \{B,bA\}, a)$	$(b, \{E,bA\}, a)$	$(b, \{bB\}, a)$
$(a, \{B,E,aB\}, b)$	$(b, \{B,bA\}, b)$	$(b, \{E,bA\}, b)$	$(b, \{bB\}, b)$
$(b, \{B,E,bC\}, a)$	$(b, \{B,bB\}, a)$	$(b, \{E,bB\}, a)$	
$(b, \{B,E,bC\}, b)$	$(b, \{B,bB\}, b)$	$(b, \{E,bB\}, b)$	

4   Reduction of the Automata

4.1   On the Minimization of Automata

Although it is not known whether the minimal automaton for every linear conjunctive language is unique, from the practical point of view it might make sense to look for *one* of the automata that generate a particular language using a minimal number of states. However, that cannot be algorithmically done; we cannot even compute this minimal size:

Theorem 3. *There is no algorithm to compute the minimal number of states in the automata for a given linear conjunctive language.*

The source of this result is the undecidability of the emptiness problem for linear conjunctive grammars [3], and the fact that the minimal number of states in automata for an arbitrary language $L \subseteq \Sigma^+$ is 1 if and only if $L = \emptyset$ or $L = \Sigma^+$.

Corollary 1. *There is no algorithm to construct one of the minimal automata for a given grammar.*

These negative results show that there is no general method to reduce size of arbitrary given automata. However, the automata that are used in practice (i.e., those that one would generally need to reduce) usually are not deliberately obfuscated, and thus the practical case does not very much resemble solving the emptiness problem. It turns out that many automata (for instance, most of those constructed by the algorithms given in Section 3) are subject to substantial reduction by quite simple methods. Let us discuss some of these methods.

4.2   Reachable States

A state $q \in Q$ is called *reachable* if there exists a string $w \in \Sigma^+$, such that $\Delta(I(w)) = q$. Obviously, unreachable states are of no use and could be safely removed from an automaton to save space. Unfortunately, by the same reasoning as above, there is no algorithm to determine them:

Observation 1 *An automaton $(\Sigma, Q, I, \delta, F)$ generates the empty language if and only if every state in F is unreachable. It is undecidable whether a given state of an arbitrary given automaton is reachable.*

However, let us turn to the practical case. The construction methods described above are based on a naïve assumption that if some two states q' and q'' are reachable, then $\delta(q', q'')$ is also a reachable state. This assumption is, in general, false, because q' and q'' could be reachable through completely different computations, and thus cannot come next to each other to make the transition $\delta(q', q'')$ ever be performed. Therefore, these algorithms are almost certain to create a lot of superfluous states, some of which are so "unrealistic" that can be filtered out by quite simple necessary conditions of reachability. Let us consider some of these conditions.

1. **State filtering.** Fix an integer $k \geqslant 2$, called *the order of the method*. The main idea is that *"if some states $q_{i_1}, \ldots, q_{i_k}$ ($q_{i_j} \in Q$) are supposed to be reachable, then the state $\Delta(q_{i_1} \ldots q_{i_k})$ can also be assumed to be reachable"*. Of course, this is not always true, because if every state q_{i_j} is reachable *in itself*, this does not guarantee that they could ever appear next to each other in some computation. Still this method allows to determine some obviously unreachable states.
   - For every nonempty terminal string $w \in \Sigma^+$ of length strictly less than k (i.e., $0 < |w| < k$), declare the state $\Delta(I(w))$ to be reachable.
   - For every string $q^{(1)} \ldots q^{(k)}$ of k supposingly reachable states, add $\Delta(q^{(1)} \ldots q^{(k)})$ to the list of reachable states.

   Let us note that the algorithms in Section 3 implicitly apply order 2 state filtering to the sets of states $\Sigma \times 2^N \times \Sigma$ and $\Sigma \times 2^{Items} \times \Sigma$.

2. **Tuple filtering.** Fix an integer $n \geqslant 1$ – the size of the tuples being considered. Out task is to determine the set $R \subseteq Q^n$ of all n-tuples of states that have a chance to be reachable.
   - For all n-tuples of terminal symbols $(a_1, \ldots, a_n) \in \Sigma^n$, declare the tuple $(I(a_1), \ldots, I(a_n))$ to be reachable.
   - For every two supposingly reachable n-tuples $(q'_1, \ldots, q'_n)$, $(q''_1, \ldots, q''_n)$, such that $q'_{j+1} = q''_j$ ($1 \leqslant j < n$), consider the n-tuple $\bar{\delta}(q'_1 q'_2 \ldots q'_{n-1} q'_n q''_n) = \delta(q'_1, q''_1) \ldots \delta(q'_n, q''_n)$ to be reachable.

3. **Tuple filtering of higher order.** Let us now consider the generalized approach that combines the ideas of tuple filtering with higher-order state filtering. Let $k \geqslant 2$ and $n \geqslant 1$. *Order k filtering of n-tuples* (or (k, n)-*filtering* for short) traces partial computations from k overlapped n-tuples to a single n-tuple:
   - For all $(n + l)$-tuples ($l < k - 1$) of symbols $(a_1, \ldots, a_{n+l})$ ($a_i \in \Sigma^n$), declare the n-tuple $\bar{\delta}^l(I(a_1), \ldots, I(a_{n+l}))$ to be reachable.

- For every k supposingly reachable n-tuples $\langle(q_1^{(i)}, \ldots, q_n^{(i)})\rangle_{i=1}^k$, such that $q_{j+1}^{(i)} = q_j^{(i+1)}$ for all $1 \leqslant i < k$ and $1 \leqslant j < n$, the n-tuple $\overline{\delta}^{k-1}(q_1^{(1)} \ldots q_n^{(1)} \ldots q_n^{(k)}) = \Delta(q_1^{(1)} \ldots q_1^{(k)}) \ldots \Delta(q_n^{(1)} \ldots q_n^{(k)})$ is also considered to be reachable.

It is easy to observe that earlier mentioned filtering of order k is in fact $(k, 1)$-filtering, while n-tuple filtering is $(2, n)$-filtering.

Turning to the automaton for the language $\{wcw \mid w \in \{a, b\}^*\}$ constructed out of the grammar given in Example 1 by the algorithm from Section 3.2, only 58 of 158 original states are found to be reachable by $(3, 2)$-filtering, and brute-force tests reveal that each of these 58 states is actually used in some real computation.

4.3   Equivalent States

In this section we generalize the known technique of finite automaton minimization [1] for the case of our automata; that is splitting the set of states into classes of equivalence. Although in our case it will not necessarily yield the minimal automaton, it can nevertheless be quite successful in reducing the number of states.

Given an automaton $M = (\Sigma, Q, I, \delta, F)$, we are looking for a partition $Q = Q_1 \cup \ldots \cup Q_n$ ($Q_i \cap Q_j = \emptyset$ for all $i \neq j$) of the set of states, such that every class of equivalence is either a subset of F or a subset of $Q \setminus F$, and for every two classes Q_i and Q_j there exists a class Q_k, such that for all $q' \in Q_i$ and $q'' \in Q_j$ it would hold that $\delta(q', q'') \in Q_k$.

The algorithm for splitting the set of states of our automata into classes of equivalence can be loosely described as a two-dimensional generalization of the unary case of the algorithm for finite automata. The set of states is initially partitioned into accepting and nonaccepting states. Then the algorithm considers all pairs of classes of equivalence, for each looking whether all possible transitions from the states of the one class by the states from the other lead to the same third class of equivalence. If not so, then one of the two source classes of equivalence can be splitted into two or more classes, and this is being done by the algorithm.

> let *partition* $= \{F, Q \setminus F\}$ be the initial partition of the set Q
> while it is possible to split the partition
> for all pairs $(Q_i, Q_j) \in$ *partition* $\times$ *partition*
> if exists $q \in Q_i$, such that $K = \{k \mid \exists q' \in Q_j : \delta(q, q') \in Q_k\}$
>   has cardinality of more than 1
> {
>   Let $Q_j^{(k)} = \{q' \mid \delta(q, q') \in Q_k\}$ for all $k \in K$
>   *partition* $= ($*partition* $\setminus \{Q_j\}) \cup \{Q_j^{(k)}\}_{k \in K}$
> }
> else if exists $q \in Q_j$, such that $K = \{k \mid \exists q' \in Q_i : \delta(q', q) \in Q_k\}$
>   has cardinality of more than 1

{
$\quad$ Let $Q_i^{(k)} = \{q' \mid \delta(q', q) \in Q_k\}$ for all $k \in K$
$\quad$ $partition = (partition \setminus \{Q_i\}) \cup \{Q_i^{(k)}\}_{k \in K}$
}

Table 1. Partition of the set of states of a sample automaton.

	States of the original automaton	Accessing strings
0	$(a, \emptyset, a), (a, \emptyset, b)$	$acca, accb, aaaca$
1	$(a, \{S, C, D, aA\}, a), (a, \{S, C, D, aA\}, b)$	$aca, aacaa, abcab$
2	$(a, \{aC\}, a), (a, \{aC\}, b)$	$aaca, aacb, abca$
3	$(b, \emptyset, a), (b, \emptyset, b)$	$bcca, bccb, baaca$
4	$(a, \{C, aA\}, a), (a, \{C, aA\}, b)$	$aacab, abcaa, aaacaab$
5	$(b, \{S, C, D, bB\}, a), (b, \{S, C, D, bB\}, b)$	$bcb, bacba, bbcbb$
6	$(a, \{D, A, aA\}, a), (a, \{D, A, aA\}, b)$	$acaa, acaaa, acbaa$
7	$(c, \{S, C, D, cE\}, c)$	c
8	$(a, \{D, B, aA\}, a), (a, \{D, B, aA\}, b)$	$acba, acaba, acbba$
9	$(b, \{bC\}, a), (b, \{bC\}, b)$	$baca, bacb, bbca$
A	$(c, \emptyset, a), (c, \emptyset, b)$	$cca, ccb, caca$
B	$(b, \{C, bA\}, a), (b, \{C, bA\}, b)$	$bca, bacaa, bacab$
C	$(a, \{C, aB\}, a), (a, \{C, aB\}, b)$	$acb, aacba, aacbb$
D	$(a, \emptyset, c)$	aac, abc, acc
E	$(a, \{aC\}, c)$	ac
F	$(b, \emptyset, c)$	bac, bbc, bcc
G	$(b, \{bC\}, c)$	bc
H	$(c, \emptyset, c)$	cc, cac, cbc
I	$(c, \{D, A, cE\}, a)$	ca, caa, cba
J	$(b, \{D, A, bB\}, a), (b, \{D, A, bB\}, b)$	$bcab, bcaab, bcbab$
K	$(a, \{E\}, a)$	a, aa, aaa
L	$(a, \{E\}, b)$	ab, aab, abb
M	$(b, \{E\}, a)$	ba, baa, bba
N	$(b, \{E\}, b)$	b, bb, bab
O	$(b, \{D, B, bB\}, a), (b, \{D, B, bB\}, b)$	$bcbb, bcabb, bcbbb$
P	$(c, \{D, B, cE\}, b)$	cb, cab, cbb
Q	$(a, \{A, aA\}, a), (a, \{A, aA\}, b)$	$aacaab, abcaaa, aacaaab$
R	$(a, \{A, aB\}, a), (a, \{A, aB\}, b)$	$acab, acaab, acbab$
S	$(a, \{B, aA\}, a), (a, \{B, aA\}, b)$	$aacbab, abcbaa, aacabab$
T	$(a, \{B, aB\}, a), (a, \{B, aB\}, b)$	$acbb, acabb, acbbb$
U	$(b, \{C, bB\}, a), (b, \{C, bB\}, b)$	$bacbb, bbcba, baacbab$
V	$(b, \{A, bA\}, a), (b, \{A, bA\}, b)$	$bcaa, bcaaa, bcbaa$
W	$(b, \{A, bB\}, a), (b, \{A, bB\}, b)$	$bacabb, bbcaba, bacaabb$
X	$(b, \{B, bA\}, a), (b, \{B, bA\}, b)$	$bcba, bcaba, bcbba$
Y	$(b, \{B, bB\}, a), (b, \{B, bB\}, b)$	$bacbbb, bbcbba, bacabbb$

Once a partition can no longer be splitted, it is of the requested form. Then, like in the case of DFAs, it suffices to construct a new automaton, in which every state represents a class of states of the original automaton.

Applying this algorithm to the mentioned automaton for the language $\{wcw \mid w \in \{a, b\}^*\}$, initially of 158 states and then reduced to 58 states by $(3, 2)$-filtering, allows to group these 58 states into 35 classes of equivalence.

Table 1 shows the states of the 58-state automaton – triples (terminal, set of items, terminal) – forming each of these classes, and several accessing strings for each class. The classes themselves are denoted with boldface digits from **0** to **9** and capital letters from **A** to **Y**. This partition can be used to construct a new automaton of 35 states out of the existing 58-state automaton. The δ function of this reduced automaton is given in Table 2; the initial function maps $I(a) = \mathbf{K}$, $I(b) = \mathbf{N}$ and $I(c) = \mathbf{7}$; the set of accepting states is $F = \{\mathbf{1}, \mathbf{5}, \mathbf{7}\}$.

These $35^2 = 1225$ entries of δ, with a small addition of a 3-entry I table and 35 bits of F, look reasonably small for practical use.

Table 2. The function δ for the sample automaton for $\{wcw \mid w \in \{a, b\}^*\}$.

	0	1	2	3	4	5	6	7	8	9	A	B	C	D	E	F	G	H	I	J	K	L	M	N	O	P	Q	R	S	T	U	V	W	X	Y
0	0	2	0	0	2	2	0	E	0	0	0	2	2	D	D	D	D	D	0	0	K	L	K	L	0	0	0	0	0	0	2	0	0	0	0
1	0	0	0	0	0	0	6	E	R	0	0	0	0	D	D	D	D	D	6	6	0	0	0	0	R	R	Q	Q	R	R	0	Q	Q	R	R
2	0	0	0	0	0	0	1	E	C	0	0	0	0	D	D	D	D	D	1	1	0	0	0	0	C	C	4	4	C	C	0	4	4	C	C
3	3	9	3	3	9	9	0	G	0	3	3	9	9	F	F	F	F	F	0	0	M	N	M	N	0	0	0	0	0	0	9	0	0	0	0
4	0	0	0	0	0	0	6	E	R	0	0	0	0	D	D	D	D	D	6	6	0	0	0	0	R	R	Q	Q	R	R	0	Q	Q	R	R
5	0	0	0	0	0	0	X	G	O	0	0	0	0	F	F	F	F	F	X	X	0	0	0	0	O	O	X	X	Y	Y	0	X	X	Y	Y
6	0	0	0	0	0	0	6	E	R	0	0	0	0	D	D	D	D	D	6	6	0	0	0	0	R	R	Q	Q	R	R	0	Q	Q	R	R
7	0	0	0	0	0	0	0	H	0	0	0	0	0	H	H	H	H	H	0	0	I	P	I	P	0	0	0	0	0	0	0	0	0	0	0
8	0	0	0	0	0	0	6	E	R	0	0	0	0	D	D	D	D	D	6	6	0	0	0	0	R	R	Q	Q	R	R	0	Q	Q	R	R
9	0	0	0	0	0	0	B	G	5	0	0	0	0	F	F	F	F	F	B	B	0	0	0	0	5	5	B	B	U	U	0	B	B	U	U
A	A	A	A	A	A	A	A	H	A	A	A	A	A	H	H	H	H	H	A	A	0	0	0	0	A	A	A	A	A	A	A	A	A	A	A
B	0	0	0	0	0	0	V	G	J	0	0	0	0	F	F	F	F	F	V	V	0	0	0	0	J	J	V	V	W	W	0	V	V	W	W
C	0	0	0	0	0	0	8	E	T	0	0	0	0	D	D	D	D	D	8	8	0	0	0	0	T	T	S	S	T	T	0	S	S	T	T
D	0	2	0	0	2	2	0	E	0	0	0	2	2	D	D	D	D	D	0	0	K	L	K	L	0	0	0	0	0	0	2	0	0	0	0
E	0	0	0	0	0	0	1	E	C	0	0	0	0	D	D	D	D	D	1	1	0	0	0	0	C	C	4	4	C	C	0	4	4	C	C
F	3	9	3	3	9	9	0	G	0	3	3	9	9	F	F	F	F	F	0	0	M	N	M	N	0	0	0	0	0	0	9	0	0	0	0
G	0	0	0	0	0	0	B	G	5	0	0	0	0	F	F	F	F	F	B	B	0	0	0	0	5	5	B	B	U	U	0	B	B	U	U
H	A	A	A	A	A	A	A	H	A	A	A	A	A	H	H	H	H	H	A	A	0	0	0	0	A	A	A	A	A	A	A	A	A	A	A
I	0	0	0	0	0	0	0	H	0	0	0	0	0	H	H	H	H	H	0	0	I	P	I	P	0	0	0	0	0	0	0	0	0	0	0
J	0	0	0	0	0	0	X	G	O	0	0	0	0	F	F	F	F	F	X	X	0	0	0	0	O	O	X	X	Y	Y	0	X	X	Y	Y
K	0	2	0	0	2	2	0	E	0	0	0	2	2	D	D	D	D	D	0	0	K	L	K	L	0	0	0	0	0	0	2	0	0	0	0
L	0	2	0	0	2	2	0	E	0	0	0	2	2	D	D	D	D	D	0	0	K	L	K	L	0	0	0	0	0	0	2	0	0	0	0
M	3	9	3	3	9	9	0	G	0	3	3	9	9	F	F	F	F	F	0	0	M	N	M	N	0	0	0	0	0	0	9	0	0	0	0
N	3	9	3	3	9	9	0	G	0	3	3	9	9	F	F	F	F	F	0	0	M	N	M	N	0	0	0	0	0	0	9	0	0	0	0
O	0	0	0	0	0	0	X	G	O	0	0	0	0	F	F	F	F	F	X	X	0	0	0	0	O	O	X	X	Y	Y	0	X	X	Y	Y
P	0	0	0	0	0	0	0	H	0	0	0	0	0	H	H	H	H	H	0	0	I	P	I	P	0	0	0	0	0	0	0	0	0	0	0
Q	0	0	0	0	0	0	6	E	R	0	0	0	0	D	D	D	D	D	6	6	0	0	0	0	R	R	Q	Q	R	R	0	Q	Q	R	R
R	0	0	0	0	0	0	8	E	T	0	0	0	0	D	D	D	D	D	8	8	0	0	0	0	T	T	S	S	T	T	0	S	S	T	T
S	0	0	0	0	0	0	6	E	R	0	0	0	0	D	D	D	D	D	6	6	0	0	0	0	R	R	Q	Q	R	R	0	Q	Q	R	R
T	0	0	0	0	0	0	8	E	T	0	0	0	0	D	D	D	D	D	8	8	0	0	0	0	T	T	S	S	T	T	0	S	S	T	T
U	0	0	0	0	0	0	X	G	O	0	0	0	0	F	F	F	F	F	X	X	0	0	0	0	O	O	X	X	Y	Y	0	X	X	Y	Y
V	0	0	0	0	0	0	V	G	J	0	0	0	0	F	F	F	F	F	V	V	0	0	0	0	J	J	V	V	W	W	0	V	V	W	W
W	0	0	0	0	0	0	X	G	O	0	0	0	0	F	F	F	F	F	X	X	0	0	0	0	O	O	X	X	Y	Y	0	X	X	Y	Y
X	0	0	0	0	0	0	V	G	J	0	0	0	0	F	F	F	F	F	V	V	0	0	0	0	J	J	V	V	W	W	0	V	V	W	W
Y	0	0	0	0	0	0	X	G	O	0	0	0	0	F	F	F	F	F	X	X	0	0	0	0	O	O	X	X	Y	Y	0	X	X	Y	Y

References

1. A. V. Aho, R. Sethi, J. D. Ullman, *Compilers: principles, techniques and tools*, Addison-Wesley, Reading, Mass., 1986.
2. A. Okhotin, "Conjunctive grammars", *Journal of Automata, Languages and Combinatorics*, 6:4 (2001), 519–535.
3. A. Okhotin, "On the closure properties of linear conjunctive languages", to appear in *Theoretical Computer Science*.
4. A. Okhotin, "On a new family of automata", Tech. Rep. 2002–456, Dept. of Computing and Information Science of Queen's University, Kingston, Ontario, Canada.
5. A. Okhotin, "Whale Calf, a parser generator for conjunctive grammars", *this volume*.

Syntactic Semiring and Language Equations

Libor Polák[*]

Department of Mathematics, Masaryk University
Janáčkovo nám 2a, 662 95 Brno, Czech Republic
polak@math.muni.cz
http://www.math.muni.cz/~polak

Abstract. A classical construction assigns to any language its (ordered) syntactic monoid. Recently the author defined the so-called syntactic semiring of a language. We show here that elements of the syntactic semiring of L can be identified with transformations of a certain modification of the minimal automaton for L.

The main issue here are the inequalities $r(x_1, \ldots, x_m) \subseteq L$ and equations $r(x_1, \ldots, x_m) = L$ where L is a given regular language over a finite alphabet A and r is a given regular expression over A in variables $x_1, \ldots, x_m$. We show that the search for maximal solutions can be translated into the (finite) syntactic semiring of the language L. In such a way we are able to decide the solvability and to find all maximal solutions effectively.

In fact, the last questions were already solved by Conway using his factors. The first advantage of our method is the complexity and the second one is that we calculate in a transparent algebraic structure.

Keywords: syntactic semiring, language equations

1 Introduction

The syntactic monoid is a monoid canonically attached to each language. In [4] the author introduced the so-called syntactic semiring of the language under the name syntactic semilattice-ordered monoid. The main result of that paper is an Eilenberg-type theorem giving a one-to-one correspondence between the so-called conjunctive varieties of regular languages and pseudovarieties of idempotent semirings. The author's next contribution [5] studies the relationships between the (ordered) syntactic monoid and the syntactic semiring of a given language. We mention here only that the first one is finite if and only if the second one is finite and that these two structures are equationally independent. Also several examples of conjunctive varieties of languages are presented there. In certain sense our notion is a modification of Reutenauer syntactic algebra for the case of the Boolean semiring.

The study of the inequalities $r(x_1, \ldots, x_m) \subseteq L$, where r is a regular expression in variables $x_1, \ldots, x_m$ (without constants) and L is a regular language, was

---

[*] Supported by the Ministry of Education of the Czech Republic under the project MSM 143100009

started already by Conway in [2]. He shows that the components of maximal solutions are among intersections of so-called factors (see Sect. 7). In particular for the equations $X \cdot Y = L$ he showed that for any languages P, Q such that $P \cdot Q = L$ there exist regular languages P', Q' such that $P \subseteq P'$, $Q \subseteq Q'$, $P' \cdot Q' = L$. This result was reproved among other things by Kari [3]. Salomaa and Yu [6] gave a direct construction of the corresponding automata. Choffrut and Karhumäki [1] generalized the result to a system of equations.

We consider here a single equation $r(x_1, \ldots, x_m) = L$ where L is a regular language over a finite alphabet A and r is a regular expression over A in variables $x_1, \ldots, x_m$. It is convenient to consider in the same time also the inequality $r(x_1, \ldots, x_m) \subseteq L$ since we show that its maximal solutions are in one-to-one correspondence with the maximal solutions of this inequality shifted into the finite syntactic semiring of the languate L, and maximal solutions of $r(x_1, \ldots, x_m) = L$ are some of the maximal solutions of $r(x_1, \ldots, x_m) \subseteq L$. Components of maximal solutions are shown to be among so-called L-closed languages, a finite family of regular languages constructed from L. Our results lead to an effective procedure for finding all maximal solutions of $r(x_1, \ldots, x_m) = L$. In fact our translation from languages to the syntactic semirings is an improvement of that from [1] where power monoids of the syntactic monoids are used. In [1] they lose the one-to-one correspondence mentioned above and the syntactic semiring is often much smaller than the power monoid of the syntactic monoid (we calculate a concrete example where the syntactic monoid has 12 elements and the syntactic semiring only 16 elements). Our methods also provide constructions of automata which correspond to components of maximal solutions in terms of the minimal automaton of the languate L. We can also deal with systems of inequalities using translations into products of syntactic semirings of languages occurring on the right hand sides.

In the next section we recall the notion of syntactic semiring and introduce the notion of L-closed languages. In Section 3 we show that for a solution of $r(x_1, \ldots, x_m) = L$ its L-closure (applied componentwise) is again a solution. Section 4 is devoted to a transition of computations from languages to the syntactic semiring of L. In Section 5 we prove the correctness of an algorithm for a computation of the syntactic semiring, in Section 6 we calculate concrete examples.

As stated above, already Conway [2] presents a method for a finding all maximal solutions of $r(x_1, \ldots, x_m) \subseteq L$. In our approach the number of candidates for components of maximal solutions is exponentially smaller. Moreover, we use transparent calculations in a finite structure whose elements are represented by mappings. The details of the comparison are explained in the last section.

2   Syntactic Semiring and Closed Languages

A structure $(O, \cdot, \leq)$ is called an *ordered monoid* if $(O, \cdot)$ is a monoid with the neutral element 1, $(O, \leq)$ is an ordered set, and $a, b, c \in O$, $a \leq b$ implies both $ac \leq bc$ and $ca \leq cb$. Further, a structure $(S, \cdot, \vee)$ is called an *idempotent semiring* if $(S, \cdot)$ is a monoid, $(S, \vee)$ is a semilattice, and $a, b, c \in S$ implies both $a(b \vee c) = ab \vee ac$ and $(a \vee b)c = ac \vee bc$. The last structure becomes an ordered monoid with respect to the relation $\leq$ defined by $a \leq b \Leftrightarrow a \vee b = b$, $a, b \in S$.

In a finite idempotent semiring $(S, \cdot, \vee)$ we can define a unary operation *; namely for $a \in S$, we have $a^* = 1 \vee a \vee a^2 \vee \ldots \vee a^k$ where k is the smallest integer such that $1 \vee a \vee a^2 \vee \ldots \vee a^k = 1 \vee a \vee a^2 \vee \ldots \vee a^{k+1}$.

A language L over A defines the so-called *syntactic congruence* on the free monoid $(A^*, \cdot)$ over A by

$$ u \approx_L v \text{ if and only if } (\forall\, p, q \in A^*) (puq \in L \iff pvq \in L) . $$

The factor-structure $(A^*, \cdot)/ \approx_L$ is called the *syntactic monoid* of L and we denote it by $(\mathsf{O}(L), \cdot)$. It is ordered by

$$ v \approx_L \,\leq\, u \approx_L \text{ if and only if } (\forall\, p, q \in A^*) (puq \in L \Rightarrow pvq \in L) $$

and we speak about the *ordered syntactic monoid*. We also write $v \preceq_L u$ instead of $v \approx_L \,\leq\, u \approx_L$.

Let $\mathsf{F}(A^*)$ be the set of all non-empty finite sets of words over A. Notice that the algebra $(\mathsf{F}(A^*), \cdot, \cup)$ is a free idempotent semiring over A. Now L defines its congruence $\sim_L$ by

$$ \{u_1, \ldots, u_k\} \sim_L \{v_1, \ldots, v_l\} \text{ if and only if} $$

$$ (\forall\, p, q \in A^*) (pu_1q, \ldots, pu_kq \in L \iff pv_1q, \ldots, pv_lq \in L) . $$

The factor-structure is called the *syntactic semiring* of L; we denote it by $(\mathsf{S}(L), \cdot, \vee)$.

Sometimes it is useful to consider $\mathsf{F}^0(A^*) = \mathsf{F}(A^*) \cup \{\emptyset\}$ and to define $\sim_L$ on $(\mathsf{F}^0(A^*), \cdot, \cup)$. The factor-structure in this case is denoted by $(\mathsf{S}^0(L), \cdot, \vee)$.

We also write $\{v\} \preceq_L \{u_1, \ldots, u_k\}$ if

$$ (\forall\, p, q \in A^*) (pu_1q, \ldots, pu_kq \in L \implies pvq \in L) . $$

In fact, it is equivalent to $\{u_1, \ldots, u_k, v\} \sim_L \{u_1, \ldots, u_k\}$ and $\{v\} \preceq_L \{u\}$ is the same as $v \preceq_L u$ defined above.

A language Q over A is called *L-saturated* if it is a union of $\approx_L$-classes, Q is said to be *L-hereditary* if $u \in Q$, $v \preceq_L u$ implies $v \in Q$, and Q is *L-closed* if $u_1, \ldots, u_k \in Q$, $\{v\} \preceq_L \{u_1, \ldots, u_k\}$ implies $v \in Q$.

Clearly, for a regular language L over a finite alphabet A,

$$ Q \text{ is } L\text{-closed} \implies Q \text{ is } L\text{-hereditary} \implies Q \text{ is } L\text{-saturated} \implies Q \text{ is regular} $$

and the language L itself is *L-closed*.

For any language P over A there exists the smallest *L-closed* language Q over A containing P; we speak about *L-closure* and we write $Q = P^L$. In fact

$$ P^L = \{ v \in A^* \mid \{v\} \preceq_L \{u_1, \ldots, u_k\} \text{ for some } u_1, \ldots, u_k \in P \} . $$

Those familiar with Conway's techniques may realize that *L-closed* sets are exactly intersections of factors – see also Section 7.

3 Inequalities and Equations

Let $A = \{a_1, \ldots, a_n\}$ $(n \geq 1)$ be a fixed finite alphabet, let $X = \{x_1, \ldots, x_m\}$ $(m \geq 0)$ be a finite set of variables. We denote by $\mathsf{Reg}\,(A, X)$ the set of all terms in the language of nullary operational symbols $0, a_1, \ldots, a_n$, binary operational symbols $\cdot, +$ and unary operational symbol * over the variables $x_1, \ldots, x_m$. The elements of $\mathsf{Reg}\,(A, X)$ are called *regular expressions* over A in X.

Let $\bar{r}$ be the realization of $r \in \mathsf{Reg}\,(A, X)$ in the algebra

$$\mathcal{L} = (2^{A^*}, \emptyset, \{a_1\}, \ldots, \{a_n\}, \cdot, \cup, ^*)$$

of all subsets of A^* where $\cdot$ is the catenation, $\cup$ is the set-theoretical union and * is the Kleene star. Notice that $\{1\} = \emptyset^*$.

For a given $r \in \mathsf{Reg}\,(A, X)$ and a regular language L over A we will consider the inequality

$$r(x_1, \ldots, x_m) \subseteq L \qquad\qquad (*)$$

and the equation

$$r(x_1, \ldots, x_m) = L . \qquad\qquad (**)$$

We could write more formally $r(x_1, \ldots, x_m) \leq l$ and $r(x_1, \ldots, x_m) = l$ where $l \in \mathsf{Reg}\,(A, \emptyset)$ is a regular expression defining the language L.

An m-tuple $(P_1, \ldots, P_m)$ of languages over A is called a *solution* of the inequality $(*)$ in $\mathcal{L}$ if $\bar{r}(P_1, \ldots, P_m) \subseteq L$ and similarly, it is a solution of $(**)$ in $\mathcal{L}$ if $\bar{r}(P_1, \ldots, P_m) = L$. A solution $(P_1, \ldots, P_m)$ of $(*)$ in $\mathcal{L}$ is *maximal* if for every other solution $(Q_1, \ldots, Q_m)$,

$$P_1 \subseteq Q_1, \ldots, P_m \subseteq Q_m \text{ implies } P_1 = Q_1, \ldots, P_m = Q_m .$$

Similarly for the equation $(**)$.

The following is a reformulation of Conway's Theorem VI.9.

Theorem 1. *Let $(P_1, \ldots, P_m)$ be a solution of the inequality $r(x_1, \ldots, x_m) \subseteq L$ in $\mathcal{L}$. Then $(P_1^L, \ldots, P_m^L)$ is again a solution of this inequality. Consequently, the components of any maximal solution are L-closed; in particular, they are regular languages.*

Proof. In fact we will prove the following:

For any languages $U, P, Q_2, \ldots, Q_m, V$ over A $(m \geq 1)$ and $r \in \mathsf{Reg}\,(A, \{x_1, \ldots, x_m\})$, we have

$$U \cdot \bar{r}(P, Q_2, \ldots, Q_m) \cdot V \subseteq L \text{ implies } U \cdot \bar{r}(P^L, Q_2, \ldots, Q_m) \cdot V \subseteq L .$$

To get the Theorem put $U = V = \{1\}$ and permute arguments in r.

We left to the reader to use induction with respect to the complexity of r, that is, to consider consecutively the cases:

$$r = 0, a_1, \ldots, a_n, \; r = x_1, \; r = x_2, \ldots, x_m, \; r = s + t, \; r = s \cdot t, \; r = s^*.$$

$\square$

4   From Languages to the Syntactic Semiring (and Back)

Theorem 2. *Let L be a regular language over a finite alphabet $A = \{a_1, ..., a_n\}$. The mapping*

$$\phi : P \mapsto \bigvee \{ \{u\} \sim_L \mid u \in P \}, \ P \subseteq A^*$$

is a surjective homomorphism of the algebra $\mathcal{L} = (2^{A^*}, \emptyset, \{a_1\}, \dots, \{a_n\}, \cdot, \cup, ^*)$ onto the algebra $\mathcal{S}^0 = (\mathsf{S}^0(L), \emptyset \sim_L, \{a_1\} \sim_L, \dots \{a_n\} \sim_L, \cdot, \vee, ^*)$. In fact, for every $r \in \mathsf{Reg}(A, \{x_1, \dots, x_m\})$, $P_1, \dots, P_m \subseteq A^*$, we have

$$\phi(\bar{r}(P_1, \dots, P_m)) = \tilde{r}(\phi(P_1), \dots, \phi(P_m)) \qquad (\star)$$

where $\tilde{r}$ is the realization of r in $\mathcal{S}^0$.

Moreover, for any $P \subseteq A^*$, its closure P^L is the largest language with its ϕ-image equal to $\phi(P)$. Consequently, ϕ is a bijection between the set $L(A)$ of all L-closed languages and the set $\mathsf{S}^0(L)$. The inverse mapping is also isotone and can be expressed as

$$\psi : \{u_1, \dots, u_k\} \sim_L \ \mapsto \ \{ v \in A^* \mid \{v\} \preceq_L \{u_1, \dots, u_k\} \} \ .$$

Proof. Note that in the formula for ϕ the join is considered in a finite structure; in fact we can take instead of P any finite set Q intersecting exactly the same $\approx_L$-classes as P does.

Clearly $\phi(\{u_1, \dots, u_k\}) = \{u_1, \dots, u_k\} \sim_L$ which gives the surjectivity.

Now $\phi(\emptyset) = \bigvee \{ \{u\} \sim_L \mid u \in \emptyset \} = \emptyset \sim_L$, a convention.

Clearly, $\phi(\{a_i\}) = \bigvee \{ \{u\} \sim_L \mid u \in \{a_i\} \} = \{a_i\} \sim_L$, $i = 1, \dots, n$.

Further, $\phi(P \cdot Q) = \bigvee \{ \{u\} \sim_L \mid u \in P \cdot Q \} = \bigvee \{ \{v \cdot w\} \sim_L \mid v \in P, w \in Q \}$ $= \bigvee \{ \{v\} \sim_L \mid v \in P \} \cdot \bigvee \{ \{w\} \sim_L \mid w \in Q \}$ due to the remark opening this proof
$= \phi(P) \cdot \phi(Q)$.

We have also $\phi(P \cup Q) = \bigvee \{ \{u\} \sim_L \mid u \in P \cup Q \}$
$= \bigvee \{ \{u\} \sim_L \mid u \in P \} \vee \bigvee \{ \{u\} \sim_L \mid u \in Q \} = \phi(P) \vee \phi(Q)$.

Finally, $\phi(P^*) = \phi(\{1\} \cup P \cup P^2 \cup \dots) = \bigvee \{ \{u\} \sim_L \mid u \in \{1\} \cup P \cup P^2 \cup \dots \}$
$= \bigvee \{ \{u\} \sim_L \mid u \in \{1\} \cup P \cup \dots \cup P^k \}$ since this expression is nondecreasing with respect to k and our calculations are in a finite structure
$= \phi(1) \vee \phi(P) \vee \dots \vee \phi(P^k)$.

On the other hand, $(\phi(P))^* = \{1\} \vee \phi(P) \vee (\phi(P))^2 \vee \dots$
$= \{1\} \vee \phi(P) \vee \phi(P^2) \vee \dots$ by the item concerning the product
$= \{1\} \vee \phi(P) \vee \dots \vee \phi(P^l)$ by the arguments as above; moreover, we can choose $k = l$.

Basics of universal algebra yield the expression $(\star)$.

If $\{v\} \preceq_L \{u_1, \dots, u_k\}$, $u_1, \dots, u_k \in P$, then $\{v\} \sim_L \leq \{u_1\} \sim_L \vee \dots \vee \{u_k\} \sim_L$ and thus $\phi(P^L) = \phi(P)$.

Conversely let $\phi(Q) \leq \phi(P)$. Then, for all $v \in Q$, we have $\{v\} \preceq_L \{u_1\} \sim_L \vee \dots \vee \{u_k\} \sim_L$ for some $u_1, \dots, u_k \in P$ (finiteness of $\mathsf{S}^0(L)$) and $v \in P^L$.

The statements about ψ are obvious. $\square$

For a regular language L over a finite alphabet A, we can translate the inequality $(*)$ and the equation $(**)$ into the inequality

$$r(x_1, \ldots, x_m) \leq \phi(L) \tag{†}$$

and the equation

$$r(x_1, \ldots, x_m) = \phi(L) . \tag{††}$$

Theorem 3. *(i) The inequality $(*)$ is solvable in $\mathcal{L}$ if and only if $(\emptyset, \ldots, \emptyset)$ is a solution.*

(ii) If $(P_1, \ldots, P_m)$ solves $(*)$ in $\mathcal{L}$, then $(\phi(P_1), \ldots, \phi(P_m))$ solves (†) in $\mathcal{S}^0$. The same is true for $(**)$ and (††).

(iii) Conversely, if $(c_1, \ldots, c_m)$ solves (†) in $\mathcal{S}^0$, then $(\psi(c_1), \ldots, \psi(c_m))$ solves $(*)$ in $\mathcal{L}$.

(iv) Maximal solutions of $(*)$ in $\mathcal{L}$ are in a one-to-one correspondence with maximal solutions of (†) in $\mathcal{S}^0$. Every solution of $(*)$ in $\mathcal{L}$ is contained (componentwise) in a maximal one.

(v) Every maximal solution of $(**)$ in $\mathcal{L}$ is also a maximal solution of $(*)$. Every solution of $(**)$ in $\mathcal{L}$ is contained in a maximal one.

Proof. The item (i) follows from the fact that $\bar{r}$ is isotone, i.e.

$$P_1 \subseteq Q_1, \ldots, P_m \subseteq Q_m \text{ implies } \bar{r}(P_1, \ldots, P_m) \subseteq \bar{r}(Q_1, \ldots, Q_m) .$$

(ii) The application of the (isotone) operator ϕ to $\bar{r}(P_1, \ldots, P_m) \subseteq L$ yields by Theorem 2 $\tilde{r}(\phi(P_1), \ldots, \phi(P_m)) \leq \phi(L)$ and the same for the equality.

(iii) Let $(c_1, \ldots, c_m)$ be a solution of (†) in $\mathcal{S}^0$. Let $Q_i = \psi(c_i), i = 1, \ldots, m$. Then $\phi(Q_i) = c_i$, $i = 1, \ldots, m$ and $\tilde{r}(\phi(Q_1), \ldots, \phi(Q_m)) \leq \phi(L)$. Consequently $\phi(\bar{r}(Q_1, \ldots, Q_m)) \leq \phi(L)$ and the application of ψ yields $(\bar{r}(Q_1, \ldots, Q_m))^L \subseteq L$ and thus $\bar{r}(Q_1, \ldots, Q_m) \subseteq L$.

(iv) Let $(P_1, \ldots, P_m)$ be a maximal solution of $(*)$. Then $P_i^L = P_i$, $i = 1, \ldots, m$ by Theorem 1. Let $(c_1, \ldots, c_m)$ be a solution of (†) such that $(\phi(P_1), \ldots, \phi(P_m)) \leq (c_1, \ldots, c_m)$ (componentwise). Application of ψ gives that $(\psi(c_1), \ldots, \psi(c_m))$ is a solution of $(*)$ which contains $(P_1, \ldots, P_m)$. Thus $P_i = \psi(c_i)$, $\phi(P_i) = c_i$, $i = 1, \ldots, m$.

Conversely, let $(c_1, \ldots, c_m)$ be a maximal solution of (†). Let $(Q_1, \ldots, Q_m)$ be a solution of $(*)$ containing $(\psi(c_1), \ldots, \psi(c_m))$. Application of ϕ gives that $(\phi(Q_1), \ldots, \phi(Q_m))$ is a solution of (†) containing $(c_1, \ldots, c_m)$. Thus $c_i = \phi(Q_i)$, $\psi(c_i) = \psi(\phi(Q_i)) \supseteq Q_i$, $i = 1, \ldots, m$.

Finally, for a solution $(P_1, \ldots, P_m)$ of $(*)$, the solution $(\phi(P_1), \ldots, \phi(P_m))$ of (†) is contained in a maximal solution $(c_1, \ldots, c_m)$ of (†) (finiteness of $\mathsf{S}^0(L)$). Now $(P_1, \ldots, P_m)$ is contained in a maximal solution $(\psi(c_1), \ldots, \psi(c_m))$ of $(*)$.

(v) The first statement is clear. For a given solution $(P_1, \ldots, P_m)$ of $(**)$ take a maximal solution of $(*)$ which contains $(P_1, \ldots, P_m)$.

$\square$

5   A Construction of the Syntactic Semiring

We extend here a well-known construction of the syntactic monoid of a regular language to the case of the syntactic semiring. This algorithm was announced in [5]; here we prove its correctness.

Let a regular language L over a finite alphabet A be given. Classically one assigns to L its minimal automaton $\mathcal{A}$ using left quotients ; namely

$D = \{ u^{-1}L \mid u \in A^* \}$ is the (finite) set of states,

$a \in A$ acts on $u^{-1}L$ by $(u^{-1}L) \cdot a = a^{-1}(u^{-1}L)$.

Denote by $[u] : d \mapsto d \cdot u$ the transformation of the set D induced by $u \in A^*$.

$d_0 = L$ is the initial state and $u^{-1}L$ is a final state if and only if $u \in L$.

Now $(\mathsf{O}\,(L), \cdot)$ is the transition monoid of $\mathcal{A}$; more precisely:

$(\mathsf{O}\,(L), \cdot)$ is isomorphic to $\{ [u] \mid u \in A^* \}$ with $[u] \cdot [v] = [u \cdot v]$ and the isomorphism is given by $u \approx_L \mapsto [u]$.

The states are ordered by the opposite inclusion:

$$u^{-1}L \leq v^{-1}L \text{ if and only if } u^{-1}L \supseteq v^{-1}L \ .$$

The order on $\mathsf{O}\,(L)$ is given by

$$[f] \leq [g] \text{ if and only if for every } d \in D \text{ we have } d \cdot f \leq d \cdot g \ .$$

Indeed, $f \preceq_L g$ iff $(\forall\, p, q \in A^*)(pgq \in L \Rightarrow pfq \in L)$, that is iff $(\forall\, p, q \in A^*)(q \in (pg)^{-1}L \Rightarrow q \in (pf)^{-1}L)$, that is iff $(\forall\, p \in A^*)((pg)^{-1}L \subseteq (pf)^{-1}L)$, that is iff $(\forall\, p \in A^*)((p^{-1}L) \cdot g \subseteq (p^{-1}L) \cdot f)$.

We extend the set of states to

$$\overline{D} = \{ d_1 \cap \ldots \cap d_m \mid m \in \mathbb{N}, \ d_1, \ldots, d_m \in D \} \ .$$

As above, $d \in \overline{D}$ is a final state if and only if $1 \in d$. The action of a letter $a \in A$ is now given by

$$(d_1 \cap \ldots \cap d_m) \cdot a = d_1 \cdot a \cap \ldots \cap d_m \cdot a \ .$$

It can be extended to transitions induced by non-empty finite sets of words by

$$d \cdot \{u_1, ..., u_k\} = d \cdot u_1 \cap \ldots \cap d \cdot u_k \text{ for } d \in \overline{D}, \ u_1, ..., u_k \in A^* \ .$$

Again, denote by $[u_1, \ldots, u_k]$ the transformation of $\overline{D}$ given by the set $\{u_1, \ldots, u_k\}$.

We show that $(\mathsf{S}\,(L), \cdot, \vee)$ is isomorphic to $\{ [u_1, \ldots, u_k] \mid u_1, \ldots, u_k \in A^* \}$ with the operations of composition and

$[u_1, \ldots, u_k] \vee [v_1, \ldots, v_l] = [u_1, \ldots, u_k, v_1, \ldots, v_l]$.

The isomorphism is given by: $\{u_1, \ldots, u_k\} \sim_L \mapsto [u_1, \ldots, u_k]$.

We have to show that $\{u_1, \ldots, u_k\} \sim_L \{v_1, \ldots, v_l\}$ is equivalent to $[u_1, \ldots, u_k] = [v_1, \ldots, v_l]$.

Indeed, $\{u_1, \ldots, u_k\} \sim_L \{v_1, \ldots, v_l\}$ if and only if $(\forall\, p, q \in A^*)\ (pu_1q, ..., pu_kq \in L \Leftrightarrow pv_1q, ..., pv_lq \in L)$, that is iff

$(\forall\, p,q \in A^*)\, (q \in (pu_1)^{-1}L \cap \ldots \cap (pu_k)^{-1}L \;\Leftrightarrow\; q \in (pv_1)^{-1}L \cap \ldots \cap (pv_l)^{-1}L),$

that is iff $(\forall\, p \in A^*)\, (pu_1)^{-1}L \cap \ldots \cap (pu_k)^{-1}L = (pv_1)^{-1}L \cap \ldots \cap (pv_l)^{-1}L ,$

that is iff $(\forall\, p \in A^*)\, p^{-1}L \cdot u_1 \cap \ldots \cap p^{-1}L \cdot u_k = p^{-1}L \cdot v_1 \cap \ldots \cap p^{-1}L \cdot v_l ,$

that is iff $(\forall\, p \in A^*)\, p^{-1}L \cdot \{u_1, \ldots, u_k\} = p^{-1}L \cdot \{v_1, \ldots, v_l\},$ that is iff

$(\forall\, d_1, \ldots, d_m \in D)\, (d_1 \cap \ldots \cap d_m) \cdot \{u_1, \ldots, u_k\} = (d_1 \cap \ldots \cap d_m) \cdot \{v_1, \ldots, v_l\} .$

Further, $(d \cdot \{u_1, \ldots, u_k\}) \cdot \{v_1, \ldots, v_l\} = (d \cdot u_1 \cap \ldots \cap d \cdot u_k) \cdot \{v_1, \ldots, v_l\}$
$= \bigcap \{d \cdot (u_i v_j) \mid i = 1, \ldots, k,\; j = 1, \ldots, l\} = d \cdot (\{u_1, \ldots, u_k\} \cdot \{v_1, \ldots, v_l\})$
and thus $[u_1, \ldots, u_k] \cdot [v_1, \ldots, v_l] = [\{u_1, \ldots, u_k\} \cdot \{v_1, \ldots, v_l\}].$

To make the computation finite, one considers instead of words from A^* their representatives in $O\,(L)$. Moreover, it suffices to take only the actions of hereditary subsets of $(O\,(L), \leq)$ (a subset H of an ordered set $(B, \leq)$ is hereditary if $b \in B, a \in H, b \leq a$ implies $b \in H$).

6 Examples

1. Let $A = \{a, b\}$ and consider the language $L = A^* aba A^*$.

Denoting $\mathbf{1} = L,\; \mathbf{p} = L \cup baA^*,\; \mathbf{q} = L \cup aA^*,\; \mathbf{0} = A^*$, we see that the minimal automaton of L looks as follows.

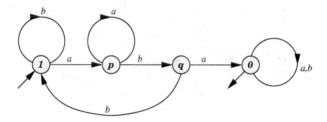

The order on states is given by $\mathbf{0} < \mathbf{p} < \mathbf{1},\; \mathbf{0} < \mathbf{q} < \mathbf{1},\; \mathbf{p}, \mathbf{q}$ incomparable. Note that $\mathbf{p} \cap \mathbf{q} = \mathbf{1}$.

Now we calculate the transitions given by $1, a, b, a^2, ab, ba, b^2, a^3, \ldots$ and regular expressions for corresponding $\approx_L$-classes.

u	$\mathbf{1}\ \mathbf{p}\ \mathbf{q}\ \mathbf{0}$	$u \approx_L$
1	$\mathbf{1}\ \mathbf{p}\ \mathbf{q}\ \mathbf{0}$	1
a	$\mathbf{p}\ \mathbf{p}\ \mathbf{0}\ \mathbf{0}$	$a^+ b^2 (b + a^+ b^2)^* + a^+$
b	$\mathbf{1}\ \mathbf{q}\ \mathbf{1}\ \mathbf{0}$	b
ab	$\mathbf{q}\ \mathbf{q}\ \mathbf{0}\ \mathbf{0}$	$a^+ b^2 (b + a^+ b^2)^* a^+ b + a^+ b$
ba	$\mathbf{p}\ \mathbf{0}\ \mathbf{p}\ \mathbf{0}$	$b(b + a^+ b^2)^* a^+$
b^2	$\mathbf{1}\ \mathbf{1}\ \mathbf{1}\ \mathbf{0}$	$b^2 (b + a^+ b^2)^*$
aba	$\mathbf{0}\ \mathbf{0}\ \mathbf{0}\ \mathbf{0}$	$A^* aba A^*$
ab^2	$\mathbf{1}\ \mathbf{1}\ \mathbf{0}\ \mathbf{0}$	$a^+ b^2 (b + a^+ b^2)^*$
bab	$\mathbf{q}\ \mathbf{0}\ \mathbf{q}\ \mathbf{0}$	$ba^+ b^2 (b + a^+ b^2)^* a^+ b + ba^+ b$
$b^2 a$	$\mathbf{p}\ \mathbf{p}\ \mathbf{p}\ \mathbf{0}$	$b^2 (b + a^+ b^2)^* a^+$
bab^2	$\mathbf{1}\ \mathbf{0}\ \mathbf{1}\ \mathbf{0}$	$ba^+ b^2 (b + a^+ b^2)^*$
$b^2 ab$	$\mathbf{q}\ \mathbf{q}\ \mathbf{q}\ \mathbf{0}$	$b^2 (b + a^+ b^2)^* a^+ b$

The syntactic monoid of L has the presentation

$$< a,b \mid a^2 = a,\ b^3 = b^2,\ aba = 0,\ ab^2a = a,\ b^2ab^2 = b^2 >$$

and its order is given componentwise according to the second column.

Some hereditary subsets of $O(L)$ act on $\overline{D}$ in the same way as some elements of $O(L)$: $[a, ba, aba] = [b^2a]$ (this means $\{b^2a\} \preceq_L \{a, ba, aba\}$); some subsets give rise to new transformations: $[a, b^2ab] : (\mathbf{1, p, q, 0}) \mapsto (\mathbf{1, 1, q, 0})$. This gives the label $\dfrac{\mathbf{1\ 1\ q\ 0}}{a,\ b^2ab}$ in the order reduct of the syntactic semiring of L depicted below.

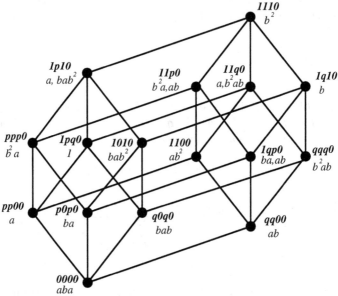

Further, $S^0(L) = S(L)$ since $\emptyset \sim_L \{aba\}$ and $\phi(L) = \{aba\} \sim_L$.

(i) Consider the inequality $x^2 \leq L$ and the equation $x^2 = L$. Write $\{u_1, \ldots, u_k\}$ instead of $\{u_1, \ldots, u_k\} \sim_L$. The elements of $S^0(L)$ with $x^2 \leq \phi(L)$ are exactly $\{aba\}$, $\{ab\}$, $\{ba\}$ (not, for instance, $\{ab, ba\}$ since $\{ab, ba\}^2 = \{bab, a, aba\} = \{1\}$). The last two are maximal solutions.

The corresponding languages are

$\psi(\{ab\}) = ab \approx_L \cup\ aba \approx_L = a^+b^2(b + a^+b^2)^*a^+b + a^+b + A^*abaA^*$,

$\psi(\{ba\}) = ba \approx_L \cup\ aba \approx_L = b(b + a^+b^2)^*a^+ + A^*abaA^*$.

In all three cases we have $x^2 = \{aba\}$ in S^0 but not $x^2 = L$ in $\mathcal{L}$.

Summarizing, $x^2 \subseteq L$ has two maximal solutions in $\mathcal{L}$ and $x^2 = L$ is not solvable there.

(ii) Clearly (A^*a, baA^*) solves $X \cdot Y = L$. We have $\{a, b\}^*\{a\} = \{b^2\}^*\{a\} = \{b^2\}\{a\} = \{b^2a\}$, $\{b\}\{a\}\{a, b\}^* = \{bab^2\}$ and thus our solution is contained in the maximal solution $(\psi(\{b^2a\}), \psi(\{bab^2\})) =$
$(b^2a \approx_L \cup\ a \approx_L \cup\ ba \approx_L \cup\ aba \approx_L,\ bab^2 \approx_L \cup\ ba \approx_L \cup\ bab \approx_L \cup\ aba \approx_L)$.

Although our first example is quite non-trivial, it demonstrates only a special case of our construction of the syntactic semiring. In the following example the set D of all states of the minimal automaton is not closed with respect to intersections.

2. Let $A = \{a, b\}$ and consider the language $L = (abA^*)'$ (the complement of abA^*).

Denoting $p = L$, $q = (bA^*)'$, $0 = A^*$, $1 = \emptyset$, $r = p \cap q$ we see that the minimal automaton of L and its extension look as follows (the covering relation of the order of $\overline{D}$ is indicated by broken lines).

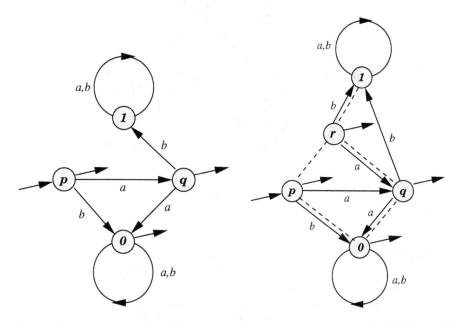

Calculations of the syntactic monoid and the syntactic semiring of L yield the following mappings from D to $\overline{D}$.

$u_1, \ldots, u_k$	p	q	0	1
1	p	q	0	1
a	q	0	0	1
b	0	1	0	1
a^2	0	0	0	1
ab	1	0	0	1
$1, a$	r	q	0	1
$1, b$	p	1	0	1
$1, ab$	1	q	0	1
a, b	q	1	0	1
b, ab	1	1	0	1
$1, a, b$	r	1	0	1

The syntactic monoid of L has the presentation

$$< \ a,b \ | \ ba = b, \ b^2 = b, \ a^3 = a^2, \ a^2b = a^2 \ > \ .$$

The order reduct of the syntactic semiring of L depicted below.

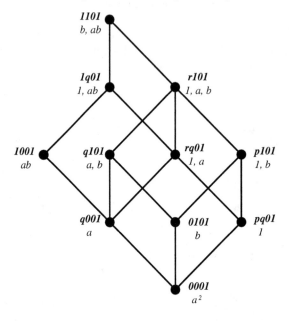

Here $S^0(L) \neq S(L)$ since there is no $u \in A^*$ satisfying
$(\ \forall \ p,q \in A^*) \ (\ puq \in L \ )$. Consequently $(S^0(L), \leq)$ is $(S(L), \leq)$ with a new bottom element which represents $\emptyset \sim_L$.

Consider the inequality $x^* \leq L$. The maximal elements of $(S^0(L), \leq)$ with the property $x^* \leq \phi(L)$ are exactly $\{1, a\} \sim_L$ and $\{1, b\} \sim_L$. The corresponding languages are $1 + a + a^2A^*$ and $1 + bA^* + a^2A^*$.

7 A Comparison of Our Results with Those by Conway

In [2] Conway studies the inequality $(*)$ in case that $r \in \mathsf{Reg} \ (\emptyset, \{x_1, \ldots, x_m\})$.

Let the maximal solutions of $x_1x_2 \subseteq L$ be exactly the pairs $(P_1, Q_1), \ldots, (P_l, Q_l)$ and let F_{ij} be the maximal solution of $P_ixQ_j \subseteq L$, $i, j = 1, \ldots, l$. He calls the components of maximal solutions of $x_1 \ldots x_k \subseteq L \ (k \in \mathbb{N})$ *factors* and their first (last) components *left (right) factors*. He shows that

(i) the maximal solutions of $PxQ \subseteq L \ (P, Q \subseteq A^*)$ are factors;

(ii) the left (right) factors are exactly $P_1, \ldots, P_l \ (Q_1, \ldots, Q_l)$ and the factors are exactly F_{ij}'s $(i, j = 1, \ldots, l)$;

(iii) the components of maximal solutions of $(*)$ are among intersections of factors.

In [2] one calculates the Q_i's as intersections of left quotients of L (in our notation $\{Q_1, \ldots, Q_l\} = \overline{D}$), then one proceeds by calculating P_i as $\bigcap_{q \in Q_i} Lq^{-1}$ and F_{ij} as $\bigcap_{p \in P_i} p^{-1} P_j$ $(i, j = 1, \ldots, l)$.

Let us compare the complexities of both approaches with respect to the number Δ of states of the minimal automaton for L, which equals to the number of left quotients of L.

The number of right factors of L equals the number of intersections of left quotients of L, which is at most 2^Δ. Thus the number of factors is less or equal to $(2^\Delta)^2 = 2^{2\Delta}$ and the Conway's number of candidates for components of maximal solutions of $(*)$, which are just intersections of factors, is at most $2^{2^{2\Delta}}$.

On the contrary, our number of candidates for components of maximal solutions of $(*)$ equals to the number of elements of the syntactic semiring of L, which is at most the number of mappings from D to $\overline{D}$ (since any transformation $[u_1, \ldots, u_k]$ of $\overline{D}$ is fully determined by its action on D). The last number is $(2^\Delta)^\Delta = 2^{\Delta^2}$. Thus we are doing exponentially better.

The second advantage of our methods is that we use transparent calculations in the finite syntactic semiring of L whose elements are represented by mappings.

Finally, it is worth noticing that every L-closed language, say Q, is an intersection of factors. Indeed, $Q = \bigcap \{ p^{-1} L r^{-1} \mid pQr \subseteq L,\ p, r \in A^* \}$ and any $p^{-1} L r^{-1}$ is a factor since it is the maximal solution of $pxr \subseteq L$.

References

1. Choffrut, C. and Karhumäki, J.; On Fatou properties of rational languages, in C. Martin-Vide and V. Mitrana (eds), *Where Mathematics, Computer Science, Linguistics and Biology Meet*, Kluwer, Dordrecht, 2000, pages 227–235
2. Conway, J.H.; *Regular Algebra and Finite Machines*, Chapman and Hall, Ltd., 1971
3. Kari, L.; On insertion and deletion in formal languages, PhD thesis, University Turku, 1991
4. Polák, L.; A classification of rational languages by semilattice-ordered monoids, http://www.math.muni.cz/~polak
5. Polák, L.; Syntactic semiring of a language, *Proc. Mathematical Foundations of Computer Science 2001*, Springer Lecture Notes in Computer Science, Vol. 2136, 2001, pages 611–620
6. Salomaa, A. and Yu, S.; On the decomposition of finite languages, in Rozenberg, G. et al (eds), *Developments in language theory. Proceedings of the 4th international conference, Aachen, Germany, July 6-9, 1999*. World Scientific, 2000, pages 22–31

Reduced Power Automata

Klaus Sutner

Computer Science Department
Carnegie Mellon University
Pittsburgh, PA 15213
sutner@cs.cmu.edu

Abstract. We describe a class of transitive semiautomata whose power automata are reduced: any two reachable sets of states have distinct behavior. These automata appear naturally in the study of one-dimensional cellular automata.

1 Motivation

The acceptance languages of transitive semiautomata enjoy a number of special properties. Notably, they are factorial, extensible and transitive (FET): $uv \in L \Longrightarrow u, v \in L$, $u \in L \Longrightarrow \exists a, b \in \Sigma \, (aub \in L)$, and $u, v \in L \Longrightarrow \exists x \, (uxv \in L)$ where Σ denotes the underlying alphabet). For languages of this type there is an alternative notion of minimal deterministic automaton, first introduced by Fischer [5] and discovered independently by Beauquier [3] in the form of the 0-minimal ideal in the syntactic semigroup of L. A *Fischer* automaton is a deterministic transitive semiautomaton. For each factorial, extensible and transitive language there is a unique Fischer automaton that minimizes the number of states. Thus, for any FET language L we can measure the state complexity in two ways: as the size $\mu(L)$ of the standard minimal DFA for L, or as the size $\mu_F(L)$ of the minimal Fischer automaton for L. The minimal Fischer automaton naturally embeds into the ordinary minimal deterministic automaton, see [9]. Thus, except in the trivial case where $L = \Sigma^*$, we have $\mu_F(L) \leq \mu(L) - 1$ and one can compute the minimal Fischer automaton in linear time given the standard minimal DFA. Note that $\mu_F(L)$ is arguably a better measure for the complexity of L than $\mu(L) - 1$ since the minimal Fischer automaton can be quite small even when the minimal DFA is large, see [11].

However, there is a fundamental obstruction to computing $\mu(L)$ or $\mu_F(L)$ for a FET language L: these languages are often given as a nondeterministic transitive semiautomaton $\mathcal{A}$. If the semiautomaton has size n, the only a priori bounds available are $\mu_F(L) \leq \mu(L) - 1$ and $\mu(L) \leq 2^n$ since the accessible part $\mathrm{pow}(\mathcal{A})$ of the Rabin-Scott power automaton of $\mathcal{A}$ has size at most 2^n. We write $\pi(\mathcal{A})$ for the size of this automaton. One can construct the minimal automaton in polynomial time from $\mathrm{pow}(\mathcal{A})$, but as shown in [11] it is PSPACE-hard to determine whether $\pi(\mathcal{A})$ is less than a given bound. Hence there is no feasible computational shortcut that would allow one to determine the size of the power automaton without actually constructing the machine. Moreover, [9,11] show

J.-M. Champarnaud and D. Maurel (Eds.): CIAA 2002, LNCS 2608, pp. 194–202, 2003.

that exponential blow-up where $\pi(\mathcal{A})$ is equal to or close to the upper bound 2^n occurs quite frequently.

We are particularly interested in the languages that arise in the study of one-dimensional cellular automata, see [14,7,2,12,6]. For our purposes here, a cellular automaton can be represented as a local map $\rho : \Sigma^w \to \Sigma$ that extends naturally to a global map on bi-infinite words on the alphabet Σ, usually referred to as configurations in this context. The cover of a configuration is the set of all its finite factors. It is easy to see that $\operatorname{cov}(\rho)$, the union of all covers of $\rho(X)$ where X ranges over all configurations, is a regular language. Indeed, the natural semiautomaton for this language is a de Bruijn automaton $B(\rho)$ whose state set is Σ^{w-1} and whose transitions are of the form $(ax, \rho(axb), xb)$ where $a, b \in \Sigma$ and $x \in \Sigma^{w-2}$, see [8,10,4]. The same holds for the cover languages $\operatorname{cov}(\rho^t)$ associated with the iterates of the global map. The de Bruijn automaton here has size $k^{t(w-1)}$ where k denotes the size of the alphabet Σ. Thus, even for binary alphabets the only obvious upper bound is

$$\mu(\operatorname{cov}(\rho^t)) \leq 2^{2^{t(w-1)}}.$$

In the mid eighties, Wolfram performed extensive calculations in an effort to understand the behavior of the sequences $\mu(\operatorname{cov}(\rho^t))$, see [13,14,15]. As shown in [9] the doubly exponential upper bound can be reached for any width w at time $t = 1$, though none of the iterates ρ^t, $t > 1$, display full blow-up.

One can characterize the cellular automata ρ for which full blow-up occurs as follows. Define a *1-permutation* automaton to be any transitive semiautomaton that is obtained by changing the label of a single transition in a permutation automaton. In a permutation automaton each symbol in Σ induces a permutation of the state set; equivalently, the automaton is deterministic, codeterministic and complete. When the selected transition is a loop we refer to the automaton as a *loop-1-permutation* automaton. For de Bruijn automaton $B(\rho)$ full blow-up occurs only for 1-permutation automata. For loop-1-permutation automata we have a particularly simple situation, see [9].

Theorem 1. *Let ρ be a binary cellular automaton such that $B(\rho)$ is a loop-1-permutation automaton of size $n = 2^{w-1}$. Then $\mu(\mathcal{A}) = \pi(\mathcal{A}) = 2^n$ and $\mu_F(\mathcal{A}) = \mu(\mathcal{A}) - 1$.*

In this paper we extend this result in two ways. First, we show that full blow-up occurs in all degenerate 1-permutation automata, see below for definitions. Second, we demonstrate that in general for any 1-permutation automaton $\mathcal{A}$ we have $\mu(\mathcal{A}) = \pi(\mathcal{A})$, regardless of the actual size of the power automaton. Hence, given the power automaton $\operatorname{pow}(\mathcal{A})$ we can compute $\mu_F(\mathcal{A})$ in linear time. In the next section we briefly introduce some terminology, but in general we refer the reader to the references for more background information. Section 3 contains the main result, and in the last section we comment on open problems.

2   One-Permutation Automata

Let $\mathcal{A} = \langle Q, \Sigma, \cdot \rangle$ be any automaton, p a state in $\mathcal{A}$. We will often abuse notation and write p rather than $\{p\}$. We denote $[p]_\mathcal{A}$ the *behavior* of state p in $\mathcal{A}$, i.e., the set of words accepted if p is chosen as initial state. Likewise $[P]_\mathcal{A}$ for $P \subseteq Q$ denotes the set of words accepted if P is chosen as set of initial states. Recall that an automaton *synchronizes (on state p)* if there exists a word w such that $Q \cdot w = p$. A *synchronizes completely* if it synchronizes on all its states. A non-empty set $P \subseteq Q$ is *rich* in $\mathcal{A}$ if $\bigcap_{p \in P} [p]_\mathcal{A} - [Q - P]_\mathcal{A} \neq \emptyset$. The automaton is rich if all its states are rich. The reversal $\mathcal{A}^{\mathrm{op}}$ of an automaton is obtained by replacing all transitions $p \xrightarrow{s} q$ by $q \xrightarrow{s} p$. Similarly, x^{op} denotes the reversal of a word x. Note that $\mathcal{A}^{\mathrm{op}}$ is a 1-permutation automaton whenever $\mathcal{A}$ is. Since $x \in [q]_\mathcal{A}$ if, and only if, $q \in Q \cdot x^{\mathrm{op}}$ in $\mathcal{A}^{\mathrm{op}}$ we have the following proposition.

Proposition 1. *State p is rich in $\mathcal{A}$ if, and only if, $\mathcal{A}^{\mathrm{op}}$ synchronizes on p. More generally, $P \subseteq Q$ is rich in $\mathcal{A}$ if, and only if, P is reachable in $\mathcal{A}^{\mathrm{op}}$.*

Hence, if $\mathcal{A}^{\mathrm{op}}$ synchronizes completely the full power automaton of $\mathcal{A}$ is reduced, and its accessible part $\mathrm{pow}(\mathcal{A})$ is the minimal automaton, so $\pi(\mathcal{A}) = \mu(\mathcal{A})$.

To simplify notation, let $\mathcal{A}_0$ be a transitive permutation automaton over the alphabet $\{a, b\}$ and fix a transition $\tau = (\alpha, b, \beta)$ in $\mathcal{A}_0$. We denote $\mathcal{A}$ the 1-permutation automaton obtained by flipping the label of that transition to a. Thus, locally the 1-permutation automaton $\mathcal{A}$ has the following structure.

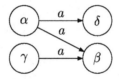

Proposition 2. *Let $\mathcal{A}$ be a 1-permutation automaton. Then $\mathcal{A}$ synchronizes on α, and β is rich in $\mathcal{A}$.*

Proof. Suppose $P \subseteq Q$ has cardinality larger than 1. Define the standard length-lex order on words to be the product order where words a first compared by length, and then each group of words of the same length is ordered lexicographically. Let x be length-lex minimal such that $\alpha \in P \cdot x$. Then $|P \cdot xb| = |P| - 1$ and $\mathcal{A}$ synchronizes on α by induction. Since $\mathcal{A}^{\mathrm{op}}$ is also a 1-permutation automaton it follows by the same argument and proposition 1 that β is rich in $\mathcal{A}$. $\qquad\square$

Proposition 1 allows us to demonstrate blow-up of machine $\mathcal{A}$ by arguing about the richness of sets of states in $\mathcal{A}^{\mathrm{op}}$. To this is end it is convenient to think of computations as moving pebbles according to some input sequence. For example, to show that p is rich we can place a red pebble on p and a black pebble on each state in $Q - p$. We then have to remove all black pebbles (by moving them to α and then firing a b transition), without losing the red one. A loss could occur because the red pebble is located at α and the next symbol is

b, or because the red pebble moves to β, but a black pebble arrives there at the same time. Of course, both red and black pebbles will split when located at α and the next symbol is an a, so there may be several red pebbles after a while.

To demonstrate this approach, consider an automaton $\mathcal{A}$ defined on a circulant graph $C(n; 1, d)$ where $1 < d < n$. Figure 1 shows a 1-permutation automaton based on $C(6; 1, 2)$.

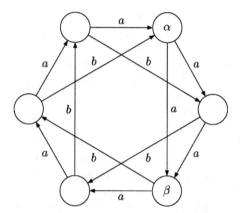

Fig. 1. A 1-permutation automaton on the circulant graph $C(6; 1, 2)$.

In this case, $\mathcal{A}$ and $\mathcal{A}^{\mathrm{op}}$ are isomorphic. To see that an arbitrary non-empty set $P \subseteq Q$ is rich place red pebbles on all the elements of P, and black pebbles on all the states in $Q - P$. We can now fire a sequence of input symbols a until a black pebble is moved to α, and then fire b. Note that no red pebbles are lost, even if the second incarnation of a pebble being placed onto β is eliminated by a black pebble arriving there at the same time. Hence, we can remove all black pebbles. It follows that $\pi(\mathcal{A}) = 2^n$ and, as we will see shortly, $\mu(\mathcal{A}) = 2^n$. However, the size of the minimal Fischer automaton is $m(2^{n/m} - 1)$ where $m = \gcd(n, d - 1)$: the states in $P \subseteq Q$ reachable from a single state p all have distances a multiple of $d - 1$, and all such P are indeed reachable.

As a first step towards our main result, let us first dispense with the case when two of the states α, β, δ or γ coincide. Let us call a 1-permutation automaton *degenerate* if either $\alpha = \beta$ or $\delta = \gamma$. Thus loop-1-permutation automata in particular are degenerate, and degenerate 1-permutation automata locally have the following structure.

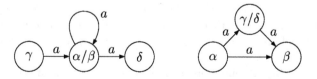

Theorem 2. *Let $\mathcal{A}$ be a degenerate 1-permutation automaton of size n. Then* $\mu(\mathcal{A}) = \pi(\mathcal{A}) = 2^n$.

Proof. By theorem 1 we only have to deal with the case $\delta = \gamma$. In theorem 3 we will show that $\mu(\mathcal{A}) = \pi(\mathcal{A})$, so it suffices to show that in $\mathcal{A}^{\mathrm{op}}$ every subset of Q is rich. But $\mathcal{A}^{\mathrm{op}}$ is again degenerate, so to simplify notation we will show that every subset of Q is rich in $\mathcal{A} = \mathcal{A}^{\mathrm{op}\,\mathrm{op}}$. To this end we show that for every R disjoint from P we have $\bigcap_{r \in R} [r]_{\mathcal{A}} - [P]_{\mathcal{A}} \neq \emptyset$.

Let A be the a-labeled cycle in $\mathcal{A}_0$ that contains the consecutive edges $\alpha \overset{a}{\to} \delta = \gamma \overset{a}{\to} \beta$. Note that in $\mathcal{A}$ there is a chord $\alpha \overset{a}{\to} \beta$ in this cycle. Define a partial order on the power set of Q by $P \prec P'$ if $|P| < |P'|$, or if $|P| = |P'|$ and the length-lex minimal word x such that $\alpha \in P{\cdot}x$ precedes the corresponding word for P', again in length-lex order.

Suppose P is $\prec$-minimal such that for some $R \cap P = \emptyset$ we have $\bigcap_{r \in R} [r]_{\mathcal{A}} \subseteq [P]_{\mathcal{A}}$. Place red pebbles on R and black pebbles on P accordingly. By the minimality of P we must have $\alpha \notin P$. Let x be the minimal witness such that $\alpha \in P \cdot x$. Then $x = bu$ and there is a red pebble on α, otherwise there would be a violation of the minimality of P.

Let m be the least common multiple of the lengths of all a-labeled cycles in $\mathcal{A}_0$. Move the pebbles according to a^m. Since P is minimal, no black pebble can be on A, so that all black pebbles return to their original positions. The red pebble originally at α now has a clone at δ. Hence we can now use b to move the black pebbles closer to α without destroying a red pebble (and all its descendants). Since $|P| = |P \cdot a^m b|$ this contradicts our minimality assumption. $\square$

Note that no claims are made about the size of the minimal Fischer automaton in the last theorem. It is not true in general that $\mu_F(\mathcal{A}) = 2^n - 1$, though in the special case of de Bruijn automata this relation obtains: in this case $\gamma = \delta = 0^k$ or 1^k, so there is a loop at $\gamma = \delta$ labeled b. From this it follows easily that $\mathcal{A}$ synchronizes on β, thus Q is reachable from α in $\mathcal{A}$.

3   Reduced Power Automata

We will now show that the power automata arising from 1-permutation automata are always reduced. $\mathcal{A}^-$ denotes the reversible automaton obtained by removing the transition τ from $\mathcal{A}_0$.

Lemma 1. *Let $\mathcal{A}$ be a 1-permutation automaton where both (α, a, δ) and (γ, a, β) lie in the same strongly connected component of $\mathcal{A}^-$. Then $\mathcal{A}$ is rich.*

Proof. First consider a cycle C of the form $\beta \longrightarrow \alpha \overset{a}{\to} \delta \longrightarrow \gamma \overset{a}{\to} \beta$. We claim that every point q on C is rich. To see this let $P \subseteq Q$ where $q \notin P$, and place red and black pebbles on Q correspondingly. We may safely assume that $q \neq \beta$ by proposition 2.

If there is no black pebble on α fire symbol s to advance the pebble from q one step towards β. If there is a black pebble on α pick $i > 0$ such that either $q \cdot b^i = q$ or $q \cdot b^i = \alpha$ depending on whether the red pebble is currently located on a b-cycle or on the open path labeled b ending at α. In both cases, we either remove at least one black pebble or we bring the red pebble closer to β on C. Our claim follows by induction.

But then every state is rich: we can move a red pebble from anywhere to the cycle C. □

Accessibility plays no role in the last argument, so we have the following corollary.

Corollary 1. *Let $\mathcal{A}$ be as in the last lemma. Then the full power automaton of $\mathcal{A}$ is reduced. In particular, $\mu(\mathcal{A}) = \pi(\mathcal{A})$.*

From now on assume that (α, a, δ) and (γ, a, β) lie in two separate transitive subautomata $\mathcal{A}_\delta$ and $\mathcal{A}_\beta$ determined by the strongly connected components of δ and β in $\mathcal{A}^-$. A typical example of this situation is shown in figure 2. The subautomaton $\mathcal{A}_\delta$ here has states $\{\alpha, \delta\}$ and all other states lie in $\mathcal{A}_\beta$.

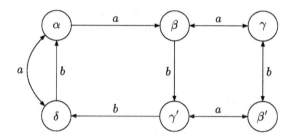

Fig. 2. A 1-permutation automaton with δ covered by $\{\beta, \beta'\}$.

In this automaton the behavior of δ is strictly contained in the behavior of $\{\beta, \beta'\}$, and the full power automaton fails to be reduced. However, we will see that $\{\beta, \beta'\}$ is not reachable, and the power automaton is still reduced. To see why, consider $P_1 \neq P_2 \subseteq Q$ but $[P_1]_{\mathcal{A}} = [P_2]_{\mathcal{A}}$. Without loss of generality assume $p \in P_1 - P_2$. Let x be length-lex minimal such that $p \cdot x = \alpha$. Since β is rich we must have $\gamma \in P_2 \cdot x$: otherwise $\beta \in p \cdot xa$ but $\beta \notin P_2 \cdot xa$. Moreover, $\delta \in p \cdot xa$ and we must have $\beta \in P_2 \cdot xau$ for any u such that $\delta \cdot u = \delta$. This is captured in the next definition. $P \subseteq Q$ *covers* δ if $\delta \notin P$ but $[\delta]_{\mathcal{A}} \subseteq [P]_{\mathcal{A}}$. A cover P is *minimal* if it is minimal with respect to cardinality.

Thus, covers form the essential obstruction to the full power automaton being reduced. We will now describe the structure of minimal covers in great detail so as to show that these sets cannot appear in the accessible part of the power automaton.

Proposition 3. *Let P be a minimal cover of δ and x in the behavior of δ. Then $|P \cdot x| = |P|$.*

Proof. By minimality, the cardinality of $P \cdot x$ cannot decrease for any $x \in [\delta]_{\mathcal{A}}$. Assume for the sake of a contradiction that $|P \cdot x| > |P|$. Let $u \in [\delta]_{\mathcal{A}}$ be the minimal prefix of x such that $\alpha \in P \cdot u$. Note that $\alpha \neq \delta \cdot u$ since no merge can occur on α. But then $ub \in [\delta]_{\mathcal{A}}$ whereas $|P \cdot ub| < |P|$, contradiction. □

Proposition 4. *Let P be a minimal cover of δ and $\delta = \delta \cdot x$. Then $P \cdot x$ is a minimal cover and x acts like a permutation on P.*

Proof. We have $[\delta]_{\mathcal{A}} = x^{-1}[\delta]_{\mathcal{A}} \subseteq x^{-1}[P]_{\mathcal{A}}$ and therefore $[\delta]_{\mathcal{A}} \subseteq [P \cdot x]_{\mathcal{A}}$. The first claim follows from the last proposition.

Since $\delta = \delta \cdot x^i$ for all $i \geq 0$ it follows that $P \cdot x^i$ is a minimal cover for all i. But then $P \cdot x^i = P \cdot x^{i+j}$ for some $i \geq 0$, $j > 0$. Hence the orbits are labeled x^j and our claim follows. □

Lemma 2. *Let P be a minimal cover of δ. Then*

$$P = \{\, \beta \cdot x \mid \delta \cdot x = \delta \text{ in } \mathcal{A}^- \,\}$$

Proof. Denote $P_0 = \{\, \beta \cdot x \mid \delta \cdot x = \delta \text{ in } \mathcal{A}^- \,\}$ and pick $x \neq \varepsilon$ such that $\delta \cdot x = \delta$ in $\mathcal{A}^-$. Clearly $x = ua$ and, by proposition 4, x permutes P. But $\delta \cdot u = \alpha$, so $\gamma \in P \cdot u$ and $\beta \in P \cdot x$. It follows that $P_0 \subseteq P$ and it suffices to show that P_0 is a cover. So suppose u is in the behavior of δ. Then for some suitable suffix v we have $\delta \in \delta \cdot (uv)^i$ for all i, and P_0 contains a cycle

$$\beta = \beta_0 \xrightarrow{uv} \beta_1 \xrightarrow{uv} \beta_2 \xrightarrow{uv} \ldots \xrightarrow{uv} \beta_{r-1} \xrightarrow{uv} \beta_r = \beta.$$

But then u is in the behavior of P_0. □

Since both subautomata $\mathcal{A}_\delta$ and $\mathcal{A}_\beta$ are reversible we have a natural partial action of the free group over $\{a, b\}$ on their state sets, see [1] for details. To avoid confusion with our π function we write $\mathbb{F}(\mathcal{A}_\delta, \delta)$ for the fundamental group of $\mathcal{A}_\delta$, and $\mathbb{F}(\mathcal{A}_\beta, P)$ for the words in the free group over $\{a, b\}$ that permute P.

Lemma 3. *Let P be a minimal cover of δ. Then $\mathbb{F}(\mathcal{A}_\delta, \delta) = \mathbb{F}(\mathcal{A}_\beta, P)$.*

Proof. We first show $\mathbb{F}(\mathcal{A}_\delta, \delta) \subseteq \mathbb{F}(\mathcal{A}_\beta, P)$. We have $\{a, b\}^* \cap \mathbb{F}(\mathcal{A}_\delta, \delta) \subseteq \mathbb{F}(\mathcal{A}_\beta, P)$ from proposition 4. For the sake of simplicity, we consider only the case where $x \in \mathbb{F}(\mathcal{A}_\delta, \delta)$ contains only one symbol $\bar{a}$, the general case is entirely analogous. So, assume $x = u\bar{a}w$ where $u, w \in \{a, b\}^*$. Since $\mathcal{A}_\delta$ is strongly connected we can choose a word $v \in \{a, b\}^*$ such that $\delta \cdot uw = \delta \cdot u\bar{a}$. But then $u(wa)^i wv$ permutes P for all $i \geq 0$. For any $p \in P$ set $q_p = p \cdot u$, so that $q_p \cdot wu = f(p)$ for some permutation f. wa permutes the set $\{\, q_p \mid p \in P \,\}$. Hence, $q_p \cdot \bar{a} = q_p \cdot (wa)^i w$ for some $i \geq 0$ and it follows that $u\bar{a}v$ permutes P.

For the opposite direction let $x \in \mathbb{F}(\mathcal{A}_\beta, P)$ and set $q = \delta \cdot x$. Since $\beta \in P \cdot x$ we must have $q = \delta \cdot b^i$ for some $i \geq 0$, so that $x\bar{b}^i \in \mathbb{F}(\mathcal{A}_\delta, \delta) \subseteq \mathbb{F}(\mathcal{A}_\beta, P)$. But then $x\bar{b}^i$ permutes P, whence $i = 0$ and we have $x \in \mathbb{F}(\mathcal{A}_\delta, \delta)$. □

Theorem 3. *Let $\mathcal{A}$ be a 1-permutation automaton. Then the accessible part of the power automaton is reduced. Hence $\mu(\mathcal{A}) = \pi(\mathcal{A})$.*

Proof. By lemma 1 we may safely assume that (α, a, β) and (γ, a, δ) do not lie in the same strongly connected component of $\mathcal{A}^-$.

First consider the case when δ has no cover, i.e., when δ is rich. Since there is a path $p \xrightarrow{x} \delta$ from any state p other than β that avoids β it follows that $\mathcal{A}$ is rich and we are done as in corollary 1.

So suppose $P_1 \neq P_2 \subseteq Q$ but $[P_1]_\mathcal{A} = [P_2]_\mathcal{A}$. Without loss of generality assume $p \in P_1 - P_2$. As mentioned previously, we must have $p \cdot xa = \delta$ and $P_2 \cdot xa$ covers δ. But covers are not reachable. To see this, assume otherwise, say $P = Q \cdot x$ for some cover P. Since $\delta \notin P$ and all states in $\mathcal{A}_\delta{}^{\mathrm{op}}$ are complete, x must be of the form $x = vbu$ where $\delta' \cdot bu = \delta$. But then $u \in \mathbb{F}(\mathcal{A}_\delta)$, so $P = Q \cdot vb$ by lemma 3, contradicting the fact that β is in P by lemma 2.

Hence P_2 cannot be reachable either, and we are done. $\square$

4 Open Problems

As pointed out in the introduction, any cellular automaton whose associated FET language has maximum complexity must be a 1-permutation automaton. Some of these automata are accounted for by theorem 2. However, computational experiments suggest that exactly half of the 1-permutation automata associated with binary cellular automata of width w demonstrate full blow-up:

Conjecture 1. There are $2^{w-1}2^{2^{w-2}}$ 1-permutation automata de Bruijn automata $\mathcal{A}$ such that

$$\mu(\mathcal{A}) = \mu_F(\mathcal{A}) + 1 = 2^{2^{w-1}}.$$

It seems that the size of the power automaton of a 1-permutation automaton $\mathcal{A}$ is usually invariant under reversal, the automaton in figure 2 being a case in point. There are exceptions, but we are unable to characterize them at this point.

Conjecture 2. In general, for a 1-permutation automaton $\mathcal{A}$ we have $\mu(\mathcal{A}) = \mu(\mathcal{A}^{\mathrm{op}})$.

Generalizing 1-permutation automata to k-permutation automata in the obvious way one can see that the corresponding cellular automata tend to have smaller μ and π values with increasing k. We do not presently understand the nature of this correlation.

References

1. E. Badouel. Representations of reversible automata and state graphs of vector addition systems. Technical Report 3490, INRIA, 1998.
2. M.-P. Beal and D. Perrin. Symbolic dynamics and finite automata. In G. Rozenberg and A. Salomaa, editors, *Handbook of Formal Languages*, volume 2, chapter 10. Springer Verlag, 1997.
3. D. Beauquier. Minimal automaton for a factorial, transitive, rational language. *Theoretical Computer Science*, 67:65–73, 1989.
4. M. Delorme and J. Mazoyer. *Cellular Automata: A Parallel Model*, volume 460 of *Mathematics and Its Applications*. Kluwer Academic Publishers, 1999.
5. R. Fischer. Sofic systems and graphs. *Monatshefte für Mathematik*, 80:179–186, 1975.

6. G. A. Hedlund. Endomorphisms and automorphisms of the shift dynamical system. *Math. Systems Theory*, 3:320–375, 1969.
7. D. Lind and B. Marcus. *Introduction to Symbolic Dynamics and Coding.* Cambridge University Press, 1995.
8. K. Sutner. De Bruijn graphs and linear cellular automata. *Complex Systems*, 5(1): 19–30, 1991.
9. K. Sutner. Linear cellular automata and Fischer automata. *Parallel Computing*, 23(11):1613–1634, 1997.
10. K. Sutner. *Linear Cellular Automata and De Bruijn Automata*, pages 303–320. Volume 460 of *Mathematics and Its Applications* [4], 1999.
11. K. Sutner. The size of power automata. In J. Sgall, Ales Pultr, and Petr Kolman, editors, *Mathematical Foundations of Computer Science*, volume 2136 of *SLNCS*, pages 666–677, 2001.
12. B. Weiss. Subshifts of finite type and sofic systems. *Monatshefte für Mathematik*, 77:462–474, 1973.
13. S. Wolfram. Twenty problems in the theory of cellular automata. *Physica Scripta*, T9:170–183, 1985.
14. S. Wolfram. *Theory and Applications of Cellular Automata.* World Scientific, 1986.
15. S. Wolfram. *A New Kind of Science.* Wolfram Media, 2002.

A Polynomial Time Algorithm for Left [Right] Local Testability

A.N. Trahtman

Bar-Ilan University, Dep. of Math. and CS,
52900, Ramat Gan, Israel
trakht@macs.biu.ac.il

Abstract. A right [left] locally testable language S is a language with the property that for some nonnegative integer k two words u and v in alphabet S are equal in the semigroup if (1) the prefix and suffix of the words of length $k-1$ coincide, (2) the set of segments of length k of the words as well as 3) the order of the first appearance of these segments in prefixes [suffixes] coincide.

We present necessary and sufficient condition for graph [semigroup] to be transition graph [semigroup] of the deterministic finite automaton that accepts right [left] locally testable language and necessary and sufficient condition for transition graph of the deterministic finite automaton with locally idempotent semigroup. We introduced polynomial time algorithms for the right [left] local testability problem for transition semigroup and transition graph of the deterministic finite automaton based on these conditions. Polynomial time algorithm verifies transition graph of automaton with locally idempotent transition semigroup.

Keywords: language, locally testable, deterministic finite automaton, algorithm, semigroup, graph

1 Introduction

The concept of local testability was first introduced by McNaughton and Papert [12] and by Brzozowski and Simon [5]. This concept is connected with languages, finite automata and semigroups and has a wide spectrum of generalizations.

The necessary and sufficient condition for local testability were investigated for both transition graph and transition semigroups of the automaton [5], [10], [13], [16]. The polynomial time algorithms solve the problem of local testability for transition graph [10] and for transition semigroups of the automaton [13]. They are polynomial in terms of the size of the semigroup or in the sum of nodes and edges.

Right [left] local testability was introduced and studied by König [9] and by Garcia and Ruiz [7]. These papers use different definitions of the conception and we follow [7] here

Theorem 11 *[7] A finite semigroup S is right [left] locally testable iff it is locally idempotent and locally satisfies the identity $xyx = xy$ [$xyx = yx$].*

J.-M. Champarnaud and D. Maurel (Eds.): CIAA 2002, LNCS 2608, pp. 203–212, 2003.

For conception of local idempotency see, for instance, [6]. The varieties of semi-groups defined by considered identities are located not far from atoms in the structure of idempotent varieties [4].

We present in this work necessary and sufficient condition for right [left] lo-cal testability for transition graph of the DFA and for the local idempotency of the transition semigroup on the corresponding transition graph. We improve necessary and sufficient condition for right [left] local testability from [7] for tran-sition semigroup. On the base of these results, we introduced a polynomial time algorithm for the right [left] local testability problem for transition semigroup and transition graph of the deterministic finite automaton and for checking the transition graph of the automaton with locally idempotent semigroup.

These algorithms are implemented in the package TESTAS. The package checks also whether or not a language given by its minimal automaton or by syn-tactic semigroup of the automaton is locally testable, threshold locally testable, strictly locally testable, or piecewise testable [2], [15].

2   Notation and Definitions

Let Σ be an alphabet and let Σ^+ denote the free semigroup on Σ. If $w \in \Sigma^+$, let $|w|$ denote the length of w. Let k be a positive integer. Let $i_k(w)$ $[t_k(w)]$ denote the prefix [suffix] of w of length k or w if $|w| < k$. Let $F_k(w)$ denote the set of segments of w of length k. A language L [a semigroup S] is called *right [left] k-testable* if there is an alphabet Σ [and a surjective morphism $\phi : \Sigma^+ \to S$] such that for all $u, v \in \Sigma^+$, if $i_{k-1}(u) = i_{k-1}(v), t_{k-1}(u) = t_{k-1}(v), F_k(u) = F_k(v)$ and the order of appearance of these segments in prefixes [suffixes] in the word coincide, then either both u and v are in L or neither is in L [$u\phi = v\phi$].

An automaton is *right [left] k-testable* if the automaton accepts a right [left] k-testable language.

A language L [a semigroup S, an automaton $\mathbf{A}$] is *right [left] locally testable* if it is right [left] k-testable for some k.

$|S|$ is the number of elements of the set S.

A semigroup S is called *semigroup of left [right] zeroes* if S satisfies the identity $xy = x$ [$xy = y$].

A semigroup S has a property ρ *locally* if for any idempotent $e \in S$ the subsemigroup eSe has the property ρ.

So a semigroup S is called *locally idempotent* if eSe is an idempotent sub-semigroup for any idempotent $e \in S$.

A maximal strongly connected component of the graph will be denoted for brevity as SCC, a finite deterministic automaton will be denoted as DFA. A node from an SCC will be called for brevity as an $SCC - node$. SCC-node can be defined as a node that has a right unit in transition semigroup of the automaton.

$|\Gamma|$ denotes the number of nodes of the graph Γ.

Γ^i denotes the direct product of i copies of the graph Γ. The edge $(\mathbf{p}_1, ..., \mathbf{p}_n) \to (\mathbf{q}_1, ..., \mathbf{q}_n)$ in Γ^i is labelled by σ iff for each i the edge $\mathbf{p}_i \to \mathbf{q}_i$ in Γ is labelled by σ.

The graph with only trivial SCC (loops) will be called *acyclic*.

If an edge $\mathbf{p} \to \mathbf{q}$ is labelled by σ then let us denote the node $\mathbf{q}$ as $\mathbf{p}\sigma$.

We shall write $\mathbf{p} \succeq \mathbf{q}$ if the node $\mathbf{q}$ is reachable from the node $\mathbf{p}$ or $\mathbf{p} = \mathbf{q}$ ($\mathbf{p} \succ \mathbf{q}$ for distinct $\mathbf{p}, \mathbf{q}$).

In the case $\mathbf{p} \succeq \mathbf{q}$ and $\mathbf{q} \succeq \mathbf{p}$ we write $\mathbf{p} \sim \mathbf{q}$ (that is $\mathbf{p}$ and $\mathbf{q}$ belong to one SCC or $\mathbf{p} = \mathbf{q}$).

3 Transition Graph of Deterministic Finite Automaton

3.1 Graph of DFA with Locally Idempotent Transition Semigroup

Lemma 31 *Let S be the transition semigroup of a deterministic finite automaton and let Γ be its transition graph. Let us suppose that for three distinct nodes $\mathbf{p}, \mathbf{q}, \mathbf{r}$ from Γ the node $(\mathbf{p}, \mathbf{q}, \mathbf{r})$ in Γ^3 is SCC-node, and $(\mathbf{p}, \mathbf{q}) \succ (\mathbf{q}, \mathbf{r})$ in Γ^2.*
Then S is not locally idempotent.

Proof. Let us suppose that for the nodes $\mathbf{p}, \mathbf{q}, \mathbf{r}$ from Γ the conditions of lemma hold. Therefore the nodes $\mathbf{p}, \mathbf{q}, \mathbf{r}$ have a right unit $e = e^2$, whence $\mathbf{p}e = \mathbf{p}$, $\mathbf{q}e = \mathbf{q}$, $\mathbf{r}e = \mathbf{r}$. In view $(\mathbf{p}, \mathbf{q}) \succ (\mathbf{q}, \mathbf{r})$, there exists an element $s \in S$ such that $\mathbf{p}s = \mathbf{q}$ and $\mathbf{q}s = \mathbf{r}$. Therefore $\mathbf{p}ese = \mathbf{q}$ and $\mathbf{q}ese = \mathbf{r}$, whence $\mathbf{p}(ese)^2 = \mathbf{r} \neq \mathbf{q} = \mathbf{p}ese$. So $\mathbf{p}(ese)^2 \neq \mathbf{p}ese$ and $(ese)^2 \neq ese$. Semigroup eSe is not an idempotent semigroup and therefore S is not locally idempotent.

Lemma 32 *Let S be the locally idempotent transition semigroup of a deterministic finite automaton and let Γ be its transition graph.*
For any SCC-node $(\mathbf{p}, \mathbf{q}) \in \Gamma^2$ and $s \in S$ from $\mathbf{p}s \succeq \mathbf{q}$ follows $\mathbf{q}s \succeq \mathbf{q}$.

Proof. Let us consider SCC-node $(\mathbf{p}, \mathbf{q})$ from Γ^2 such that $\mathbf{p}s \succeq \mathbf{q}$. The node $(\mathbf{p}, \mathbf{q})$ has a right unit $e = e^2$, so $\mathbf{p}e = \mathbf{p}$, $\mathbf{q}e = \mathbf{q}$. For some $b \in S$ we have $\mathbf{p}sb = \mathbf{q}$. We can assume $s = es$, $b = be$. $esbe = (esbe)^2$ in locally idempotent semigroup S. Therefore $\mathbf{q} = \mathbf{p}esbe = \mathbf{p}(esbe)^2 = \mathbf{q}esbe = \mathbf{q}sbe$. Thus we have $\mathbf{q}s \succeq \mathbf{q}$.

Lemma implies

Corollary 33 *Let S be the locally idempotent transition semigroup of a deterministic finite automaton and let Γ be its transition graph.*
Let us suppose that in Γ^2 we have $(\mathbf{p}, \mathbf{q}) \succ (\mathbf{q}, \mathbf{r})$ and the node $(\mathbf{p}, \mathbf{q})$ is an SCC-node. Then $\mathbf{r} \sim \mathbf{q}$.

Lemma 34 *Let S be transition semigroup of a deterministic finite automaton and suppose that in Γ^2 we have $(\mathbf{p}, \mathbf{q}) \succ (\mathbf{q}, \mathbf{p})$ for two distinct nodes $\mathbf{p}, \mathbf{q}$.*
Then S is not locally idempotent.

Proof. We have $\mathbf{p}s = \mathbf{q}$ and $\mathbf{q}s = \mathbf{p}$ for some $s \in S$. So $\mathbf{p}s^2 = \mathbf{p} \neq \mathbf{p}s = \mathbf{q}$ and $\mathbf{p} = \mathbf{p}s^{2n} \neq \mathbf{p}s^{2n-1} = \mathbf{q}$. Therefore $s^{2n} \neq s^{2n-1}$ for any integer n because of $\mathbf{p} \neq \mathbf{q}$. Finite semigroup S contains therefore non-trivial subgroup, whence S is not locally idempotent.

Let us formulate the necessary and sufficient conditions for graph to be transition graph of DFA with locally idempotent transition semigroup.

Theorem 35 *Transition semigroup S of a deterministic finite automaton is locally idempotent iff*

    1. $(\mathbf{p}, \mathbf{q}) \not\sim (\mathbf{q}, \mathbf{p})$ in Γ^2 for any two distinct nodes $\mathbf{p}, \mathbf{q}$,

    2. for any SCC-node $(\mathbf{p}, \mathbf{q}) \in \Gamma^2$ and $s \in S$ from $\mathbf{p}s \succeq \mathbf{q}$ follows $\mathbf{q}s \succeq \mathbf{q}$ and

    3. for any SCC-node $(\mathbf{p}, \mathbf{q}, \mathbf{r})$ of Γ^3 with distinct components holds $(\mathbf{p}, \mathbf{q}) \not\sim (\mathbf{q}, \mathbf{r})$ in Γ^2.

Proof. If S is locally idempotent then the condition 1 follows from lemma 34, condition 2 follows from lemma 32, condition 3 follows from lemma 31.

Suppose now that S is not locally idempotent. Then for some node $\mathbf{p}$ from Γ, idempotent e and element s from S we have $\mathbf{p}(ese)^2 \neq \mathbf{p}ese$. Hence $\mathbf{p}e \neq \mathbf{p}ese$ and at least one of two nodes $\mathbf{p}(ese)^2$, $\mathbf{p}ese$ exists. If exists the node $\mathbf{p}(ese)^2$ then the node $\mathbf{p}ese$ exists too. So $\mathbf{p}ese$ exists anyway. Therefore $\mathbf{p}e$ exists too and from $(\mathbf{p}e, \mathbf{p}ese)ese = (\mathbf{p}ese, \mathbf{p}(ese)^2)$ in view of condition 2 follows $\mathbf{p}(ese)^2 \succ \mathbf{p}ese$, whence the node $\mathbf{p}(ese)^2$ exists.

The node $(\mathbf{p}e, \mathbf{p}ese, \mathbf{p}(ese)^2)$ is an SCC-node of Γ^3 because all components of the node have common right unit e. Let us notice that $\mathbf{p}(ese)^2 \neq \mathbf{p}ese$ and $\mathbf{p}e \neq \mathbf{p}ese$. We have $(\mathbf{p}e, \mathbf{p}ese) \succ (\mathbf{p}ese, \mathbf{p}(ese)^2)$. In the case $\mathbf{p}e = \mathbf{p}(ese)^2$ we have contradiction with condition 1, in opposite case we have contradiction with condition 3.

3.2   Right Local Testability

Theorem 36 *Let S be transition semigroup of deterministic finite automaton with state transition graph Γ. Then S is right locally testable iff*

    1. for any SCC-node $(\mathbf{p}, \mathbf{q})$ from Γ^2 such that $\mathbf{p} \sim \mathbf{q}$ holds $\mathbf{p} = \mathbf{q}$.

    2. for any SCC-node $(\mathbf{p}, \mathbf{q}) \in \Gamma^2$ and $s \in S$ from $\mathbf{p}s \succeq \mathbf{q}$ follows $\mathbf{q}s \succeq \mathbf{q}$.

Proof. Suppose semigroup S is right locally testable.

Condition 1. Let $(\mathbf{p}, \mathbf{q})$ be an SCC-node with distinct components. Then for some idempotent $e \in S$ holds $(\mathbf{p}, \mathbf{q})e = (\mathbf{p}, \mathbf{q})$. If $\mathbf{p} \sim \mathbf{q}$ then for some $a, b \in S$ holds $\mathbf{q}a = \mathbf{p}$ and $\mathbf{p}b = \mathbf{q}$, whence $\mathbf{q}eae = \mathbf{p}$ and $\mathbf{p}ebe = \mathbf{q}$. So $\mathbf{q}eaebe = \mathbf{q}$ and $\mathbf{p}ebeae = \mathbf{p}$. Semigroup S is right locally testable and therefore the subsemigroup eSe satisfies identity $xyx = xy$ [7]. Consequently, $\mathbf{q} = \mathbf{q}eaebe = \mathbf{q}eaebeae = \mathbf{p}ebeae = \mathbf{p}$.

Condition 2 follows from lemma 32 because right locally testable semigroup S is locally idempotent.

Suppose now that both conditions of the theorem are valid. Let us begin from the local idempotency of S.

If the identity $x^2 = x$ is not valid in eSe for some idempotent e then for some node $\mathbf{v} \in \Gamma$ and some element $a \in S$ we have $\mathbf{v}eae \neq \mathbf{v}eaeae$. At least one of two considered nodes exists. In view of $\mathbf{v}e \succeq \mathbf{v}eae \succeq \mathbf{v}eaeae$ the nodes $\mathbf{v}eae, \mathbf{v}e$ exist. Let us denote $\mathbf{p} = \mathbf{v}e$, $\mathbf{q} = \mathbf{v}eae$. Therefore $(\mathbf{p}, \mathbf{q})$ is an SCC-node. Notice that $\mathbf{p}eae \succeq \mathbf{q}$. Hence, by condition 2, $\mathbf{q}eae \succeq \mathbf{q}$. Now, by by condition 1, in view of $\mathbf{q} \succeq \mathbf{q}eae$, we have $\mathbf{q}eae = \mathbf{q}$. So $\mathbf{v}eae = \mathbf{v}eaeae$ in spite of our assumption.

Thus the transition semigroup S is locally idempotent.

If the identity $xyx = xy$ [7] is not valid in eSe then for some node $\mathbf{v} \in \Gamma$, some idempotent e and elements $a, b \in S$ holds $\mathbf{v}eaebe \neq \mathbf{v}eaebeae$. So the node $\mathbf{v}eaebe$ exists. Let us denote $\mathbf{p} = \mathbf{v}eaebe$. S is locally idempotent and therefore $\mathbf{p} = \mathbf{v}eaebeaebe$. Consequently, the node $\mathbf{q} = \mathbf{v}eaebeae$ exists too. We have $\mathbf{p} \neq \mathbf{q}$. The node $(\mathbf{v}eaebe, \mathbf{v}eaebeae) = (\mathbf{p}, \mathbf{q})$ is an SCC-node from Γ^2. It is clear that $\mathbf{p} = \mathbf{v}eaebe \succeq \mathbf{v}eaebeae = \mathbf{q}$. Then $\mathbf{q} = \mathbf{v}eaebeae \succeq \mathbf{v}eaebeaebe = \mathbf{v}eaebe = \mathbf{p}$. So $\mathbf{p} \sim \mathbf{q}$ and $\mathbf{p} \neq \mathbf{q}$ in spite of the condition 1.

3.3   Left Local Testability

Lemma 37 *Let reduced DFA $\mathbf{A}$ with state transition graph Γ and transition semigroup S be left locally testable. Suppose that for SCC-node $(\mathbf{p}, \mathbf{q})$ of Γ^2 holds $\mathbf{p} \succeq \mathbf{q}$.*

Then for any $s \in S$ holds $\mathbf{p}s \succeq \mathbf{q}$ iff $\mathbf{q}s \succeq \mathbf{q}$.

Proof. Suppose $\mathbf{A}$ is left locally testable. Then the transition semigroup S of the automaton is finite, aperiodic and for any idempotent $e \in S$ the subsemigroup eSe is idempotent [7].

For some $a, e = e^2 \in S$ holds $\mathbf{p}a = \mathbf{q}$, $(\mathbf{p}, \mathbf{q})e = (\mathbf{p}, \mathbf{q})$. So we have $\mathbf{p}es = \mathbf{p}s$ and $\mathbf{q}es = \mathbf{q}s$.

If we assume that $\mathbf{p}s \succeq \mathbf{q}$, then for some b from S holds $\mathbf{p}sb = \mathbf{q}$, whence $\mathbf{p}esbe = \mathbf{q}$. In idempotent subsemigroup eSe we have $esbe = (esbe)^2$. Therefore $\mathbf{q}esbe = \mathbf{p}(esbe)^2 = \mathbf{p}esbe = \mathbf{q}$ and $\mathbf{q}es = \mathbf{q}s \succeq \mathbf{q}$.

If we assume now that $\mathbf{q}s \succeq \mathbf{q}$, then for some $d \in S$ holds $\mathbf{q}sde = \mathbf{q}$. For some $a \in S$ holds $\mathbf{p}a = \mathbf{q}$ because of $\mathbf{p} \succeq \mathbf{q}$. So $\mathbf{q}sde = \mathbf{q}esde = \mathbf{q}$ and $\mathbf{p}eaesde = \mathbf{q}$. The subsemigroup eSe satisfies identity $xyx = yx$, therefore $eaesde = esdeaesde$. So $\mathbf{q} = \mathbf{p}eaesde = \mathbf{p}esdeaesde$. Hence, $\mathbf{p}es = \mathbf{p}s \succeq \mathbf{q}$.

Lemma 38 *Let reduced DFA $\mathbf{A}$ with state transition graph Γ be left locally testable.*

If the node $(\mathbf{p}, \mathbf{q}, \mathbf{r})$ is an SCC-node of Γ^3, $(\mathbf{p}, \mathbf{r}) \succeq (\mathbf{q}, \mathbf{r})$ and $(\mathbf{p}, \mathbf{q}) \succeq (\mathbf{r}, \mathbf{q})$ in Γ^2, then $\mathbf{r} = \mathbf{q}$.

Proof. Suppose **A** is left locally testable. Then the transition semigroup S of the automaton is finite, aperiodic and for any idempotent $e \in S$ the subsemigroup eSe is idempotent [7].

Let us consider the nodes $\mathbf{p}, \mathbf{q}, \mathbf{r}$ from Γ such that the conditions of lemma are valid for them. From $(\mathbf{p}, \mathbf{r}) \succeq (\mathbf{q}, \mathbf{r})$ and $(\mathbf{p}, \mathbf{q}) \succeq (\mathbf{r}, \mathbf{q})$ follows $(\mathbf{p}, \mathbf{r})s = (\mathbf{q}, \mathbf{r})$ and $(\mathbf{p}, \mathbf{q})t = (\mathbf{r}, \mathbf{q})$ for some $s, t \in S$ and $(\mathbf{p}, \mathbf{q}, \mathbf{r})e = (\mathbf{p}, \mathbf{q}, \mathbf{r})$, for some idempotents $e \in S$. We can take s, t from eSe. Therefore
$$ese = s, ete = t, s^2 = s, t^2 = t$$
So $\mathbf{p}s = \mathbf{q}$, $\mathbf{r}s = \mathbf{r}$, $\mathbf{p}t = \mathbf{r}$, $\mathbf{q}t = \mathbf{q}$. Let us notice that $\mathbf{q}s = \mathbf{p}s^2 = \mathbf{p}s = \mathbf{q}$. Analogously, $\mathbf{r}t = \mathbf{r}$.

We have $\mathbf{p}sts = \mathbf{q}ts = \mathbf{q}s = \mathbf{q}$. Then $\mathbf{p}ts = \mathbf{r}s = \mathbf{r}$. The identity $xyx = yx$ is valid in subsemigroup eSe, whence $\mathbf{q} = \mathbf{p}sts = \mathbf{p}ts = \mathbf{r}$.

Let us formulate the necessary and sufficient conditions for graph to be transition graph of DFA with left locally testable transition semigroup.

Theorem 39 *Let S be transition semigroup of a deterministic finite automaton with state transition graph Γ.*

Then S is left locally testable iff

1. S is locally idempotent,

2. for any SCC-node $(\mathbf{p}, \mathbf{q})$ of Γ^2 such that $\mathbf{p} \succeq \mathbf{q}$ and for any $s \in S$ we have $\mathbf{p}s \succeq \mathbf{q}$ iff $\mathbf{q}s \succeq \mathbf{q}$ and

3. If for arbitrary nodes $\mathbf{p}, \mathbf{q}, \mathbf{r} \in \Gamma$ the node $(\mathbf{p}, \mathbf{q}, \mathbf{r})$ is SCC-node of Γ^3, $(\mathbf{p}, \mathbf{r}) \succeq (\mathbf{q}, \mathbf{r})$ and $(\mathbf{p}, \mathbf{q}) \succeq (\mathbf{r}, \mathbf{q})$ in Γ^2, then $\mathbf{r} = \mathbf{q}$.

Proof. Suppose semigroup S is left locally testable. Then S is locally idempotent [7]. Second and third conditions of our theorem follow from lemmas 37 and 38, correspondingly.

Suppose now that the conditions of the theorem are valid but for an arbitrary node $\mathbf{p}$, an arbitrary idempotent $e \in S$ and two elements $s, t \in eSe$ holds $\mathbf{p}sts \neq \mathbf{p}ts$. By condition 1,
$$s^2 = s, \ t^2 = t, \ tsts = ts, \ stst = st, \ tssts = ts$$
At least one of two nodes $\mathbf{p}sts = \mathbf{q}$ and $\mathbf{p}ts = \mathbf{r}$ exists. Therefore $\mathbf{p}e$ exists too. We have $(\mathbf{p}e, \mathbf{p}ts)sts = (\mathbf{p}sts, \mathbf{p}ts)$. Therefore the existence of the node $\mathbf{p}ts = \mathbf{r}$ implies by condition 2 the existence of the node $\mathbf{p}sts = \mathbf{q}$. Analogously, from $(\mathbf{p}e, \mathbf{p}sts)ts = (\mathbf{p}ts, \mathbf{p}sts)$ and existence of the node $\mathbf{p}sts = \mathbf{q}$ follows by condition 2 the existence of the node $\mathbf{p}ts = \mathbf{r}$.

The node $(\mathbf{p}e, \mathbf{q}, \mathbf{r})$ is an SCC-node because all his components have common right unit e. We have $(\mathbf{p}, \mathbf{r})sts = (\mathbf{p}sts, \mathbf{p}tssts) = (\mathbf{q}, \mathbf{p}ts) = (\mathbf{q}, \mathbf{r})$. Analogously, $(\mathbf{p}, \mathbf{q})ts = (\mathbf{p}ts, \mathbf{p}ststs) = (\mathbf{r}, \mathbf{p}sts) = (\mathbf{r}, \mathbf{q})$. Thus,
$$(\mathbf{p}e, \mathbf{r}) \succ (\mathbf{q}, \mathbf{r}), \ (\mathbf{p}e, \mathbf{q}) \succ (\mathbf{r}, \mathbf{q})$$
Now by the third condition of the theorem, $\mathbf{r} = \mathbf{q}$. Therefore $\mathbf{p}sts = \mathbf{p}ts$. The node $\mathbf{p}$ is an arbitrary node, whence $sts = ts$ for every two elements $s, t \in eSe$. Consequently, the subsemigroup eSe satisfies identity $xyx = yx$. Thus the semigroup S is left locally testable.

4 Semigroups

Lemma 41 *Let S be a finite locally idempotent semigroup. The following two conditions are equivalent in S:*

a) *S satisfies locally the identity $xyx = xy$ (S is right locally testable).*

b) *No two distinct idempotents e, i from S such that $ie = e, ei = i$ have a common right unit in S. That is, there is no idempotent $f \in S$ such that $e = ef$ and $i = if$.*

Proof. Suppose the identity $xy = xyx$ is valid in subsemigroup uSu for any idempotent u and for some idempotents e, i in S we have $ie = e$, $ei = i$. Suppose f is a common right unit of e, i. The identity $xyx = xy$ in fSf and equality $ei = i$ imply $i = ei = efefif = efefifef = eie = e$. Thus the idempotents e, i are not distinct.

Suppose now that uSu does not satisfy the identity $xyx = xy$ for some idempotent u. Notice that uSu is an idempotent semigroup. So for some a, b of S, $uaubuau \neq uaubu$. For two distinct idempotents $i = uaubuau$ and $e = uaubu$ with common right unit u we have $ie = uaubuauuaubu = uaubuaubu = uaubu = e$ and $ei = uaubuaubuau = uaubua = i$.

So two distinct idempotents e, i from S such that $ie = e, ei = i$ have a common right unit u in S.

The following lemma is proved analogously:

Lemma 42 *Let S be a finite locally idempotent semigroup. The following two conditions are equivalent in S:*

a) *S satisfies locally the identity $xyx = yx$ (S is left locally testable).*

b) *No two distinct idempotents e, i from S such that $ie = i, ei = e$ have a common left unit in S. That is, there is no idempotent $f \in S$ such that $e = fe$ and $i = fi$.*

Recall that a semigroup A is a right [left] zero semigroup if A satisfies the identity $xy = y[xy = x]$. A right [left] locally testable semigroup is locally idempotent [7]. Then from the last two lemmas follows

Theorem 43 *A finite semigroup S is right [left] locally testable iff S is locally idempotent and no two distinct idempotents e, i from right [left] zero subsemigroup have a common right [left] unit in S.*

5 An Algorithm for Semigroup

The following proposition is useful for the algorithm.

Lemma 51 *[13] Let E be the set of idempotents of a semigroup S of size n represented as an ordered list. Then there exists an algorithm of order n^2 that reorders the list so that the maximal left [right] zero subsemigroups of S appear consecutively in the list.*

1. *Testing whether a finite semigroup S is right [left] locally testable.*

Suppose $|S| = k$. We begin by finding the set of idempotents E. This is a linear time algorithm. Then let us verify local idempotency. For every $e \in E$ and every $s \in S$ let us check condition $ese = (ese)^2$. If the condition does not hold for some pair, the semigroup is not locally idempotent and therefore not right locally testable (theorem 43). This takes $O(k^2)$ steps.

Now we reorder E according to lemma 51 in a chain such that the subsemigroups of right [left] zeroes form intervals in this chain. We note the bounds of these intervals. We find for each element e of E the first element i in the chain such that e is a right [left] unit for i. Then we find in the chain the next element j with the same unit e. If i and j belong to the same subsemigroup of right [left] zeroes we conclude that S is not right [left] testable (Lemma 41) and stop the process. If they are in different right [left] zero semigroups, we replace i by j and continue the process of finding a new j. This takes $O(k^2)$ steps.

Finding the maximal subsemigroup of right [left] zeroes containing a given idempotent needs k steps. So for to reorder E we need at most k^2 steps. The time and the space complexity of the algorithm is $O(k^2)$.

6   Graph Algorithms

Let n be the sum of the nodes and edges of Γ. The first-depth search ([1], [10] or [15]) will be used for SCC search, for reachability table for triples and for checking condition 2 of theorems 35 and 36.

Table of reachability for triples.

Suppose SCC of Γ, Γ^3 and the table of reachability are known. For every SCC-node $\mathbf{q}$ of the graph Γ let us form by help of the first-depth search on Γ^2 the following relation L [I] on Γ: $\mathbf{p}L\mathbf{r}$ if $(\mathbf{p}, \mathbf{q}) \succeq (\mathbf{r}, \mathbf{q})$ [$\mathbf{p}I\mathbf{r}$ if $(\mathbf{p}, \mathbf{q}) \succeq (\mathbf{q}, \mathbf{r})$]. For every node $(\mathbf{p}, \mathbf{q})$ we form set of nodes $\mathbf{r}$ such that $\mathbf{p}L\mathbf{r}$ [$\mathbf{p}I\mathbf{r}$]. We use an auxiliary array for this aim: for every node $(\mathbf{p}, \mathbf{q})$ and for every node $\mathbf{s}$, we form set of pointers to nearest successors $(\mathbf{t}, \mathbf{s})$ [$(\mathbf{s}, \mathbf{t})$] of $(\mathbf{p}, \mathbf{q})$.

If $(\mathbf{p}, \mathbf{q}, \mathbf{r})$ is an SCC-node with distinct components and $\mathbf{p}L\mathbf{r}$ [$\mathbf{p}I\mathbf{r}$] then we add the triple $(\mathbf{p}, \mathbf{q}, \mathbf{r})$ to the set $Left$ [$LocId$]. ($O(n^3)$ time and space complexity).

6.1   Graph of Automaton with Locally Idempotent Transition Semigroup

The algorithm is based on the theorem 35. Let us recognize the reachability on the graph Γ and form the table of reachability for all pairs of Γ. The time required for this step is $O(|\Gamma|^2)$.

We find graph Γ^2 and all SCC of the graph ($O(n^2)$ time complexity). If the nodes $(\mathbf{p}, \mathbf{q})$ and $(\mathbf{q}, \mathbf{p})$ belong to common SCC then the transition semigroup is not locally idempotent (condition 1).

For check the condition 2 of the theorem let us add to the graph Γ^2 new node $(\mathbf{0}, \mathbf{0})$ with edges from this node to every SCC-node $(\mathbf{p}, \mathbf{q})$ from Γ^2 such that $\mathbf{p} \succeq \mathbf{q}$. Let us consider first-depth search from the node $(\mathbf{0}, \mathbf{0})$ (the unique starting point of any path).

Let us fix the node $\mathbf{q}$ after going through the edge $(\mathbf{0}, \mathbf{0}) \rightarrow (\mathbf{p}, \mathbf{q})$. We do not visit edges $(\mathbf{r}, \mathbf{s}) \rightarrow (\mathbf{r}, \mathbf{s})\sigma$ such that $\mathbf{r}\sigma \not\succeq \mathbf{s}$. In the case that for the node $(\mathbf{r}, \mathbf{s})$ from two conditions $\mathbf{r}\sigma \succeq \mathbf{q}$ and $\mathbf{s}\sigma \succeq \mathbf{q}$ only the first is valid the condition 2 does not hold, the transition semigroup is not locally idempotent and the algorithm stops.

Let us find graph Γ^3, all SCC of the graph Γ^3 and mark all SCC-nodes with three distinct components such that the first component is ancestor of two others. $(O(n^3)$ time complexity).

Let us go to the condition 3 of the theorem 35. We form a table of triples $LocId$ (see algorithm for table of reachability above). If some SCC-node $(\mathbf{p}, \mathbf{q}, \mathbf{r})$ from Γ^3 with distinct components belongs to $LocId$ then the condition 3 does not hold and the semigroup is not locally idempotent.

The whole time and space complexity of the algorithm is $O(n^3)$.

6.2   Right Local Testability of DFA

The algorithm is based on the theorem 36. Let us form a table of reachability of the graph Γ, find all SCC of Γ, Γ^2 and all SCC-nodes of Γ^2. $(O(n^2)$ time complexity).

Let us verify the condition 1 of the theorem. For every SCC-node $(\mathbf{p}, \mathbf{q})$ $(\mathbf{p} \neq \mathbf{q})$ from Γ^2 let us check the condition $\mathbf{p} \sim \mathbf{q}$. If the condition holds the automaton is not right locally testable. $(O(n^2)$ time complexity).

For check the condition 2 of the theorem let us add to the graph Γ^2 new node $(\mathbf{0}, \mathbf{0})$ with edges from this node to every SCC-node $(\mathbf{p}, \mathbf{q})$ from Γ^2 such that $\mathbf{p} \succeq \mathbf{q}$. Let us consider first-depth search from the node $(\mathbf{0}, \mathbf{0})$ (the unique begin of any path).

Let us fix the node $\mathbf{q}$ after going through the edge $(\mathbf{0}, \mathbf{0}) \rightarrow (\mathbf{p}, \mathbf{q})$. We do not visit edges $(\mathbf{r}, \mathbf{s}) \rightarrow (\mathbf{r}, \mathbf{s})\sigma$ such that $\mathbf{r}\sigma \not\succeq \mathbf{s}$. In the case that for the node $(\mathbf{r}, \mathbf{s})$ from two conditions $\mathbf{r}\sigma \succeq \mathbf{q}$ and $\mathbf{s}\sigma \succeq \mathbf{q}$ only the first is valid the algorithm stops and the condition 2 does not hold. The automaton is not right locally testable in this case. $(O(n^2)$ time complexity).

The whole time and space complexity of the algorithm is $O(n^2)$.

6.3   Left Local Testability of DFA

The algorithm is based on the theorem 39. Let us form a table of reachability on the graph Γ and find all SCC of Γ. Let us find Γ^2 and all SCC of Γ^2. $(O(n^2)$ time complexity).

Let us check the local idempotency $(O(n^3)$ time complexity).

For check the condition 2 of the theorem let us add to the graph Γ^2 new node $(\mathbf{0}, \mathbf{0})$ with edges from this node to every SCC-node $(\mathbf{p}, \mathbf{q})$ from Γ^2 such that $\mathbf{p} \succeq \mathbf{q}$. Let us consider first-depth search from the node $(\mathbf{0}, \mathbf{0})$.

We do not visit edges $(\mathbf{r}, \mathbf{s}) \to (\mathbf{r}, \mathbf{s})\sigma$ such that $\mathbf{r}\sigma \not\succeq \mathbf{s}$ and $\mathbf{s}\sigma \not\succeq \mathbf{s}$. In the case that for the node $(\mathbf{r}, \mathbf{s})$ from two conditions $\mathbf{r}\sigma \succeq \mathbf{s}$ and $\mathbf{s}\sigma \succeq \mathbf{s}$ only one is valid the algorithm stops and the condition 2 does not hold.

Condition 3 of the theorem 39. Let us find Γ^3 and all SCC-nodes of Γ^3 ($O(n^3)$ time complexity).

Let us recognize the relation $\succ$ on the graph Γ^2 and find set $Left$ of triples $\mathbf{p}, \mathbf{q}, \mathbf{r}$ such that $(\mathbf{p}, \mathbf{q}) \succ (\mathbf{r}, \mathbf{q})$ (see algorithm for table of reachability above).

If for some SCC-node $(\mathbf{p}, \mathbf{u}, \mathbf{v})$ of Γ^3 both triples $(\mathbf{p}, \mathbf{u}, \mathbf{v})$ and $(\mathbf{p}, \mathbf{v}, \mathbf{u})$ belong to the set then the condition 3 does not hold, the automaton is not left locally testable and the algorithm stops.

The whole time and space complexity of the algorithm is $O(n^3)$.

References

1. A. Aho, J. Hopcroft, J. Ulman, The Design and Analisys of Computer Algorithms, Addison-Wesley, 1974.
2. D. Belostotski, D. Kravtsov, A. Shemshurenko, M. Sobol, A.N. Trahtman, Sh. Yakov, A package for checking some kinds of testability. 6-th Int. Conf. on Impl. and Appl. of Automata, CIAA2001, Pretoria, 2001.
3. J.-C. Birget, Strict local testability of the finite control of two-way automata and of regular picture description languages, *J. of Alg. Comp.* 1, **2**(1991), 161–175.
4. A.P. Biryukov, Varieties of idempotent semigroups, Algebra i logika, 9, 3(1970), 255–273.
5. J.A. Brzozowski, I. Simon, Characterizations of locally testable events, *Discrete Math.* 4, (1973), 243–271.
6. J.C. Costa, Free profinite R-trivial , locally idempotent and locally commutative semigroups. Sem. Forum, 58, 3(1999), 423–444.
7. P. Garcia, J. Ruiz, Right and left locally testable languages, *Theoret. Comput. Sci.*, **246**(2000), 253–264.
8. T. Head, Formal languages theory and DNA: an analysis of the generative capacity of specific recombinant behaviors, *Bull. Math. Biol.* **49**(1987), 4, 739–757.
9. R. König, Reduction algorithm for some classes of aperiodic monoids, R.A.I.R.O. Theor.Inform., 19, **3**(1985), 233–260.
10. S. Kim, R. McNaughton, R. McCloskey, A polynomial time algorithm for the local testability problem of deterministic finite automata, *IEEE Trans. Comput.* **40**(1991) N10, 1087–1093.
11. Lallement, G., Semigroups and Combinatorial Applications, Wiley, N.Y., 1979.
12. R. McNaughton, S, Papert, *Counter-free automata* M.I.T. Press. Mass., 1971.
13. A.N. Trahtman, A polynomial time algorithm for local testability and its level. Int. J. of Algebra and Comp., vol. 9, 1(1998), 31–39.
14. A.N. Trahtman, Identities of locally testable semigroups. Comm. in Algebra, v. 27, 11(1999), 5405–5412.
15. A.N. Trahtman, Piecewise and local threshold testability of DFA. Lect. Notes in Comp. Sci., 2138(2001), 347–358.
16. Y. Zalcstein, Locally testable language, *J. Comp. System Sci.* **6**(1972), 151–167

Whale Calf, a Parser Generator for Conjunctive Grammars

Alexander Okhotin

Department of Computing and Information Science,
Queen's University, Kingston, Ontario, Canada K7L 3N6.
okhotin@cs.queensu.ca

Abstract. *Whale Calf* is a parser generator that uses *conjunctive grammars*, a generalization of context-free grammars with an explicit intersection operation, as the formalism of specifying the language. All existing parsing algorithms for conjunctive grammars are implemented – namely, the tabular algorithm for grammars in the binary normal form, the tabular algorithm for grammars in the linear normal form, the tabular algorithm for arbitrary grammars, the conjunctive LL, the conjunctive LR and the algorithm based on simulation of the automata equivalent to linear conjunctive grammars. The generated C++ programs can determine the membership of strings in the language and, if needed, create parse trees of these strings.

1   Introduction

Conjunctive grammars were introduced in [2] as a generalization of context-free grammars that allows the use of an explicit operation of conjunction within the formalism of rules, which has semantics of intersection of languages.

Conjunctive grammars inherit all descriptive capabilities of context-free grammars (since context-free grammars can be viewed as a particular case of conjunctive grammars), while the additional operation can be used anywhere within the grammar. The rules in conjunctive grammars are of the form

$$A \to \alpha_1 \& \ldots \& \alpha_n, \tag{1}$$

where A is a nonterminal symbol, $n \geqslant 1$ and α_i are strings comprised of terminal and nonterminal symbols. Informally, a rule (1) means that every string that can be separately derived from each α_i can also be derived from A; the objects of the form $A \to \alpha_i$ are called *conjuncts*. A formal definition of conjunctive grammars can be found in the paper [7] published in this volume.

Besides the obvious increase in descriptional capabilities in comparison with context-free grammars, it turns out that conjunctive grammars retain many attractive properties of theirs, such as efficient recognition algorithms and tree representation of derivations.

The papers [2,3,4,5,6,7] define several efficient recognition and parsing algorithms for conjunctive grammars, which are briefly described in Section 2 of this

J.-M. Champarnaud and D. Maurel (Eds.): CIAA 2002, LNCS 2608, pp. 213–220, 2003.

paper. Most of these algorithms in this or that sense generalize some known context-free parsing methods; somewhat surprisingly, in almost every case the computational complexity of a generalization is the same as the complexity of its context-free prototype. This suggests that the new algorithms could be applied for solving practical problems of syntax analysis, and gives a motivation for developing software implementing these algorithms.

The parser generator Whale Calf, which is discussed in this paper, does implement all the algorithms introduced in [2,3,4,5,6,7].

2   Parsing Algorithms

2.1   Algorithms for Grammars in Normal Forms

Two of these were developed in the initial paper [2] to prove upper bounds for the complexity of conjunctive and linear conjunctive languages. They are: (i) the algorithm for grammars in the binary normal form and (ii) the algorithm for grammars in the linear normal form.

It is known [2] that every conjunctive grammar can be transformed to the binary normal form and every linear conjunctive grammar can be transformed to the linear normal form. These two parsing algorithms are of entirely theoretical value and are supported in Whale Calf for the sake of completeness. Both, similarly to the classical Cocke–Kasami–Younger context-free algorithm, construct the $n \times n$ upper-triangular matrix $T_{ij} = \{A \mid A \in N, A \Longrightarrow^* a_i \ldots a_j\}$ of nonterminals that derive the substrings of the input string $a_1 \ldots a_n$. The construction starts from the elements $T_{11}, \ldots, T_{nn}$ and ends with T_{1n}; the string is then accepted if and only if the start symbol of the grammar is in T_{1n}.

The binary normal form algorithm uses $O(n^3)$ time and $O(n^2)$ space, while the linear normal form algorithm uses $O(n^2)$ time and $O(n)$ space.

2.2   Tabular Algorithm for Arbitrary Grammars

This algorithm is based upon the general idea of the well-known context-free parsing algorithm due to Graham, Harrison and Ruzzo, which, given an input string of length $a_1 \ldots a_n$, constructs an upper-triangular matrix $\{t_{ij}\}_{0 \leqslant i \leqslant j \leqslant n}$ of sets of *dotted rules* of the form $A \to \alpha \cdot \beta$ (where $A \to \alpha\beta$ is a rule of the grammar), such that $A \to \alpha \cdot \beta \in t_{ij}$ if only if α derives the substring $a_{i+1} \ldots a_j$ of the input string and at the same time $S \Longrightarrow^* a_1 \ldots a_i A \gamma$ for some string γ.

The generalizion of the GHR algorithm for the case of conjunctive grammars [4] creates a similar matrix $\{t_{ij}\}$ of *dotted conjuncts* of the same form $A \to \alpha \cdot \beta$, such that there exists a rule $A \to \gamma_1 \& \ldots \& \alpha\beta \& \ldots \gamma_m$. A dotted conjunct $A \to \alpha \cdot \beta$ is in t_{ij} if and only if α derives $a_{i+1} \ldots a_j$ and there exists a finite sequence of *conjuncts* $C_{t-1} \to \gamma_t C_t \delta_t$ ($0 < t \leqslant k$, where $k \geqslant 0$ is some number), such that $C_0 = S$, $C_k = A$ and there exists a factorization $a_1 \ldots a_i = u_1 \ldots u_k$, where γ_t derives u_t for every t.

The algorithm is applicable to any conjunctive grammar, works in cubic time and uses quadratic space. If the grammar is linear – i.e., every rule are either of the form $A \to w$ ($w \in \Sigma^*$) or of the form $A \to u_1 B_1 v_1 \& \ldots \& u_n B_n v_n$ ($n \geqslant 1$, $u_i, v_i \in \Sigma^*$, $B_i \in N$) – then the complexity is reduced to quadratic time and $O(n)$ space.

However, in order to achieve $O(n)$ space upper bound, one has to sacrifice the possibility of parse tree construction. The implementation of the algorithm in Whale Calf uses $O(n^2)$ time and $O(n^2)$ space in the case of linear conjunctive grammars, but always allows to construct parse trees.

Two methods of parse tree construction for this algorithm have been developed in [4]. Using the *bottom-up* method, the tree is constructed along with the creation of the recognition matrix, and the algorithm is slowed down by a constant factor. The *top-down* method constructs the parse tree out of the matrix $\{t_{ij}\}$ after the string is successfully recognized; this method works fast on "reasonable" grammars, but can use exponential time or even go into an infinite loop on "unreasonable" ones. Only the top-down method is implemented in Whale Calf parser generator.

2.3 Top-Down Conjunctive SLL(k) Algorithm

A context-free *strong LL(k)* top-down parser attempts to construct the leftmost derivation of an input string, using k lookahead symbols to determine the rules to apply to nonterminals, and a pushdown store to hold the right parts of the sentential forms forming the derivation. Left parts of sentential forms are prefixes of the input string that are being compared with the input symbols and then discarded.

The conjunctive generalization of this algorithm [3] uses *tree-structured pushdown* to handle multiple branches of computation simultaneously, thus ensuring that substrings of the input string are derived from every conjunct of a rule. The parsing table used by this algorithm is a mapping from $N \times \Sigma^{\leqslant k}$ to the set of rules of the grammar, where $\Sigma^{\leqslant k}$ denotes $\{w \mid w \in \Sigma^*, |w| \leqslant k\}$.

In its deterministic case the algorithm is applicable to a subclass of conjunctive grammars. Although there exist grammars even for the simplest languages, on which the algorithm works in exponential time and uses exponential space, its complexity is nevertheless linear for the practical cases, which include the intersection closure of context-free LL(k) languages.

Similarly to context-free LL, the conjunctive LL parsing method can be implemented manually using a variation of the recursive descent technique; this kind of implementation is not supported in Whale Calf.

2.4 Bottom-Up Conjunctive LR Algorithm

The Generalized LR parsing algorithm for context-free grammars, introduced by Tomita in 1986, is a polynomial-time implementation of nondeterministic LR parsing that uses graph-structured stack to represent the contents of the nondeterministic parser's pushdown for all possible branches of computation at a single computation step.

The same idea of graph-structured pushdown turns out to be suitable for parsing conjunctive grammars. While generalized LR uses graph-structured pushdown merely to simulate nondeterminism whenever it arises, the extension of this algorithm for the conjunctive case [5] additionally relies on doing several computations at once in order to implement the conjunction operation. In order to reduce by a rule, it requires multiple paths corresponding to the conjuncts of the rule to be present in the graph at the same time. Instead of defining a particular way of constructing a parsing table, the algorithm was proved correct for any table that satisfies the requirements listed in [5], and an extension of context-free SLR(k) method conforming to these requirements was developed. The latter method is used in the implementation in Whale Calf parser generator.

Although internally the algorithm is somewhat different from the context-free generalized LR, it looks very much the same from the user's side, and hence one could expect it to be as suitable for practical use as the context-free generalized LR has proved to be.

The algorithm is applicable to any grammar and can be implemented to work in no more than $O(n^3)$ time. In many common cases it is even faster: for instance, it is known to work in linear time for the Boolean closure of deterministic context-free languages. The implementation used by Whale Calf has $O(n^4)$ complexity upper bound, but in practical cases it works better than the other implementation with worst case cubic time performance proposed in [5].

2.5   Automaton-Based Algorithm for Linear Conjunctive Grammars

In the paper [6], a very simple family of cellular automata was found to be computationally equivalent to linear conjunctive grammars. Several practical algorithms for creating these automata and reducing their size were proposed in [7]. Once constructed out of grammars, these automata can then be simulated in $(n^2 + n)/2 + C$ elementary table lookup operations (where n is the length of the input string), using space of no more than n.

Although the tabular algorithm for arbitrary grammars of [4] also works in $O(n^2)$ time and $O(n)$ space, the present algorithm is many times (constant times) faster and requires much less memory.

3   Implementation

Whale Calf software consists of two distinct components: the parser generator that converts a text-based description of a conjunctive grammar into a set of C++ structures containing information necessary to parse the language, and a C++ class library that uses this information to do the actual parsing. All the user has to do is to write one or more grammar files; use the Whale Calf parser generator to translate them into C++ files, which will define a grammar object; define a parser object within the main program, passing the grammar object to its constructor; use a parser class method to load a string into the parser; and finally invoke one more method to recognize or parse the string.

3.1   Input File Format

A Whale Calf input file consists of a declaration of the parsing method used, of some parameters for this parsing method (where applicable), of the list of terminal symbols and of the set of rules. The specification of the parsing algorithm is of the form `algorithm=value`, where `value` must be one of the following: `tabular`, `SLL1`, `SLLk`, `LR`, `linear_automaton`, `binary`, `linear`. The default parsing algorithm is `tabular`.

If `algorithm=SLLk`, then the value of the parameter k can be set using the statement of the form `SLLk_lookahead_length=k`; the default value is 2. The size of the parsing table grows exponentially with k.

If `algorithm=linear_automaton`, then some parameters for automaton creation procedure can be configured through variables `automaton_filtering_order` and `automaton_filtering_tuple_size` (these control state filtering; the default is order 2 filtering of pairs – i.e., both equal 2), and `automaton_accessing_string_max_length` and `automaton_number_of_accessing_strings`, that, once set, instruct Whale Calf to compile the list of accessing strings of states at the stage of parser generation, which might be useful for the user and proved to be useful for the author (see the table in [7]).

Consider the following input file for Whale Calf that denotes a grammar for the language $\{wcw \mid w \in \{a, b\}^*\}$ [2] and instructs the parser generator to use the LR algorithm:

```
algorithm=LR;

terminal a, b, c;

S -> C & D;
C -> a C a | a C b | b C a | b C b | c;
D -> a A & a D | b B & b D | c E;
A -> a A a | a A b | b A a | b A b | c E a;
B -> a B a | a B b | b B a | b B b | c E b;
E -> a E | b E | e;
```

Whale Calf will process this file and create two C++ source files with the names of the form `filename.cpp` and `filename.h`. These two files, together with the runtime library files, `whalecalf_rtl.cpp` and `whalecalf_rtl.h`, form a parser for this language.

3.2   Use of Generated Parsers

All six algorithms are implemented in a uniform manner; the difference is mainly between the names of the parser classes. These names are `WhaleCalfTabularParser`, `WhaleCalfLL1Parser`, `WhaleCalfLLkParser`, `WhaleCalfLRParser`, `WhaleCalfBinaryParser`, `WhaleCalfLinearParser` and `WhaleCalfLinearAutomatonParser`.

It suffices to create a parser object, use the method **read()** to pass the input string to the parser, and then either call the method **recognize()** to determine whether the string is in the language, or the method **parse()** to construct the parse tree of the string.

The string is supplied to the method **read()** either as a pair of pointers (or STL iterators) to integers, which mark the beginning and the end of the string, or as an **std::vector<int>**. In both cases the terminal symbols are encoded as numbers, enumerated starting from zero in the order of their definition: for instance, if the declaration

```
terminal a, b, c;
```

is used, then the numbers 0, 1 and 2 correspond to the symbols a, b and c respectively.

The method **recognize()** takes no arguments and returns a value of type **bool**, which is **true** if and only if the string is in the language. The method **parse()** also takes no arguments and returns a pointer to the top node of the constructed tree if the input string is in the language, or **NULL** pointer otherwise. The nodes of the tree are represented in memory using the following predefined data structure:

```
struct TreeNode
{
    int rn;                 // rule number
    int tn;                 // terminal number
    int position;           // of a terminal in the input string
    std::vector<std::vector<TreeNode *> > descendants;
};
```

For internal nodes, the data member **rn** contains the number of the rule

$$A \to s_{0,0} \ldots s_{0,l_0-1} \& \ldots \& s_{m-1,0} \ldots s_{m-1,l_{m-1}-1} \quad (m \geqslant 1,\ l_i \geqslant 1,\ s_{ij} \in \Sigma \cup N)$$

used at this node, **tn** equals **-1**, and **descendants** is a vector of size m, such that every **descendants[i]** $(0 \leqslant i < m)$ is a vector of integers of size l_i, and for every j $(0 \leqslant j < l_i)$ the element **descendants[i][j]** contains a pointer to the descendant of the current node corresponding to the symbol s_{ij}.

For the leaves, **rn** is **-1**, while **tn** holds the number of the terminal symbol, **position** gives the position of this terminal in the input string and the vector of descendants is empty.

The creation of parse trees is only supported in the LL, LR and Tabular parsing algorithms. In case of LL and LR, using the generated program in the parser mode slows down its execution by a constant factor. For the Tabular algorithm, the construction of a parse tree is preceded by ordinary recognition; as noted in Section 2.2, this construction works efficiently for most grammars, while for some grammars it can work very slow or even fail to terminate.

The following example uses the parser given in Section 3.1 to construct the derivation tree of *abcab* according to the grammar for $\{wcw \mid w \in \{a,b\}^*\}$.

```
#include "grammar.h"              // The generated header file.

WhaleCalfLRParser whale_calf(Grammar::grammar);

int x[]={0, 1, 2, 0, 1};         // Let the input string be "abcab".
whale_calf.read(x, x+5);         // Any pair of STL iterators can come here.
WhaleCalf::TreeNode *tree=whale_calf.parse();
if(tree) whale_calf.print_parse_tree(tree, ofstream("parse_tree.dot"));
```

The generated parsers are capable of exporting some of their static and dynamic data structures, such as LR and LL parsing tables, tables constructed by the tabular algorithm, contents of tree-structured or graph-structured pushdown, etc. Tables are printed as TEX sources, while graphs are printed as text-based graph descriptions for consequent processing by the **dot** application from Graphviz graph drawing software [1], which converts them directly to eps figures.

The constructed parse trees can also be exported in **dot** format. For instance, the tree produced by the parser from the example above and converted to eps format is given in unaltered form in Figure 1.

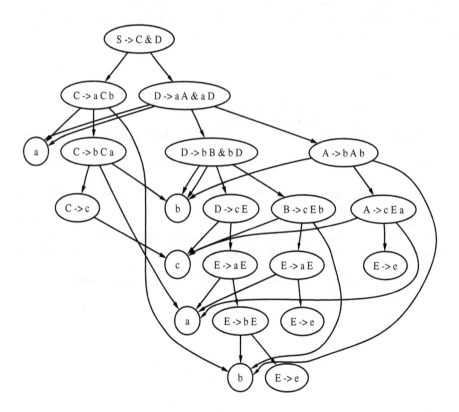

Fig. 1. A parse tree constructed by LR parser ($abcab \in \{wcw \mid w \in \{a, b\}^*\}$).

4 Conclusion

The present version of the program implements all existing parsing algorithms for conjunctive grammars and provides a primitive programmer's interface to these algorithms. Although this interface lacks flexibility required for industrial programming, its simplicity can be valuable for a scientist interested in the very concept of conjunctive grammars.

The software may be freely used for educational and research purposes and is available from

`http://www.cs.queensu.ca/home/okhotin/whalecalf/`

In the future versions it is planned to enhance the programmer's interface of the generated parsers and thus make the program usable for practical parser generation. Although it cannot possibly rival context-free LALR(1) parser generators in terms of the speed of the generated parsers, it is likely to be useful for the applications where general context-free parsing methods are now being used, because the algorithms implemented in Whale Calf have basically the same computational complexity, but are applicable to a wider class of languages and allow the use of a convenient logical operation of intersection.

It is also planned to implement the results of ongoing research on a further extension of conjunctive grammars with negation.

References

1. Graphviz – open source graph drawing software, available at
   `http://www.research.att.com/sw/tools/graphviz/`.
2. A. Okhotin, "Conjunctive grammars", *Journal of Automata, Languages and Combinatorics*, 6:4 (2001), 519–535.
3. A. Okhotin, "Top-down parsing of conjunctive languages", *Grammars*, 5:1 (2002), 21–40.
4. A. Okhotin, "A recognition and parsing algorithm for arbitrary conjunctive grammars", to appear in *Theoretical Computer Science*.
5. A. Okhotin, "LR parsing for conjunctive grammars", *Grammars*, 5:2 (2002), 81–124.
6. A. Okhotin, "On a new family of automata", Technical Report 2002–456, Department of Computing and Information Science of Queen's University, Kingston, Ontario, Canada.
7. A. Okhotin, "Efficient automaton-based recognition for linear conjunctive languages", *this volume*.

automata, a Hybrid System for Computational Automata Theory

Klaus Sutner*

Computer Science Department
Carnegie Mellon University
Pittsburgh, PA 15213
sutner@cs.cmu.edu

Abstract. We present a system that performs computations on finite state machines, syntactic semigroups, and one-dimensional cellular automata.

1 Sample Computations

The automata system facilitates computation on finite state machines, syntactic semigroups, and one-dimensional cellular automata. Unlike some other systems such as Grail, AUTOMATE, Amore, see [6] for detailed references, the automata package is a hybrid system that is built around a commercial computer algebra system. Specifically, the current implementation uses version 4.1 of *Mathematica* by Wolfram Research, Inc., see [14]. Before commenting more on this approach, we present two typical sample sessions. Fairly detailed descriptions of earlier versions of the package can be found in [8,9].

1.1 Entropy of Sofic Shifts

Suppose you wish to determine the entropy of the sofic subshift associated with a particular one-dimensional cellular automaton, see [5,1] for more background information). Here is a short session in automata that shows the necessary calculations. The dialogue is captured the way it would appear in the plain text interface. For more elaborate examples using the notebook frontend, see my home page http://www.cs.cmu.edu/~sutner. The first command converts the elementary cellular automata number 92 into a de Bruijn semiautomaton, which is then converted into the corresponding minimal Fischer automaton, see [2,10]. We extract the transition matrix from the latter, construed as a non-negative integer matrix, and determine its Perron eigenvalue.

---

* Supported in part by NSF-ITR 0113919.

J.-M. Champarnaud and D. Maurel (Eds.): CIAA 2002, LNCS 2608, pp. 221–227, 2003.

```
sa = ToSA[ CA[ 92, 3, 2 ] ];
mf = MinimalFischerFA[ sa ]

    SA[ 8, 2, {{1, 1, 1}, {2, 1, 4}, {3, 1, 1}, {4, 1, 6},
    {5, 1, 1}, {6, 1, 6}, {7, 1, 8}, {1, 2, 2}, {2, 2, 3},
    {3, 2, 5}, {4, 2, 2}, {6, 2, 7}, {7, 2, 5}, {8, 2, 2}} ]

M = FullTransitionMatrixFA[ mf ];
Log[ 2, Max[ Abs[ N[ Eigenvalues[M] ] ] ] ]

    0.900537
```

In the formatting mode chosen here the semiautomaton mf is shown in abbreviated form. There are two invisible fields indicating the actual state set (a set of size 8 according to the first field in the automaton, see section 2 below), and the elements of the alphabet (a set of size 2 according to the second field in the automaton). The first three commands use operations defined in the package, whereas computation of the eigenvalues is handled entirely by *Mathematica*.

1.2   Preserving Regularity

As a second example, consider regularity preserving operations on regular languages. There is a family of such operations based on existential quantification over strings of a certain length. In particular, a function $f : \mathbb{N} \to \mathbb{N}$ is regularity preserving if for any regular language L the language

$$T(L, f) = \{ x \in \Sigma^* \mid \exists y \in \Sigma^* (|y| = f(|x|) \wedge xy \in L) \}$$

is again regular. For specific functions f, the construction of the corresponding machines can be expressed easily in terms of Boolean matrices, see also [4]. For example, consider the function $f(i) = 2^i$. Here is the construction of a DFA for $T(L, f)$ where L is the language of all strings over $\{a, b\}$ whose length is divisible by 3. We construct a DFA for L by hand and define symbol B to be the natural homomorphism $\beta : \Sigma^* \to \mathbb{B}^{Q \times Q}$ from words to Boolean matrices of size $Q \times Q$. The ability to use higher type objects in this effortless way is a significant advantage in actual interactive, experimental computations. Of course, in this particular case this is a bit of overkill, the Boolean sum $\beta(a) + \beta(b)$ is a simple circulant matrix here.

```
m = DFA[ 3, 2, {{2,3,1},{2,3,1}}, 1, {1} ]

  DFA[3, 2, {{2, 3, 1}, {2, 3, 1}}, 1, {1}]

TransitionMatrixFA[ m, B, Type->Boolean ];
M = BooleanUnion[ B[a], B[b]]

  {{0, 1, 0}, {0, 0, 1}, {1, 0, 0}}
```

We can now define an action dot that turns $Q' = Q \times \mathbb{B}^{Q \times Q}$ into a semimodule over Σ^*. First, the transition function of the DFA is assigned to the symbol delta. Operation dot then applies delta to the first component of any pair $(p, A) \in Q'$, and squares the Boolean matrix. The sub-semimodule generated by (q_0, M) provides the state set for the DFA mm recognizing $T(L, f)$. During the generation of the sub-semimodule we also produce the transition function for mm. Lastly, the final states (p, A) can be determined by the condition that $I_p \cdot A \cdot I_F$ not be the null vector.

```
TransitionFunctionFA[ m, delta ];
F = ToBitVector[ Final[m], Range[3] ];
dot[{p_,P_},s_] :=
    { delta[p,s], BooleanComposition[P,P] };
final[{p_,P_}] := ToBitVector[p,Range[3]].P.F > 0;
{Q,W,mm} = GenerateDFA[ {{1},M}, dot, 2, final ];
mm

  DFA[ 6, 2, {{2, 3, 4, 5, 6, 1}, {2, 3, 4, 5, 6, 1}},
      1, {2, 3} ]

W

  {Eps, a, aa, aaa, aaaa, aaaaa}
```

The other fields Q and W contain the carrier set of the semimodule and a collection of corresponding witnesses, respectively. Either one could be used as the underlying state set of mm if need be. At any rate, the resulting machine has 6 states and a little arithmetic shows that $T(L, f)$ should consist of all words of length i where $i \equiv 1, 2 \pmod 6$. We can verify this computationally by generating a few words in the language, or by evaluating its census function up to length 20.

```
LanguageFA[ mm,  -6 ]
LanguageFA[ mm,  -20, SizeOnly->True ]
```

```
{{}, {a, b}, {aa, ab, ba, bb}, {}, {}, {}, {}}
```

```
{0, 2, 4, 0, 0, 0, 0, 128, 256, 0, 0, 0, 0, 8192, 16384,
    0, 0, 0, 0, 524288, 1048576}
```

1.3   Syntactic Semigroups

As a last example, we calculate the syntactic semigroup of a regular language. Consider $L = \{ x \in \{a,b\}^* \mid x_{-3} = a \}$, the set of all words having an a in the third position from the end.

```
m = MinimizeFA[ IthSymbolFA[ a, -3 ] ];
{S,W,eq} = SyntacticSG[ m, Equations->True ];
S
```

```
SG[ T[2, 3, 5, 7, 5, 7, 3, 2], T[1, 4, 6, 8, 6, 8, 4, 1],
    T[3, 5, 5, 3, 5, 3, 5, 3], T[4, 6, 6, 4, 6, 4, 6, 4],
    T[2, 7, 7, 2, 7, 2, 7, 2], T[1, 8, 8, 1, 8, 1, 8, 1],
    T[5, 5, 5, 5, 5, 5, 5, 5], T[6, 6, 6, 6, 6, 6, 6, 6],
    T[7, 7, 7, 7, 7, 7, 7, 7], T[8, 8, 8, 8, 8, 8, 8, 8],
    T[3, 3, 3, 3, 3, 3, 3, 3], T[4, 4, 4, 4, 4, 4, 4, 4],
    T[2, 2, 2, 2, 2, 2, 2, 2], T[1, 1, 1, 1, 1, 1, 1, 1]]
```

The semigroup is presented as an explicit set of transformations, i.e., functions $[8] \to [8]$. Since we chose the option `Equations->True`, the operation also generates the canonical rewrite system for the semigroup, which turns out to consist of all directed equations of the form $xyzu = yzu$. There are 8 idempotents in the semigroup, and they happen to coincide with the right nulls.

```
id = IdemSG[S]
```

```
{ T[5, 5, 5, 5, 5, 5, 5, 5], T[6, 6, 6, 6, 6, 6, 6, 6],
    ..., T[1, 1, 1, 1, 1, 1, 1, 1]}
```

```
id == RightNullSG[S]
```

```
True
```

In a similar fashion we can generate the D-class decomposition of the semi-group. In the visual frontend, the classes can then be rendered in their natural two-dimensional representation, either using transformations or their witnesses.

2   Experimentation, Prototyping, and Production Code

One of the goals of `automata` is to demonstrate the feasibility of a computational environment that supports interactive computation, rapid prototyping of complicated algorithms, and the use of production scientific code. As a case in point, take the function `MinimalFischerFA` that was used in the entropy computation. Originally this function consisted of a short segment of *Mathematica* code, interactively developed and based on primitives provided by the package, whose sole purpose it was to compute a few Fischer automata arising from a some examples. The code was later collected into an experimental function available in the package, but not yet officially supported. In the last step, the function became a fully supported part of the package, complete with an implementation as external C++ code. It can now be used both from within the package, as a part of a C++ library, in the form of shell scripts, or as a command in an interactive calculator written entirely in C++.

Similar comments apply to all the other crucial operations that tend to be computational bottlenecks: in our case, computation of a power automaton, minimization, generation of syntactic semigroups, to name a few. All these operations are implemented both in *Mathematica* and externally in C++. Note that this double implementation has some advantages with respect to checking correctness: the implementation languages *Mathematica* and C++ are sufficiently different to make it unlikely that the same error would appear in both implementations. Of course, there is no safeguard against structurally wrong implementations in any language. As indicated in the semimodule computation above, some operations can optionally produce certificates that can be used to verify the correctness of the output.

Considerable effort has gone into integrating the two components as tightly as possible. For example, the internal algorithms dealing with finite state machines support an option `Normalize` which allows the user to preserve the natural state set of a machine. Thus, in a power automaton construction the state set of the new machine is naturally a subset of $\mathrm{pow}(Q)$, where Q is the state set of the nondeterministic machine. In a product automaton, the state set is a subset of $Q_1 \times Q_2$ and minimization produces a partition of the state set of the given machine. By default the state set is always normalized to $[n]$, but whenever necessary we can preserve the structure even during nested operations:

```
m1 = ToDFA[ InfixFA[ aba ], Normalize->1 ];
MinimizeFA[ m1, Normalize->2 ] // States
```

```
{{{1}}, {{1, 2}}, {{1, 3}}, {{1, 2, 4}, {1, 3, 4}, {1, 4}}}
```

The same options are also available in the external code; indeed, nested lists of atoms (integers, strings, finite state machines, semigroups, cellular automata) are the basic data structure in the external code.

Another important point is the quality of the frontend. In principle, modern user-interface tools make it feasible to construct relatively sophisticated front-ends from scratch. However, these front-ends inevitably lack versatility, and often are indeed limited to a narrow collection of operations. The visual presentation of mathematical information is a challenging task, and one should not expect satisfactory solutions from ad-hoc efforts. The *Mathematica* frontend on the other hand produces near-publication quality results, and provides easy access to a large array of operations. When the data produced by the core algorithms of the system are complicated in nature (e.g., the D-class decomposition of a semigroup), the notebook frontend greatly helps to display, manipulate and further analyze the data, conveniently within the whole system.

For research applications yet another aspect of considerable importance is the archiving of data. Often the actual calculation of the data requires a relatively small program based on the machinery in the system. Ideally, the program, accompanying text, the actual data, and their analysis should all be bundled in a single unit. Dealing with collections of separate files becomes quickly unwieldy, and often forces tedious and time-consuming recomputation. A coherent, platform independent interface such as a *Mathematica* notebook addresses all these issues.

Efforts are currently under way to develop an XML standard for the representation and exchange of finite state machines, regular expressions, and transformation semigroups. The purpose of the standard is two-fold: first of all, it allows communication between software systems that are currently isolated from each other. For example, it should be straightforward to generate a finite state machine on one system, pipe the output to another to have it minimized there, and then have a third system generate the corresponding syntactic semigroup. Secondly, representing mathematical objects in XML and building on existing standards such as OpenMath, one can easily communicate these objects over the internet, so that the three systems cooperating in the computation of the semigroup might well be located on three separate machines. The most recent version web browsers are capable of rendering a good amount of mathematics, hence the results of the computation can be observed and controlled in a browsers. The latest version of Mathematica offers a lot of XML support and makes it fairly easy to generate and convert XML based material. A prototype of the DTD and sample conversion routines between the XML format and the `automata` format are available at the website below.

Needless to say, maintenance of a hybrid system poses significant challenges. The latest version of `automata` uses XML as the sole repository for the *Mathematica* code. The various components are automatically assembled into a so-called add-on package via XSL style-sheets. This bundling process produces a software package that can simply be deposited in the user's home directory, and that will then load automatically whenever a command in the package is used. Short help on a per-function basis is available from the notebook interface, and there is a large collection of notebooks that demonstrate the use of the package. The latest version is fully integrated with the extensible *Mathematica* help-browser and provides interactive help for all the commands in the package.

As far as the external code is concerned, it is the usual collection of header-, implementation- and make-files. The STL is used as the main source for standard data structures, see [7,3]. If desired, the user can provide memory managers to speed up the external code (the standard memory manager is taken from the STL). Apart from the nested lists of atoms the external code tries to avoid inheritance in favor of parametrized types; thus it is relatively easy to read, extend, and modify.

The package has been brought to bear on a number of problems that might otherwise well have proven intractable, see [11,12,10,13]. The code is available at http://www.cs.cmu.edu/~sutner.

References

1. M.-P. Beal and D. Perrin. Symbolic dynamics and finite automata. In G. Rozenberg and A. Salomaa, editors, *Handbook of Formal Languages*, volume 2, chapter 10. Springer Verlag, 1997.
2. R. Fischer. Sofic systems and graphs. *Monatshefte für Mathematik*, 80:179–186, 1975.
3. G. Glass and B. Schuchert. *The STL <Primer>*. Prentice Hall, 1996.
4. D. Kozen. Lower bounds for natural proof systems. In *Proc. 18-th Ann. Symp. on Foundations of Computer Science*, pages 254–266. IEEE Computer Society, 1977.
5. D. Lind and B. Marcus. *Introduction to Symbolic Dynamics and Coding*. Cambridge University Press, 1995.
6. R. Raymond, D. Wood, and S. Yu. *First International Workshop on Implementing Automata*, volume 1260 of *Lecture Notes in CS*. Springer Verlag, 1997.
7. B. Stroustrup. *The C++ Programming Language*. Addison-Wesley, 1997.
8. K. Sutner. Finite state machines and syntactic semigroups. *The Mathematica Journal*, 2(1):78–87, 1992.
9. K. Sutner. Implementing finite state machines. In N. Dean and G. Shannon, editors, *Computational Support for Discrete Mathematics*, volume 15, pages 347–365. DIMACS, 1994.
10. K. Sutner. Linear cellular automata and Fischer automata. *Parallel Computing*, 23(11):1613–1634, 1997.
11. K. Sutner. σ-automata and Chebyshev polynomials. *Theoretical Computer Science*, 230:49–73, 2000.
12. K. Sutner. Decomposition of additive cellular automata. *Complex Systems*, 13(3):245–270, 2001.
13. K. Sutner. The size of power automata. In J. Sgall, Ales Pultr, and Petr Kolman, editors, *Mathematical Foundations of Computer Science*, volume 2136 of *SLNCS*, pages 666–677, 2001.
14. S. Wolfram. *The Mathematica Book*. Wolfram Media, Cambridge UP, 4th edition, 1999.

A Package TESTAS for Checking Some Kinds of Testability

A.N. Trahtman

Bar-Ilan University, Dep. of Math. and St.,
52900,Ramat Gan,Israel
trakht@macs.biu.ac.il

Abstract. We implement a set of procedures for deciding whether or not a language given by its minimal automaton or by its syntactic semigroup is locally testable, right or left locally testable, threshold locally testable, strictly locally testable, or piecewise testable. The bounds on order of local testability of transition graph and order of local testability of transition semigroup are also found. For given k, the k-testability of transition graph is verified. Some new effective polynomial time algorithms are used. These algorithms have been implemented as a C/C^{++} package.

1 Introduction

Locally testable and piecewise testable languages with generalizations are the best known subclasses of star-free languages with wide spectrum of applications.

Membership of a long text in a locally testable language just depends on a scan of short subpatterns of the text. It is best understood in terms of a kind of computational procedure used to classify a two-dimensional image: a window of relatively small size is moved around on the image and a record is made of the various attributes of the image that are detected by what is observed through the window. No record is kept of the order in which the attributes are observed, where each attribute occurs, or how many times it occurs. We say that a class of images is locally testable if a decision about whether a given image belongs to the class can be made simply on the basis of the set of attributes that occur.

Kim, McNaughton and McCloskey have found necessary and sufficient conditions of local testability for the state transition graph Γ of deterministic finite automaton [9]. By considering the cartesian product $\Gamma \times \Gamma$, we modify these necessary and sufficient conditions and the algorithms used in the package are based on this approach.

The locally threshold testable languages were introduced by Beauquier and Pin [1]. These languages generalize the concept of locally testable language and have been studied extensively in recent years.

Right [left] local testability was introduced and studied by König [11] and by Garcia and Ruiz [8]. These papers use different definitions of the conception and we follow here [8]:

A finite semigroup S is right [left] locally testable iff it is locally idempotent and locally satisfies the identity $xyx = xy$ [$xyx = yx$].

J.-M. Champarnaud and D. Maurel (Eds.): CIAA 2002, LNCS 2608, pp. 228–232, 2003.
© Springer-Verlag Berlin Heidelberg 2003

We introduced polynomial time algorithms for the right [left] local testability problem for transition graph and transition semigroup of the deterministic finite automaton. Polynomial time algorithm verifies transition graph of automaton with locally idempotent transition semigroup.

There are several systems for manipulating automata and semigroups. The list of these systems is following [7] and preprint of [3]:

REGPACK [12] AUTOMATE [5] AMoRE [13] Grail [17] The FIRE Engine [27] LANGAGE [3]. APL package [6]. Froidure and Pin package [7]. Sutner package [20]. Whale Calf [16].

Some algorithms concerning distinct kinds of testability of finite automata were implemented by Caron [3], [4]. His programs verify piecewise testable, locally testable, strictly and strongly locally testable languages.

In our package TESTAS (testability of automata and semigroups), the area of implemented algorithms was essentially extended. We consider important and highly complicated case of locally threshold testable languages [25]. The transition semigroups of automata are studied in our package at the first time [22]. Some algorithms (polynomial and even in some way non-polynomial) check the order of local testability [24]. We implement a new efficient algorithm for piecewise testability improving the time complexity from $O(n^5)$ [3], [19] to $O(n^2)$ [25]. We consider algorithms for right local testability ($O(n^2)$ time and space complexity), for left local testability ($O(n^3)$ time and space complexity) and the corresponding algorithms for transition semigroups ($O(n^2)$ time and space complexity). The graphs of automata with locally idempotent transition semigroup are checked too ($O(n^3)$ time complexity). All algorithms dealing with transition semigroup of automaton have $O(n^2)$ space complexity.

2   Algorithms Used in the Package

Let the integer a denote the size of alphabet and let g be the number of nodes. By n let us denote here the size of the semigroup.

The syntactic characterization of locally threshold testable languages was given by Beauquier and Pin [1]. From their result follow necessary and sufficient conditions of local threshold testability for transition graph of DFA [25] and used in our package a polynomial time algorithm for the local threshold testability problem for transition graph and for transition semigroup of the language.

Let us notice here that the algorithm for transition graph from [25] ([26]) is valid only for complete graph. Of course, the general case can be reduced to the case of complete graph by adding of a sink state. Let us notice also another error from [25] ([26]): in the Theorem 16 (17) in the list of the conditions of local threshold testability, the property that any T_{SCC} is well defined is missed.

The time complexity of the graph algorithm for local threshold testability is $O(ag^5)$. The algorithm is based on consideration of the graphs Γ^2 and Γ^3 and therefore has $O(ag^3)$ space complexity. The time complexity of the semigroup algorithm is $O(n^3)$.

Polynomial time algorithms for the local testability problem for semigroups [22] of order $O(n^2)$ and for graphs [25] of order $O(ag^2)$ are implemented in the package too. We use in our package a polynomial time algorithm of worst case asymptotic cost $O(ag^2)$ for finding the bounds on order of local testability for a given transition graph of the automaton [24] and a polynomial time algorithm of worst case asymptotic cost $O(ag^3)$ for checking the 2-testability [24]. Checking the k-testability for fixed k is polynomial but growing with k. For checking the k-testability [24], we use an algorithm of worst case asymptotic cost $O(g^3 a^{k-2})$. The order of the last algorithm is growing with k and so we have non-polynomial algorithm for finding the order of local testability. The algorithms are based on consideration of the graph Γ^2 and have $O(ag^2)$ space complexity. The 1-testability is verified by help of algorithm of cost $O(a^2 g)$.

The situation in semigroups is more favorable than in graphs. We implement in our package a polynomial time algorithm of worst case asymptotic cost $O(n^2)$ for finding the order of local testability for a given semigroup [22]. The class of locally testable semigroups coincides with the class of strictly locally testable semigroups [23], whence the same algorithm of cost $O(n^2)$ checks strictly locally testable semigroups.

Stern [19] modified necessary and sufficient conditions of piecewise testability of DFA (Simon [18]) and described a polynomial time algorithm to verify piecewise testability.

We use in our package a polynomial time algorithm to verify piecewise testability of deterministic finite automaton of worst case asymptotic cost $O(ag^2)$ [25]. In comparison, the complexity of Stern's algorithm [19] is $O(ag^5)$. Our algorithm uses $O(ag^2)$ space. We implement also an algorithm to verify piecewise testability of a finite semigroup of cost $O(n^2)$

3   Description of the Package TESTAS

The package includes programs that analyze:
   1) an automaton of the language presented as oriented labeled graph;
   2) an automaton of the language presented by its syntactic semigroup,
   and find
   3) the direct product of two semigroups or of two graphs,
   4) the syntactic semigroup of an automaton presented by its transition graph.

First two programs are written in C/C^{++} and can by used in WINDOWS environment. The input file may be ordinary txt file. We open source file with transition graph or transition semigroup of the automaton in the standard way and then check different properties of automaton from menu bar. Both graph and semigroup are presented on display by help of rectangular table.

First two numbers in input graph file are the size of alphabet and the number of nodes. Transition graph of the automaton is presented by the matrix:

nodes X labels

where the nodes are presented by integers from 0 to n-1. i-th line of the matrix is a list of successors of i-th node according the label in row. The (i,j) cell contains number of the node from the end of the edge with label from the j-th row and beginning in i-th node. There exists opportunity to define the number of nodes, size of alphabet of edge labels and to change values in the matrix.

The input of semigroup algorithms is Cayley graph of the semigroup presented by the matrix:

$$\text{elements X generators}$$

where the elements of the semigroup are presented by integers from 0 to $n-1$ with semigroup generators in the beginning. i-th line of the matrix is a list of products of i-th element on all generators.

Set of generators is not necessarily minimal, therefore the multiplication table of the semigroup (Cayley table) is acceptable too. Comments without numerals may be placed in the input file as well.

The program checks local testability, local threshold testability and piecewise testability of syntactic semigroup of the language. Strictly locally testable and strongly locally testable semigroups are verified as well. The level of local testability of syntactic semigroup is also found. Aperiodicity and associative low can be checked too. There exists possibility to change values of products in the matrix of the Cayley graph.

The checking of the algorithms is based in particular on the fact that the considered objects belong to variety and therefore are closed under direct product. Two auxiliary programs written in C that find direct product of two semigroups and of two graphs belong to the package. The input of semigroup program consists of two semigroup presented by their Cayley graph with generators in the beginning of the element list. The result is presented in the same form and the set of generators of the result is placed in the beginning of the list of elements. The number of generators of the result is $n_1 g_2 + n_2 g_1 - g_1 g_2$ where n_i is the size of the i-th semigroup and g_i is the number of its generators. The components of direct product of graphs are considered as graphs with common alphabet of edge labels. The labels of both graphs are identified according their order. The number of labels is not necessary the same for both graphs, but the result alphabet used only common labels from the beginning of both alphabets. Big size semigroups and graphs can be obtained by help of these programs.

An important verification tool of the package is the possibility to study both transition graph and semigroup of an automaton. The program written in C finds syntactic semigroup from the transition graph of the automaton.

Maximal size of semigroups we consider on standard PC was about some thousands elements. Maximal size of considered graphs was about some hundreds nodes. The program used in such case memory on hard disc and works some minutes.

References

1. D. Beauquier, J.E. Pin, Factors of words, Lect. Notes in Comp. Sci., 372(1989), 63–79.
2. J.A. Brzozowski, I. Simon, Characterizations of locally testable events, Discrete Math. 4(1973), 243–271.

3. P. Caron, LANGAGE: A Maple package for automaton characterization of regular languages, Springer, Lect. Notes in Comp. Sci., 1436(1998), 46–55.
4. P. Caron, Families of locally testable languages, Theoret. Comput. Sci., 242(2000), 361–376.
5. J.M. Camparnaud, G. Hansel, Automate, a computing package for automata and finite semigroups, J. of Symbolic Comput., 12(1991), 197–220.
6. G. Cousineau, J.F. Perrot, J.M. Rifflet, APL programs for direct computation of a finite semigroup, APL Congress 73, Amsterdam, North Holl. Publ., (1973) 67–74.
7. V.Froidure,J.-E. Pin, Algorithms for computing finite semigroups. F. Cucker and M. Shub eds., Foundations of Comp. Math. (1997), 112–126.
8. P. Garcia, Jose Ruiz, Right and left locally testable languages, *Theoret. Comput. Sci.*, **246**(2000), 253–264.
9. S. Kim, R. McNaughton, R. McCloskey, A polynomial time algorithm for the local testability problem of deterministic finite automata, IEEE Trans. Comput., N10, 40(1991) 1087–1093.
10. S. Kim, R. McNaughton, Computing the order of a locally testable automaton, Lect. Notes in Comp. Sci., 560(1991) 186–211.
11. R. König, Reduction algorithm for some classes of aperiodic monoids, R.A.I.R.O. Theor.Inform., 19, **3**(1985), 233–260.
12. E. Leiss, Regpack, an interactive package for regular languages and finite automata, Research report CS-77-32, Univ. of Waterloo, 1977.
13. O. Matz, A. Miller, A. Potthoff, W. Thomas, E.Valkema, Report on the program AMoRE, Inst. inf. und pract. math., Christian-Albrecht Univ. Kiel, 1995.
14. R. McNaughton, Algebraic decision procedure for local testability, Math. Syst. Theory, 8(1974), 60–76.
15. R. McNaughton, S. Papert, Counter-free automata, M.I.T. Press Mass., (1971).
16. A. Okhotin, Whale Calf, a parser generator for conjunctive grammars. 7-th Int. Conf. on Impl. and Appl. of Automata, CIAA2002, Tours, 2002, 211–216.
17. D. Raymond, D. Wood, Grail, a C^++ library for automata and expressions, J. of Symb. Comp., 17(1994) 341–350.
18. I. Simon, Piecewise testable events, Lect. Notes in Comp. Sci., 33(1975), 214–222.
19. J. Stern, Complexity of some problems from the theory of automata. Inf. and Control, 66(1985), 163–176.
20. K. Sutner, Finite State Mashines and Syntactic Semigroups, The Mathematica J., 2(1991), 78–87.
21. A.N. Trahtman, The varieties of testable semigroups. Semigroup Forum, 27, (1983), 309–318.
22. A.N. Trahtman, A polynomial time algorithm for local testability and its level. Int. J. of Algebra and Comp., vol. 9, 1(1998), 31–39.
23. A.N. Trahtman, Identities of locally testable semigroups. Comm. in Algebra, v. 27, 11(1999), 5405–5412.
24. A.N. Trahtman, Algorithms finding the order of local testability of deterministic finite automaton and estimation of the order, Th. Comp. Sci., 235(2000), 183–204.
25. A.N. Trahtman, Piecewise and local threshold testability of DFA. Lect. Notes in Comp. Sci., 2138(2001), 347–358.
26. A.N. Trahtman, An algorithm to verify local threshold testability of deterministic finite automata. Lect. Notes in Comp. Sci., 2214(2001), 164–173.
27. B.W. Watson, The design and implementation of the FIRE Engine: A C^++ toolkit for Finite Automata and Regular Expressions, Comp. Sci. Rep. 94722, Endhoven Univ. of Techn. 1994.

DAWG versus Suffix Array

Miroslav Balík[*]

Department of Computer Science and Engineering, Czech Technical University,
Karlovo nám. 13, CZ-121 35, Prague 2, Czech Republic
balikm@fel.cvut.cz

Abstract. This paper shows a comparison of two data structures used
for indexing of input texts. The first structure is the Suffix Array and
the second is the Directed Acyclic Word Graph (*DAWG*). We present
an efficient *DAWG* implementation. This implementation is compared
with other structures used for text indexing. The construction time and
speed of searching of a set of substrings are shown for the *DAWG* and
the Suffix Array.

1 Introduction

Indexing structures support pattern matching in a linear time with respect to the
length of the pattern are constructed for static texts. Although some indexing
structures have a linear size with respect to the length of the text, this size is
high enough to prevent practical implementation and usage. For the *suffix tree*
the size is rarely smaller than $10n$ bytes, where n is the length of the text. Other
structures are a Directed Acyclic Word Graph (*DAWG*) (size about $30n$ bytes)
and its compact version *CDAWG* (size about $10n$ bytes). Other types of indexing
structures are usually smaller, *suffix arrays* [6] (size $5n$ bytes), level compressed
tries [1] (size about $11n$ bytes), *suffix cactuses* - a combination of suffix trees and
suffix arrays [10] (size $9n$ bytes), and *suffix binary search trees*[9] (size about $10n$
bytes).

We have used a set of 31 files in the experiments. 17 files are taken from the
Calgary Corpus and 14 files from the Canterbury Corpus [5]. Both Corpora are
widely used to compare lossless data compression programs. These files are also
used in [11], and therefore our results can be compared to the previous work.

2 Basic Definitions

An alphabet is a finite set of symbols. A *string* over a given alphabet is a finite
sequence of symbols. Let $T = t_1 t_2 \ldots t_n$ be a string (*text*) over a given alphabet
A. A pattern P of length m is a substring of a text T if $P = t_i t_{i+1} \ldots t_{i+m-1}$. A
pattern $P = t_i t_{i+1} \ldots t_n$ is called i-th suffix of the text. To determine whether a

---

[*] This research has been partially supported by the Ministry of Education, Youth,
and Sports of Czech Republic under research program No J04/98:212300014 and by
the Grant Agency of Czech Republic under research program No 102/01/1433.

J.-M. Champarnaud and D. Maurel (Eds.): CIAA 2002, LNCS 2608, pp. 233–238, 2003.
© Springer-Verlag Berlin Heidelberg 2003

pattern P is a substring (subpattern, subword, factor) of a text T is a pattern matching problem. $DAWG(T)$ is a minimal automaton that accepts all suffixes of a text T. The second structure to be compared is a suffix array. Suffix array is an array of pointers to the text. Each pointer represent one suffix of the text, its beginning in the text. That pointers are ordered in increasing lexicographical order of pointed suffixes.

3   Construction of *DAWG* and Suffix Array

There are many ways of constructing *DAWG* from text. More details can be found for example in [3]. The method used here is the on-line construction algorithm. An example of *DAWG* constructed using this algorithm for an input text $T = acagac$ is shown in Fig. 1.

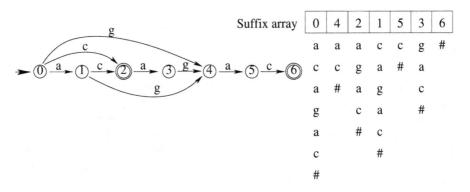

Suffix array	0	4	2	1	5	3	6
	a	a	a	c	c	g	#
	c	c	g	a	#	a	
	a	#	a	g		c	
	g		c	a		#	
	a		#	c			
	c			#			
	#						

Fig. 1. *DAWG(acagac)* and Suffix array*(acagac)*.

An implementation of *DAWG* presented in this paper uses a compression of elements of the graph that represents the automaton to decrease space requirements. The 'compression' is not a compression of the whole data structure, which would mean to perform decompression to be able to work with it, but it is a compression of individual elements, so it is necessary to decompress only those elements that are necessary during a specific search. This method is applicable to all homogenous automata[1] and it can be generalized to all automata that accept a finite set of strings and to all structures, which can be drawn as an acyclic graph.

The whole graph is a sequence of bits in a memory that can be referenced by pointers. A vertex is a position in the bit stream where a sequence of edges originating from the vertex begins. These edges are pointers into the bit stream. They point to memory cells where the corresponding terminal vertices cells are

---

[1] Homogenous automata have all transitions to a specific state labelled with the same symbol.

located. Vertices are stored in a topological order[2], which ensures that a search for a pattern is a one-way pass through the implementation of the graph structure.

Each vertex contains an information about labels of all edges that lead to it and the number of edges that start from it. Since it is possible to construct a statistical distribution of all symbols in the text, we can store edge labels using a Huffman code [8]. We also use a Huffman code to encode the number of edges that start from a vertex. The most frequent case of a node having only one outgoing edge is then dealt with as a special case.

The last part of the vertex contains references to vertices that can be accessed from the current vertex. These references are realized as relative addresses with respect to the beginning of the next element.

We will use an address consisting of two parts: the first part (of length s) will determine the number of bits of the second part, the second part will determine the distance of the ending vertex in bits. The best results are obtained for $s = 3$. This value is sufficient for a wide range of input text file lengths, which guarantees a simple implementation. This observation is based on experimental evaluation. Suppose $s = 3$, $t = 32$. This encoding regularly divides address codes into eight categories by four bits. The longest address is 32 bits long. It corresponds to the maximal size of the text of about 100 MB long.

The approach presented here creates a $DAWG$ structure in three phases. The first phase is the construction of the usual $DAWG$, the second phase is the topological ordering (or re-ordering) of vertices, which ensures that no edge has a negative "length", where the length is measured as a difference of vertex numbers. The final phase is the encoding and storing the resulting structure. The first phase uses an on-line construction algorithm and takes the space peak in the construction of the $DAWG$. This creates a large space overhead. This overhead depends on the type of the text, but the whole working space can be bounded by $64 * n$, where n is the size of the text.

In the Suffix array suffixes of the text are represented by the position of their beginnings in the text. The i-th field of the suffix array is initialized with the number i. All suffixes of the text are represented in the suffix array, the longest suffix is represented with number 1 and the shortest suffix is represented with number n. The construction of the suffix array consists of ordering initialized suffix array. The sorting operation between two fields of suffix array compares corresponding suffixes and the resulting value depends on its lexicographical order. The resultant suffix array represents the list of suffixes of the text and performs binary searches on them. An example of suffix array constructed for an input text $T = acagac$ is shown in Fig. 1.

---

[2] A topological ordering of a graph is a numbering of vertices that ensures that each edge starts from a vertex with a lower number and ends at a vertex with a higher number.

Table 1. Relative space requirements (in bytes per input symbol) of *DAWG* and other structures,**File** ... the name of the testing file; **Source** ... CL – Calgary Corpus, CN – Canterbury Corpus; **Length** ... the size of the text; |**A**| ... the size of the input alphabet;(***DAWG***,***CDAWG***, and ***Suff. Tree***) cite the results of the implementation published by Kurtz in [11] and show the relative space requirement *CDAWG* and suffix tree use the original text for string matching, but the length of the text is not scored up to the shown ratio; **S.Array** ... the lower bound of the size of suffix array using the shortest pointers. Whole pointers have the same size and this size is $\lceil log_2(n) \rceil$ bits. ***DAWG1*** corresponds to the addresses that use eight categories (three bits per category code). These categories regularly divide possible lengths from the length 0 bits to the maximal size of 32 bits. The first category corresponds to addresses 4 bits long, the second corresponds to addresses 8 bits long, etc. This means that this address encoding is sufficient for texts less than approximately 100 MB. Some categories are not used if the *DAWG*1 is created for a small text. ***DAWG2*** is obtained for a code with eight categories, where the first category denotes the address of length zero, i.e. no address is stored and the referred element leads to the next processed element. The next categories regularly divide possible lengths from 4 bits to the maximal size.

File	Source	Length	|A|	DAWG	CDAWG	S.Tree	S.Array	DAWG.1	DAWG.2
book1	CL	768771	81	30.35	15.75	9.83	**3.50**	3.75	3.66
book2	CL	610856	96	29.78	12.71	9.67	3.50	3.25	**3.17**
paper1	CL	53161	95	30.02	12.72	9.82	3.00	3.09	**2.98**
paper2	CL	82199	91	29.85	13.68	9.82	3.13	3.19	**3.06**
paper3	CL	46526	84	30.00	14.40	9.80	**3.00**	3.24	3.12
paper4	CL	13286	80	30.34	14.76	9.91	**2.75**	3.21	3.04
paper5	CL	11954	91	30.00	14.04	9.80	**2.75**	3.14	2.97
paper6	CL	38105	93	30.29	12.80	9.89	3.00	3.08	**2.96**
alice29	CN	152089	74	30.27	14.14	9.84	3.25	3.34	**3.20**
lcet10	CN	426754	84	29.75	12.70	9.66	3.38	3.21	**3.12**
plrabn12	CN	481861	81	29.98	15.13	9.74	**3.38**	3.60	3.52
bible	CN	4047392	63	29.28	10.87	7.27	3.75	3.01	**2.94**
world192	CN	2473400	94	27.98	7.87	9.22	3.75	2.58	**2.53**
bib	CL	111261	81	28.53	9.94	9.46	3.13	2.76	**2.68**
news	CL	377109	98	29.48	12.10	9.54	3.38	3.25	**3.15**
progc	CL	39611	92	29.73	11.87	9.59	3.00	2.98	**2.87**
progl	CL	71646	87	29.96	8.71	10.22	3.13	2.48	**2.40**
progp	CL	49379	89	30.21	8.28	10.31	3.00	2.44	**2.35**
trans	CL	93695	99	30.47	6.69	10.49	3.13	2.41	**2.35**
fields	CN	11150	90	29.86	9.40	9.78	2.75	2.54	**2.43**
cp	CN	24603	86	29.04	10.44	9.34	2.88	2.75	**2.64**
grammar	CN	3721	76	29.96	10.60	10.14	2.50	2.48	**2.36**
xargs	CN	4227	74	30.02	13.10	9.63	**2.63**	2.90	2.75
asyoulik	CN	125179	68	29.97	14.93	9.77	**3.13**	3.49	3.34
geo	CL	102400	256	26.97	13.10	7.49	**3.13**	3.27	3.18
obj1	CL	21504	256	27.51	13.20	7.69	**2.88**	3.12	2.98
obj2	CL	246814	256	27.22	8.66	9.30	3.25	2.75	**2.67**
ptt5	CN	513216	159	27.86	8.08	8.94	3.38	1.70	**1.63**
kennedy	CN	1029744	256	21.18	7.29	4.64	3.50	1.65	**1.57**
sum	CN	38240	255	27.79	10.26	8.92	3.00	2.62	**2.53**
ecoli	CN	4638690	4	34.01	23.55	12.56	**3.75**	4.59	4.46

4 Results

The space needed for a suffix array construction depends on the size of the text and on the sorting algorithm. The text size determines the size of pointers to the text. There are 32 bit long pointers used in our experiments to achieve simple implementation. The space occupied by the suffix array is $4 * n$ bytes, and $5 * n$ bytes after adding the text needed for string matching. We use a standard quick sort algorithm, which does not need extra space for sorting. The quick sort algorithm works in $\mathcal{O}(n * n)$ time in the worst case, but in $(n * log(n))$ on average. The $DAWG$ can be created using the on-line construction algorithm in $\mathcal{O}(n)$ time [3]. Vertex re-ordering can also be done in $\mathcal{O}(n)$ time, the encoding of $DAWG$ elements as described above can also be done in $\mathcal{O}(n)$ time. This means that the described $DAWG$ construction can be performed in $\mathcal{O}(n)$ time. The time of construction is similar for both structures.

The space requirements are a very important qualifier of the implementation. Table 1 shows the results for the set of test files.

The time complexity of searching in such an encoded $DAWG$ is $\mathcal{O}(m)$, see [2]. This complexity supposes that the time of decoding of individual parts is constant with respect to the size of the text. Next, it is supposed that the time of searching for the appropriate transition is done in a constant time, but this is done in a time linear with respect to the size of the alphabet using our implementation. So we made some tests to compare the time of string searching.

In experiments there are patterns that occur in texts. The lengths of the patterns range between 4 and 20 symbols. There were 1000 patterns prepared for each file, and this set was searched ten times to measure the time. We used PC computer, the Linux operating system, a Pentium processor and 500MB RAM. The search time was relatively constant, for suffix array it was about 0.5 second, for the $DAWG$ in our implementation about 15 seconds. The suffix array is better, but the set of patterns could be preprocessed using a trie automaton. Then the task of searching a set of pattern could be solved by intersection of the trie and $DAWG$ automaton. This technique is used for solving more complex tasks, see [7].

5 Conclusion

A new method of $DAWG$ implementation is presented and compared to the implementation of the *suffix array*. The results show that the ratio of code file size to the input file size is about 3:1.

It was shown that the suffix array is simpler to implement, it is faster to construct and the search time is also shorter. The $DAWG$ is a more complex structure and is more suitable for complex tasks, for example approximate string matching.

References

1. Anderson A, Nilson S. *Efficient implementation of suffix trees.* Software-Practice and Experience, 25(1995); 129–141.
2. Balík M. *String Matching in a Text.* Diploma Thesis, CTU, Dept. of Computer Science & Engineering, Prague, 1998.
3. Crochemore M, Rytter W. *Text Algorithms.* Oxford University Press, New York, 1994.
4. Crochemore M, Vérin R. *Direct Construction Of Compact Directed Acyclic Word Graphs.* CPM97, A. Apostolico and J. Hein, eds., LNCS 1264, Springer–Verlag, 1997; 116–129.
5. http://corpus.canterbury.ac.nz/.
6. Gonnet G.H, Baeza-Yates R. *Handbook of Algorithms and Data Structures - In Pascal and C.* Addison - Wesley, Wokingham, UK, 1991.
7. Holub J., Melichar B.: *Approximate String Matching using Factor Automata.* Theoretical Computer Science, Vol. 249 (2), Elsevier Science, 2000, pp. 305–311.
8. Huffman, D.A. *A method for construction of minimum redundancy codes.* Proceedings of IRE, Vol.40, No.9, Sept.1952; 1098–1101.
9. Irving R.W. *Suffix binary search trees.* Technical report TR-1995-7, Computing science Department, University of Glasgow, Apr.95.
10. Kärkkäinen J. *Suffix cactus: A cross between suffix tree and suffix array.* in Proc. 6th Symposium on combinatorial Pattern Matching, CPM95, 1995; 191–204.
11. Kurtz S. *Reducing the Space Requirement of Suffix Trees.* Software–Practice and Experience, 29(13), 1999; 1149–1171.

On Predictive Parsing and Extended Context-Free Grammars

Anne Brüggemann-Klein[1] and Derick Wood[2]

[1] Institut für Informatik, Technische Universität München,
Arcisstr. 21, 80290 München, Germany
brueggem@informatik.tu-muenchen.de
[2] Department of Computer Science,
Hong Kong University of Science & Technology,
Clear Water Bay, Kowloon, Hong Kong SAR
dwood@cs.ust.hk

Abstract. Extended context-free grammars are context-free grammars in which the right-hand sides of productions are allowed to be any regular language rather than being restricted to only finite languages. We present a novel view on top-down predictive parser construction for extended context-free grammars that is based on the rewriting of partial syntax trees. This work is motivated by our development of ECFG, a Java toolkit for the manipulation of extended context-free grammars, and by our continuing investigation of XML.

1 Introduction

We have been investigating XML [2], the Web language for encoding structured documents, its properties and use for a number of years [4,5,11]. The language XML itself, the document grammars that XML defines, and various other Web languages are defined by extended context-free grammars; that is, context-free grammars in which the right-hand sides of productions are allowed to be any regular language rather than being restricted to only finite languages. Hence, we became interested in factoring out all grammar processing that Web applications are based on and need to perform, into a separate toolkit that we call ECFG.

A cornerstone of ECFG is to be able to generate parsers from grammars. We present in this paper the principles of generating strong LL(1) parsers from a subset of the extended context-free grammars that is pertinent to Web grammars. We call these parsers **eSLL(1) parsers**. In particular, we contribute a novel view to predictive parsing that is based on what we call partial syntax trees. The parser generator is intended to be one tool among many in our toolkit.

LaLonde [12] appears to have been the first person to seriously consider the construction of parsers for extended context-free grammars. The construction of LL(1)-like parsers for extended context-free grammars has been discussed by Heckmann [9], by Lewi and his co-workers [13], and by Sippu and Soisalon-Soininen [16]. Warmer and his co-workers [18,19] and Clark [6] have developed SGML parsers based on LL(1) technology. Mössenböck [14] and Parr and

J.-M. Champarnaud and D. Maurel (Eds.): CIAA 2002, LNCS 2608, pp. 239–247, 2003.
© Springer-Verlag Berlin Heidelberg 2003

Quong [15] have implemented LL(1) parser generators for extended context-free grammars.

We give, in Section 2, some general background information on extended context-free grammars and Web languages and discuss the level of support that is currently available for grammar manipulation. We then define the basic notation and terminology that we need, in Section 3, before introducing partial syntax trees, in Section 4. In Section 5, we describe a nondeterministic algorithm eNSLL to compute a sequence of leftmost partial syntax trees for a given input string. We define an extended context-free grammar to be an **eSLL(1) grammar** if and only if the algorithm eNSLL is actually deterministic and we characterize eSLL(1) grammars in terms of first and follow sets. We mention further results in the final section.

2   The Grammar Toolkit

Starting with XML, we present in this section some general background information on extended context-free grammars and Web languages and discuss the level of support that is currently available for grammar manipulation. We focus on the facts that have led to our decision to develop the grammar toolkit ECFG and to equip it with a predictive-parser generator.

XML is defined by an extended context-free grammar. The XML grammar derives XML documents that consist of an optional Document Type Definition (DTD) and the document proper, called the document instance. The XML grammar describes the syntax for DTDs and instances in general terms. The DTD is specific to an application domain and not only defines the vocabulary of elements, attributes and references in the document but also specifies how these constructs may be combined. The DTD is again an extended context-free grammar.

There are a number of XML parsers that read a DTD and a document instance, and are able to determine whether both follow the general rules of the XML grammar and whether the instance conforms to the DTD. Furthermore, there are two well-established means for application programs to access XML data; namely DOM, a W3C standard, and SAX, an industry standard. XML parsers typically support both of these Application Programming Interfaces (APIs).

It is curious that none of the XML tools we are aware of provide API access to the DTD of an XML document. This limits and hinders the development of XML tools that are customized for the application domain and of tools that read and manipulate DTDs such as DTD-aware editors for document instances, DTD-browsers, DTD-analyzers and DTD-aware query optimizers for XML documents. State-of-the-art XML tools treat DTDs as black boxes; they may be able to handle DTDs but they do not share their knowledge!

For this reason we propose a more transparent approach to the development of XML tools that is based on ECFG, a Java toolkit for the manipulation of extended context-free grammars, that we are currently implementing.

Grammars are ubiquitous. In the Web context alone, we have not only the XML grammar and XML DTDs but also XML Schemas, the CSS grammar, the XPath grammar, and specific DTDs or quasi-DTDs such as MathML and XSLT. Web tools such as a CSS processor, an XPath query optimizer and an XML processor that validates a document instance against its DTD are very different applications. With ECFG we aspire to support any grammar manipulations that these diverse tools might need to perform.

The cornerstone of grammar manipulation is to generate parsers automatically from grammars. The theory of parser generators is well understood and has been explored, at least for the case of nonextended grammars, in a number of textbooks [1,17,20]. Furthermore, this knowledge is embodied in generator tools such as lex, flex, bison, yacc, Coco/R and ANTLR. A parser generator constructs a parser from a given grammar. The parser in turn converts a symbol stream into a syntax tree or some other structure that reflects the phrase structure of the symbol stream; alternatively and more commonly, the parser does not expose the parse tree itself but triggers semantic actions that are coded into its grammar for each phrase that it recognizes in the symbol stream.

In the context of Web languages, the languages that a grammar derives are often grammars once more, as exemplified by the XML grammar that derives DTDs; that is, document grammars. These grammars not only need to be turned into parsers again, which would be in the scope of standard parser generators, but they also need to be analyzed and transformed in complex ways. The analysis requires, in some cases, computations that parser generators perform but do not expose; for example, computations of first and follow sets. For this reason, we have decided to design and implement our own parser generator in ECFG. In our domain of applications, grammars need to be first-class citizens.

It is be a common assumption that XML documents are easy to parse; whereas this assumption has not been formally verified, is obviously true for document instances, which are fully bracketed. Hence, of all the alternative parsing strategies that are in use, our parser generator employs the simplest one, namely the strong LL approach to parsing with a one-symbol lookahead, generalizing it from "normal" to extended context-free grammars.

3 Notation and Terminology

An **extended context-free grammar** G is specified by a tuple of the form (N, Σ, P, S), where N is a nonterminal alphabet, Σ is a terminal alphabet, P is a set of **production schemas** of the form $A \longrightarrow L_A$, such that A is a nonterminal and L_A is a regular language over the alphabet $\Sigma \cup N$, and S, the sentence symbol, is a nonterminal. Given a production schema $A \longrightarrow L_A$ such that α is a string in L_A, we say that $A \longrightarrow \alpha$ is a **production** of G. We call L_A the **rhs-language** of A. Since the rhs-languages of extended grammars are regular, extended and "normal" grammars derive the same class of languages, namely the context-free languages [10].

We represent the set of production schemas P of an extended context-free grammar $G = (N, \Sigma, P, S)$ as a transition diagram system [7,8] which provides a nondeterministic finite automata (NFAs) for the rhs-language of each nonterminal. We require the automata to be of Glushkov type so that each state is labeled by a symbol in $N \cup \Sigma$ and each incoming transition bears that state's label.

In practice, the rhs-languages of an extended grammar are given as regular expressions. A regular expression can, however, be transformed into a Glushkov-type NFA in linear time [3].

A **transition diagram system** DS $= (Q, \mathbf{label}, F, \mathbf{init}, \mathbf{trans}, \mathbf{belongs})$ over N and Σ has a set of states Q, a relation **label** $\subseteq Q \times (N \cup \Sigma)$ that maps each state to at most one symbol, a set of final states $F \subseteq Q$, a relation **init** $\subseteq N \times Q$ that assigns exactly one initial state to each nonterminal, a relation **trans** $\subseteq Q \times Q$ for the transitions between states and a relation **belongs** $\subseteq Q \times N$ that maps each state to the unique nonterminal to whose rhs-automaton the state belongs.

A relationship $p\,\mathbf{trans}\,q$ implies that q has some label X (that is, $q\,\mathbf{label}\,X$) and means that there is a transition from p to q on the symbol X. This notion of transition relation accounts for the Glushkov property. A production $A \longrightarrow \alpha$ of the grammar G translates into a string α of the NFA $M_A = (N \cup \Sigma, Q, p_A, F, \mathbf{trans})$ such that $A\,\mathbf{init}\,p_A$. Each state in the transition diagram system is uniquely assigned to some nonterminal via the relation **belongs**. A state that is reachable from a nonterminal's initial state must belong to that same nonterminal. When we construct the automata from the rhs-expressions of a grammar, the sets of states must hence be chosen to be disjoint.

For the remainder of the paper, let Σ denote a set of terminals and N denote a set of nonterminals; their union $\Sigma \cup N$ forms a **vocabulary**. An extended context-free grammar is given as $G = (N, \Sigma, P, S)$; its set of production schemas P is represented by the transition diagram system DS $= (Q, \mathbf{label}, F, \mathbf{init}, \mathbf{trans}, \mathbf{belongs})$ over N and Σ.

Names A and B denote nonterminals, a and b denote terminals, X denotes a symbol in the vocabulary $\Sigma \cup N$, p denotes a state, α, β and γ denote strings over the vocabulary, whereas u, v and w denote strings over Σ. If we need additional names of any of these types, we use embellishments.

4   Partial Syntax Trees

We base our approach to parsing on the use of **partial syntax trees** whose nodes are **labeled** with symbols in the vocabulary $\Sigma \cup N$ and some of whose nodes are **annotated** with states in Q. Internal nodes are always labeled with nonterminal symbols from N; external nodes are labeled with symbols from either alphabet. Only nodes that have a nonterminal label may have an annotation. We call those nodes **active**.

A partial syntax tree represents the progress a parser has made in constructing a syntax tree for a given input string of terminals in a top-down manner. An active node represents a construction site where the parser may append further nodes to the list of child nodes, thus gradually expanding the active node. When the parser has completed the expansion work at a construction site, it will remove the annotation to make the node inactive. The goal is to construct a partial syntax tree without any active nodes such that its terminal-labeled leaves spell out the input string that is to be parsed. Leaves that are inactive and labeled with a nonterminal are not expanded and thus contribute the empty string to the input string.

A grammar, particularly its transition diagram system, constrains the work of a parser and determines if the partial syntax tree that is constructed **conforms** to the grammar: First of all, the tree's root must be labeled with the grammar's sentence symbol. Furthermore, the labels and annotations in the tree must conform to the grammar in the following way:

- For each inactive node v, the labels of the children of v must spell out a string in the rhs-language of v's label.
- For each active node v, its state annotation is reachable from the node label's initial state by the input string formed by the sequence of labels of v's children.

Particularly, each external active node must be annotated with the initial state of the node's label and the language of an inactive external node's label must contain the empty string.

Since we wish to explore top-down left-to-right parsing, we are particularly interested in **leftmost** partial syntax trees in which the active nodes form a prefix of the rightmost branch of the tree. A leftmost construction is the analog of a leftmost derivation for "normal" context-free grammars. The frontier of a leftmost partial syntax tree is a sequence, from left to right, of inactive nodes, followed by at most one active node. The sequence of nodes in the frontier that have *terminal labels* yields a terminal string over Σ, which we call the **yield** of the leftmost partial syntax tree.

We call a partial syntax tree on which all work has been completed (that is, which has no active nodes left) just a **syntax tree**. Whereas a partial syntax tree represents a parser's work-in-progress, a syntax tree represents the finished product that may then be exposed to application programs.

A partial syntax tree of grammar G can be constructed incrementally by beginning with an initial one-node partial syntax tree and then, step by step, adding nodes, changing the states that are associated with nodes and making active nodes inactive. Rather than applying a whole production $A \longrightarrow \alpha$, $\alpha = x_1 \cdots x_n$, in a single step to a node v with label A, we add n children to v one after the other, in n steps, labeling the children with $x_1, \ldots, x_n$ and keeping track in the state annotation of v how far we have progressed. We can view this process as a sequence of transformations on partial syntax trees.

A single **transformation** manipulates, nondeterministically, an *active node v* of a partial syntax tree in one of the following three ways, where we assume that v is labeled with a nonterminal A and is annotated with a state p that belongs to A:

1. If p is a final state, then v is made inactive by removing the state p from v. We call this transformation a **reduce step**.

2. If there is a transition from p to p' and if the label of state p' is a terminal a, then a new node v' is added as a new rightmost child of v. The new node is labeled with a and v is annotated with state p'. We call this transformation a **shift step**.

3. If there is a transition from p to p' and if the label of state p' is on a nonterminal B then a new active node v' is added as a new rightmost child of v. The new node is labeled with B and is annotated with the initial state which is associated with B. Futhermore, v is annotated with state p'. We call this transformation an **expand step**.

A **construction** of a partial syntax tree is a sequence of transformations that begins with the initial partial syntax tree whose one node is active, is labeled with the sentence symbol S and is annotated with the initial state of S and that ends with the partial syntax tree itself.

A **leftmost construction** is a construction that begins with the initial partial syntax tree and consists only of leftmost partial syntax trees. (Note that the initial partial syntax tree and all syntax trees are leftmost.)

Theorem 1. *The language of a grammar consists of the yields of the grammar-conformant syntax trees. Furthermore, for each such syntax tree there is a leftmost construction.*

5   Predictive Parsing

This section focuses on parsing; that is, for each terminal string u of a grammar, we construct a syntax tree whose yield is u. Our approach to parsing is top-down with a look-ahead of one symbol; that is, we do left-most constructions and read the input string from left to right, advancing at most one position at each transformation step. At each step, the choice of transformation is guided by the current input symbol.

A leftmost partial syntax tree is **compatible** with a given terminal string if its yield is a prefix of the string.

As our parsing strategy, we present a nondeterministic algorithm eNSLL to compute a leftmost construction in which each leftmost partial syntax tree is compatible with a given input string $a_1 \cdots a_n$ of terminals. The algorithm generalizes strong LL(1) parsing for extended grammars, which accounts for its name.

When given a leftmost partial syntax tree that is compatible with the input string, the algorithm expands the tree's deepest active node using one of the three transformation types given in Section 4. When choosing a transformation type, the algorithm eNSLL is guided by the input symbol immediately to the right of the partial syntax tree's yield. We call this symbol the **current input symbol.** If the algorithms has moved beyond the end of the input string, we set the current input symbol to the empty string, thus signaling to the algorithm that it has read the full input string.

We need to introduce a number of concepts to describe the behaviour of eNSLL:

First, for each pair of states p and p' such that p **trans** p' let $L(p, p')$ be the language of all strings over Σ that are the yields of syntax trees constructed from the one-node initial tree whose label is the symbol that is associated with p and whose state annotation is p such that the first transformation is to add a child to the root that is labeled with the symbol of p' and to annotate the root with state p'. Formally, $L(p, p')$ is the union of all languages $L(X\alpha)$ such that p' **label** X and α in $(N \cup \Sigma)^*$ moves the grammar's transition diagram system from p' to some final state.

Next, $follow(A)$ is the set of all terminals that can occur immediately after A in a string that G can derive from S. More formally, $follow(A)$ consists of all a in Σ such that G derives $\alpha A a \beta$ from S, for some α and β in $(N \cup \Sigma)^*$. In addition, we add the empty string to $follow(A)$ for each A for which G derives some αA.

Finally, we consider every leftmost partial syntax tree whose deepest active node v is annotated with some state p and labeled with the symbol of p, and any construction whose first transformation step adds a new rightmost child to v and that annotates v with some state p' such that p **trans** p' while labeling the new node with the symbol of p. The first terminals that are derived by such constructions form the set $first(p, p')$. To be precise, $first(p, p')$ consists of the first symbols of the strings in $L(p, p') follow(A)$; note that we consider the empty string to be the first symbol of the empty string. Furthermore, $first(p)$ is the union of all $first(p, p')$ such that p **trans** p'.

The algorithms eNSLL computes a leftmost construction for a syntax tree whose yield is a given input string of terminals. The algorithm starts with the initial one-node partial syntax tree that each construction starts with. At each step of the construction, it chooses nondeterministically a reduce, shift, or expand step to continue its computation, but the choice is constrained by the next input symbol and by the first and follow sets.

In order to be more precise, let us look at the following scenario: We are given a leftmost partial syntax tree t that is compatible with some terminal string. Furthermore, we assume that we can continue any leftmost construction of t until we reach a syntax tree for the terminal string. Let the tree's deepest active node v have label A and annotation p. Finally, let a be the current input symbol. In this situation, eNSLL performs a reduce step only if a is in $follow(A)$, it performs a shift step only if p' **label** a, and it performs an expand step only if a is in $first(p, p')$.

An eNSLL computation **terminates** if no further transformation steps are possible. The eNSLL algorithm **accepts** an input string if it terminates with a partial syntax tree that is, in fact, a syntax tree and whose yield is the complete input string.

Theorem 2. *The eNSLL algorithm of a grammar accepts exactly the strings of the grammar.*

We say that a grammar is **eSLL(1)** if and only if the eNSLL algorithm for the grammar is deterministic.

Theorem 3. *An extended context-free grammar is eSLL(1) if and only if it satisfies the following two conditions:*

1. *For each final state p such that p **belongs** A, the sets $first(p)$ and $follow(A)$ are disjoint.*
2. *For each pair of different states q, q' to which there are transitions from p, the sets $first(q)$ and $first(q')$ are disjoint.*

Theorem 4. *We can test if a grammar is eSLL(1) in worst-case time $O(|\Sigma| \cdot |G|)$.*

Theorem 5. *Let the rhs-languages of an extended context-free grammar be defined by regular expressions and let the grammar's transition diagram system be computed with the Glushkov construction [3]. If the grammar is eSLL(1), then the transition diagram system must be deterministic.*

6   Further Results

In addition to providing the proofs for the theorems in this paper, the full version of this paper investigates two related topics:

First, it is straightforward to build a parsing table of parse actions from the first and follow sets that drive the eNSLL algorithm. There is at most one parse action in each table cell if and only if the grammar is eSLL(1). We can build the parse table in worst-case time $O(|\Sigma| \cdot |G|)$.

Second, "normal" context-free grammar are a special case of extended grammar. This carries over to strong LL(1)-grammars. In the full version of this paper, we characterize SLL(1) grammars in terms of eSLL(1) extended grammars.

We discuss implementation and application issues in a separate paper.

Acknowledgements. The work of both authors was supported partially by a joint DAAD-HK grant. In addition, the work of the second author was supported under a grant from the Research Grants Council of Hong Kong.

References

1. A. V. Aho, R. Sethi, and J. D. Ullman. *Compilers: Principles, Techniques, and Tools.* Addison-Wesley Series in Computer Science. Addison-Wesley Publishing Company, Reading, MA, 1986.

2. T. Bray, J. P. Paoli, and C. M. Sperberg-McQueen. Extensible Markup Language (XML) 1.0.
http://www.w3.org/TR/1998/REC-xml-19980210/, February 1998.

3. A. Brüggemann-Klein. Regular expressions into finite automata. *Theoretical Computer Science*, 120:197–213, 1993.

4. A. Brüggemann-Klein and D. Wood. One-unambiguous regular languages. *Information and Computation*, 140:229–253, 1998.

5. A. Brüggemann-Klein and D. Wood. Caterpillars: A context specification technique. *Markup Languages: Theory & Practice*, 2(1):81–106, 2000.

6. J. Clark, 1992. Source code for SGMLS. Available by anonymous ftp from ftp.uu.net and sgml1.ex.ac.uk.

7. D.J. Cohen and C.C. Gotlieb. A list structure form of grammars for syntactic analysis. *Computing Surveys*, 2:65–82, 1970.

8. D. Giammarresi and D. Wood. Transition diagram systems and normal form transformations. In *Proceedings of the Sixth Italian Conference on Theoretical Computer Science*, pages 359–370, Singapore, 1998. World Scientific Publishing Co. Pte. Ltd.

9. R. Heckmann. An efficient ELL(1)-parser generator. *Acta Informatica*, 23:127–148, 1986.

10. J. E. Hopcroft and J. D. Ullman. *Introduction to Automata Theory, Languages and Computation*. Addison-Wesley Series in Computer Science. Addison-Wesley Publishing Company, Reading, MA, 1979.

11. P. Kilpeläinen and D. Wood. SGML and XML document grammars and exceptions. *Information and Computation*, 169:230–251, 2001.

12. W. R. LaLonde. Regular right part grammars and their parsers. *Communications of the ACM*, 20:731–741, 1977.

13. J. Lewi, K. de Vlaminck, E. Steegmans, and I. van Horebeek. *Software Develepment by LL(1) Syntax Description*. John Wiley & Sons, Chichester, UK, 1992.

14. H. Mössenböck. A generator for production quality compilers. In *Lecture Notes in Computer Science 471*, Berlin, 1990. Springer-Verlag. Proceedings of the Third International Workshop on Compiler-Compilers.

15. T. J. Parr and R. W. Quong. ANTRL: A predicated-LL(k) parser generator. *Software—Practice and Experience*, 25(7):789–810, 1995.

16. S. Sippu and E. Soisalon-Soininen. *Parsing Theory, Volume 1, Languages and Parsing, Volume 2, LL(k) and LR(k) Parsing,*. EATCS Monographs on Theoretical Computer Science. Springer-Verlag, Berlin, 1988.

17. P. D. Terry. *Compilers and Compiler Generators*. Out of print, available on the Web, 2000.

18. J. Warmer and S. Townsend. The implementation of the Amsterdam SGML parser. *Electronic Publishing, Origination, Dissemination, and Design*, 2:65–90, 1989.

19. J. Warmer and H. van Vliet. Processing SGML documents. *Electronic Publishing, Origination, Dissemination, and Design*, 4(1):3–26, March 1991.

20. R. Wilhelm and D. Maurer. *Compiler Design*. Addison-Wesley, Reading, MA, 1995.

Star Normal Form, Rational Expressions, and Glushkov WFAs Properties

Pascal Caron[1] and Marianne Flouret[2]

[1] LIFAR, Université de Rouen,
76134 Mont-Saint-Aignan Cedex, France
Pascal.Caron@dir.univ-rouen.fr
[2] LIH, Université du Havre,
76058 Le Havre Cedex, France
Marianne.Flouret@univ-lehavre.fr

Abstract. In this paper, we extend the characterisation of Glushkov automata to multiplicities. We consider automata obtained from rational expressions in star normal form. We show that for this class of automata, the graphical Boolean properties are preserved. We prove that this new characterization only depends on conditions on coefficients and we explicit these conditions.

1 Introduction

The extension of Boolean algorithms (over languages) to multiplicities (over series) has always been a central point in theoretical research. First, Schützenberger [14] has given an equivalence between rational and recognizable series extending the classical Kleene's theorem [11]. Recent works have been done in this area. The authors have extended the Glushkov construction to automata with multiplicities [6]. Lombardy and Sakarovitch have given an extension [12] of Antimirov's algorithm based on partial derivatives [2]. The SEA software [1] suits to this kind of problems by allowing us to work on both Boolean and multiplicity automata.

Caron and Ziadi have provided a characterisation of Boolean Glushkov automata [7]. After some theoretical recalls, we extend this result to multiplicities in the case of rational expressions on star normal form.

2 Definitions

2.1 Classical Notions

Let Σ be a finite alphabet, ε the empty word, and $(\mathbb{K}, \oplus, \otimes)$ be a semiring where 0 is the neutral element of $(\mathbb{K}, \oplus)$ and 1 the one of $(\mathbb{K}, \otimes)$. A *formal series* [3] is a mapping S from Σ^* into $\mathbb{K}$ usually denoted by $S = \sum_{w \in \Sigma^*} \langle S|w \rangle w$ (where $\langle S|w \rangle := S(w) \in \mathbb{K}$ is the coefficient of w in S). *Rational expressions* are obtained

J.-M. Champarnaud and D. Maurel (Eds.): CIAA 2002, LNCS 2608, pp. 248–254, 2003.
© Springer-Verlag Berlin Heidelberg 2003

from the letters by a finite number of combinations of rational laws ($+$, $\cdot$, $*$, and an external product $\times$). *Rational series* are formal series that can be described by *rational expressions*. When $\mathbb{K} = \mathbb{B}$, the external product can be omitted and then we talk about regular languages and regular expressions.

A Boolean automaton $\mathcal{M}$ over an alphabet Σ is usually defined [8,10] as a 5-tuple $(\Sigma, Q, I, F, \delta)$ where Q is a finite set of states, $I \subseteq Q$ the set of initial states, $F \subseteq Q$ the set of final states, and $\delta \subseteq Q \times \Sigma \times Q$ the set of edges. We denote by $L(E)$ the language represented by the regular expression E and by $L(\mathcal{M})$ the language recognized by the automaton $\mathcal{M}$. A weighted finite automaton (WFA) [8] over an alphabet Σ is then a 5-tuple $(\Sigma, Q, I, F, \delta)$ on a semiring $\mathbb{K}$, and the sets I, F and δ are rather viewed as mappings $I : Q \to \mathbb{K}$, $F : Q \to \mathbb{K}$, and $\delta : Q \times \Sigma \times Q \to \mathbb{K}$. In the following of this paper, we will need the original construction of Glushkov [9,13] which is summarized as follows. The first step is to mark out each occurrence of the same symbol in a rational expression E. Therefore, each occurrence of letter will be indexed by its position in the expression. The resulting will be denoted $\overline{E}$, defined over the alphabet of indexed symbols $\overline{\Sigma}$, each one appearing at most once in $\overline{E}$. Glushkov defines four functions on E in order to compute a non necessarily deterministic automaton. $First(E)$ represents the set of initial positions of words of $L(E)$, $Last(E)$ the set of final positions of words of $L(E)$, $Follow(E, i)$ the set of positions which immediately follows the position i in the expression E. $Null(E)$ returns $\{\varepsilon\}$ if the language $L(E)$ recognizes the empty word, $\emptyset$ otherwise. These functions allow us to define the automaton $\overline{\mathcal{M}} = (\overline{\Sigma}, Q, 0, F, \overline{\delta})$ where

1. $\overline{\Sigma}$ is the indexed alphabet,
2. 0 is the single initial state with no incoming edge,
3. $Q = Pos(E) \cup \{0\}$
4. $\forall i \in First(E), \overline{\delta}(0, a_i) = \{i\}, \ a_i \in \overline{\Sigma}$
5. $\forall i \in Pos(E), \forall j \in Follow(E, i), \overline{\delta}(i, a_j) = \{j\}, \ a_j \in \overline{\Sigma}$
6. $F = Last(E) \cup Null(E) \cdot 0$

The Glushkov automaton $\mathcal{M} = (\Sigma, Q, 0, F, \delta)$ of E is computed from $\overline{\mathcal{M}}$ by replacing the indexed letters on edges by the corresponding letters in the expression E.

We will also need the Glushkov construction defined by the authors in the case of multiplicities [6]. This construction is obtained from the previous one by associating a coefficient to each element of every set.

2.2   Extended Notions

We have to define the casting $\widetilde{\mathcal{M}}$ (resp. $\widetilde{E}$) of a WFA $\mathcal{M}$ (resp. a rational expression E) in $\mathbb{B}$. Similarly, Buchsbaum et al [5] define the topology of a graph. The automaton $\widetilde{\mathcal{M}} = (\Sigma, Q, \widetilde{I}, \widetilde{F}, \widetilde{\delta})$ is then defined with $\widetilde{I}, \widetilde{F} \subset Q$ and $\widetilde{I} = \{q \in Q \mid I(q) \neq 0\}$, $\widetilde{F} = \{q \in Q \mid F(q) \neq 0\}$, and $\widetilde{\delta} = \{(p, a, q) \mid p, q \in Q, \ a \in \Sigma \text{ and } \delta((p, a, q)) \neq 0\}$. The regular expression $\widetilde{E}$ is obtained from E without respect to the weights. Brüggemann-Klein defines expressions in *star normal* *form* (SNF) [4] as expressions for which all unions of *First* are disjoint. Formally, for all subexpression H^* in E, we have $\forall x \in Last(H)$, $Follow(H,x) \cap First(H) = \emptyset$. We extend this definition to multiplicities. A rational expression E is in SNF if $\widetilde{E}$ is in SNF.

The computation of the Glushkov (resp. extended Glushkov) automaton from a regular (resp. rational) expression E is denoted by $\mathcal{M}_b(E)$ (resp. $\mathcal{M}_k(E)$).

Lemma 1. *Let E be a rational expression. If E is in SNF, then*

$$\widetilde{\mathcal{M}_k(E)} = \mathcal{M}_b(\widetilde{E}).$$

3   Characterization of Glushkov Boolean Automata

An automaton $\mathcal{M} = (\Sigma, Q, I, F, \delta)$ is *homogeneous* if for all (p, a, q), $(p', a', q') \in \delta$, $q = q' \Rightarrow a = a'$. As the Glushkov automaton $\mathcal{M} = (\Sigma, Q, 0, F, \delta)$ of an expression E is homogeneous, we can define the Glushkov graph as $G = (X, U)$ with X the set of vertices $(Pos(E) \cup \{\Phi\} \cup \{0\})$, and U the set of edges (edges of $\mathcal{M}$ without label and edges from final states of $\mathcal{M}$ to Φ). A *hammock* is a graph $G = (X, U)$ without loop if $|X| = 1$, otherwise it has two distinguished vertices i and t such that, for any vertex x of X, (1) there exists a path from i to t going through x, (2) there is no path from t to x nor from x to i. $\mathcal{O} \subseteq X$ is a *maximal orbit* of G if and only if it is a strongly connected component with at least one edge. The set of direct successors (resp. direct predecessors) of $x \in X$ is denoted by $Q^+(x)$ (resp. $Q^-(x)$). For an orbit $\mathcal{O} \subset X$, $\mathcal{O}^+(x)$ denotes $Q^+(x) \cap (X \setminus \mathcal{O})$ and $\mathcal{O}^-(x)$ denotes the set $Q^-(x) \cap (X \setminus \mathcal{O})$. In other words, $\mathcal{O}^+(x)$ is the set of vertices which are directly reached from x and which are not in $\mathcal{O}$. $In(\mathcal{O}) = \{x \in \mathcal{O} \mid \mathcal{O}^-(x) \neq \emptyset\}$ and $Out(\mathcal{O}) = \{x \in \mathcal{O} \mid \mathcal{O}^+(x) \neq \emptyset\}$ denote the *input* and the *output* of the orbit $\mathcal{O}$. A maximal orbit $\mathcal{O}$ is *stable* if $Out(\mathcal{O}) \times In(\mathcal{O}) \subset U$. A maximal orbit $\mathcal{O}$ is *transverse* if for all $x, y \in Out(\mathcal{O})$, $\mathcal{O}^+(x) = \mathcal{O}^+(y)$ and for all $x, y \in In(\mathcal{O})$, $\mathcal{O}^-(x) = \mathcal{O}^-(y)$.

A maximal orbit $\mathcal{O}$ is *strongly stable* (resp. *transverse*) if it is stable (resp. transverse) and if after deleting the edges in $Out(\mathcal{O}) \times In(\mathcal{O})$ every maximal suborbit is strongly stable (resp. transverse).

Let G be a graph in which all the orbits are strongly stable. We call graph without orbit of G the acyclic graph obtained by recursively deleting, for every maximal orbit $\mathcal{O}$ of G, the edges in $Out(\mathcal{O}) \times In(\mathcal{O})$.

A graph G is *reducible* if it has no orbit and if it can be reduced to one vertex by iterated applications of any of the three rules R_1, R_2, R_3 described below.
Rule R_1: If x and y are vertices such that $Q^-(y) = \{x\}$ and $Q^+(x) = \{y\}$, then delete y and define $Q^+(x) := Q^+(y)$.

Rule R_2: If x and y are vertices such that $Q^-(x) = Q^-(y)$ and $Q^+(x) = Q^+(y)$, then delete y and any edge connected to y.

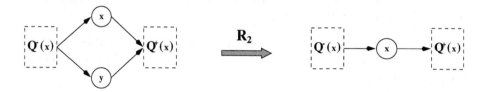

Rule R_3: If x is a vertex such that for all $y \in Q^-(x)$, $Q^+(x) \subset Q^+(y)$, two cases have to be distinguished :
If $0 \notin Q^-(x)$ or $\Phi \notin Q^+(x)$ or $|X| = 3$ then delete edges in $Q^-(x) \times Q^+(x)$. If $0 \in Q^-(x)$, $\Phi \in Q^+(x)$ and $|Q^-(x) \times Q^+(x)| \neq 1$ then delete edges in $Q^-(x) \times Q^+(x) \setminus \{(0, \Phi)\}$.

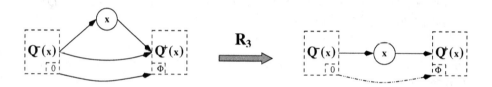

Theorem 1 ([7]). $G = (X, U)$ *is a Glushkov graph if and only if the three following conditions are satisfied:*

- *G is a hammock.*
- *Each maximal orbit in G is strongly stable and strongly transverse.*
- *The graph without orbit of G is reducible.*

4   Glushkov WFA Properties for Star Normal Form Rational Expressions

From now, we restrict $\mathbb{K}$ to a field in order to compute our characterization. Let us consider $\mathcal{M}$ a WFA without orbit. Our aim here is to give conditions on weights in order to check whether $\mathcal{M}$ is a Glushkov WFA. Relying on the Boolean characterization, we can deduce that (1) $\mathcal{M}$ is homogeneous and (2) the Glushkov graph of $\widetilde{\mathcal{M}}$ is reducible.

We now define a $\mathbb{K}$-*graph* as a graph labeled with coefficients in $\mathbb{K}$, that is $G_k = (X, U)$ where X is the set of vertices and $U : X \times X \to \mathbb{K}$ is the label associated with each edge. When there is no edge between two vertices p and q, we have $U(p, q) = 0$. In case an input value is associated to the initial state, it is distributed on the edges linking its successors. A left multiplication by the input value of coefficients of successors is applied. A *Glushkov* $\mathbb{K}$-*graph* is a $\mathbb{K}$-graph and a Glushkov graph in which output costs of final states label edges to Φ. We now give the conditions on coefficients for applying rules, and how to obtain the new label on the edge $(0, \Phi)$ when it exists.

Proposition 1. *For a regular expression E, each edge of its Glushkov graph G_E is computed only once, excepting edges induced by a star and the edge between the states 0 and Φ.*

Definition 1. *A $\mathbb{K}$-graph is $\mathbb{K}$-reducible if it has no orbit and if it can be reduced to one vertex by iterated applications of the three rules R_1, R_2 and R_3 where the following conditions are checked.*

- *If there exists two states x and y such that we can apply the rule R_2, then $\exists k \in \mathbb{K} \mid \forall p \in Q^-(x), \forall q \in Q^+(x), \frac{U(p,x) \times U(x,q)}{U(p,y) \times U(y,q)} = k$.*
- *If there exists a state x satisfying the rule R_3 conditions, then $\exists k \in \mathbb{K} \mid \forall p \in Q^-(x), \forall q \in Q^+(x), \frac{U(p,x) \times U(x,q)}{U(p,q)} = k$, and if $0 \in Q^-(x)$ and $\Phi \in Q^+(x)$ then $U(0, \Phi) := U(0, \Phi) - 1/k$.*

Proposition 2. *If $G = (X, U)$ is a Glushkov $\mathbb{K}$-graph without orbit then it is $\mathbb{K}$-reducible.*

We can notice that when an expression is in SNF, the proposition 1 extends the single computation of edges to the star operation.

We will now consider a graph which has at least one maximal orbit. We extend the notions of strong stability and strong transversality for $\mathbb{K}$-graph obtained from rational expressions in SNF. We have to give a characterization on coefficients only. Stability and transversality notions for WFAs are very linked.

Definition 2. *Let G_k be a Glushkov $\mathbb{K}$-graph. Let $\mathcal{O}$ be a maximal orbit. Let s be a state of $Out(\mathcal{O})$ and e a state of $In(\mathcal{O})$. Let $(p_1, \cdots, p_m)$ (resp. $(q_1, \cdots, q_n)$) be the ordered states of $\mathcal{O}^-(e)$ (resp. $\mathcal{O}^+(s)$). Let $(c_1, \cdots, c_n)$ (resp. $(c'_1, \cdots, c'_m)$) the set of coefficients from the state s (resp. to the state e). G_k is $\mathbb{K}$-transverse if (1) $\widetilde{G_k}$ is strongly transverse and (2) $\forall s_i \in Out(\mathcal{O})$ (resp. $\forall e_j \in In(\mathcal{O})$), its set of successors' (resp. predecessors) coefficients is $k_i(c_1, \cdots, c_n) = (k_i c_1, \cdots, k_i c_n)$ (resp. $(c'_1, \cdots, c'_m)k'_j = (c'_1 k'_j, \cdots, c'_m k'_j)$). $k_i \in \mathbb{K}$ is called the output cost of s_i (resp. $k'_j \in \mathbb{K}$ the input cost of e_j).*

Definition 3. *Let G_k be a Glushkov $\mathbb{K}$-graph. Let G be a maximal orbit. Let s be a state of $Out(\mathcal{O})$. Let $(e_1, \cdots, e_m)$ be the ordered states of $In(\mathcal{O})$. Let $(c_1, \cdots, c_m)$ the set of coefficients from the state s. G_k is $\mathbb{K}$-stable if (1) $\widetilde{G_k}$ is strongly stable and (2) $\forall s_i \in Out(\mathcal{O})$, its set of successors'coefficients is $k_i(c_1, \cdots, c_m) = (k_i c_1, \cdots, k_i c_m)$. k_i is called the orbit coefficient of s_i*

We can now define the recursive version of WFA transversality and stability.

Definition 4. *A $\mathbb{K}$-graph is strongly $\mathbb{K}$-transverse (resp. strongly $\mathbb{K}$-stable) if it is $\mathbb{K}$-transverse (resp. $\mathbb{K}$-stable) and if after deleting every edge of $Out(\mathcal{O}) \times In(\mathcal{O})$, it is strongly $\mathbb{K}$-transverse (resp. $\mathbb{K}$-stable).*

Proposition 3. *A Glushkov $\mathbb{K}$-graph in SNF is strongly $\mathbb{K}$-stable and strongly $\mathbb{K}$-transverse.*

Proposition 4. *Let $G = (X, U)$. G is a Glushkov $\mathbb{K}$-graph if and only if*

- *G is a hammock.*
- *G is strongly $\mathbb{K}$-stable and strongly $\mathbb{K}$-transverse.*
- *The graph without orbit of G is $\mathbb{K}$-reducible.*
- *For each maximal orbit $\mathcal{O}$ the set of output coefficients is exactly the set of orbit coefficients. After deleting $Out(\mathcal{O}) \times In(\mathcal{O})$ edges, this property is preserved.*

5   Conclusion

We have extended here the characterization of Glushkov automata to multiplicities in the SNF case. As far as non-SNF expressions are concerned, the difficulty lies in the fact that when computing the automaton, some edges may be computed several times (coefficients are added) and some may be deleted.

References

1. P. Andary, P. Caron, J.-M. Champarnaud, G. Duchamp, M. Flouret, and E. Laugerotte. SEA: A symbolic environment for automata theory. In *Automata Implementation : Fourth International Workshop on Implementing Automata, WIA'99*, Lecture Notes in Computer Science, 1999. To be published.
2. V. Antimirov. Partial derivatives of regular expressions and finite automaton constructions. *Theoret. Comput. Sci.*, 155:291–319, 1996.
3. J. Berstel and C. Reutenauer. *Rational series and their languages*. EATCS Monographs on Theoretical Computer Science. Springer-Verlag, Berlin, 1988.
4. A. Brüggemann-Klein. Regular expressions into finite automata. *Theoret. Comput. Sci.*, 120(1):197–213, 1993.
5. A. Buchsbaum, R. Giancarlo, and J. Westbrook. On the determinization of weighted finite automata. *SIAM J. Comput.*, 30(5):1502–1531, 2000.
6. P. Caron and M. Flouret. Glushkov construction for multiplicities. In *Fifth International Conference on Implementation and Application of Automata, CIAA'00*, volume 2088 of *Lecture Notes in Computer Science*, pages 67–79, London, Ontario, 2001. Springer-Verlag, Berlin.
7. P. Caron and D. Ziadi. Characterization of Glushkov automata. *Theoret. Comput. Sci.*, 233(1–2):75–90, 2000.
8. S. Eilenberg. *Automata, languages and machines*, volume A. Academic Press, New York, 1974.

9. V. M. Glushkov. On a synthesis algorithm for abstract automata. *Ukr. Matem. Zhurnal*, 12(2):147–156, 1960. In Russian.

10. J. E. Hopcroft and J. D. Ullman. *Introduction to Automata Theory, Languages and Computation*. Addison-Wesley, Reading, MA, 1979.

11. S. Kleene. Representation of events in nerve nets and finite automata. *Automata Studies*, Ann. Math. Studies 34:3–41, 1956. Princeton U. Press.

12. S. Lombardy and J. Sakarovitch. Derivatives of regular expression with multiplicity. Technical Report 2001D001, ENST, Paris, 2001.

13. R. F. McNaughton and H. Yamada. Regular expressions and state graphs for automata. *IEEE Transactions on Electronic Computers*, 9:39–57, March 1960.

14. M. P. Schützenberger. On the definition of a family of automata. *Inform. and Control*, 4:245–270, 1961.

Comparison of Construction Algorithms for Minimal, Acyclic, Deterministic, Finite-State Automata from Sets of Strings

Jan Daciuk

Alfa-Informatica, Rijksuniversiteit Groningen
j.daciuk@let.rug.nl

Abstract. This paper compares various methods for constructing minimal, deterministic, acyclic, finite-state automata (recognizers) from sets of words. Incremental, semi-incremental, and non-incremental methods have been implemented and evaluated.

1   Motivation

During last 12 years, one could see emergence of construction methods specialized for minimal, acyclic, deterministic, finite-state automata. However, there are various opinions about their performance, and how they compare to more general methods. Only partial comparisons are available. What has been compared so far was complete programs, which performed not only construction, but computation of a certain representation (e.g. space matrix representation, or various forms of compression).

The aim of this paper is to give answers to the following questions:

- What is the fastest construction method?
- What is the most memory-efficient method?
- What is the fastest method for practical applications?
- Do incremental methods introduce performance overhead?

The third question is not the same as the first one, because one has to take into account the size of data and available main memory. Even the fastest algorithm may become painfully slow during swapping.

2   Construction Methods

Due to lack of space, the construction methods under investigation have only been enumerated here. The reader is referred to the bibliography for proper descriptions. Some of the methods use a structure called the *register* of states. In those algorithms, states in an automaton are divided into those that have been minimized, i.e. they are unique in that part, and other states, i.e. those that are to be minimized. The register is a hash table, and two states are considered

J.-M. Champarnaud and D. Maurel (Eds.): CIAA 2002, LNCS 2608, pp. 255–261, 2003.

Table 1. Characteristics of data used in experiments

	strings			automaton	
	words	characters	av. len.	states	trans.
German words	716 273	10 221 410	14.27	45 959	97 239
morph.	3 977 448	364 681 813	91.69	107 198	435 650
French words	210 284	2 254 846	10.72	16 665	43 507
morph.	235 566	17 111 863	72.64	32 078	66 986
Polish words	74 434	856 176	11.50	5 289	12 963
morph.	92 568	5 174 631	55.90	84 382	106 850
/usr/dict/words	45 407	409 093	9.01	23109	47346

equivalent if they are either both final or both non-final, and they have the same transitions (the same number, labels, and targets). Methods 1, 3, and 4 require sorted data; the strings must be sorted lexicographically, lexicographically on reversals of strings, and on decreasing lengths respectively. The following methods have been investigated:

1. Incremental construction for sorted data ([2]).
2. Incremental construction for unsorted data ([2]).
3. Semi-incremental construction by Bruce Watson ([7]).
4. Semi-incremental construction by Dominique Revuz ([4]).
5. Building a trie and minimizing it using the Hopcroft algorithm ([3], [1]).
6. Building a trie and minimizing it using the minimization phase from the incremental construction algorithms (postorder minimization).
7. Building a trie and minimizing it using the minimization phase from the algorithm by Dominique Revuz (lexicographical sort [5]).

3   Experiments

Data sets for evaluation were taken from the domain of Natural language Processing (NLP). Acyclic automata are widely used as dictionaries. Both word lists, and morphological dictionaries, for German, French, and Polish, as well as a word list for English were used. Word lists and morphological dictionaries have different characteristics. Strings in word lists are usually short, sharing short suffixes. Strings in morphological dictionaries are much longer, with long suffixes shared between entries. The data is summarized in Table 1.

All methods were implemented in a single program, with data structures and most functions shared among different algorithms. Unfortunately, there is not enough space in a short paper to describe the implementation in detail. In the experiments, the hash function had 10001 possible values. The register was implemented with an overflow area for each hash value being a set class from the C++ standard template library - a tree-like structure.

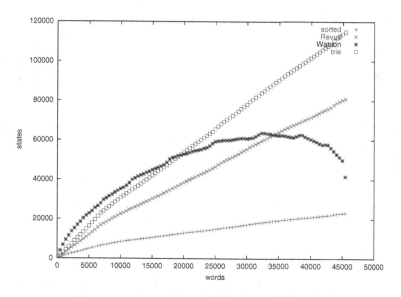

Fig. 1. Memory requirements for English words.

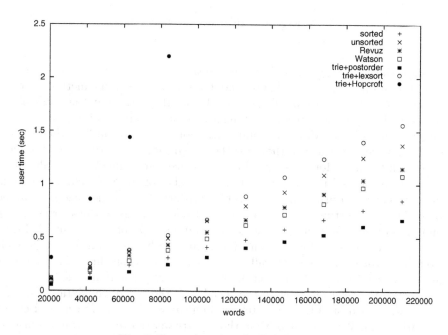

Fig. 2. Execution time for Polish words

Figure 1 shows how the number of states grows during construction of an automaton for a representative data set using various algorithms. The points labeled "trie" represent non-incremental methods. Memory requirements for construction algorithms are proportional to the number of states of the largest au-

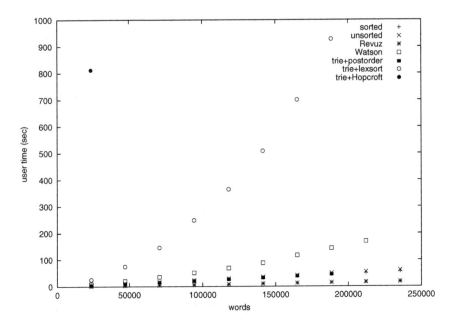

Fig. 3. Execution time for French morphology

tomaton during construction. The diagram shows that only incremental methods keep the automaton minimal throughout the process – other methods require memory for additional redundant states before they arrive at the minimal automaton. The intermediate automaton for non-incremental methods can be much larger than minimal. Memory requirements for the incremental method for unsorted data are identical to those for the sorted method on the same data, and only slightly higher for data sorted for other methods. The Watson's algorithm displays an unusual behavior. The largest number of states is achieved approximately half way during the construction process. This phenomenom is caused by two factors: sorting of input data (from longest strings to the shortest ones), and minimization scheme (prefixes cause minimization of larger words). Initial memory requirements for Watson's algorithm are higher than for a trie made from data sorted lexicographically, as longer words come first. They become lower towards the end of data, as shorter words trigger minimization.

To test the relation between the speed, and the size of the data, each algorithm was tested on 0.1, 0.2, ... 0.9, and on the whole data. In case of Revuz's algorithm, and Watson's algorithm, those parts were sorted accordingly, instead of taking the same number of words from the beginning of the whole file sorted according to the requirements. This is different than measurements of memory requirements, because they were all taken during a single run on the whole appropriate file. Also, due to multiuser, multitask unix environment, only processor times were measured, not the elapsed "real" time. It means that the effects of swapping do not show up on diagrams. Only initial values for trie + Hopcroft minimization algorithm are shown to underline differences between other algorithms. For most data, the trie + postorder minimization method was the fastest. It was slightly faster than the algorithm for sorted data, and in some cases their values are not distinguishable on diagrams. For morphological dictionaries, Revuz's algorithm was faster (Fig 3). This happens because in that data very long common suffixes were present. The INTEX program [6] uses Revuz's algorithm without pseudo-minimization phase to save both time and disk space, but annotations are kept short, and their expansions are kept elsewhere.

4   The Fastest Algorithm

Surprisingly, the fastest construction algorithm is not yet described in literature. This is probably due to its simplicity. We define a deterministic finite state automaton as $M = (Q, \Sigma, \delta, q_0, F)$, where Q is the set of states, Σ is the alphabet, $\delta \in Q \times \Sigma \longrightarrow Q \cup \{\bot\}$ is the transition function, q_0 is the initial state, and $F \subseteq Q$ is the set of final states. A somewhat formally awkward notation of assignment to the delta function in the algorithm below means creating or modifying a transition. This algorithm has exactly the same complexity as both incremental algorithms from [2].

```
func trie_plus_postorder_minimization;
    start_state := construct_trie; Register := ∅;
    postorder_minimize(start_state);
    return start_state;
cnuf

func construct_trie();
    start := new state;
    while file not empty
        word := next word form file; i := 0; s := start;
        while i < length(word)
            if δ(s, word_i) ≠ ⊥ → δ(s, word_i) := new state; fi
            s := δ(s, word_i); i := i + 1;
        elihw
        F := F ∪ {s};
    elihw
cnuf

proc postorder_minimize(s);
    foreach a ∈ Σ : δ(s, a) ≠ ⊥
        postorder_minimize(δ(s, a));
        if ∃_{q∈Register} δ(s, a) ≡ q → δ(s, a) = q;
        else Register := Register ∪{s}; fi
    hcaerof
corp
```

5   Conclusions

- For unsorted data, the trie + postorder register-based minimization algorithm is the fastest, provided that we have enough memory to use it. The difference between the minimal automaton and the corresponding trie can be huge.
- All but incremental methods produce intermediate automata much larger than the minimal ones. All alternatives to the incremental algorithm for unsorted data build a trie first – the worst possible case from the point of view of memory efficiency. Therefore, the incremental algorithm for unsorted data is the fastest algorithm for unsorted data in practical applications, and in fact the only algorithm for that purpose.
- For typical sorted data, the trie + postorder register-based minimization algorithm can be used, but as it builds a trie, it requires huge amounts of memory. The incremental algorithm for sorted data can be used instead with almost no performance penalty. For sorted data where strings share long suffixes, like in certain morphological data, Revuz's algorithm is the fastest. However, such data can easily be transformed so that the long suffixes are stored separately (as it is done e.g. in INTEX). For the transformed data, Revuz's algorithm is no longer the fastest one. It also requires non-standard sorting that cannot be performed efficiently using ready-made programs. Moreover, tools for constructing natural language morphologies have additional data that can be used for faster construction algorithms. The author has implemented such an algorithm.
- Both fully incremental algorithms are the most economical in their use of memory. They are orders of magnitude better than other, even semi-incremental methods. Even for a very small data set, like the one presented on Figure 1, the intermediate automata in semi-incremental methods are 3-4 times larger than the minimal ones.
- Both incremental algorithms are the fastest in practical applications, i.e. for large data sets. The algorithm for sorted data is the fastest, but if data is not sorted, sorting it (and storing it in memory) may be more costly than using the algorithm for unsorted data. However, when the same data is used repeatedly, sorting is always beneficial.
- It seems that incremental algorithms do not introduce much overhead when compared to non-incremental methods. The differences between the incremental sorted data algorithm and its non-incremental counterpart are minimal. The non-incremental version of the semi-incremental Revuz's algorithm (trie + lexical sort) is sometimes faster than the original version for words, and always slower for morphologies.
- Trie + Hopcroft minimization is the slowest algorithm. While all other algorithms are linear, this one has an additional $\mathcal{O}(\log(n))$ overhead, and it is quite complicated compared to register-based algorithms.

Acknowledgements. The outline of experiments was discussed with Bruce Watson. This research was carried out within the framework of the PIONIER

Project *Algorithms for Linguistic Processing*, funded by NWO (Dutch Organization for Scientific Research) and the University of Groningen. The program used in the experiments is available from
http://www.eti.pg.gda.pl/~jandac/adfa.html.

References

1. A. V. Aho, J. E. Hopcroft, and J. D. Ullman. *The Design and Analysis of Computer Algorithms*. Addison-Wesley Publishing Company, 1974.
2. Jan Daciuk, Stoyan Mihov, Bruce Watson, and Richard Watson. Incremental construction of minimal acyclic finite state automata. *Computational Linguistics*, 26(1):3–16, April 2000.
3. John E. Hopcroft. An n log n algorithm for minimizing the states in a finite automaton. In Z. Kohavi, editor, *The Theory of Machines and Computations*, pages 189–196. Academic Press, 1971.
4. Dominique Revuz. *Dictionnaires et lexiques: méthodes et algorithmes*. PhD thesis, Institut Blaise Pascal, Paris, France, 1991. LITP 91.44.
5. Dominique Revuz. Minimisation of acyclic deterministic automata in linear time. *Theoretical Computer Science*, 92(1):181–189, 1992.
6. Max Silberztein. INTEX tutorial notes. In *Workshop on Implementing Automata WIA99 – Pre-Proceedings*, pages XIX–1 – XIX–31. 1999.
7. Bruce Watson. A fast new (semi-incremental) algorithm for the construction of minimal acyclic DFAs. In *Third Workshop on Implementing Automata*, pages 91–98, Rouen, France, September 1998. Lecture Notes in Computer Science, Springer.

Term Validation of Distributed Hard Real-Time Applications

Gaëlle Largeteau and Dominique Geniet

Laboratoire d'Informatique Scientifique et Industrielle,
Université de Poitiers & ENSMA,
Téléport 2 - 1 avenue Clément Ader
BP 40109 86961 Futuroscope Chasseneuil cédex, France
{largeteau,dgeniet}@ensma.fr

Abstract. To validate real-time systems, one must especially validate on the one hand its functional behaviours (by proving that it does what it must do), and on the other hand its operational behaviours (by proving that it respects its time specifications). Here, we deal with the operational aspects. In previous works, we presented a technique, based on finite automata, to validate real-time systems designed to run on a centralised architecture. Here, we extend this approach to distributed systems. The main contribution of this work is to show that, when the modeled physical process is closed, finite automata and product operators are sufficient to valid distributed systems on an operational way.

1 Introduction

A real-time system is **reactive** and **concurrent** (all operations associated with a process managing have to run simultaneously). It is a set of elementary **tasks**, each of them coding a reaction to incoming events. This set is composed of **periodic** and **non periodic** tasks (related to alarm signals and user actions). Validity of a real-time system is based on both the correctness of its results and its conformity to timing constraints. There are two classes of real-time systems: **hard** and **soft** systems. If not respecting terms implies irretrievable consequences, the system is **hard**, otherwise the system is **soft**. Here, we deal with hard real-time systems composed of periodic tasks.

Validating a real-time system consists in proving that it will always be able to react in conformity with its timing constraints, whatever the incoming event flow. The term validation is then a decision process related to task scheduling sequences. It usually follows two main approaches: first, *in-line* approach consists in choosing the task to elect for any context switch during the application run. Since computing task system scheduling issue with critical resources is NP-complete [2], this approach is not optimal[1] for almost every task configuration, and it has an exponential complexity. To solve this problem, the *off-line*

---

[1] A scheduling algorithm is optimal if and only if it gives a valid scheduling sequence when there exists one.

J.-M. Champarnaud and D. Maurel (Eds.): CIAA 2002, LNCS 2608, pp. 262–269, 2003.

approach uses formal models to search for existence of at least one scheduling sequence satisfying constraints (through model checking techniques).

The fast technological evolution in recent years (especially in network communications) has resulted in using distributed systems as a base for hard real-time applications more and more frequently. These systems stand founded on real-time protocols integrating timing constraints for messages transmissions. Since scheduling distributed systems is NP-difficult, the *in-line* approach is still not optimal. We use the *off-line* approach defined in [3][4] to suggest a method that validates distributed systems on an operational way. Its principle is to integrate communication protocols in the model and to adapt the model to targets with different processor speeds. The physical architecture is composed of a set of sites, that communicate through a network. Each site dispose of many processors, and of a RAM shared between its processors. All the processors follow the local clock of the site. Moreover, each site dispose of a network board, which contains a specialised processor. Real-time system validation involves the foreseeability of behaviors. Since using cache or pipeline induces nondeterminism, they are always disabled in real-time systems: here, we make the assumption, in the framework of validation, that none are used.

Firstly, the model is presented in the framework of centralised real-time systems with fixed execution time tasks. Then, we describe a modelling technique for distributed real-time systems integrating speed differences. We show how product automata can be used to model simultaneity in distributed systems. We assume that there is no task migration. The task placement is not considered.

2 Centralised Systems Validation

2.1 Task Temporal Modelling

A real-time software is a set of atomic tasks. We denote $(\tau_i)_{i \in [1,n]}$ such a system. Each task τ_i is specified by: its arrival time r_i, its deadline D_i, its period T_i, and C_i, the CPU execution time of each instance of the task. Parameters r_i, D_i and T_i come from the specifications of the external system, but C_i depends on both the code of the task and the performances of the target processor. We assume that all atomic statements have the same duration of one *time unit*[2]. Hence, C_i is constant in time units. On the opposite, r_i, D_i and T_i do not depend on the CPU frequency: they are not fixed in time unit. In the following, we use this property to build a model language which takes into account both term specifications, and performances of the processor.

Let τ be a task of timing constraints r, D and T. The code ξ of τ is a word over the set P of atomic statements. The execution duration C of τ is extracted from this code. During its execution, τ can be active or suspended whether it owns the processor or not. Then, for each time unit, observing τ state allows to build an activity/inactivity sequence for τ. The set of sequences that respects the specified timing constraints is the τ temporal model. Our aim is to build this

---

[2] Time unit is the duration of a non-preemptive instruction (assembler).

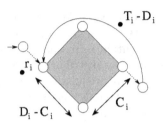

Fig. 1. Task Model

set, i.e to build the regular language $L(\tau)$. We consider time as implicit: each task processes one action by time unit. Letter a models the activity state of τ for one time unit, and $\bullet$ models its suspended state for one time unit. We note $\Sigma=\{a, \bullet\}$. The temporal model associated with ξ is the word $\phi(\xi)$, where ϕ is the concatenation morphism $P \to \{a\}$. The length of $\phi(\xi)$ is the duration C of τ. The τ temporal model $L_u(\tau)$ is obtained by given the system inactivity periods (using $\bullet$). We use the *Shuffle*[3] operator $\amalg$, the generic expression of the model is given in [3] by[4] $L(\tau) = Center(\bullet^r((\bullet^{D-C}\amalg\phi(\xi))\bullet^{T-D})^*)$. Each word **w** of this language has got the same length T and is called **valid temporal behavior** of τ. The automaton associated with $L(\tau)$ have a generic pattern that depends on the temporal features of the application (see figure1).

Task τ is running on a processor with particular temporal features : we define a **time unit** as the time interval between two clock ticks, and a **cadence** as the inverse of its duration. In the multi-processor case, all processors of a same site work in a synchronous way. The duration of τ is then equal to $\mid \phi(\xi) \mid \times u_S$ on site S, and $\mid \phi(\xi) \mid \times u_T$ on site T. The τ temporal features (D, T, etc.) are no longer expressed in the language directly as the occurrence number of $\bullet$, but as the occurrence number of $\bullet$ that is necessary to model the inactivity time corresponding to the target processor. We note $L_u(\tau)$ the set of τ valid temporal behaviors on a processor that have **u** for time unit.

Example 1. Let be τ with $(r,D,T,C)=(3ms,8ms,10ms,3t.u.[5])$. A τ model can be $L_{1ms}(\tau) = Center(\bullet^3((\bullet^5\amalg a^3)\bullet^2)^*)$, or $L_{250\mu s}(\tau) = Center(\bullet^{12}((\bullet^{29}\amalg a^3)\bullet^8)^*)$.

The rate between **a**'s and $\bullet$'s depend on the target *cadence*. In the following, we show that task τ, defined with temporal characteristics (r,D,T,C), and designed to run on a processor with a cadence **c(u=1/c)**, can always be associated with a regular language $L_u(\tau)$. In order to integrate processor features in the model, values expressed in seconds (r, D, T) have to be converted in time units. Let u be the time unit associated with the processor, x seconds correspond to $\frac{x}{u}$ t.u.

---

[3] *Shuffle*($\amalg$), is defined by the formula: $\forall a \in \Sigma$, a $\amalg \varepsilon = a$ and $\forall(a,b,w,w') \in \Sigma^2 \times (\Sigma^*)^2$, aw $\amalg$bw'= a (w $\amalg$bw') $\cup$ b (aw $\amalg$w').

[4] The L *center* is the set of L prefixes indefinitely extendable in L, algebraically, Center(L^*)=L^*.LeftFactors(L).

[5] t.u. for time unit

on this processor. The values in seconds of r, D and T equal respectively to $\frac{r}{u}$, $\frac{D}{u}$ and $\frac{T}{u}$ t.u.. Usually, timing constraints r, D and T are of the order of 10^{-1}s and the time unit **u** is of the order of 10^{-5}s. Since $\mathbb{Q}$ is dense in $\mathbb{R}$, we can assume that $\frac{r}{u}$, $\frac{D}{u}$ and $\frac{T}{u}$ are integers. By using the same approach than in [3], we get $L_u(\tau)= \text{Center}(\bullet^{\frac{r}{u}}((\bullet^{(\frac{D}{u}-C)}\amalg\phi(\xi))\bullet^{(\frac{T-D}{u})})^*)$ as task model. We note $\dot{\tau}$ the set $\{L_u(\tau), u \in \mathbb{Q}^{*+}\}$.

2.2   Validation

We have defined in [3][4] a technique, based on the Arnold-Nivat [1] model, to collect all valid scheduling sequences of a task system. The principle consists first in associating each critical resource R_j (processor, resource, message, etc.) with a virtual task V_{Rj} (modeled by a regular language $L(V_{Rj})$), and then associating the system $(\tau_i)_{i\in I}$ with the homogeneous product Ω of the $L(\tau_i)$ and the $L(V_{Rj})$. Let call S the subset of $\prod_{i\in I}(\Sigma_i)$ of vectors describing valid configurations (respecting mutual exclusion on processors or resources). We prove in [4] that language[6] $\text{Proj}_I(\text{Center}(L(\tau)_{i\in I}\cap S^*))$ collects the set of valid scheduling sequences, from resources management and timing constraints point of view.

Validating a real-time tasks system $(\tau_i)_{i\in I}$ consists in deciding if the configuration $(\tau_i)_{i\in I}$ can be scheduled in conformity with its time constraints. This decision is reached by evaluating the predicate $(center(\Omega_{i\in I}s(L(\tau_i))) = \emptyset)$ using an automaton associated with the language. If the language is empty, there exists a valid temporal behavior, then the configuration can be scheduled, otherwise there is no way to schedule the system.

3   Model for Distributed Systems

A distributed system is defined by a lack of common memory, a use of communication system and by the fact that there is no global state that can be observed [5]. Such a system is characterised by a set of sites, running with different speeds. Each site has a local clock that does not depend on others and that is the reference for every processor of the site. A clock is defined as an increasing sequence depending on time. A model that collects behaviors of a distributed system must be able to express simultaneity of different tasks placed on different sites, with no assumption concerning both a *global* time and correlations between the different speeds of the sites.

The model presented in section 2 is useful to validate real-time systems placed on a single site, possibly multi-processor. The speed of the site is implicitly modeled by the the time unit associated with the labels of the edges of the product automaton which models the software. A distributed system can be viewed (on a model way) as a set of such automata, each automaton being associated with its own time unit. As far as the target architecture is known and static, we know a priori the different speeds of the differents sites. To build an

---

[6] $\text{Proj}_I(\text{Center}(L(\tau)_{i\in I}\cap S^*))$ is noted $\Omega_{i\in I}s(L(\tau_i))$ in the following.

automaton that collects all behaviors of the system, we need two tools. First, a *zoom* technique, to accord the different automata with the same time semantics: we can not give a semantics to a product automaton $A\Omega B$, when A and B do not share the same time semantics. Second, a *start* result, to show that respective starting times of different sites have no incidence on the time validity of the software. The *zoom* technique is presented in section 3.1. The *start* result is obtained as an obvious corollary of properties of words of a regular language center.

3.1 *Zoom Languages*

In $\dot{\tau}$ building process (recall that $\dot{\tau}=\{L_u(\tau), u \in \mathbb{Q}^{*+}\}$), we take various CPU speeds into account. We obtain a language class which satisfies the following property: for each word of each language of $\dot{\tau}$, the rate between **a**'s and •'s is a function of the cadence. Consider $L_u \in \dot{\tau}$. We call **granularity** the time associated with each letter duration into L_u words. It is the time semantics of each edge of the automaton. We note $_gL_u$ the observation of L_u with the granularity g (i.e. the *zoom rate* $\frac{g}{u}$).

Example 2. : let $L = \{a\}$ be a language associated with the time unit *1ms*: the duration of **a** is 1ms. Consider the language M=$\{a^n\}$ associated with the duration $\frac{1}{n}$ ms. L and M share the same semantics, because they both contain the same behaviour, which semantics is "τ is in the a state during 1ms": $|a| \times 1 = |a^n| \times \frac{1}{n}$. On the opposite, we observe that N=$\{a^n\}$associated with a duration of $\frac{1}{(n-1)}$ is not equivalent to L : $|a|\times 1 \neq |a^n| \times \frac{1}{(n-1)}$. M is the observation of L with the **granularity** $\frac{1}{n}$.

To build the product $L_u\Omega L_v$, L_u and L_v must be observed with the same granularity. Then, we must be able to get $g \in \mathbb{Q}$ such that both $_gL_u$ and $_gL_v$ exist. Then, we must build the set $\overline{L_u(\tau)}$ of languages that collects behaviors of L_u in different granularities, i.e. the set of $_gL_u(\tau)$ associated with task τ running on a site that has **u** as a time unit and observed with a granularity **g**. To build $\overline{L_u(\tau)}$, we use the isomorphism ψ, defined by:

$$\psi_{u,g} : P_c \cup \{a, \bullet\} \rightarrow (P_c \cup \{a, \bullet\})^k \text{ such that } k = u/g,$$
$$\forall x \notin P_c, \psi(x) = x^k ;$$
$$\forall x \in \{P, S\}, \psi(x) = a^{k-1}.x ;$$
$$\forall x \in \{V, R\}, \psi(x) = x.a^{k-1}.$$

Then $\overline{L_u(\tau)}=\{_gL_u(\tau), _gL_u(\tau) \subset \Sigma^* / \exists g \in \mathbb{Q}^{+*}, u \in g\mathbb{N}^*, _gL_u(\tau)=\psi_{u,g}(L_u(\tau))\}$. Given $_{g_1}L_{u_1}$ and $_{g_2}L_{u_2}$. We remark that $_{g_1}L_{u_1}\Omega_{g_2}L_{u_2}$ have a time semantics if and only if $g_1=g_2$. The model expresses simultaneity through the homogeneous product Ω of languages, our goal is then to find a granularity g which, applied to all sites, gives a temporal semantics to the product. To reach this aim, we extend in a natural way the GCD notion to $\mathbb{Q}$ (GCD operator is noted $\wedge$).

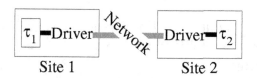

Fig. 2. Distributed application example

Theorem 1. *Given $L_{u_1}(\tau_1)$ and $L_{u_2}(\tau_2)$. Then, $\exists g \in \mathbb{Q}^{+*}$, $g = u_1 \wedge u_2$ and $_gL_{u_1}(\tau_1) \subset \Sigma^*$, $_gL_{u_2}(\tau_2) \subset \Sigma^*$ such that $_gL_{u_1}(\tau_1) \in \overline{L_{u_1}(\tau_1)}$ and $_gL_{u_2}(\tau_2) \in \overline{L_{u_2}(\tau_2)}$*

Obtained languages are maximal: $\not\exists g' > g /_{g'}L_{u_1}(\tau_1) \in \overline{L_{u_1}(\tau_1)}$, $_{g'}L_{u_2}(\tau_2) \in \overline{L_{u_2}(\tau_2)}$. Moreover, ψ gives a constructing algorithm for this languages class. This theorem gives a technique to build a set of languages sharing the same granularity. This set allows to use homogeneous product for the composition of systems placed on different sites. This approach stands whatever the site speeds and start times and it can be used in the frame of multi-processor centralised systems that do not have a global clock.

3.2 Communication Integration

In the previous part, we have established our model validity in the distributed case. We apply the homogeneous product to languages corresponding to each site. We note $L_{u_n}(S_n)$ the language associated to the site S_n.

Let $(L_{u_i}(S_i))_{i \in J}$ be the set of languages associated with sites. We use Theorem 1 (section 3.1): let be $G = \wedge_{i \in J}(u_i)$, and $(_GL(S_i))_{i \in J}$ the set of languages such that: $\forall i \in J$, $L(S_i) = \psi_{u_i,G}(L_{u_i}(S_i))$. Languages $(_GL(S_i))_{i \in J}$ are all built on the same granularity G, we can therefore build $_GL = (\Omega(_GL(S_i))_{i \in J})$. $_GL$ gives the system $(\tau_i)_{i \in I}$ model on sites $(S_j)_{j \in J}$.

To temporarily validate this system, we have to integrate communication protocols into the model. Our aim is to warrant that message transmissions stay in temporal terms.

Then, it is necessary to have a model for network behaviors (see figure 2). To obtain the model for all the drivers, we first model one of them, and then their simultaneous run using the Arnold-Nivat's product. The driver task is duplicated in order to run on each site of the system, on a dedicated processor (the network board CPU). The model language that collects driver behaviors is called D, it is built on the network. The language D has the granularity g_D of one bit transmission duration.

For all j in J, $_{g_D}D_{g_D}$ is the driver i associated language. All drivers share the same code and then the same language. Let *Prot* be the synchronisation set expressing protocol communication constraints. Then $_{g_D}R = \Omega_{i \in I} Prot(_{g_D}D)$, is the model for the network (see figure3). This method can be used for any protocol that supports an automaton based model.

We check then the compatibility of message transmission and application timing constraints. To warrant application terms, a message must be transmitted

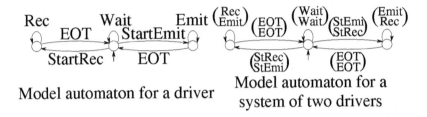

Fig. 3. Driver and Network automata

in a limited time: it has a deadline. We use a virtual task Stw (stopwatch) that keeps a record of the elapsed time between a message *Send* and its *Receive*.

This deadline, associated with a network model, allows to decide the compatibility between transmission and timing constraints. Granularity of Stw is G. Let $_G$Msg=Proj$_{Stw}$($_G$L Ω_{Sr} $_G$Stw), computed with a resource synchronisation (Sr) on the stopwatch [sec.2.2]. To test transmission validity, we must compute the languages $_G$Msg and $_{g_D}$R homogeneous product. We apply Theorem 1: using H=G∧g, we get $_H$Msg and $_H$R.

Language $_H$L=Center($_H$Msg$\Omega_{Sr}$$_H$R) collects the set of valid messages scheduling (respecting timing constraints) on the network. The validity test is the same as in centralised system validation: If $_H$L=∅ then there is no valid behavior, otherwise, there exists at least one.

4   Conclusion

Languages $L_u(\tau)$ are useful to validate hard real time distributed systems, if they are based on protocols that can be modeled by regular languages. The centralised model was extended by considering processors speed and by defining a *zoom* operation on languages. This last tool, associated with a generalisation of GCD to ℚ, is useful to model with finite automata distributed systems with no addition of restrictive hypothesis (the only one is the closure of the modeled system: this is not a restriction when considering real-time systems!).

The result is a schedulability decision for the application on a distributed architecture. One of the central corollaries of this approach is the cyclicity of scheduling sequences in distributed multi-processor environnement: this result is an immediate corrolary (star lemma) of the fact that valid scheduling set is a regular language.

This work is ongoing. Our present studies concern both the integration of task migration and the integration of a small level of non determinism by considering alarm events.

References

1. A.Arnold: Finite transition systems. Prentice Hall. (1994).
2. S.K.Baruah, L.E.Rosier, R.R.Howell: Algorithms and Complexity Concerning the Preemptive Scheduling of Periodic Real-Time Tasks on one Processor. Real Time Systems. Teknea. (1990).
3. D.Geniet: Validation d'applications temps réel à contraintes strictes à l'aide de languages rationnels. Real Time Systems. Teknea. (2000).
4. D.Geniet, G.Largeteau: Validation d'applications temps réel strictes à durées variables à l'aide de languages rationnels. Modélisation des Systèmes Réactifs. Hermes sciences. Toulouse. (2001).
5. M.Raynal: Synchronisation et état global dans les systèmes répartis. Eyrolles.(1992).

Common Subsequence Automaton*

Zdeněk Troníček

Dept. of Comp. Science and Eng., FEE CTU Prague
Karlovo nám. 13, 121 35 Prague 2, Czech Republic
tronicek@fel.cvut.cz

Abstract. Given a set of strings, a common subsequence of this set is a string that is a subsequence of each string in this set. We describe an on-line algorithm building the finite automaton that accepts all common subsequences of the given set of strings.

1 Introduction

A *subsequence* of a string T is any string obtainable by deleting zero or more symbols from T. Given a set P of strings, a *common subsequence* of P is a string that is a subsequence of every string in P. Problems on subsequences arise in many areas, *e.g.* in molecular biology and coding theory. One of the problems with great practical impact is the longest common subsequence (LCS) problem. The problem is to find, given a set P of strings, a common subsequence of P that has maximal length among all common subsequences of P. If the number of strings in P is not bounded, the problem is NP-complete, as was shown by Maier [9].

The algorithms for the LCS problem are usually divided into two groups in literature: the algorithms for the LCS of two strings, and the algorithms for the LCS of three or more strings. This separation is sensible, because many algorithms from the former group do not have any straightforward generalization for three or more strings. We shortly mention several algorithms from both groups.

The first solution of the LCS problem of two strings was probably dynamic programming, which was discovered independently by several scientists. Improvements were described by Hirschberg [4] and Hunt and Szymanski [7]. An algorithm with the best known worst-case time complexity was given by Masek and Paterson [10]. Itoga [8] extended the dynamic programming for the case of arbitrary number of strings. Hsu and Du [6] introduced a common subsequence tree. Crochemore and Troníček [2] described an automaton that accepts all common subsequences of the given strings and gave an off-line algorithm for its building.

Another problem on subsequences is to decide, for a string S and a set P of strings, whether S is a subsequence of P. Preprocessing strings in P allows to solve the problem in time linear in the length of S. Baeza-Yates [1] described the

---

* This research has been supported by GAČR grant No. 201/01/1433.

J.-M. Champarnaud and D. Maurel (Eds.): CIAA 2002, LNCS 2608, pp. 270–275, 2003.

automaton accepting all subsequences of given set of strings and a right-to-left algorithm for its building. This automaton is called Directed Acyclic Subsequence Graph (DASG). Crochemore and Troníček [2] gave a left-to-right algorithm. An on-line algorithm is from Hoshino *et al.* [5].

In this paper, we describe an on-line algorithm building the CSA. The language accepted by the CSA is a subset of the language accepted by the DASG for the same strings. This implies similarity between the CSA and DASG. The on-line algorithm building the CSA described below is modification of the algorithm from [5]. A possible application of the CSA is the LCS problem or the problem of separating two sets of strings. Given two sets P and N of strings, we say that a string S separates P and N if S is a subsequence of P and simultaneously S is not a subsequence of any string in N. The problem has application in discovery science and machine learning [3]. We slightly reformulate the problem: given two sets P and N of strings and a string S, we ask if S separates P and N. We assume that the problem should be answered for several different strings S. Then it makes sense to preprocess strings in P and N. With the CSA for P and the DASG for N, we are able to answer the question in time linear in the length of S.

The paper is organized as follows. In section 2 we recall the definition of the CSA from [2], in section 3 we prove two properties of the CSA, and in section 4 we describe an on-line algorithm building the CSA.

Let Σ be a finite alphabet of size σ and ε the empty word. A finite automaton is, in this paper, a 5-tuple $(Q, \Sigma, \delta, q_0, F)$, where Q is a finite set of states, Σ is an input alphabet, $\delta : Q \times \Sigma \to Q$ is a transition function, q_0 is the initial state, and $F \subseteq Q$ is the set of final states. Notation $\langle i, j \rangle$ means the interval of integers from i to j, including both i and j. All strings in this paper are considered on alphabet Σ.

2 Definition of CSA

Let P denote a set of strings $T_1, T_2, \ldots, T_k$. Let n_i be the length of T_i and $T_i[j]$ be j-th symbol of T_i for all $j \in \langle 1, n_i \rangle$ and all $i \in \langle 1, k \rangle$. Given $T = t_1 t_2 \ldots t_n$ and $i, j \in \langle 1, n \rangle, i \leq j$, notation $T[i \ldots j]$ means the string $t_i t_{i+1} \ldots t_j$.

Definition 1. *We define a position point of the set P as an ordered k-tuple $[p_1, p_2, \ldots, p_k]$, where $p_i \in \langle 0, n_i \rangle$ is a position in string T_i. If $p_i \in \langle 0, n_i - 1 \rangle$ then it denotes the position in front of $(p_i + 1)$-th symbol of T_i, and if $p_i = n_i$ then it denotes the position behind the last symbol of T_i for all $i \in \langle 1, k \rangle$.*

A position point $[p_1, p_2, \ldots, p_k]$ is called *initial position point* if $p_i = 0$ for all $i \in \langle 1, k \rangle$. We denote by *ipp* the initial position point and by $Pos(P)$ the set of all position points of P.

Definition 2. *For a position point $[p_1, p_2, \ldots, p_k] \in Pos(P)$ we define the common subsequence position alphabet as the set of all symbols which are contained simultaneously in $T_1[p_1+1 \ldots n_1], \ldots, T_k[p_k+1 \ldots n_k]$, i.e. $\Sigma_{cp}([p_1, p_2, \ldots, p_k]) = \{a \in \Sigma : \forall i \in \langle 1, k \rangle \exists j \in \langle p_i + 1, n_i \rangle : T_i[j] = a\}$.*

Definition 3. *For* $a \in \Sigma$ *and a position point* $[p_1, p_2, \ldots, p_k] \in Pos(P)$ *we define the common subsequence transition function:*
$csf([p_1, p_2, \ldots, p_k], a) = [r_1, r_2, \ldots, r_k]$, *where* $r_i = min\{j : j > p_i \text{ and } T_i[j] = a\}$ *for all* $i \in \langle 1, k \rangle$ *if* $a \in \Sigma_{cp}([p_1, p_2, \ldots, p_k])$, *and*
$csf([p_1, p_2, \ldots, p_k], a) = \emptyset$ *otherwise.*
Let csf^* *be reflexive-transitive closure of* csf.

Lemma 1. *The automaton* $(Pos(P), \Sigma, csf, ipp, Pos(P))$ *accepts a string* S *iff* S *is a subsequence of* P.

Proof. See [2]. □

The automaton from lemma 1 is called *Common Subsequence Automaton* (CSA) for strings $T_1, T_2, \ldots, T_k$.

We briefly describe an off-line algorithm building the CSA. The algorithm generates step by step all reachable position points (states). At each step we process one position point. First, we will find the common subsequence position alphabet for this point and then determine the common subsequence transition function for each symbol of that alphabet. When the position point has been processed, we continue with a next point until transitions of all reachable position points are determined. The complexity of the algorithm depends on the number of states of the outcoming automaton. If the total number of states is $O(t)$ then the algorithm requires $O(k\sigma t)$ time.

An ℓ-dominant match (also called minimal) of two strings is an ordered pair $[i_1, i_2]$ such that $T_1[i_1] = T_2[i_2]$, the length of the LCS of $T_1[1 \ldots i_1], T_2[1 \ldots i_2]$ is equal to ℓ, and the length of the LCS of pairs $T_1[1 \ldots i_1 - 1], T_2[1 \ldots i_2]$ and $T_1[1 \ldots i_1], T_2[1 \ldots i_2 - 1]$ is less than ℓ. We recall generalization of dominant matches for more than two strings: an ℓ-dominant match of $T_1, \ldots, T_k$ is an ordered k-tuple $[i_1, \ldots, i_k]$ such that $T_1[i_1] = \ldots = T_k[i_k]$, the length of the LCS of $T_1[1 \ldots i_1], \ldots, T_k[1 \ldots i_k]$ is equal to ℓ, and for arbitrary permutation $[j_1, \ldots, j_k]$ of $[1, 0, 0, \ldots, 0]$ is the length of the LCS of $T_1[1 \ldots i_1 - j_1], \ldots, T_k[1 \ldots i_k - j_k]$ less than ℓ.

3   Properties of CSA

First, we show the correspondence between the dominant matches and states of the CSA.

Lemma 2. *Given a set* P *of strings, a position point* $p \in Pos(P)$ *is reachable iff* p *is a dominant match of strings in* P.

Proof. We prove two implications:
1. If p is a dominant match of strings in P then p is reachable. Let $p = [p_1, p_2, \ldots, p_k]$ be an ℓ-dominant match and let $a_1 a_2 \ldots a_\ell$ be the longest common subsequence of strings $T_1[1 \ldots p_1], T_2[1 \ldots p_2], \ldots, T_k[1 \ldots p_k]$. If the longest common subsequence is not determined uniquely, we can choose an arbitrary

one. Obviously, $a_1 a_2 \ldots a_\ell$ determines the ℓ-dominant match. For two distinct ℓ-dominant matches we obtain the distinct longest common subsequences. Hence, $csf^*(ipp, a_1 a_2 \ldots a_\ell) = [p_1, p_2, \ldots, p_k]$ and so each dominant match is also a reachable position point.

2. If p is a reachable position point then p is a dominant match of strings in P. Since p is reachable, there exists path $a_1 a_2 \ldots a_\ell$ such that $csf^*(ipp, a_1 a_2 \ldots a_\ell) = p$. This path is a common subsequence of strings in P. We find the shortest prefix of each string in P such that this prefix contains the common subsequence. A dominant match is determined by these prefixes.   □

We will show that the number of dominant matches of two strings can be quadratic in the length of the input strings. The proof is based on the same idea as the proof of quadratic growth of the number of states for the DASG in [2].

Lemma 3. *Let* $T_1 = (ab)^{2x}, T_2 = (bab)^x$, *where* $x \in Z, x \geq 1$ *and let* R *denote the set of all reachable position points of* T_1, T_2. *Then,* R *contains the position points* $[2(i+j) - 3, 3i - 1]$ *for all* $i \in \langle 1, x \rangle$ *and all* $j \in \langle 1, i + 1 \rangle$.

Proof. (by induction):

1. $i = 1$: Clearly, $[1, 2], [3, 2] \in R$.

2. We write the position points for i (from the lemma): $[2i - 1, 3i - 1], [2i + 1, 3i - 1], \ldots, [4i - 1, 3i - 1]$. Further, we find out the transitions for each of these position points and generate new points:

$[2i - 1, 3i - 1] \xrightarrow{a} [2i + 1, 3i + 2]$

$[2i + 1, 3i - 1] \xrightarrow{a} [2i + 3, 3i + 2]$

$\vdots$

$[4i - 1, 3i - 1] \xrightarrow{a} [4i + 1, 3i + 2]$

$[4i - 1, 3i - 1] \xrightarrow{b} [4i, 3i] \xrightarrow{b} [4i + 2, 3i + 1] \xrightarrow{a} [4i + 3, 3i + 2]$

The new generated points $[2i + 1, 3i + 2], [2i + 3, 3i + 2], \ldots, [4i + 1, 3i + 2], [4i + 3, 3i + 2]$ are exactly the same as the points from the lemma for $i + 1$.   □

4   Building CSA

We will describe (informally) an on-line algorithm building the CSA for a set of strings $T_1, T_2, \ldots, T_k$. In the first step, we build the DASG for T_1 (which is also the CSA for T_1), and then in each subsequent step we load the next string. That is, after loading i-th string, we have the CSA for $T_1, T_2, \ldots, T_i$.

We will explain the idea of loading a string into the automaton. The states of the automaton are divided to active and non-active. At the beginning, before appending the first character of the string, only the initial state is active. Once a state becomes active, it remains active until the whole string is processed. We process each string character by character. When a character is being loaded, we examine transitions from all active states labeled with this character. Let q be a state where any (one or more) such transitions end. Two situations can occur: (1) all the transitions that lead to q start in active states – then no splitting of

q is needed, or (2) at least one input transition of q starts in a non-active state – then q must be split to two states. In this case, we create a new state with the same output transitions, and redirect all transitions leading to q and starting in an active state to the copy. The new active states are found as targets of transitions that start in an active state and are labeled with actual character. When the whole string is loaded, all states that are not active will be removed.

In general case, the automaton built by the presented algorithm is not minimal and can be minimized using a standard approach. The time complexity of loading string depends on the number of states of the automaton. We have not found any tight upper bound for the number of states. Providing that $n_1 = n_2 = \ldots = n_k = n$, the trivial upper bound is $1 + n^k$. If the number of states of the CSA after loading string T is $O(v)$ and we implement the set operations in logarithmic time, loading a string T requires $O(v\sigma \log v)$ time.

5   Conclusion

We have described the on-line algorithm building the CSA for a set of strings. We have also proven that the maximum number of states of the CSA for two strings is at least quadratic in the length of the input strings. However, the problem of tight upper bound for the number of states remains open.

Acknowledgment. Leszek Gąsieniec deserves many thanks for giving me the idea to deal with this automaton.

References

1. R. A. Baeza-Yates. Searching subsequences. *Theor. Comput. Sci.*, 78(2):363–376, 1991.
2. M. Crochemore and Z. Troníček. Directed acyclic subsequence graph for multiple texts. Rapport I.G.M. 99-13, Université de Marne-la-Vallée, 1999.
3. M. Hirao, H. Hoshino, A. Shinohara, M. Takeda, and S. Arikawa. A practical algorithm to find best subsequence patterns. In *Proceedings of the 3rd International Conference on Discovery Science*, volume 1967, pages 141–154. Springer-Verlag, Berlin, 2000.
4. D. S. Hirschberg. A linear space algorithm for computing maximal common subsequences. *Commun. ACM*, 18(6):341–343, 1975.
5. H. Hoshino, A. Shinohara, M. Takeda, and S. Arikawa. Online construction of subsequence automata for multiple texts. In *Proceedings of the String Processing and Information Retrieval: A South American Symposium 2000*, La Coruña, Spain, 2000. IEEE Computer Society Press.
6. W. J. Hsu and M. W. Du. Computing a longest common subsequence for a set of strings. *BIT*, 24:45–59, 1984.
7. J. W. Hunt and T. G. Szymanski. A fast algorithm for computing longest common subsequences. *Commun. ACM*, 20(5):350–353, 1977.
8. S. Y. Itoga. The string merging problem. *BIT*, 21:20–30, 1981.

9. D. Maier. The complexity of some problems on subsequences and supersequences. *J. Assoc. Comput. Mach.*, 25(2):322–336, 1978.

10. W. J. Masek and M. S. Paterson. A faster algorithm for computing string edit distances. *J. Comput. Syst. Sci.*, 20(1):18–31, 1980.

Searching for Asymptotic Error Repair⋆

Manuel Vilares, Victor M. Darriba, and Miguel A. Alonso

Department of Computer Science, University of A Coruña
Campus de Elviña s/n, 15071 A Coruña, Spain
{vilares,alonso}@udc.es,
darriba@dc.fi.udc.es

Abstract. We work in the domain of a regional least-cost strategy with
dynamic validation in order to avoid cascaded errors [3], extending the
theoretical model to illustrate its asymptotic equivalence with global
repair algorithms. This is an objective criterion to measure the quality of
an error repair algorithm, since the point of reference is a technique that
guarantees the best quality for a given error metric when all contextual
information is available. To the best of our knowledge, it is the first
time that such a discussion takes place. We also reformulate the parsing
framework using parsing schemata [1], simplifying the description.

1   The Parsing Model

Our aim is to parse a sentence $w_{1...n} = w_1 \ldots w_n$ according to an unrestricted
context-free grammar $\mathcal{G} = (N, \Sigma, P, S)$, where the empty string is represented by
ε. We generate from $\mathcal{G}$ a *push-down automaton* (PDA) for the language $\mathcal{L}(\mathcal{G})$. In
practice, we chose an LALR(1) device generated by ICE [2], although any shift-
reduce strategy is adequate. A PDA is a 7-tuple $\mathcal{A} = (Q, \Sigma, \Delta, \delta, q_0, Z_0, Q_f)$
where: Q is the set of states, Σ the set of input symbols, Δ the set of stack
symbols, q_0 the initial state, Z_0 the initial stack symbol, Q_f the set of final
states, and δ a finite set of transitions of the form $\delta(p, X, a) \ni (q, Y)$ with
$p, q \in Q$, $a \in \Sigma \cup \{\varepsilon\}$ and $X, Y \in \Delta \cup \{\varepsilon\}$.

To get polynomial complexity, we avoid duplicating stack contents when am-
biguity arises, storing them in a table $\mathcal{I}$ of *items*, $\mathcal{I} = \{[q, X, i, j],\ q \in Q,\ X \in$
$\{\varepsilon\} \cup \{\nabla_{r,s}\},\ 0 \le i \le j\}$; where q is the current state, X is the top of the
stack, and the positions i and j indicate the substring $w_{i+1} \ldots w_j$ spanned by
the last category pushed onto the stack. The symbol $\nabla_{r,s}$ indicates that the part
$A_{r,s+1} \ldots A_{r,n_r}$ of a rule $A_{r,0} \to A_{r,1} \ldots A_{r,n_r}$ has been recognized.

We describe the parser using *parsing schemata* [1]. A *parsing schema* is a
triple $\langle \mathcal{I}, \mathcal{H}, \mathcal{D} \rangle$, with $\mathcal{H} = \{[a, i, i+1],\ a = w_i\}$ an initial set of items called
hypothesis that encodes the sentence to be parsed[1], and $\mathcal{D}$ a set of *deduction*

⋆ Research partially supported by the Spanish Government under projects TIC2000-
  0370-C02-01 and HP2001-0044, and the Autonomous Government of Galicia under
  project PGIDT01PXI10506PN.
[1] The empty string, ε, is represented by the empty set of hypothesis, $\emptyset$. An input string
  $w_{1...n}$, $n \ge 1$ is represented by $\{[w_1, 0, 1], [w_2, 1, 2], \ldots, [w_n, n-1, n]\}$.

J.-M. Champarnaud and D. Maurel (Eds.): CIAA 2002, LNCS 2608, pp. 276–281, 2003.

steps that allow new items to be derived from already known items. Deduction steps are of the form $\{\eta_1, \ldots, \eta_k \vdash \xi \,/\, conds\}$, meaning that if all antecedents η_i are present and the conditions *conds* are satisfied, then the consequent ξ should be generated. In our case, $\mathcal{D} = \mathcal{D}^{\mathrm{Init}} \cup \mathcal{D}^{\mathrm{Shift}} \cup \mathcal{D}^{\mathrm{Sel}} \cup \mathcal{D}^{\mathrm{Red}} \cup \mathcal{D}^{\mathrm{Head}}$, where:

$$\mathcal{D}^{\mathrm{Shift}} = \{[q, X, i, j] \vdash [q', \varepsilon, j, j+1] \left/ \begin{array}{l} \exists\, [a, j, j+1] \in \mathcal{H} \\ shift_{q'} \in action(q, a) \end{array} \right.\}$$

$$\mathcal{D}^{\mathrm{Sel}} = \{[q, \varepsilon, i, j] \vdash [q, \nabla_{r,n_r}, j, j] \left/ \begin{array}{l} \exists\, [a, j, j+1] \in \mathcal{H} \\ reduce_r \in action(q, a) \end{array} \right.\}$$

$$\mathcal{D}^{\mathrm{Red}} = \{[q, \nabla_{r,s}, k, j][q', \varepsilon, i, k] \vdash [q', \nabla_{r,s-1}, i, j] \,/\, q' \in reveal(q)\}$$

$$\mathcal{D}^{\mathrm{Init}} = \{\vdash [q_0, \varepsilon, 0, 0]\} \qquad \mathcal{D}^{\mathrm{Head}} = \{[q, \nabla_{r,0}, i, j] \vdash [q', \varepsilon, i, j] \,/\, q' \in goto(q, A_{r,0})\}$$

with $q_0 \in \mathcal{Q}$ the initial state, and *action* and *goto* entries in the PDA tables. We say that $q' \in reveal(q)$ iff $\exists Y \in N \cup \Sigma$ such that $shift_q \in action(q', Y)$ or $q \in goto(q', Y)$, that is, when there exists a transition from q' to q in $\mathcal{A}$. A deduction step *Init* is in charge of starting the parsing process. The step *Shift* corresponds to pushing a terminal a onto the top of the stack when the action to be performed is a shift to state st'. A step *Sel* corresponds to pushing the ∇_{r,n_r} symbol onto the top of the stack in order to start the reduction of a rule r. The reduction of a rule of length $n_r > 0$ is performed by a set of n_r steps *Red*, each of them corresponding to a pop transition replacing the two elements $\nabla_{r,s} X_{r,s}$ placed on the top of the stack by the element $\nabla_{r,s-1}$. The reduction of a rule r is finished by a step *Head* corresponding to a swap transition that recognizes the top element $\nabla_{r,0}$ as equivalent to the left-hand side $A_{r,0}$ of that rule, and performs the corresponding change of state. The parse attains a worst case time (resp. space) complexity $\mathcal{O}(n^3)$ (resp. $\mathcal{O}(n^2)$). The input string has been recognized iff the final item $[q_f, \nabla_{0,0}, 0, n]$, $q_f \in \mathcal{Q}_f$ has been generated.

2   The Error Repair Algorithm

We first assume that we are dealing with the first error detected, using the terminology introduced in [3]. We extend the item structure with the accumulated error counter e, resulting in items $[p, X, i, j, e]$. Once the detection items have been fixed, we apply the set of deduction steps in error mode, $\mathcal{D}_{\mathrm{error}}$, that follows:

$$\mathcal{D}_{\mathrm{error}}^{\mathrm{Shift}} = \{[q, X, i, j, 0] \vdash [q', a, j, j+1, 0] \left/ \begin{array}{l} \exists [a, j, j+1] \in \mathcal{H} \\ shift_{q'} \in action(q, a) \end{array} \right.\}$$

$$\mathcal{D}_{\mathrm{error}}^{\mathrm{Insert}} = \{[q, \varepsilon, i, j, 0] \vdash [q, \varepsilon, j, j, I(a)] \,/\, \not\exists\, shift_{q'} \in action(q, a)\}$$

$$\mathcal{D}_{\mathrm{error}}^{\mathrm{Delete}} = \{[q, \varepsilon, i, j, 0] \vdash [q, \varepsilon, j, j+1, D(w_i)]\}$$

$$\mathcal{D}_{\mathrm{error}}^{\mathrm{Replace}} = \{[q, \varepsilon, i, j, 0] \vdash [q, \epsilon, j, j+1, R(a)] \,/\, \not\exists\, shift_{q'} \in action(q, a)\}$$

This process continues until a repair covers both error and detection items. Once this has been performed on each detection item, we select the corresponding regional repairs and the parse goes back to standard mode. Error counters are summarized at the time of reductions by adding counters on popped items:

$$\mathcal{D}_{\mathrm{error}}^{\mathrm{Sel}} = \{[q, \varepsilon, i, j, e] \vdash [q, \nabla_{r,n_r}, j, j, e], \; reduce_r \in action(q, a)\}$$

$$\mathcal{D}_{\mathrm{error}}^{\mathrm{Red}} = \{[q, \nabla_{r,s}, k, j, e][q', \varepsilon, i, k, e'] \vdash [q', \nabla_{r,s-1}, i, j, e+e'] \,/\, q' \in reveal(q)\}$$

$$\mathcal{D}_{\mathrm{error}}^{\mathrm{Head}} = \{[q, \nabla_{r,0}, i, j, e] \vdash [q', \varepsilon, i, j, e] \,/\, q' \in goto(q, A_{r,0})\}$$

with $\mathcal{D}_{error}^{Init} = \mathcal{D}^{Init}$. When the current repair is not the first one, it can modify a previous repair in order to avoid cascaded repairs by adding the cost of the new error hypotheses to profit from the experience gained from previous ones.

3 Asymptotic Behavior

We consider the arithmetical expressions to illustrate this point. In the worst case, when the error repair zone becomes the entire input string, performance and cost are the same as for global error repair. We introduce two deterministic grammars, $\mathcal{G}_L$ and $\mathcal{G}_R$, and a non-deterministic one $\mathcal{G}_N$:

$$\mathcal{G}_L: \text{E} \rightarrow \text{E} + \text{T} \mid \text{T} \qquad \mathcal{G}_R: \text{E} \rightarrow \text{T} + \text{E} \mid \text{T} \qquad \mathcal{G}_N: \text{S} \rightarrow \text{S} + \text{S} \mid (\text{S}) \mid \text{number}$$
$$\text{T} \rightarrow (\text{E}) \mid \text{number} \qquad \text{T} \rightarrow (\text{E}) \mid \text{number}$$

As $\mathcal{G}_N$ contains a rule "$S \rightarrow S+S$", sentences of the form $b_1+b_2+\ldots+b_{i+1}$ have a number of exponential parses, which allows us to evaluate strongly ambiguous contexts. In the deterministic case, parses are built from the left-associative (resp. right-associative) interpretation for $\mathcal{G}_L$ (resp. $\mathcal{G}_R$), in order to estimate the impact of traversal orientation. Erroneous input strings are of the form: "$b_1 + \ldots+b_{i-1}+(b_i+\ldots+(b_{[n/3]}+b_{[n/3]+1}b_{[n/3]+2}+\ldots+b_\ell b_{\ell+1}+b_{\ell+2}+\ldots+b_n$", where $i \in \{[n/3], \ldots, 1\}$ and $\ell = 3[n/3]-2i+1$, with $[n/3]$ being the integer part of $n/3$. Given i, regional repairs are obtained by replacing tokens b_{3i} by closed brackets to obtain "$b_1+\ldots+b_{i-1}+(b_i+\ldots+(b_{[n/3]}+b_{[n/3]+1})+\ldots+b_\ell)+b_{\ell+2}+\ldots+b_n$".

3.1 The Error Repair Region

We focus on the evolution of this region in relation to the location of the point of error, in opposition to static strategies associated to global repair approaches.

Location of Points of Detection. As is shown in the left-hand-side of Fig. 1, when we deal with global approach all input positions are points of detection. In the regional case, results depend on the grammar. So, although the number of points of detection grows with i because of the increase in the number of points of error, this number is higher for $\mathcal{G}_N$ (resp. $\mathcal{G}_R$). This is due to the right-associativity introduced by the rule "$S \rightarrow S + S$" (resp. "$E \rightarrow T + E$"), which generates a reduction for each "+" operator in the parsed prefix, illustrating the convergence of regional repairs with global ones. The reason for which results for $\mathcal{G}_N$ and $\mathcal{G}_R$ do not agree with results for the global case is because in regional repairs, operators "+" are not points of detection, while this is possible in a global one. The maximal number of points for $\mathcal{G}_N$ and $\mathcal{G}_R$, corresponding to the maximum size of the repair region as is shown in the right-hand-side of Fig. 1, is approximately half of those related to the global case.

Factors Determining the Size. We first focus on the case of $\mathcal{G}_R$ (resp. $\mathcal{G}_N$), profiting from the sequence of cascaded errors raised by the repair process exemplified. When the algorithm detects the first point of error at $b_{[n/3]+1}$, it takes

$b_{[n/3]}$ as point of detection and proposes as regional repair the replacement of $b_{[n/3]+2}$ by a closed bracket. Once this has been done, the algorithm returns the control to the parse until a new point of error is detected at $b_{[n/3]+3}$. In this case, "$(b_{[n/3]}$" is taken as the point of detection, which implies that we have moved back to a point previous to that proposed for the first error detected at $b_{[n/3]+1}$.

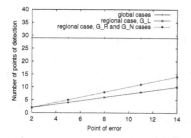 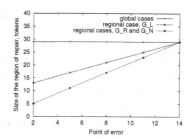

Fig. 1. Points of detection (resp. repair scope) *vs.* position of the point of error

More exactly, the algorithm asks whether the first regional repair applied was not optimal, taking into account the information about the parsing process now available. Perhaps the best solution for this first error would have been either to delete $b_{[n/3]+2}$ or to insert "+" between $b_{[n/3]+1}$ and $b_{[n/3]+2}$, which at that moment were not considered because the reductions defining the scopes of these repairs were not minimal in relation to that of the regional repair finally applied.

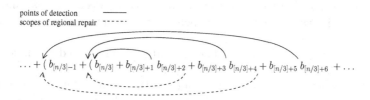

Fig. 2. An example on cascaded errors for $\mathcal{G}_R$ and $\mathcal{G}_N$

We then repeat the same steps as in the first case, proposing the regional repair that replaces $b_{[n/3]+4}$ by a closed bracket, followed by a shift over "+". So, the frontier of the new error repair region is "$(b_{[n/3]-1} + (b_{[n/3]} + b_{[n/3]+1}) + b_{[n/3]+3})$", which includes the scope of the previous regional repair, whose frontier was "$(b_{[n/3]} + b_{[n/3]+1})$"; as is shown in Fig. 2. The algorithm continues to apply the previous process for all $i \in \{[n/3], \ldots, 1\}$, until the size of the repair region extends to the whole original input string, as is shown in Fig. 1.

In the case of $\mathcal{G}_L$, the size of the repair region grows with the position of the point of error, b_l, $l \in \{[n/3] + 1, [n/3] + 3, \ldots, 3[n/3] - 2i + 1\}$. This behavior is also a consequence of the presence of cascaded errors, as is shown in Fig. 3. In comparison with previous results, when the algorithm detects the first point of error at $b_{[n/3]+1}$, it takes $b_{[n/3]}$ as the point of detection and proposes as regional

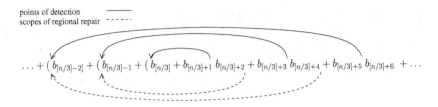

Fig. 3. An example on cascaded errors for $\mathcal{G}_L$

repair the replacement of $b_{[n/3]+2}$ by a closed bracket, as was the case for $\mathcal{G}_R$ and $\mathcal{G}_N$. As for $\mathcal{G}_R$, the rule providing the reduction is "$F \rightarrow (E)$". However, in this case, this reduction does not characterize a regional repair because it is followed by a chain of reductions in $\mathcal{G}_L$ previous to the next shift action, and not by an immediate shift action. These reductions are given by the rules "$T \rightarrow F$" and "$E \rightarrow E + T$", and the frontier of the repair region associated to this first error is "$b_{[n/3]-1} + (b_{[n/3]} + b_{[n/3]+1})$". Applying a similar reasoning to the next errors in the input string, we conclude that the sizes of the error repair regions are now larger, as is shown in the right-hand-side of Fig. 1, which also illustrates the asymptotic convergence with global repairs. So, the repair region when the last point of error, b_ℓ, is to the right of the input, includes the total input string.

3.2   The Computational Cost

Items are the basis for showing the computational behavior of our proposal. The cost of the algorithm is, in the worst case, given by the cost of global error repair approaches, due to asymptotic equivalence between regional and global repairs. Our aim is to focus on the dependency of grammar design.

The Case of Global Repairs. The generation is illustrated in the left-hand-side of Fig. 4. In all cases the number of items generated remains constant because it is only dependent on the length of the input string. These strategies expend equal effort on all parts of the program, including areas without errors. The situation of the curve for $\mathcal{G}_N$ is justified by subsumption phenomena between items generated by the parse process. In effect, the compact representation of $\mathcal{G}_N$ in relation to $\mathcal{G}_R$ and $\mathcal{G}_L$ in terms of the number of rules facilitates the application of such mechanisms. The greater cost of $\mathcal{G}_R$ in relation to $\mathcal{G}_L$ is due to the introduction of a non-determinism by the error hypotheses. When a token "b_l" is shifted in $\mathcal{G}_L$, the only PDA action available is the reduction of all or part of the analyzed prefix, since we can assume that the lookahead is "$+$", "$)$" or $\dashv$. For $\mathcal{G}_R$, two possibilities exist. When the lookahead is a "$+$", a shift takes place; but when it is a "$)$" or $\dashv$, a reduction is made. Thus, in the case or $\mathcal{G}_R$, the error repair algorithm introduces a larger number of parse conflicts, and hence items.

The Case of Regional Repairs. The generation is discussed with reference to the right-hand-side of Fig. 4. The general distribution of curves for $\mathcal{G}_R$, $\mathcal{G}_L$

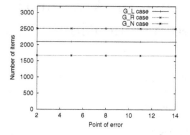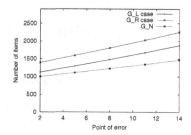

Fig. 4. Items for global (resp. regional) repairs *vs.* position of the point of error

and $\mathcal{G}_N$ is the same as mentioned for global repairs and it can be justified in the same manner. It is of interest to compare the results for global and regional repairs. So, Fig. 5 shows the number of items whose generation has been saved going from global to regional repair, illustrating the asymptotic convergence. The difference in terms of items generated is minor when the point of error is situated to the right of the input string, enlarging the repair region. This difference does not reach zero, which is in apparent contradiction with the above-mentioned convergence. We should take here into account that even though the size of the repair region can be the same for both global and regional repairs, the latter are not forced to apply the error hypotheses on all the error parse branches.

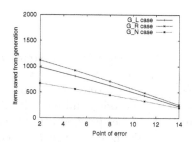

Fig. 5. Saved items from global to regional repair *vs.* position of the point of error

References

1. K. Sikkel. *Parsing Schemata.* PhD thesis, Univ. of Twente, The Netherlands, 1993.
2. M. Vilares. *Efficient Incremental Parsing for Context-Free Languages.* PhD thesis, University of Nice. ISBN 2-7261-0768-0, France, 1992.
3. M. Vilares, V.M. Darriba, and F.J. Ribadas. Regional least-cost error repair. In S. Yu and A. Păun, editors, *Implementation and Application of Automata*, volume 2088 of *LNCS*, pages 293–301. Springer-Verlag, Berlin-Heidelberg-New York, 2001.

Automata-Based Representations for Arithmetic Constraints in Automated Verification[*]

Constantinos Bartzis and Tevfik Bultan

Department of Computer Science
University of California
Santa Barbara CA 93106, USA
{bar,bultan}@cs.ucsb.edu

Abstract. In this paper we discuss efficient symbolic representations for infinite-state systems specified using linear arithmetic constraints. We give new algorithms for constructing finite automata which represent integer sets that satisfy linear constraints. These automata can represent either signed or unsigned integers and have a lower number of states compared to other similar approaches. We experimentally compare different symbolic representations by using them to verify non-trivial specification examples. In many cases symbolic representations based on our construction algorithms outperform the polyhedral representation used in Omega Library, or the automata representation used in LASH.

1 Introduction

Symbolic representations enable verification of systems with large state spaces which cannot be analyzed using enumerative approaches. Recently, symbolic model checking has been applied to verification of infinite-state systems using symbolic representations that can encode infinite sets [8,5,7]. One class of infinite-state systems are systems that can be specified using linear arithmetic formulas on unbounded integer variables. Verification of such systems have many interesting applications such as monitor specifications, mutual exclusion protocols [5,7], and parameterized cache coherence protocols [6]. In this paper we present new symbolic representations for linear arithmetic formulas and experimental results on efficiency of different symbolic representations.

There are two basic approaches to symbolic representation of linear arithmetic constraints in verification: 1) *Polyhedral representation*: In this approach linear arithmetic formulas are represented in a disjunctive form where each disjunct corresponds to a convex polyhedron. Each polyhedron corresponds to a conjunction of linear constraints [8,7]. This approach can be extended to full Presburger arithmetic by including divisibility constraints (which can be represented as an equality constraint with an existentially quantified variable) [5,2]. 2) *Automata representation*: An arithmetic constraint on v integer variables can

---

[*] This work is supported in part by NSF grant CCR-9970976 and NSF CAREER award CCR-9984822.

be represented by a v-track automaton that accepts a string if it corresponds to a v-dimensional integer vector (in binary representation) that satisfies the corresponding arithmetic constraint [4,11]. For both of these symbolic representations one can implement algorithms for intersection, union, complement, existential quantifier elimination operations, and subsumption, emptiness and equivalence tests, and therefore use them in model checking.

In this paper we present new construction algorithms for the automata representation and also experimentally compare these different approaches. We give a new algorithm for constructing a finite automata representation for sets satisfying Presburger arithmetic formulas. The size of the resulting automaton in our construction has the same upper bound as the construction given in [4], however, our construction is also able to handle negative integers. The size of the resulting automaton in our construction is different than the construction given in [11]. We implemented our construction algorithm using the MONA tool [9] and integrated it to a set of tools for infinite-state model checking [12]. We experimented with a large set of examples. To compare the performance of our construction algorithm to other approaches we also integrated the LASH tool [1] which uses the automata construction given in [11], and Omega Library [2] which uses a polyhedral representation to the same set of tools and ran them on the same set of examples. Our experimental results show that our construction algorithm produces more compact representations than the construction algorithm given in [11]. Also automata representation is more efficient compared to the polyhedral representation used in [2].

2   Finite Automata Representation for Presburger Formulas

In this section we give a brief description of our algorithm for constructing a finite automaton that accepts the set of natural number tuples that satisfy a Presburger arithmetic formula on v variables. A full description and analysis of the algorithm and a comparison to other approaches is given in [3]. We encode numbers using their binary representation. A v-tuple of natural numbers $(n_1, n_2, ..., n_v)$ is encoded as a word over the alphabet $\{0, 1\}^v$, where the i_{th} letter in the word is $(b_{i1}, b_{i2}, ..., b_{iv})$ and b_{ij} is the i_{th} least significant bit of number n_j.

The construction relies on a basic state machine (BSM) that performs linear arithmetic on non-negative integer variables. Each state of the BSM for $\sum_{i=1}^{v} a_i \cdot x_i$ is associated with a carry value. At any point, the BSM adds up the bit of the i_{th} variable of the current symbol a_i times for each i, plus the carry value of the current state. It writes the resulting bit to the output and moves to a new state according to the value of the new carry. The number of possible values of the carry (and thus the number of states) is $\sum_{i=1}^{v} |a_i|$.

A finite automaton (FA) for $\sum_{i=1}^{v} x_i = 0$ is similar to the BSM but has an extra sink state. Whenever the resulting bit is 1, the FA moves to the sink state, otherwise it continues as described before. The only initial and accepting state is the one associated with 0 carry. A FA for $\sum_{i=1}^{v} x_i < 0$ has no sink state. The accepting states are those associated with negative carries. The construction of FA for all other kinds of linear constraints ($\leq, >, \geq$) is similar. If the right hand side of the equations or inequations is a non-zero constant c, the state with carry value of $-c$ will be the initial state of the FA. If no such state exists, we need to introduce more states corresponding to carry values between $-c$ and the carry value closest to $-c$. Thus the number of states now becomes at most: $S = |\min(-c, \sum_{a_i<0} a_i)| + |\max(-c, \sum_{a_i>0} a_i)|$. This is a tighter upper bound than the one given in [4], even though the construction algorithms are similar. An alternative way to cope with the constant term c is to stack $\log_2 c + 1$ BSMs, where the i_{th} BSM compares the resulting bit against the i_{th} bit of c. Now the total number of states is at most $(\log_2 c + 1) \cdot \sum_{i=1}^{v} |a_i|$. We can choose which alternative to use depending on the expected upper bound on the number of states. Finally, after constructing FA for atomic linear constraints (equations and inequations) we can construct FA for any Presburger formulas using standard automata operations such as intersection, union, complementation and projection.

Based on the same ideas we can construct FA for formulas on all integers (including negative), using 2's complement arithmetic. The procedure is based on the fact that in order for the FA to accept the encoding of a tuple of numbers, it must also accept the encoding of the same numbers with arbitrarily many sign bits (i.e. the most significant bit of each number repeated arbitrarily many times). The FA contains two clones of each state of the BSM, one accepting and one rejecting. For equations, looping transitions in the BSM that write 0 go to the according accepting clone. All other transitions that write 0 go to the rejecting clone. All transitions that write 1 in the BSM go to the sink state. For inequations, looping transitions that write 1 go to the accepting clone and those which write 0 go to the rejecting clone. Any other transition goes to the appropriate accepting clone, iff by repeatedly receiving the same combination of bits the BSM will eventually enter a loop which writes 1. Otherwise it goes to the rejecting clone. These FA are only twice as large as those for non-negative integers described before.

Note that our construction algorithm and the one in [11] result in different automata, because the accepted languages are different (one is the reverse of the other). Moreover, we can prove the same or lower upper bound on the size of the resulting automata. Finally, in our algorithm, once a state has been created, all transitions originating from it can be computed immediately (as opposed to [11]), which is more convenient when transitions are stored using BDDs.

3   Implementation and Experiments

In [10] polyhedral and automata representation for arithmetic constraints are compared experimentally for reachability analysis of several concurrent systems. The results show no clear winner. On some problem instances the polyhedral representation is superior, on some others automata representation is. Our experimental setup is more reliable compared to [10]. In [10] boolean variables are mapped to integer variables when polyhedral representation is used. This is an inefficient encoding which gives an unfair advantage to the automata representation. In our experiments boolean variables are not mapped to integers in any representation. Also, our tools perform full CTL model checking including liveness properties instead of just reachability analysis discussed in [10].

We integrated our construction algorithms to an infinite state CTL model checker built on top of the Composite Symbolic Library [12]. The Composite Symbolic Library defines an abstract interface for the operations used in symbolic verification [12]. To integrate a new symbolic representation to the Composite Symbolic Library one implements this abstract interface with specialized operations. Composite Symbolic Library supports a disjunctive composite representation for formulas on integer and boolean variables. A disjunctive composite representation is in the form $\bigvee_{i=1}^{n} \bigwedge_{t \in T} p_{it}$ where p_{it} denotes the formula of type t (which could be integer or boolean) in the ith disjunct, and n and T denote the number of disjuncts and the set of variable types ($T = \{integer, boolean\}$)), respectively. The methods such as intersection, union, complement, satisfiability check, subsumption test, which manipulate composite representations in the above form are implemented in the Composite Symbolic Library by calling the operations on integer and boolean formula representations [12].

We integrated five different symbolic representations to the Composite Symbolic Library. The first three use the disjunctive composite representation described above to combine formulas on integer and boolean variables. We used the BDD representation for boolean formulas. We implemented three different integer formula representations using LASH [1]) (version V3), Omega [2] (version V2), and our automata construction algorithm (version V1) which uses MONA automata package [9] as an automata manipulator. We also implemented two automata based representations using LASH (version V5) and our construction algorithms (version V4) again built on top of MONA automata package, for both boolean and integer variables without using the disjunctive composite representation. The states of both boolean and integer variables can be represented in an automaton, hence one can avoid using the disjunctive composite representation.

We experimented with a large set of examples. Specification of the examples and properties are available at: http://www.cs.ucsb.edu/~bultan/composite/.

The results of our experimental evaluation of different representations for linear integer arithmetic constraints are shown in Table 1. We obtained the experimental results on a SUN ULTRA 10 work station with 768 Mbytes of memory, running SunOs 5.7. For each version of the verifier we recorded the following statistics: 1) Time elapsed during the construction of the symbolic representation of the transition system, shown in the table as CT. 2) Time elapsed during the verification process, shown as VT. It includes the time needed for forward or backward fixpoint computations, however, it excludes the construction time (CT). 3) The maximum amount of memory used by the verifier, shown as Mem. Also for V1, V3, V4 and V5 that use automata as a symbolic representation we recorded the size (number of states) of the automaton representing the transition

Table 1. Experimental results for performance of different symbolic representations for integer arithmetic constraints. Time measurements appear in seconds and memory measurements in Mbytes. For each problem instance the following values are shown: time elapsed during the construction of the symbolic representation of the transition system (CT), time elapsed during verification process (VT), the maximum amount of memory used by the verifier (Mem). For the automata representations we also give the number of states in the automata representing the transition relation (TRS) and the number of states in the automata representing the fixpoint iterate with the maximum size (MS). The instances marked ↑ ran out of memory or did not converge in 5000 seconds.

Problem Instance	V1 - Automata					V2 - Omega				V3 - LASH					V4 - Automata					V5 - LASH				
	CT	VT	Mem	TRS	MS	CT	VT	Mem	MS	CT	VT	Mem	TRS	MS	CT	VT	Mem	TRS	MS	CT	VT	Mem	TRS	MS
BARBERM2-1	0.13	0.07	8	184	26	0.22	0.11	7	26	0.31	0.23	6	198	25	0.05	0.01	0.45	115	40	1.71	0.22	0.36	276	46
BARBERM3-1	0.14	0.08	9	241	26	0.2	0.11	7	26	0.39	0.29	6	257	25	0.07	0.01	0.46	124	42	2.39	0.26	0.4	311	52
BARBERM4-1	0.15	0.09	9	298	26	0.21	0.13	7	26	0.44	0.36	6	316	25	0.07	0.02	0.5	133	44	3.1	0.28	0.43	346	58
BARBERM2-2	0.12	0.08	8	184	26	0.18	0.11	7	26	0.31	0.25	6	198	25	0.05	0.01	0.45	115	40	1.72	0.22	0.36	276	46
BARBERM3-2	0.13	0.09	9	241	26	0.19	0.12	7	26	0.37	0.31	6	257	25	0.06	0.02	0.46	124	42	2.3	0.26	0.4	311	52
BARBERM4-2	0.15	0.1	9	298	26	0.21	0.13	7	26	0.44	0.36	6	316	25	0.07	0.02	0.5	133	44	3.09	0.29	0.43	346	58
BARBERM2-3	0.12	0.08	8	184	26	0.19	0.11	7	26	0.31	0.25	6	198	25	0.06	0.01	0.45	115	40	1.71	0.22	0.36	276	46
BARBERM3-3	0.14	0.08	8	241	26	0.19	0.12	7	26	0.37	0.31	6	257	25	0.06	0.02	0.46	124	42	2.39	0.26	0.4	311	52
BARBERM4-3	0.14	0.1	10	298	26	0.22	0.13	7	26	0.45	0.37	6	316	25	0.07	0.02	0.5	133	44	3.1	0.28	0.04	346	52
BARBERMP-1	0.2	0.22	9	1266	131	0.23	0.33	7	131	1.01	1.45	6	1282	139	0.2	0.12	0.7	1103	131	7.92	1.19	2.7	1544	156
BARBERMP-2	0.21	0.21	9	1266	131	0.23	0.33	7	131	1.01	1.46	6	1282	139	0.2	0.12	0.7	1103	131	7.93	1.21	0.27	1544	156
BARBERMP-3	0.2	0.22	9	1266	131	0.22	0.33	7	131	1.01	1.45	6	1282	139	0.19	0.12	0.7	1103	131	7.91	1.22	2.7	1544	156
BAKERY2-1	0.1	0.04	8	80	31	0.13	0.11	7	31	0.18	0.24	6	96	42	0.06	0.04	0.38	117	36	1.56	0.27	0.27	236	73
BAKERY2-2	0.11	0.08	9	80	21	0.13	0.16	7	21	0.18	0.47	6	96	25	0.05	0.04	0.42	117	28	1.53	0.51	0.26	236	55
BAKERY3-1	0.17	1.52	33	558	306	0.3	3.92	10	306	0.64	10.39	6	569	424	0.37	0.77	0.64	646	382	6.22	6.5	1.83	1247	588
BAKERY3-2	0.16	3.6	100	558	305	0.3	13.1	20	305	0.64	23.78	7	569	340	0.36	1.64	0.79	646	117	6.14	13.61	1.76	1247	230
BAKERY4-1	0.49	38.21	420	3284	2437	1.09	142.96	43	2437	2.61	340.02	10	2691	3321	12.14	60.5	1.82	3444	6010	63.48	273.01	30.38	5542	5667
BAKERY4-2	↑														12.15	113	1.74	3444	869	63.45	546.81	29.75	5542	1027
TICKET2-1	0.1	0.18	10	168	117	0.13	0.22	7	117	0.26	0.57	6	188	116	0.07	0.1	0.56	179	132	2	1.04	0.43	263	161
TICKET2-2	0.11	0.18	10	168	117	0.13	0.22	7	117	0.27	1.15	6	188	116	0.06	0.11	0.56	179	132	1.99	1.05	0.43	263	161
TICKET3-1	0.13	0.91	33	315	107	0.17	1.99	10	107	0.46	4.51	7	354	627	0.16	1.36	0.93	333	562	4.78	8.93	1.93	492	839
TICKET3-2	0.14	1.67	33	315	107	0.18	1.99	13	107	0.45	12.34	8	354	627	0.16	1.3	0.93	333	562	4.78	8.93	1.93	492	839
TICKET4-1	0.16	17.24	221	504	2775	0.23	27	27	2775	0.7	116.97	8	568	2961	0.66	14.6	2.09	531	2336	11.86	74.72	10.2	789	4103
TICKET4-2	0.16	17.29	221	504	2775	0.23	26.94	27	2775	0.71	116.79	17	568	2961	0.66	14.6	2.09	531	2336	11.86	74.74	10.2	789	4103
COHERENCE-1	0.19	0.25	10	1150	102	0.26	0.28	7	102	0.19	5.92	6	1203	263	0.11	0.33	0.7	730	86	3.56	4.51	1.52	1377	237
COHERENCE-2	0.2	0.52	15	1150	51	0.27	1.99	10	51	0.2	8.49	7	1203	568	0.11	0.51	0.74	730	161	3.57	5.78	1.67	1377	472
COHERENCE-3	0.21	2.46	30	1150	1013	0.26	7.3	14	1013	0.2	47.16	14	1203	2019	0.11	22.2	0.98	730	544	3.55	25.27	3.8	1377	1216
COHERENCE-4	0.19	22.43	334	1150	448	0.27	42.91	39	448	1.04	206.13	12	1203	746	0.11	31.4	2	730	239	3.57	196.63	2.58	1377	641
PC5	0.13	0.03	8	440	54	0.15	0.05	7	54	0.43	0.92	6	587	74	0.09	0.04	0.55	244	61	4.26	0.61	0.94	680	144
PC10	0.19	0.06	8	700	54	0.22	0.08	7	54	0.62	1.55	7	917	74	0.19	0.06	0.79	283	61	11.9	0.7	1.26	811	166
RW4	0.09	0.01	7	50	3	0.12	0.01	6	3	0.12	0.01	6	40	3	0.02	0.01	0.03	71	5	0.63	0.03	0.17	136	18
RW8	0.13	0.01	8	100	3	0.18	0.01	7	3	0.2	0.02	7	80	3	0.04	0.01	0.31	143	5	2.61	0.05	0.24	256	30
RW16	0.23	0.02	10	200	3	0.36	0.02	7	3	0.42	0.05	7	160	3	0.12	0.01	0.04	287	5	13.01	0.09	0.41	496	54
RW32	0.65	0.03	19	400	3	1	0.03	7	3	1.2	0.09	7	320	3	0.38	0.02	0.07	575	5	76.28	0.17	0.76	976	102
RW64	2.83	0.06	49	800	3	3.86	0.06	13	3	4.61	0.18	10	640	3	1.82	0.07	1.33	1151	5	536.96	0.35	1.77	1936	198
SIS	694.87	0.34	19	107873	422	2.31	0.06	12	422	3.49	0.04	7	192	19	20.7	0.69	1.26	54568	431	152.85	1.92	39.22	95617	850
LIGHTCONTROL	0.2	0.08	10	108	12	0.18	0.07	7	12	0.28	0.2	6	72	12	0.07	0.02	0.04	187	27	2.41	0.3	0.34	301	70
INSERTIONSORT	0.11	0.01	7	140	13	0.11	0.15	7	13	0.21	0.67	6	173	86	0.06	0.02	0.46	127	19	1.5	0.77	0.43	231	101

system, shown as TRS, and the size of the largest automaton computed during the fixpoint computation, shown as MS. As discussed above our automata construction algorithm used in versions V1 and V4 uses MONA automata package. MONA automata package uses BDDs to store the transition relation of the automata. Therefore, to make the comparison with LASH fair, instead of giving the number of automaton states for versions V1 and V4, we give the total number of BDD nodes used in the MONA representation. For the barber and ticket problems we used forward fixpoint computation, while for all other problems backward fixpoint computations were used.

By carefully inspecting Table 1 one can make the following remarks. Versions V4 and V5 that use only automata as a single representation for both integer and boolean variables require less memory, both for the transition relation and the fixpoint iterates, than V1, V2 and V3 that use disjunctive representations. This can be explained by the fact that deterministic minimal automata are canonical, while the composite symbolic representation is not. For most of the examples but not all, V4 performs better than V5 both in construction and verification times and memory requirements. This is in accordance to the measured sizes of the two automata implementations. On the other hand, by inspecting the data for V1, V2, V3, we can see a clear manifestation of time-memory tradeoff. For most examples V1 is faster than V2 and V3, but uses more memory. V3 consumes less memory, but is usually slower than the other two. V2 appears to be a good compromise between time and memory efficiency. Now, when comparing the composite versions V1 and V3 with their "pure automata" counterparts V4 and V5 respectively, we can conclude that the later generally perform better than the earlier, with the exception of most construction time measurements for V5 being greater that those for V3.

Based on these results we conclude that the versions based on our automata construction algorithms for linear integer arithmetic formulas and implemented using MONA automata package (V1 and V4) are the most time efficient of all, with V4 being more memory efficient than V1. If a composite representation must be used, Omega library based V2 can be a good time-memory compromise. Finally LASH based V5 is a close competitor to V4, but suffers from high construction times.

References

1. The Liège Automata-based Symbolic Handler (LASH). Available at
   http://www.montefiore.ulg.ac.be/~boigelot/research/lash/.
2. The Omega project. http://www.cs.umd.edu/projects/omega/.
3. C. Bartzis and T. Bultan. Efficient symbolic representations for arithmetic constraints in verification. Technical Report TRCS-2002-16, Computer Science Department, University of California, Santa Barbara, June 2002.
4. A. Boudet and H. Comon. Diophantine equations, Presburger arithmetic and finite automata. In H. Kirchner, editor, *Proceedings of the 21st International Colloquium on Trees in Algebra and Programming - CAAP'96*, volume 1059 of *Lecture Notes in Computer Science*, pages 30–43. Springer-Verlag, April 1996.

5. Tevfik Bultan, Richard Gerber, and William Pugh. Model-checking concurrent systems with unbounded integer variables: symbolic representations, approximations, and experimental results. *ACM Transactions on Programming Languages and Systems*, 21(4):747–789, 1999.

6. G. Delzanno and T. Bultan. Constraint-based verification of client-server protocols. In *Proceedings of the 7th International Conference on Principles and Practice of Constraint Programming*, 2001.

7. Giorgio Delzanno and Andreas Podelski. Constraint-based deductive model checking. *Journal of Software Tools and Technology Transfer*, 3(3):250–270, 2001.

8. T. A. Henzinger, P. Ho, and H. Wong-Toi. Hytech: a model checker for hybrid systems. *Software Tools for Technology Transfer*, 1:110–122, 1997.

9. Nils Klarlund and Anders Møller. *MONA Version 1.4 User Manual*. BRICS Notes Series NS-01-1, Department of Computer Science, University of Aarhus, January 2001.

10. T. R. Shiple, J. H. Kukula, and R. K. Ranjan. A comparison of Presburger engines for EFSM reachability. In *Proceedings of the 10th International Conference on Computer-Aided Verification*, 1998.

11. P. Wolper and B. Boigelot. On the construction of automata from linear arithmetic constraints. In S. Graf and M. Schwartzbach, editors, *Proceedings of the 6th International Conference on Tools and Algorithms for the Construction and Analysis of Systems*, Lecture Notes in Computer Science, pages 1–19. Springer, April 2000.

12. T. Yavuz-Kahveci, M. Tuncer, and T. Bultan. Composite symbolic library. In *Proceedings of the 7th International Conference on Tools and Algorithms for the Construction and Analysis of Systems*, volume 2031 of *Lecture Notes in Computer Science*, pages 335–344. Springer-Verlag, April 2001.

On the Implementation of Compact DAWG's

Jan Holub[1*] and Maxime Crochemore[2**]

[1] Department of Computer Science and Engineering, Czech Technical University,
Karlovo nám. 13, CZ-121 35, Prague 2, Czech Republic
http://cs.felk.cvut.cz/~holub
[2] Gaspard-Monge Institute, University of Marne-la-Vallée,
F-77454 Marne-la-Vallée CEDEX 2, France
and King's College London
http://www-igm.univ-mlv.fr/~mac

Abstract. There are several data structures that allow searching for a pattern P in a preprocessed text T in time dependent just on the length of P. In this paper we present an implementation of CDAWG's— Compact Direct Acyclic Word Graphs. While the previous implementations of CDAWG's required from $7n$ to $23n$ bytes of memory space, ours achieves $1.7n$ to $5n$ for a text T of length n. The implementation is suitable for large data files, since it minimizes the number of disk accesses. If disk accesses are not to be optimized, space requirements can be further decreased.

1 Introduction

Finding pattern $P = p_1 p_2 \ldots p_m$ (of length m) in a text $T = t_1 t_2 \ldots t_n$ (of length n) is a very important task for any data retrieval system. There is a huge amount of unstructured texts, where one needs to find an information, and other types of texts appear at a steady rate. If we know the text T in advance, we can preprocess it and build a complete index over T. In such a way we improve searching times up to $\mathcal{O}(m)$ (on a fixed alphabet, which is the standard practical situation). Several data structures have been developed for that purpose (see [7], [10] or [6]). Kurtz [12] presents implementation experiments on several of them (DAWG–Directed Acyclic Word Graph, CDAWG–Compact DAWG, suffix tree). In this paper we discuss CDAWG implementation.

A CDAWG may be regarded as the compaction of a DAWG. A DAWG [3, 5] is a structure that can answer a query in time $\mathcal{O}(m)$. The size of DAWG's is linear with n as well as their construction time. In order to decrease the number of states of DAWG's, a data structure called Compact DAWG (CDAWG) was developed [3,4]. This CDAWG was built by compaction of DAWG. Direct

* This research has been partially supported by MŠMT research program No MSM 212300014 and by GAČR research programs No GP201/01/P082 and GA201/01/1433.
** Work by this author is partially supported by CNRS action AlBio, NATO Science Programme grant PST.CLG.977017, and Wellcome Trust Foundation.

J.-M. Champarnaud and D. Maurel (Eds.): CIAA 2002, LNCS 2608, pp. 289–294, 2003.
© Springer-Verlag Berlin Heidelberg 2003

constructions, avoiding a preliminary DAWG construction, has been designed in [9] and [11].

In the present paper we describe our implementation of CDAWG and compare it with other similar structures allowing fast pattern searching. While previous implementations of CDAWG's required from $7n$ to $23n$ bytes of memory space, we show that ours achieves $1.7n$ to $5n$ bytes for a text T of length n. This proves that the implementation is suitable for large data files, since it minimizes the number of disk accesses.

2   CDAWG

One way to develop a complete index over a text T is to construct its suffix trie. We can build the suffix trie by merging finite automata of suffixes of T (each accepting a suffix) giving to all these automata the same initial state.

If we replace sequence of transitions with single-symbol labels that do not fork by one transition with a string label (operation called compaction), we get a suffix tree. If we minimize the suffix trie, we get DAWG. Finally, if we minimize a suffix tree, we get a CDAWG. If we compact DAWG, we get the same CDAWG. This approach is used in [11].

Another way is to construct a simple non-deterministic finite automaton (NFA) accepting T. Then we connect the initial state with all the other states using ε-transitions and transform this NFA to the equivalent deterministic finite automaton. Thus we get a DAWG that can be further compacted to get a CDAWG.

An algorithm for direct construction of CDAWG without constructing DAWG first was introduced in [8] while an algorithm for on-line construction of CDAWG was introduced in [11].

3   Implementation

The algorithm at the origin of our implementation of CDAWG's processes in two steps: first, we construct a CDAWG as described in [8] and we sort states according to their topological order; then, we classify the states into three classes according to their maximum length of incoming transition label ($maxLen$) and we add fourth class for the terminal state q_T, from which no transition leads:

- Class I (Q_{I}): the initial state q_0 and the states with $maxLen = 1$,
- Class II (Q_{II}): the states with $1 < maxLen \leq Limit$,
- Class III (Q_{III}): the states with $maxLen > Limit$,
- Class IV (Q_{IV}): the terminal state q_T (no transition leads from q_T).

The typical distribution of states according to $maxLen$ is shown in Table 1. As we can see the most of the labels are very short. That is the reason, why we have decided to create Classes. The most frequent Class I occupies the smallest part of memory. For each state with $maxLen > 1$, a parameter $Limit$ distinguishes what implementation (either Class II or III) is more space-efficient.

Table 1. Distribution of states according to their *maxLen* in Calgary Corpus file paper4. The maximum *maxLen* for file paper4 is 28.

maxLen	1	2	3	4	5	6	7	8	9	10	11	12	13	14	15	16	17	18	19	20	21	···
no. of states	2546	464	231	142	86	57	40	27	25	16	5	3	11	6	3	1	2	0	2	1	0	···

For states Q_I we store just outgoing transitions. For states Q_II and Q_III we have to store also incoming transition label. While in Class II we store the whole label (the longest one), in Class III we store only a pointer to the source text (*EndPos*). The terminal state (the state in Q_IV) is not memorized.

We can also store some optional additional data. In Classes I, II, and III we can store one bit indicating, whether the corresponding state is final or not. Doing so, the CDAWG recognizes all suffixes of T, otherwise it recognizes all factors of T considering that all states are final. In Classes I and II we can also memorize the corresponding position in text (*EndPos*). The terminal state is always final and has $EndPos = n$.

Then we store outgoing transitions. We store the number of outgoing transitions and the first symbol of each of outgoing transition labels (string of first symbols—*SFS*). Then we store the outgoing transition records.

At the beginning of each outgoing transition we store the number of Class of the destination state. For Classes I, II, and III we store a pointer to the beginning of the destination state (number of bits to be skipped to reach the destination state). For Classes II, III, and IV we store also the length of outgoing transition label ($Len - 1$).

We do not store the first symbol of the label since it is already stored in the *SFS*. Removing the *SFS* and storing entire label strings in destination states, could decrease space requirements, but using the CDAWG and searching for the desired transition, would force to read from as many parts of the CDAWG datafile as the number of outgoing transitions. Thus this is likely to require more disk accesses and would significantly increase the resulting searching time.

4   Results

We made some experiments on Calgary and Canterbury Corpora test files[1] [1]. The comparison with other methods is shown in Table 2. Value for DAWG, CDAWG, and Suffix Tree are taken from [12]; DAWG.B is the implementation of DAWG's designed by M. Balík [2]; finally, CD.HC1 is our implementation. If we do not care for the number of disk accesses, we can move symbols from the *SFS* to the destination state. The space requirements further decrease as we can see in column CD.HC2. The best results are highlighted.

A single character in the table denotes the type of file: *e* for English text, *f* for formal text (like programs), *b* for binary files (i.e. containing 8-bit symbols), and *d* for DNA sequences.

---

[1] File `ptt5` from Canterbury Corpus and `pic` from Calgary Corpus are the same.

Table 2. Space requirements for suffix data structures applied to files of the Calgary and Canterbury Corpora (values are in bytes per symbol of text).

file	type	$|\Sigma|$	length	DAWG	CDAWG	Suff.Tree	DAWG.B	CD.HC1	CD.HC2
book1	e	81	768771	30.35	15.75	9.83	**3.66**	4.42	3.78
book2	e	96	610856	29.78	12.71	9.67	3.17	3.67	**3.14**
paper1	e	95	53161	30.02	12.72	9.82	2.98	3.26	**2.72**
paper2	e	91	82199	29.85	13.68	9.82	3.06	3.58	**3.01**
paper3	e	84	46526	30.00	14.40	9.80	3.12	3.62	**3.02**
paper4	e	80	13286	30.34	14.76	9.91	3.04	3.46	**2.82**
paper5	e	91	11954	30.00	14.04	9.80	2.97	3.34	**2.72**
paper6	e	93	38105	30.29	12.80	9.89	2.96	3.27	**2.73**
alice29	e	74	152089	30.27	14.14	9.84	**3.20**	3.82	3.23
lcet10	e	84	426754	29.75	12.70	9.66	3.12	3.56	**3.03**
plrabn12	e	81	481861	29.98	15.13	9.74	**3.52**	4.15	3.53
bible	e	64	4047392	29.28	10.87	7.27	2.94	3.26	**2.88**
world192	e	94	2473400	27.98	7.87	9.22	2.53	2.43	**2.09**
bib	f	81	111261	28.53	9.94	9.46	2.68	2.68	**2.24**
news	f	98	377109	29.48	12.10	9.54	3.15	3.44	**2.91**
progc	f	92	39611	29.73	11.87	9.59	2.87	3.06	**2.54**
progl	f	87	71646	29.96	8.71	10.22	2.40	2.39	**2.03**
progp	f	89	49379	30.21	8.28	10.31	2.35	2.28	**1.92**
trans	f	99	93695	30.47	6.69	10.49	2.35	1.95	**1.66**
fields.c	f	90	11150	29.86	9.40	9.78	2.43	2.39	**1.96**
cp.html	f	86	24603	29.04	10.44	9.34	2.64	2.58	**2.12**
grammar	f	76	3721	29.96	10.60	10.14	2.36	2.44	**1.97**
xargs	f	74	4227	30.02	13.10	9.63	2.75	2.99	**2.40**
asyoulik	f	68	125179	29.97	14.93	9.77	3.34	3.84	**3.23**
geo	b	256	102400	26.97	13.10	7.49	3.18	2.66	**1.92**
obj1	b	256	21504	27.51	13.20	7.69	2.98	2.39	**1.67**
obj2	b	256	246814	27.22	8.66	9.30	2.67	1.96	**1.51**
pic	b	159	513216	27.86	8.08	8.94	**1.63**	2.17	1.79
kennedy	b	256	1029744	21.18	7.29	4.64	1.57	1.65	**1.10**
sum	b	255	38240	27.79	10.26	8.92	2.53	2.86	**2.29**
E.coli	d	4	4638690	34.01	23.55	12.56	**4.46**	5.46	5.24

We made also experiments on several other DNA sequences (of size $n = 40$ kB to 1.5 MB) and the space requirements were about $4.5n$ (CD.HC1: 4.21–5.15, CD.HC2: 3.99–4.92).

Further decrease of space requirements can be achieved, if we store states at even addresses or addresses divisible by 4 or 8.

In addition to the difference between DAWG and CDAWG structures, we can discuss a difference between implementation of DAWG.B and CD.HC. DAWG.B was developed for the minimum space requirements, therefore it uses some compression techniques (for alphabet symbols, number of edges, edges, etc.). The CD.HC was developed for the speed, therefore it uses the *SFS* and no compression. It also needs the source text to be stored out of the data structure.

5 Conclusion

In the paper we presented an efficient implementation of CDAWG's. The space requirements are much lower than in the previous works and vary from 1.65 to 5.46 bytes per symbol of input text. The implementation requires that the source text is stored, so the total space increases by one byte per character, but other implementations also need the source text. Only [2] can reconstruct the source text from its implementation of DAWG's but it takes some time.

The space requirements can be further decreased. For instance we can compress the labels or we can remove the *SFS* and store all incoming transition labels in the destination states (CD.HC2). But as mentioned above, it would increase number of disk accesses. In our implementation we require at most $m + 1$ disk accesses[2] when searching for a pattern of length m—we traverse at most $m + 1$ states (including the initial state) and all outgoing transitions are located with the state. But in case of CD.HC2, we would get $(m\tau + 1)$ disk accesses, where τ is the average number of outgoing transitions. In such a case we need, for each outgoing transition, to look at the destination state to find out the transition label.

The goal of this work is to implement CDAWG so that it can be used for large source texts. In such a case we require minimum disk accesses that are in the worst case (the required data are not in disk cache) 100,000 times slower than memory accesses. When running CDAWG, we traverse the resulting data-file forward (we do not go backward). We can also set any size of CDAWG buffer (the part of CDAWG stored in main memory) and thus control space requirements when running CDAWG.

References

1. http://corpus.canterbury.ac.nz.
2. M. Balík. Implementation of DAWG. In J. Holub and M. Šimánek, editors, *Proceedings of the Prague Stringology Club Workshop '98*, pages 26–35, Czech Technical University, Prague, Czech Republic, 1998. Collaborative Report DC–98–06.
3. A. Blumer, J. Blumer, A. Ehrenfeucht, D. Haussler, M. T. Chen, and J. Seiferas. The smallest automaton recognizing the subwords of a text. *Theor. Comput. Sci.*, 40(1):31–55, 1985.
4. A. Blumer, J. Blumer, A. Ehrenfeucht, D. Haussler, and R. McConnel. Complete inverted files for efficient text retrieval and analysis. *J. Assoc. Comput. Mach.*, 34(3):578–595, 1987.
5. M. Crochemore. Transducers and repetitions. *Theor. Comput. Sci.*, 45(1):63–86, 1986.
6. M. Crochemore, C. Hancart, and T. Lecroq. *Algorithmique du texte*. Vuibert, 2001. 347 pages.
7. M. Crochemore and W. Rytter. *Text algorithms*. Oxford University Press, 1994.

---

[2] The worst case is, when no traversed state is in disk cache, which is unlikely to happen.

8. M. Crochemore and R. Vérin. Direct construction of compact directed acyclic word graphs. In A. Apostolico and J. Hein, editors, *Proceedings of the 8th Annual Symposium on Combinatorial Pattern Matching*, number 1264 in Lecture Notes in Computer Science, pages 116–129, Aarhus, Denmark, 1997. Springer-Verlag, Berlin.

9. M. Crochemore and R. Vérin. On compact directed acyclic word graphs. In J. Mycielski, G. Rozenberg, and A. Salomaa, editors, *Structures in Logic and Computer Science*, number 1261 in Lecture Notes in Computer Science, pages 192–211. Springer-Verlag, Berlin, 1997.

10. D. Gusfield. *Algorithms on strings, trees and sequences: computer science and computational biology*. Cambridge University Press, Cambridge, 1997.

11. S. Inenaga, H. Hoshino, A. Shinohara, M. Takeda, S. Arikawa, G. Mauri, and G. Pavesi. On-line construction of compact directed acyclic word graphs. In *Proceedings of the 12th Annual Symposium on Combinatorial Pattern Matching*, number 2087 in Lecture Notes in Computer Science, pages 169–180. Springer-Verlag, Berlin, 2001.

12. S. Kurtz. Reducing the space requirements of suffix trees. *Softw. Pract. Exp.*, 29(13):1149–1171, 1999.

Dynamic Programming – NFA Simulation

Jan Holub[*]

Department of Computer Science and Engineering, Czech Technical University,
Karlovo nám. 13, CZ-121 35, Prague 2, Czech Republic
holub@fel.cvut.cz
http://cs.felk.cvut.cz/~holub

Abstract. Nondeterministic finite automaton (*NFA*) cannot be directly used because of its nondeterminism. One way how to use *NFA* is to determinize *NFA* and the second way is to use one of simulation methods. This paper deals with one of the simulation method called dynamic programming. We present the method on one of the pattern matching problems as well as modifications for several other tasks.

1 Introduction

In Computer Science there is a class of problems that can be solved by finite automata. For some of these problems one can construct directly a deterministic finite automaton (*DFA*) that solve them. For other problems it is easier to build a nondeterministic finite automaton (*NFA*). Since one cannot use *NFA* directly because of its nondeterminism, one should transform it to the equivalent *DFA* using the standard subset construction [9,10] or one should simulate a run of the *NFA* using one of the simulation methods [6].

When transforming *NFA*, one can get the *DFA* with a huge amount of states (up to $2^{|Q_{NFA}|}$, where $|Q_{NFA}|$ is the number of states of *NFA*). The time complexity of the transformation is proportional to the number of states of *DFA*. The run is then very fast (linear with the length of an input text). On the other hand, when simulating the run of *NFA*, the time and space complexities are given by the number of states of *NFA*. The run of the simulation is then slower.

There are known three simulation methods [6]: *basic simulation method*, *dynamic programming*, and *bit parallelism*. All of these methods use breadth-first search for traversing the state space. The first overview of the simulation methods was presented in [8]. This paper is a continuation of [7], where the basic simulation method and the bit parallelism were described in detail.

The dynamic programming was firstly used for the approximate string matching using the Levenshtein distance in [12]. It just computed edit distance between the pattern and the text. In [13], each configuration of integer vector of the dynamic programming was considered as a state of *DFA* and in such a way the

---

[*] This research has been partially supported by MŠMT research program No MSM 212300014 and by GAČR research programs No GP201/01/P082 and GA201/01/1433.

J.-M. Champarnaud and D. Maurel (Eds.): CIAA 2002, LNCS 2608, pp. 295–300, 2003.

DFA was constructed (the size of the DFA is $\mathbf{min}(3^m, (k+1)!(k+2)^{m-k})$ [13, 11], where m is the length of the pattern and k is the maximum number of differences allowed). Then in [11,3,4] it was shown that the dynamic programming is a simulation of NFA.

2   Definitions

Let Σ be a nonempty input alphabet, Σ^* be the set of all strings over Σ, ε be the *empty string*, and $\Sigma^+ = \Sigma^* \setminus \{\varepsilon\}$. If $a \in \Sigma$, then $\bar{a} = \Sigma \setminus \{a\}$ denotes a *complement* of a over Σ.

Nondeterministic finite automaton (NFA) is a 4-tuple $(Q, \Sigma, \delta, q_0, F)$, where Q is a set of states, Σ is a set of input symbols, δ is a mapping $Q \times (\Sigma \cup \{\varepsilon\}) \mapsto 2^{|Q|}$, q_0 is an initial state, $F \subseteq Q$ is a set of final (accepting) states. *Deterministic finite automaton* (DFA) is NFA, where δ is a mapping $Q \times \Sigma \mapsto Q$. We can extend δ to $\hat{\delta}$ mapping $Q \times \Sigma^* \mapsto 2^{|Q|}$ for NFA or $Q \times \Sigma^+ \mapsto Q$ for DFA respectively. DFA (resp. NFA) accepts a string $w \in \Sigma^*$ if and only if $\hat{\delta}(q_0, w) \in F$ (resp. $\hat{\delta}(q_0, w) \cap F \neq \emptyset$).

An *active state* of NFA, when the last symbol of a prefix w of an input string is processed, denotes each state q, $q \in \hat{\delta}(q_0, w)$. At the beginning, only q_0 is an active state.

A *depth of state* q in NFA is the minimum number of moves that are needed to get from an initial state q_0 to this state q without using ε-transitions. A *level of state* q in NFA is the minimum among the numbers of differences associated with all final states reachable from q. In the figures of this paper, the states of the same depth are in the same column and the states of the same level are in the same line (row).

An algorithm $\mathcal{A}$ *simulates a run of an NFA*, if $\forall w$, $w \in \Sigma^*$, it holds that $\mathcal{A}$ with given w at the input reports all information associated with each final state q_f, $q_f \in F$, after processing w, if and only if $q_f \in \hat{\delta}(q_0, w)$.

3   Dynamic Programming

The basic simulation method described in [6,7] maintains a set of active states during the whole simulation process. While in bit parallelism this set is represented by bit vectors, in the dynamic programming this set is represented by a vector of integer variables. We divide all states into some subsets and each of the subsets is represented by one integer. The value of this integer then holds the information, what states of the subset are active.

The simulation using the dynamic programming will be shown on the NFA for the approximate string matching using the Levenshtein distance. This problem is defined as a searching for all occurrences of pattern $P = p_1 p_2 \ldots p_m$ in text $T = t_1 t_2 \ldots t_n$, where the found occurrence X (substring of T) can have at most k differences. The number of differences is given by the Levenshtein distance $D_L(P, X)$, which is defined as the minimum number of edit operations *replace*, *insert*, and *delete*, that are needed to convert P to X.

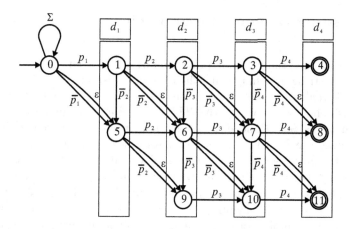

Fig. 1. Dynamic programming uses for each depth of states of *NFA* one integer variable *d*.

Figure 1 shows the *NFA* constructed for this problem ($m = 4$, $k = 2$). The horizontal transitions represent matching, the vertical transitions represent *insert*, the diagonal ε-transitions represent *delete*, and the remaining diagonal transitions represent *replace*. The self-loop of the initial state provides skipping the prefixes of T located in front of the occurrences. Formula 1 simulates the run of the *NFA* in Figure 1.

$$
\begin{aligned}
&d_{j,0} \leftarrow j, && 0 \leq j \leq m \\
&d_{0,i} \leftarrow 0, && 0 \leq i \leq n \\
&d_{j,i} \leftarrow \mathbf{min}(\text{if } t_i = p_j \text{ then } d_{j-1,i-1} \text{ else } d_{j-1,i-1} + 1, && \hspace{2cm}(1)\\
&\qquad\quad \text{if } j < m \text{ and } t_i \neq p_{j+1} \text{ then } d_{j,i-1} + 1, && 0 < i \leq n, \\
&\qquad\quad d_{j-1,i} + 1), && 0 < j \leq m
\end{aligned}
$$

In the dynamic programming for the approximate string matching using the Levenshtein distance there is for each depth j, $0 < j \leq m$, of *NFA* in each step i of the run one integer variable $d_{j,i}$ that contains level number of the topmost active state in j-th depth of *NFA*. Each value of $d_{i,j}$ greater than $k + 1$ can be replaced by value $k + 1$ and it represents that there is no active state in j-th depth of *NFA* in i-th step of the run.

Term $d_{j-1,i-1}$ represents matching transition, term $d_{j-1,i-1} + 1$ represents transition *replace*, term $d_{j,i-1} + 1$ represents transition *insert*, and term $d_{j-1,i} + 1$ represents transition *delete*.

The self-loop of the initial state is represented by setting $d_{0,i} \leftarrow 0$, $0 \leq i \leq n$. Only the states reachable from q_0 by ε-transitions are active at the beginning. Thus all transitions (paths) of the *NFA* are considered.

Each element $d_{m,i} \leq k$ shows an occurrence of P with at most $d_{m,i}$ differences—the final state in level $d_{m,i}$ is active.

In [2] they compress the matrix D since they use the property that $(d_{j,i} - d_{j-1,i-1}) \in \{0, 1\}$.

4   Adjusting Dynamic Programming

Now, we show how the dynamic programming can simulate other *NFA*s. In the approximate string matching using the Hamming distance, the only allowed edit operation is *replace*. By omitting transitions *insert* and *delete* from the *NFA* for the Levenshtein distance we get the *NFA* for the Hamming distance. By omitting terms simulating *insert* and *delete* transitions in Formula 1 we get the formula for simulating the *NFA* for the Hamming distance. In such a case we also have to change the initial setting of the vector, since only the initial state is active at the beginning (there are no ε-transitions in such *NFA*).

If we label *replace* and *insert* transitions by Σ (i.e., the transitions are used even if t_i is the matching symbol), we get so called Σ version of *NFA* [6]. This *NFA* has a little simpler formula, but it has a little bit different behavior. The original dynamic programming algorithm [12,13][1] for the approximate string matching using the Levenshtein distance simulates the Σ version of *NFA*.

If we introduce transition *transpose* (two adjacent symbols are exchanged) into the *NFA* for the Levenshtein distance, we get the *NFA* for the generalized Levenshtein distance [4]. This transition leads from a state q of level l and depth j to an auxiliary state q' and then to the state q'' of level $l + 1$ and depth $j + 2$. It reads two symbols: p_{j+2} and p_{j+1}.

To get formula for the approximate string matching using the generalized Levenshtein distance we have to insert Term 2 simulating transition *transpose* into Formula 1.

$$\text{if } i > 1 \text{ and } j > 1 \text{ and } t_{i-1} = p_j \text{ and } t_i = p_{j-1}\text{then } d_{j-2,i-2} + 1 \qquad (2)$$

We get the sequence matching from the string matching, if we allow any number of symbols to be located between two adjacent symbols of the pattern. The *NFA* for the sequence matching we get from the *NFA* for the string matching just by inserting self-loop to each nonfinal state. Such self-loop of state q is then labeled by $\bar{p}_j$, where p_j is a label of the match transition leading from q [4]. To get the formula for sequence matching, we should insert term **if** $j < m$ **and** $t_i \neq p_{j+1}$ **then** $d_{j,i-1}$ (which simulates the self-loop) in formula for string matching.

If we do not care about the exact number of differences in the found string and we only want to be sure that the number of differences is less or equal to k, we can use the reduced *NFA* [5][2]. The reduced *NFA* for the approximate string matching contains in each level only the first $(m - k + 1)$ states. Other states are removed, since they are needed only to determine the exact number of differences in the found string. For the simulation of this *NFA*, we can use

---

[1] In origin, it was designed in order to directly compute the edit distance, which in the Σ version of *NFA* exactly corresponds to the values of the integer vector. Later it was shown that it simulates the corresponding *NFA*.

[2] A similar simulation of reduced *NFA*s (Σ-version) for the approximate string matching using the Levenshtein distance was independently presented in [1].

another approach. We have one integer variable for each ε-diagonal[3]. See [6] for details.

Weighted approximate string and sequence matching introduces for each edit operation (*replace*, *insert*, *delete*, and *transpose*) its weight (w_R, w_I, w_D, and w_T respectively). It can be either independent on the symbol being edited or it can vary according to the symbol. In the *NFA* it is represented in such a way that transitions representing various edit operations lead to states in various levels according to their weights. In formulae for simulating *NFA* it is represented in such a way that instead of increasing the value $d_{j,i}$ by one, we increase the value by the weight of the corresponding edit operation. For details see [6].

5   Conclusion

In this paper we presented the simulation method the called dynamic programming. The method was demonstrated on the *NFA* for the approximate string matching using the Levenshtein distance. The way how to use the method for other problems is also demonstrated.

The time complexity of the dynamic programming for the presented tasks is $\mathcal{O}(mn)$ ($\mathcal{O}(m|\Sigma| + (m-k)n)$ for the reduced *NFA*) and the space complexity is $\mathcal{O}(m)$ ($\mathcal{O}(m|\Sigma| + m - k)$ for the reduced *NFA*).

Together with other simulation methods the dynamic programming creates an alternate to *DFA* when deciding, how to use *NFA*.

References

1. R. A. Baeza-Yates and G. Navarro. A faster algorithm for approximate string matching. In *Proceedings of the CPM'96*, no. 1075 in LNCS, pages 1–23, Laguna Beach, CA, 1996. Springer-Verlag, Berlin.
2. Z. Galil and K. Park. An improved algorithm for approximate string matching. In *Proceedings of the 16th ICALP*, no. 372 in LNCS, pages 394–404, Stresa, Italy, 1989. Springer-Verlag, Berlin.
3. J. Holub. Approximate string matching in text. Master's thesis, Faculty of Electrical Engineering, Czech Technical University, Prague, Czech Republic, 1996.
4. J. Holub. Simulation of NFA in approximate string and sequence matching. In *Proceedings of the Prague Stringology Club Workshop '97*, pages 39–46, Czech Technical University, Prague, Czech Republic, 1997.
5. J. Holub. Dynamic programming for reduced NFAs for approximate string and sequence matching. In *Proceedings of the Prague Stringology Club Workshop '98*, pages 73–82, Czech Technical University, Prague, Czech Republic, 1998.
6. J. Holub. *Simulation of Nondeterministic Finite Automata in Pattern Matching*. Ph.D. Thesis, Czech Technical University, Prague, Czech Republic, 2000.
7. J. Holub. Bit parallelism—NFA simulation. In *Proceedings of the 6th CIAA*, Pretoria, South Africa, 2001. University of Pretoria.

---

[3] This kind of simulation cannot be used for the approximate string and sequence matching that uses the Hamming distance, since there are no ε-diagonals there.

8. J. Holub and B. Melichar. Implementation of nondeterministic finite automata for approximate pattern matching. In *Proceedings of the WIA'98*, no. 1660 in LNCS, pages 92–99, Rouen, France, 1999. Springer-Verlag, Berlin.

9. J. E. Hopcroft and J. D. Ullman. *Introduction to automata, languages and computations*. Addison-Wesley, Reading, MA, 1979.

10. D. C. Kozen. *Automata and Computability*. Springer-Verlag, Berlin, 1997.

11. B. Melichar. Approximate string matching by finite automata. In *Computer Analysis of Images and Patterns*, no. 970 in LNCS, pages 342–349. Springer-Verlag, Berlin, 1995.

12. P. H. Sellers. The theory and computation of evolutionary distances: Pattern recognition. *J. Algorithms*, 1(4):359–373, 1980.

13. E. Ukkonen. Finding approximate patterns in strings. *J. Algorithms*, 6(1–3):132–137, 1985.

Deterministic Parsing of Cyclic Strings*

Bořivoj Melichar

Department of Computer Science and Engineering
Czech Technical University
Karlovo nám. 13, CZ-121 35, Prague 2, Czech Republic
phone: ++420 2 24357287
fax: ++420 2 24923325
melichar@fel.cvut.cz

Abstract. A technique of parsing of cyclic strings using an adapted strong LR parser is described. The adapted parser is able to find the starting point of the normal form of cyclic string. The resulting algorithm of parsing has linear time complexity.

1 Introduction

One technique used for the recognition of two-dimensional shapes consists in a description of the contour of the shape by a linear string of primitives. A number of approaches exists to obtain such a representation [FY86].

The linear string representing the planar object must be invariant with respect to the starting point. For instance, if we have a set of planar objects and the used primitives are symbols a and b, the strings *ababaab*, *babaaba* and *abaabab* represent the same object. It is useful to write all strings representing some class of objects in a normal form. Then it is possible to find a formal description of a set of strings written in a normal form in a given class. One of useful formal system for the description of sets of strings is a grammar. Having a grammar it is possible to use a parser for the decision whether a given string belongs to the language described by the grammar provided that the string is in the normal form. Therefore it is necessary for such a decision to put the strings in normal form. On the other hand, it is very useful to adapt the parser to be able to learn if there exists a cyclic rotation of the string such that it is a member of the language described by the grammar. Oncina [ON96] has described an adaptation of the Cocke-Younger-Kasami context-free grammar parser in order to use it with cyclic strings. The obtained parser has the same time complexity as the original one ($\mathcal{O}(n^3)$).

In this paper, an adaptation of strong LR parser is described in order to use it for cyclic strings. The adapted parser has linear time complexity.

* This research was partially supported by grants 201/02/0125 of the Grant Agency of Czech Republic and by the Ministry of Education, Youth, and Sports of the Czech Republic under research program No. J04/98:212300014 (Research in the area of information technologies and communications).

J.-M. Champarnaud and D. Maurel (Eds.): CIAA 2002, LNCS 2608, pp. 301–306, 2003.

A (right) cyclic shift is a mapping $\sigma : T^* \to T^*$, defined by $\sigma(a_1 \ldots a_n) = a_n a_1 \ldots a_{n-1}$. Let σ^m denote the composition for all $m \geq 0$ and let σ^0 denote the identity. Two strings x and y in T^* are equivalent if $x = \sigma^m(y)$ for some $m \geq 0$, where m is the length of the cyclic shift. Clearly, this defines an equivalence relation in T^*. The equivalence class of a string x will be denoted with $[x]$, and will be called a cyclic string. Let $A \subset T^*$, then $[A] = \bigcup_{x \in A} [x]$.

2   Strong LR Parsing

We use standard notation as defined in [AV71]. Let $G = (N, T, P, S)$ be a context-free grammar. The *augmented grammar* for G is $G' = (N \cup \{S'\}, T, P \cup \{S' \to S\}, S')$, where $S' \notin N$. All derivations used in this paper are the rightmost derivations. Let $k \geq 0$. A grammar G is said to be strong $LR(k)$ if, in the augmented grammar G' for G, the conditions

$\quad S' \Rightarrow^* \alpha_1 A w \Rightarrow \alpha_1 \beta w = \alpha_1' X_1 w,$

$\quad S' \Rightarrow^* \gamma B x \Rightarrow \alpha_2 \beta y = \alpha_2' X_2 y,$

$\quad X_1 = X_2$ and $FIRST_k(w) = FIRST_k(y)$

always imply that $A = B$ and $x = y$.

The strong LR parsing is described in [MEL88]. The construction of the parsing table is based on the collection L of sets of strong $LR(0)$ items. The construction of this collection is similar to the construction of canonical collection of sets of $LR(0)$ items.

The symbol to the left of the dot in an $LR(0)$ item is used as the name of the set of strong $LR(0)$ items in the collection L. This symbol is unique for each item in the collection with the only exception of the initial set. Its name is $\#$ in all cases. The difference between canonical collection and the collection L is: If two sets with the same name X are in L then replace both such sets by the union of them. So the collection L contains the initial set and just one set for each grammar symbol. The goto table is not necessary and only the parsing table is used. It is constructed as is usual for simple LR grammars. The parser for strong LR grammars has not the correct prefix property, because of doing union of some sets during the construction of the collection L. The standard LR parser must be modified in order to obtain the strong LR parser in this way: During the operation *reduce* it must check if the right hand side of the reduction rule is at the top of the pushdown store. If not, the parsing ends with the error signalization.

3   Parsing of Cyclic Strings

The parsing of cyclic strings in the normal form starts with the initial symbol $(\#)$ on the pushdown store and the first k symbols of the input string as the lookahead string. The parsing of a cyclic string can start in an arbitrary point of the input string. Let us use two observations:

1. We can divide a sequence of configurations of the parser parsing some input string on a number of subsequences each one starting in a configuration

with the terminal symbol on the top of the pushdown store (with an exception of the first subsequence). Each such subsequence consists of some number of transitions corresponding to reductions followed by a transition corresponding to the shift of one terminal symbol (with an exception of the last subsequence).

2. There is for each terminal symbol on the top of the pushdown store and for each lookahead string at most one non error entry in the strong LR parsing table.

Using these observations, we can start parsing of the input string in an arbitrary point provided that a substring of $k + 1$ terminal symbols is seen by the parser. The first symbol of this substring is the symbol on the top of the pushdown store and the rest is the lookahead string of the length k.

A configuration of cyclic parser is a quadruple $(\#\omega, x, \pi, \alpha)$, where $\#\omega$ is the contents of the pushdown store, x is the rest of the input string, π is the concatenation of the substring of the right parse and the prefix of it, and α is the expected string.

The expected string α is created during reductions. Let the cyclic string with normal form $x = a_1 a_2 \cdots a_n$ be $x^m = a_{n-m+1} \cdots a_n a_1 a_2 \cdots a_{n-m}$, where m is the length of the cyclic shift. It is composed of two parts. The first part $a_{n-m+1} \cdots a_n$ is a suffix of x and it is parsed starting with symbol a_{n-m+1}. There is possible that during the parsing of this suffix a reduction needs some string of symbols, which is expected on the top of the pushdown store but which was not pushed on it. This is a string which can be obtained during parsing of the prefix of x which will be parsed later. Therefore the parser is creating the expected string in order to check the correctness of the cyclic string and to compute the length of the cyclic shift.

To continue parsing after the suffix $a_{n-m+1} a_{n-m+2} \ldots a_n$ is already parsed, we must ensure that parsing with symbol a_i, $i = n - k + 1, n - k + 2, \ldots, n$, at the top of the pushdown store and the $FIRST_k(a_{i+1} \ldots a_n a_1 a_2 \ldots a_m)$ as the lookahead string is possible. The starting point of classical LR parsing is the configuration $(\#, x_1 x_2 \ldots x_n, \varepsilon)$. Therefore we must simulate this situation during the parsing of cyclic string in the configuration $(\#\omega a_i, a_{i+1} \ldots a_n a_1 a_2 \ldots a_{n-m} \cdot a_{n-m+1} \cdots a_{n-m+k}, \pi)$. For this reason we must modify the parsing table.

We restrict our further explanation to the case $k = 1$.

The modification of the parsing table consists of two moving operations:

1. The moving of reduction operations which are performed at the end of the standard parsing (in the column for ε) to the column for symbols in $FIRST(S)$ in the same row.
2. The moving of operations which are performed at the beginning of the standard parsing (operations in the row for the initial symbol $\#$) to the row, where is the operation accept.

The target entry of these moving operations can contain three possible values:

1. It is an error entry.
2. It contains the same operation as is the moved operation.
3. It contains another operation (shift or reduce) than is the moved operation.

The moving operation is simply possible in the first two cases. It is even empty operation in the second case. There is the conflict in the third case and the moving is not possible. We obtain the modified parsing table MC from the parsing table M by performing of moving operations and the removal of the row of M for the initial symbol #. If there is some conflict then the cyclic parsing is not deterministic. Otherwise the cyclic strong LR parsing is deterministic using an adapted strong LR parser. The adaptation of a strong LR parser to obtain a cyclic parser consists of the following changes:

1. Variable C is introduced as a counter of positions in the input string.
2. The starting and ending positions of symbols pushed to the pushdown store (*start* and *end*, respectively) are added. Let $A \to \beta = B\beta'D$ be a rule used for reduction of string β to a nonterminal A, where $B, D \in (N \cup T)$, then $start(A) = start(B)$ and $end(A) = end(D)$. The starting and ending positions of terminal symbol are the same and they are equal to the position of this symbol in the input string. If the starting position is not defined for some nonterminal symbol X, then $start(X) = -1$.
3. The positional information is added also to the elements of the right parse. The ending position of the nonterminal symbol which is the result of some reduction, is added to the corresponding element of the right parse.
4. An input of the parser is an input string with its first symbol appended at the end as a lookahead string.
5. The first operation of the parser is shift. This enables to start the parsing with a terminal symbol on the top of the pushdown store.
6. A reconstruction of the configuration of the parser is performed after parsing of the input string. The result of this reconstruction is a configuration of the parser parsing the input string in the normal form just after the shift of the last symbol.

Next algorithm is the strong $LR(1)$ parser adapted for parsing of cyclic strings.

Algorithm
Cyclic strong $LR(1)$ parsing.
Input: Cyclic parsing table MC for grammar $G = (N, T, P, S)$, cyclic string x.
Output: Right parse for x in the normal form or error signalization.
Method: String y is the lookahead string. Symbol X will be the top symbol of the pushdown store. String $x' = x.FIRST(x)$ will be the input string. The dot (.) is used for the separation of the cyclic string and the appended string.

1. Set $\alpha = \varepsilon$, $\pi = \varepsilon$, $C = 1$.
2. Read the first input symbol and push it on the pushdown store with its position equal to one.
3. Repeat next steps until the input is parsed or an error signalization appears:
   a) String y is the lookahead string (first input symbol from the rest of the input string). The appended string ($FIRST(x)$) is used only in case when the expected string α is not empty. Otherwise it is supposed to be empty and the cyclic shift is equal to zero.
   b) If $MC(X, y) = $ *shift*, read the input symbol $z = FIRST(y)$, $C := C + 1$ and push $z(C, C)$ to the pushdown store.

c) If $MC(X, y) = reduce\ (i)$, where $A \rightarrow \beta, \beta = B\beta'D$ is the i-th rule in P, where $B, D \in N \cup T$, then:

    i. If string β is on the top of the pushdown store, then pop it and push symbol A on the top of the pushdown store with $start(A) = start(B)$ and $end(A) = end(D)$.

    ii. If only the suffix β_2 of $\beta = \beta_1\beta_2$ is on the top of the pushdown store, then set $\alpha := \beta_1\alpha$, pop β_2 from the pushdown store, and push symbol A on the top of the pushdown store with $start(A) = -1$ and $end(A) = end(D)$.

    In both cases, add $R_i(C)$ to the right parse: $\pi := \pi R_i(C)$, where $C = end(A)$.

d) If $MC(X, y) = error$ then finish with an error signalization.

4. If string α is a suffix of ω in the configuration $(\#\omega, \varepsilon, \pi, \alpha)$, e.g. $\omega = \gamma\alpha$, then the length of the cyclic shift is equal to m, which is the ending length of input string minus the position of the rightmost symbol of γ, else finish with error signalization. Divide π into two parts $\pi = \pi_1\pi_2$ so that the first symbol of π_2 corresponds to the reduction made in some position which is greater then the length of the cyclic shift. The next configuration will be $(\#\gamma, \varepsilon, \pi_2\pi_1, \varepsilon)$.

5. Do all possible reductions:
If $M(X, \varepsilon) = reduce(i)$, $A \rightarrow \beta = B\beta'D$ is the ith rule in P, then pop string β and push symbol A on the top of the pushdown store with $start(A) = start(B)$ and $end(A) = end(C)$. Add $R_i(C)$ to the right parse: $\pi := \pi R_i(C)$.

6. If $M(X, \varepsilon) = accept$ then finish. π is the right parse of input string in the normal form. Symbol $S(p, m)$ is in the pushdown store. The cyclic shift of the input string is its length minus m.

4   Example

Consider the augmented strong $LR(1)$ grammar $G = (\{S', S, A\}, \{a, b, c, d\}, P, S')$ where P consists of the rules:

(0) $S' \rightarrow S$ (2) $A \rightarrow aAb$
(1) $S \rightarrow cA$ (3) $A \rightarrow d$

This grammar generates language $L(G) = \{ca^n db^n : n \geq 0\}$.
The collection of sets of strong $LR(0)$ items for G contains the following sets:

$\# = \{[\, S' \rightarrow .S$ $A = \{\, S \rightarrow cA.$ $b = \{\, A \rightarrow aAb.\}$
     $S \rightarrow .cA\}$ $A \rightarrow aA.b\}$ $d = \{\, A \rightarrow d.\}$

$c = \{\, S \rightarrow c.A$ $a = \{\, A \rightarrow a.Ab$ $S = \{\, S' \rightarrow S.\}$
     $A \rightarrow .aAb$ $A \rightarrow .aAb$
     $A \rightarrow .d\}$ $A \rightarrow .d\}$

The parsing of string $adbbca$ using table MC will be performed in the following way:

$(\#,$	$adbbca.a, \varepsilon,$	$\varepsilon)$
$\vdash(\#a(1, 1),$	$dbbca.a, \varepsilon,$	$\varepsilon)$
$\vdash(\#a(1, 1)d(2, 2),$	$bbca.a, \varepsilon,$	$\varepsilon)$

$$\vdash(\#a(1,1)A(2,2), \qquad bbca.a, R_3(2), \qquad\qquad\qquad \varepsilon)$$
$$\vdash(\#a(1,1)A(2,2)b(3,3), \quad bca.a, R_3(2), \qquad\qquad\qquad \varepsilon)$$
$$\vdash(\#A(1,3), \qquad\qquad bca.a, R_3(2)R_2(3), \qquad\qquad \varepsilon)$$
$$\vdash(\#A(1,3)b(4,4), \qquad ca.a, R_3(2)R_2(3), \qquad\qquad \varepsilon)$$
$$\vdash(\#A(-1,4), \qquad\qquad ca.a, R_3(2)R_2(3)R_2(4), \qquad a)$$
$$\vdash(\#S(-1,4), \qquad\qquad ca.a, R_3(2)R_2(3)R_2(4)R_1(4), ca)$$
$$\vdash(\#S(-1,4)c(5,5), \qquad a.a, R_3(2)R_2(3)R_2(4)R_1(4), ca)$$
$$\vdash(\#S(-1,4)c(5,5)a(6,6), \quad .a, R_3(2)R_2(3)R_2(4)R_1(4), ca)$$

Now the parsing of input string stops and after the reconstruction of the configuration the parsing continues:

$$\vdash (\#S(-1,4), \quad \varepsilon, R_3(2)R_2(3)R_2(4)R_1(4), \varepsilon)$$

The parsing finishes by operation *accept* and the cyclic shift is 2.
The parsing table M and the modified parsing table MC are:

M	a	b	c	d	ε
$\#$		s			
a	s			s	
b		R_2			R_2
c	s			s	
d		R_3			R_3
A		s			R_1
S					A

MC	a	b	c	d	ε
a	s			s	
b		R_2	R_2		R_2
c	s			s	
d		R_3	R_3		R_3
A			s	R_1	R_1
S				s	A

In these tables, the abbreviations are used: A for *accept*, s for *shift*, and R_i for *reduction* by rule (i), error entries are empty.

5   Conclusion

We have shown how the deterministic parsing of cyclic strings can be done. Strong LR parsing is the method used as a base. The time complexity of cyclic string parsing is linear $(\mathcal{O}(n))$. The open question is the extension of presented approach in two ways. The first one is the extension of the used method in order to use more than one lookback symbol. The second one is the adaptation of top down parser for parsing of cyclic strings.

References

[AU71]   Aho, A.V, Ullman, J.D.: *The Theory of Parsing, Translation and Compiling.* Volume I: Parsing, Volume II: Compiling. Prentice Hall, Inc. 1971, 1972.

[FY86]   Fu, K., Young, T.: *Handbook of Pattern Recognition and Image Processing.* Academic Press, 1986.

[MEL88]   Melichar, B.: *Strong LR Grammars.* In: Proceedings of Workshop on Compiler Compilers and High-speed Compilation, Berlin, October 1988, Akademie der Wissenschafften der DDR, Berlin 1989, pp. 259–274.

[ON96]   Oncina, J.: *The Cocke-Younger-Kasami Algorithm for Cyclic Strings.* In: Proceedings of ICPR'96, IEEE, Computer Society Press, 1996, pp. 413–416.

Author Index